Brother Paul's

Mormon Bathroom Reader

Amazing Mormon History, Stories,
Quips & Quotes

By Paul B. Skousen
Cedar Fort, Inc.
Springville, Utah

Other books by Paul B. Skousen

The Skousen Book of Mormon World Records (2004)

Brother Paul's
MORMON BATHROOM READER
Amazing Mormon History, Stoies, Quips & Quotes

ISBN 1-55517-895-2

Cover design by Nikki Williams
Layout by Paul B. Skousen

Distributed by:

Cedar Fort, Inc. / November 2005
www.cedarfort.com

PRINTED IN THE UNITED STATES OF AMERICA
10 9 8 7 6 5 4 3 2 1

Brother Paul's

Mormon Bathroom Reader

Amazing Mormon History,
Stories, Quips & Quotes

Published November 2005

DO YOU HAVE A STORY TO TELL?

I t's backwards to talk about a book's second edition when you haven't even read the first. But let's do.

IN THE FOLLOWING PAGES you will find many of the lost gospel and Church history gems and treasures that you might have once known and forgotten, or simply never asked about. There are thousands of such stories—histories, events, testimony-building experiences, and more—that could inspire, help, instruct, edify and strengthen others if only such stories had an outlet. Well, that outlet is here—in the future editions of this book.

YOU ARE INVITED TO BE IN PRINT
Your compensation would be a byline as an author, contributor or source, and a chance to go down in history. All books find their way into the dusty stream of historical knowledge exchange, and this is your chance to be a part. Your story or contribution could be something of immense value to others, but also a means to pass along to the next generations a part of you that will outlive most people's memories—if you put it in writing in a book.

SO, HERE'S THE PLAN
Enjoy this first edition of *Brother Paul's Mormon Bathroom Reader*, and notice the many kinds of information that are presented. Does any of this trigger a memory or question? Make a note of it. Write it in the margins of this book. Scribble some notes. Your good idea can be as short as a one liner or quote, or as long as a 3 or 4 page article. And if you have specific knowledge that elaborates on one of these articles, or corrects it, please send it in.

AND THEN CONTACT THE AUTHOR
You can reach Brother Paul at Cedar Fort, Inc., or at www.mormonworldrecords.com.

INSTRUCTIONS:
HOW TO USE THIS BOOK

THIS BOOK IS CLEVERLY ORGANIZED ON A THREE-TIERED TIMED BASIS.

IN GENERAL, the articles in *Brother Paul's Mormon Bathroom Reader* are disbursed with great enthusiasm throughout in three taunting lengths: short, medium, and long.

STAGGERED READING TIMES

This book need not be read from front to back in the usual fashion for this is not a fashionable book. To the contrary, it is meant to be picked up and read from any page.

Some articles delving into a rather convoluted or involved subject have been broken into convenient chapters so as not to wear out their welcome when the allotted time for casual reading is exhausted. It is wise and appropriate to keep a sturdy and durable, preferably laminated, bookmark handy.

The following is your guide for estimated length and value of any particular sized article. Please memorize the following as there will be a quiz at the conclusion of the reading:

SHORT STOP—Timely one-pagers for people in a hurry.
WHISTLE STOP—Intermediate length of 2-3 pages when urgency is not an issue.
WATER STOP—Long articles for extended periods of concentration.
MIND-NUMBING MARATHONS—Multipage articles guaranteed to burn off some serious time for needful reading excursions.

Dedicated to our six amazing story-loving grandchildren:
Christian, Jessica, Laurie, Jackson, Kayla, & Katrina

Brother Paul's Mormon Bathroom Reader was renamed 44 times!

6

BATTLESTAR GALACTICA!

From 1978-79, Latter-day Saint Glen Larson's huge science fiction television series won a sizeable audience. The 1980 World Almanac *ranked it 20th out of 100 based on Nielsen ratings. It was too costly for ABC, and they cancelled it after 17 episodes and an eight-month run. It sputtered to life in 1980 with six more episodes and then died.*

MORMON THEMES
For Latter-day Saints who enjoyed *Battlestar Galactica*, Brother Larson made many references to Church doctrine. Can you spot the veiled references in the following?

PLOT: The whole series centers on a huge war that destroyed the original 12 colonies of man. (Hint: Tribes of Israel)
• The last remnants escaped and went hunting for a lost tribe spoken of in ancient traditions as "the colony of earth."
• The home world for all humanity was called "Kobol."
• A spaceship upon which peace talks take place was also named "Star Kobol."
• The colonies of humans were ruled by a Council of Twelve, headed by a president.
• The human's leader was named Commander Adama.
• An evil overlord tried to persuade the humans to give him total complete power, authority, and control in exchange for him plotting a path to the lost colony of earth and saving them all.
• Angelic beings of light influenced the humans and warned them but wouldn't interfere in their exercise of free agency.
• These angelic messengers of light traveled as pairs—a man and woman flitting about as one—unseen, but doing good.
• Explaining themselves, one of the angelic beings said he was simply an advanced form of humanity: "As you are now, we once were; as we are now, you may become."
• When Commander Adama performed the marriage of Captain Apollo and Serina, he said, "A union between this man and this woman not only for now but for all eternities."
• In the episode "The Super Scouts," this statement was made: "The glory of the universe is intelligence."

Oliver Cowdery transcribed about 500 pages of the Book of Mormon.

MORONI'S PROMISE!

PART I

It's an act of faith to pick up a scripture of another religion and explore it for truth and understanding. Moroni promised great things to those who tried. Here are a few famous people who did!

READER: Abraham Lincoln
DATE: November 18, 1861
CIRCUMSTANCE: President Lincoln was into the Civil War only six months when he went to the Library of Congress and borrowed a copy of the Book of Mormon. Over a period of several weeks, he checked out four other books on Mormonism. He returned them on July 29, 1862.

READER: Ronald Reagan
DATE: July 1967
CIRCUMSTANCE: LDS members of the California Legislature and full-time elders serving in the Sacramento area presented then-Governor Reagan with his first Book of Mormon in 1967. Said Governor Reagan, "I have always admired the tremendous personal integrity and self-initiative of the Latter-day Saint people, and on a number of occasions I refer to programs of your Church as outstanding examples of what I feel to be the true American way." Over the years he received additional copies, including a copy given him by President Hinckley during President Reagan's visit to Salt Lake City in 1981.

READER: Senator Ted Kennedy
DATE: January 1989
CIRCUMSTANCE: While sharing the podium with Utah Senator Orrin Hatch for a fireside in Boston, Massachussets, Senator Kennedy was asked if he had a copy of the Book of Mormon. He replied, "No," then turning to Hatch, continued, "But I bet there's a copy on my desk Monday morning."

To read more about Moroni's promise, see page 130.

The Bible was written in three languages: Hebrew, Aramaic, and Greek.

OH, YOU BEAUTIFUL BABY!

Brother Paul has welcomed ten babies into his family (one at a time, thank goodness!), and each has been an amazing miracle. What other miracle babies are there in the Church?

MOST AT ONE TIME

With the help of a fertility clinic, Samuel and Patti Oragenson Frustaci of Riverside, California gave birth to septuplets (7) on May 21, 1985. Three of the seven survived, and they averaged around 1 pound 2 ounces each. In 1990, Sister Frustaci gave birth to a set of twins.

QUINTUPLETS

It happened a world apart, but it was five times the joy. On Oct. 12, 2004, Joshua Horton lay wounded in Iraq with his foot so severely damaged, amputation was being considered. Meanwhile, his wife was preparing to deliver five babies (quintupletes) at Edward Hospital just outside of Chicago. By the time Brother Horton was transferred to a hospital in Maryland, Sister Horton gave birth. The family was eventually reunited, and Brother Horton was able to keep his foot.

Nathan and Nichole Faylor of Austin, Texas, welcomed three boys and two girls on Sept. 2, 2002. The children averaged about 3 pounds. Diaper and bottle duty became a stake-wide project with two sets of sisters coming daily to help Sister Faylor with the chores.

MOST EVER

Delos and Allice Dodge of Mesa, Arizona, welcomed 18 children into their family. There were ten single births intermingled with four sets of twins. Great-grandson Richard Dodge said only a few of the original 18 lived to see the year 2000, but the family was always very close and frequently met for reunions.

By the time Brigham arrived in Salt Lake, potatoes and corn were already planted.

HEAVIEST

Who is the heaviest baby born into the Church? In Utah, the heaviest tipped the scales at 16 pounds 13 ounces. Mrs. Renee Kelsch of Salt Lake City gave birth to Jodie K., her twelfth child, at Cottonwood Hospital on Jan. 25, 1979.

BORN IN A TEMPLE

The Bennetts had an unusual experience during the April 7, 1893, session of the dedication of the Salt Lake Temple – Sister Bennett went into labor! She was escorted to another room in the Temple where she gave birth to a healthy baby boy. Joseph F. Smith's wife, an experienced mid-wife, helped with the delivery. The boy was named Joseph Temple Bennett.

FIRST "TEST TUBE"

The first test-tube baby born to LDS parents, and the 14th test-tube baby born in the U.S., was a healthy 7 pound 9 ounce, 20 1/2-inch boy. He was delivered Jan. 11, 1983, at 8:08 a.m., to Claudia and Steven Allen, of Centerville, Utah.

THE FIRST TEST-TUBE TWINS were born to Michael and Shauna Poulsen of Cody, Wyoming. The boy and girl were born April 8, 1984. He weighed in at 6 pounds 2 ounces, and his sister, Apryl Shanel, arrived at 5 pounds 3 ounces.

ARITHMETIC PROGRESSION

Michael and Laura Daut, of the Littleton 6th Ward in the Columbine Colorado Stake were not too sure if they wanted a fourth pregnancy. The first pregnancy produced one baby, the second produced two babies, and the third produced, yes—you guessed it—three babies. The family of six children, all under age four, attracted much attention. "We love them and they love us," the parents said. "All of us have to work hard and nurture one another."

****

Brazil got its name from the nut, not the other way around.

LET'S END THE FLAT-EARTH MYTH!

*We all "know" it's true, so how could
six billion people be wrong?*

Pretty much *everybody* thinks that during the Middle Ages and before, the earth's ignorant masses believed the earth was flat and thought that anybody venturing beyond the known lands would fall off. Even among readers of the Book of Mormon, those passages about a man becoming inspired of the Spirit to venture forth upon the open seas to find the promised land are viewed by some as the means to overcome the concept of flat-earth allegedly widespread at the time. But it just isn't so.

This silly "flat-earth" idea has been in the American mainstream of thought since about 1860. The truth is, ancient civilizations always knew the earth was round. What they didn't know, and tried to figure out, was just how BIG around (the circumference) it was.

GLOBAL THINKING

As far back as 500 BC, great thinkers used math to figure out the size of our globe. Pythagoras, Euclid, Aristotle, Ptolemy and others worked from 500 BC until 150 AD on the problem and came within a thousand miles of the correct answer. Augustine (AD 350), John Scotus Eriugena (AD 850), and Columbus and Cabot (1480s and 1490s) all used the stars, math, and the sun to estimate the earth's size.

INTENTIONAL MYTHDEEDS!

If the ancients knew the earth was round, why do we teach that they didn't? Dr. Jeffrey B. Russell, a history professor and author at the University of California at Santa Barbara, points to Antoine-Jean Letronne and American author Washington Irving for the myth.

• In 1828, Washington Irving wrote that Columbus promised Spain's king and queen that he would prove the earth was round

---

by sailing west across the ocean. This was pure fiction.

• In 1834, Letronne wrote that the Catholic Church tried to keep people living in the Middle Ages from exploring by frightening them with tales of a flat-earth— the Church never taught this.

• In 1848, Irving apologized for the myth, saying, "Neither did I conceive I was committing any grievous historical sin in helping out the few facts I could collect ... with figments of my own brain."

• By the 1860s, these stories were injected into the American school system, and teachers started sharing the tales as fact. Even many modern books still contain the myth. However, most newer books do not.

TRUTH IN ADVERTISING GETS KILLED

By the 1980s, most textbooks and encyclopedias had corrected the myth, but then Daniel Boorstein, the former Librarian of Congress, re-stated the myth as fact in his book, *The Discoverers* (New York, 1983). Said he, "A Europe-wide phenomenon of scholarly amnesia ... afflicted the continent from 300 A.D. to at least 1300. During those centuries, Christian faith and dogma suppressed the useful image of the world that had been so slowly, so painfully, and so scrupulously drawn by ancient geographers." And with that, the myth was given a breath of fresh air.

READ ALL ABOUT IT

Dr. Russell documents the known facts about knowledge of the earth's shape and traces where the flat-earth myth started and how it was perpetuated in his short book, *Inventing the Flat Earth—Columbus and Modern Historians* (Praeger Publishers). It's a great read and answers all the questions about ancient maps that purported to show a flat-earth belief, and other "evidences" brought forth by the myth purveyors.

So, if anybody ever tells you Columbus sailed the oceans to prove the earth was round, you can tell them that is not true. There is no evidence, no record, no corroboration of anybody teaching flat-earth in Columbus' day or prior—no school, no Bible expert, no historian, no mathematician, no sailor, no newspaper, nobody. Let's credit our ancestors for being smart enough to figure out the earth's circumference using just a piece of parchment, a quill pen or charcoal, and their very own brains.

****

When David O. McKay toured the missions of the Church in 1921, he stopped in Puketapu, Huntly, Waikato, to address hundreds of Maoris at a conference. He felt impressed to ask his interpreter Stuart Meha to sit out this particular speech. For the full 40 minutes of his English talk, the entire congregation knew every word that Elder McKay said. For decades afterwards, the older members always spoke with reverence of the day the "spirit of interpretation" came to their islands.

****

George Washington pled for clean speech from his troops during the Revolutionary War: "The General is very sorry to be informed that the foolish and wicked practice of profane cursing and swearing, a vice heretofore little known in an American Army, is growing into fashion. He hopes the officers will, by example as well as by influence, endeavor to check this, and that both they and the men will reflect that we can have little hope of the blessings of heaven on our arms if we insult it by our unpiety and folly. Added to this, it is a vice so mean and low without any temptation that every man of sense and character detests and despises it."

****

Two elders were tracting in deepest Africa when they came across a large lion. The elders began to run. The slower of the two realized that he would not be able to outrun the lion. He dropped to his knees and prayed for the Lord to convert the lion. When he opened his eyes he saw the lion on his knees also and heard him say, "Lord, please bless this food I am about to consume."

THE MYSTERY OF DESERET

PART I

*So, what's with all the beehive symbolism the pioneers brought
to Utah? Turns out there's a lot more there than
meets the eyes—all five of them.*

WE READ IN ETHER 2:3 that deseret means "honey-bee," and the Jaredites carried deseret with them during their trek through the old world. Tracing this brief mention of our happy insect, the honeybee, opens up an amazing cult of secrecy dating back to pre-Egyptian royalty and ceremonies, possibly as far back as 6000 B.C. Before we explore that mystery, have you ever wondered where we got that shape for the beehive used to adorn Utah buildings and architecture, not to mention the famous beehive hairdo of the 1960s?

TAMING NATURE'S CANDY MAKER

Beehives have been around since the first flowering plants appeared, a date some scientists guess at about 160 million years ago. Whatever the dates might be, for thousands of years bee-keepers have sought creative ways to raise honeybees. A painting in Spain showing beekeeping has been dated to 7000 B.C. The Egyptians used fire-baked clay cylinders for their bees, blowing smoke in at one end to drive the bees out so they could safely retrieve the honey. Others used sticks or pieces of wood. But the simplest method didn't require anything except a knowledge of what branch or tree hollow to exploit sometime in mid-August when the bulk of the bees' work was done.

DON'T SKIP THE SKEP

The bushel basket of the masses has been around thousands of years. In the middle ages, probably before 1000 A.D., the Anglo-Saxons were using their own bushel basket that more or less was a unit of measure that they called a skep (skeppe). These baskets were easy to make. Lengths of twisted or braided straw

The honeybee is the only bee that dies after stinging.

were coiled to make the familiar dome-shaped containers patterned after Mom's high school photo hairdo. These skeps could carry a skepful of whatever. And that's what the ages-old beehive started to be called—a skep—probably by accident.

HOME SWEET HOME

Sometime during those Middle Ages, some bees probably found an abandoned upside-down skep and decided to move in. They started making wax that they scraped off their bellies and fashioned into close-hanging panels of honeycomb. These large frames of six-sided wax cells served as storage containers for honey sealed with a thin layer of wax. In other cells, the queen would lay eggs to grow her brood (baby bees). She could lay 2,000 eggs a day. A typical skep could not accommodate a lot of bees, but still they might have 20,000-40,000 honeybees working it at any given time.

WORTH ITS WEIGHT IN HONEY

Early beekeepers could lift a skep and tell by its weight if it was loaded with honey worth harvesting (40-50 pounds), if it was only partially full, or if it was too light to survive the winter. If it was light, there probably wasn't enough honey for the bees to eat until spring and still leave the skep owner with something to harvest. Beekeeping had always been a popular industry wherever weather permitted, and using the skep was perfect. The basket was cheap to make and reusable. It protected the bees from the weather, and the bees would seal up all the cracks with their wax. They also set guards to warn away any large or small threat. And anybody could entice some bees into it with a little sugar water.

WAY TO BEE The pattern of the skep was carried by early settlers from Europe to the U.S., and from this, we get the famous shape for pioneer-era beehives.

But the skep created a problem—how do you get the honey out? There was only one way: you had to turn it over and scrape it out. This destroyed the hive, and the bees had to build a new one, or that particular group would have to swarm with the queen and find a new home before winter set in. Oftentimes beekeepers would set up more than one skep or stack two or three of them, so as one filled, the bees would move to another.

Once the honeycomb was all scraped out and the brood cells separated out (yuck), the beekeepers pressed the wax to squeeze out the honey. In early days, there was always much more wax produced than honey from such beehives.

DESERET MEANS INDUSTRY?

That the pioneers equated Deseret, or honeybees, to industriousness makes a lot of sense. These little creatures perform a lot of work. The pioneers brought five skeps with them to Utah in 1848 and found symbolism of successful colonization in the way bees worked, cooperated, and organized themselves.

- Honeybees never sleep. They'll rest in a cell but won't sleep.
- Their wings beat 180 times a second, and they'll travel up to eight miles from the hive, at 22 miles an hour, in search of nectar.
- Each trip back to the hive includes a load of carefully collected nectar and pollen weighing about one-sixth of the bee's weight. All of this hard work burns out a bee's life in about two months during the summer. The queen lives up to 8 years.
- It takes 1/3 ounce of honey to make enough wax for one birthday cake candle.
- A modern beehive can have up to 60,000 bees, the giant majority of them female. The males (drones) number less than 300, and are kept around to impregnate a new queen if the original is killed. In the winter, most of the drones are kicked out. Drones don't gather honey, and they're a great liability for the hive when it comes to food shortages in the winter.
- A bee colony is extremely organized. Every member has jobs and chores and purpose. In the winter, they all clump in a big ball with the queen in the middle to keep her warm. As the temperature drops, bees on the outside die and drop to the bottom of the hive. Come spring, the dead bees are all cleaned out, and as the weather warms, the honey-hunting work resumes.

Now, how about that strange word, *Deseret?* What's the story with that? Find out by turning to page 363.

Elizabeth Steele, the first pioneer baby, was born on Aug. 9, 1847, on Temple Square.

THE BRETHREN SAID IT!

PART I

All is not always sober and somber at the podium, as evidenced by these humorous anecdotes from the brethren.

"Adam found himself in a very favorable set of circumstances. He was resting comfortably in the garden. He had a job; yes, the Lord had told him to dress and keep the garden. That is all he had to do. That is no big deal if you don't have weeds growing in the garden, and there were no briars, thistles, and noxious weeds growing in the Garden of Eden. I rather imagine if you looked very closely you would find that Adam was playing around with a stick that was kind of crooked on the end, looking very much like a golf club."—*Hartman Rector, Jr.*

"IN THE DAYS OF THE PIONEER SETTLEMENTS, it was not uncommon to have a ward marshal whose assignment it was, under the direction of the bishop, to maintain orderly conduct among the teenagers.

"On a Sunday evening after sacrament meeting, the ward marshal at the little settlement of Corinne came upon a buggy with some teenagers. Since it was his responsibility to check on the young people, he stealthily crept near the buggy just as the moon came out. He had to stand more or less at attention to keep from being seen, but he could easily hear all that was transpiring in the buggy.

"Later, in reporting it to the bishop, he told of what had gone on. There had been some jokes told, much laughter, and the usual teen-age chatter. He said they sang several songs. The bishop interrupted his report with the question, 'Well, was there anything out of order in that situation?' His answer, 'Yes! me behind that blamed tree.'"—*Boyd K. Packer*

"I HAVE, all the days of my life, enjoyed singing very much. When I was a little boy ten years of age I joined a singing class, and the professor told me that I could never learn to sing. Some years ago I had my character read by a phrenologist and he told me that I could sing, but he said he would like to be forty miles away while I was doing it. I was practicing singing a few weeks ago in the Templeton building, and the room where I was doing so was next to that of a dentist. The people in the hall decided that some one was having his teeth extracted."—*Heber J. Grant*

WHAT WE NEED TO DO, brethren and sisters, is to work for salvation—the greatest gift of God to the children of men, and as my father said: 'If you are saved, no one will be more surprised than you are.'"—*J. Golden Kimball*

"I WANT TO CALL YOUR ATTENTION to a remark that was made by a son of Heber C. Kimball some years ago, in speaking in this great Tabernacle, he said: 'If you Latter-day Saints would but put yourselves in a position to fulfil prophecy, after it had been made by the servants of God, they would not be so afraid to prophesy!'"—*James G. Duffin*

"ONE OF THE SISTERS, gathering the little tots around her on the stand, told them the story of Jesus feeding the multitude in the miraculous manner set forth in the New Testament. Going home that night, one of the mothers, anxious to impress the lesson upon the mind of her little son, asked him certain questions concerning it.

'What did Sister Blank tell us this evening?'

The boy replied: 'She told us how the Savior fed the people.'

'How many people?'

'Five thousand.'

'And what did he feed them with?'

'Five loaves of bread and two fishes.'

'Well, now,' said the mother, 'How do you suppose he could do that?'

The little fellow mused a moment, and then blurted out: 'Well, I don't believe those in the middle got any.'"—*Orson F. Whitney*

For more of "The Brethren Said It!", go to page 45.

... food, clothing and medicine to 147 countries—and the giving continues.

WHERE WE GOT 'EM: THE PEARL OF GREAT PRICE

Aptly named, the Pearl of Great Price is exactly that, a real find for anybody taking time to consider the amazing things contained between its covers.

THE PEARL OF GREAT PRICE is an amazing little book loaded with insight, answers, and history. It started out as a collection of odds and ends that didn't have a good home among Church scripture, yet promised keen insight into many scriptural topics.

THE BOOK WAS CREATED in 1851 by Elder Franklin D. Richards, a member of the Twelve who was serving as president of the British Mission. He said the Church needed additional material for new converts who wanted to learn more about their newfound Church. This first edition contained

• A few of the revelations from Genesis that were part of the Joseph Smith Translation of the Bible. These dealt with Moses and remained without a title until the 1878 edition of the Pearl of Great Price identified them as *Visions of Moses* and *Writings of Moses*. Today, it's simply called the *Book of Moses*.

• The Book of Abraham, translated from scrolls of papyri that Joseph worked on beginning in 1835.

• Matthew 24 as it was revealed to the Prophet Joseph in 1831.

• A section called *A Key to the Revelations of St. John*, that has since been removed and put into the Doctrine and Covenants as Section 77.

• Another revelation also moved to the D&C as Section 87.

In 1834, the Church had 2 stakes; in 1934, 110 stakes; in 2004, 2,665 stakes.

- Joseph Smith's history starting with the first vision, visits from Moroni, and his translation of the Book of Mormon.

- Other revelations that make up parts of today's Doctrine and Covenants Sections 20, 27, and 107.

- The thirteen Articles of Faith were included, but these were untitled at the time and showed up as a list of statements. These had been earlier published in the *Times and Seasons* in 1842.

- A poem originally called, "Truth," but we know it today as a favorite LDS hymn, "Oh Say, What Is Truth?"

IN 1902, James E. Talmage finished his assigned work to divide the book into chapters and verses, and to give titles to the other unnamed portions. He removed some things, including items duplicated in the Doctrine and Covenants.

- In 1976, a revelation given to Joseph Smith on the Celestial Kingdom (1836) and Joseph F. Smith's vision of the redemption of the dead (1913) were added. Three years later, these were moved to the Doctrine and Covenants as Sections 137 and 138.

BROTHER PAUL HAS SEVERAL FAVORITES from this great little book. For example,

- God defines the source of his power in Moses 4:1-3, where Satan demands, "Wherefore, give me thine honor." God explains what that actually means in verse 3, where he says his honor is "my own power." That word *honor* is a very valuable key to understanding how the Atonement works.

- Our fanciful imagination about God sometimes overwhelms reality. Is everything God wants and commands performed or done instantly, as we see in movies and books about genies and fairies (or orcs and druids)? No. All things require time to obey, an outcome of all things having a degree of agency, even the very elements. This amazing idea is tucked away in Abraham 4:18, in the middle of several verses about the creation of the world. "And the Gods watched those things which they had ordered until they obeyed." The words *watched* and *until* mean a passage of time was required.

• Great information about the make up of the universe is in Abraham 3, especially verses 22-23, where intelligences are described as being organized; some were even spirits from which God chose his leaders: "Now the Lord had shown unto me, Abraham, the intelligences that were organized before the world was; and among all these there were many of the noble and great ones; And God saw these souls that they were good, and he stood in the midst of them, and he said: These I will make my rulers; for he stood among those that were spirits, and he saw that they were good; and he said unto me: Abraham, thou art one of them; thou wast chosen before thou wast born."

THE DOCTRINE & COVENANTS is is a wonderful little book—a quick read, informative, satisfying, meaty. Brother Paul highly recommends this book for repeated reading, and it only takes a couple of hours to read it. Be sure to take notes; it's worth it.

****

Please sing it ain't so!

LDS SINGERS AND BANDS have sold a lot of gold and platinum records, but how many were actually among the top ten best musical hits by the end of any given year?

In a forty-year span, from 1956 to 1996, these three groups with Latter-day Saint ties made it into the top ten. Have there been others?

• The Guess Who (founding member Randy Bachman joined the Church in 1970) for "American Woman," 1970, ranked #3.
• The Osmonds for "One Bad Apple," 1971, ranked #5.
• Donny Osmond (solo) for "Go Away Little Girl," 1971, ranked #8.5

JACK MORMON

Be it Jack or Jane Mormon, today's connotation of Jack Mormon is far different than when it was first coined 160 years ago.

The first use of anything remotely using "jack" as an adjective was around 1362 when it meant "any common fellow." It also meant an everyday regular guy, a generalist, run-of-the-mill, ordinary, not refined or specialized (jack-of-all-trades, jackrabbit, jackass, jackdaw). In 1387, Chaucer used the word in *The Canterbury Tales* as "Jakke fool." Some 200 years later, the jack was included in a deck of playing cards as the foolishly painful or dramatically powerful surprise card.

• **B.H. ROBERTS** reported that in the 1840s, Thomas C. Sharpe, editor of an Illinois anti-Mormon newspaper called the *Warsaw Signal*, used the term Jack Mason to refer to non-Masons who were friendly towards the Masons of the 1830s.
• **SHARPE LATER COINED** the term Jack Mormon to label any non-Mormon who was friendly towards the Church or otherwise refused to participate in acts of anti-Mormon terrorism. For decades afterwards, a Jack Mormon was somebody friendly or sympathetic towards the Latter-day Saints.
• **IN 1845,** the *Quincy Whig* in Illinois said "Jack Mormons, and sympathizers abroad may croak and groan over the poor Mormons."
• **IN 1846,** Sharpe's *Warsaw Signal* mocked "A certain Jack-mormon of Hancock county, we won't call him big-head, (but the Saints used to) is in the habit of shaving the hair off his forehead, in order to give it an intellectual appearance."
• **BY THE TURN OF THE CENTURY,** Jack Mormon had evolved from meaning a friendly gentile, to a non-practicing Latter-day Saint, usually somebody who drank, smoked, never went to Church, or otherwise didn't live up to his religion.
• **IN 1971,** a good brother named Jack Mormonn was baptized with his wife and became members of the Audubon 2nd Ward, Philadelphia Pennsylvania Stake. His devoted service and positive example gives the term a much more positive spin!

The Declaration of Independence was written on hemp (marijuana) paper.

MORMON MYTH BUSTERS, PART I

Brother Paul has enjoyed the many faith-promoting rumors that frequent the e-mail in-boxes of Saints and friends alike. Here are a few of his favorites.

CLAIM: The LDS Church owns the Coca-Cola or Pepsi Companies

STATUS: False

STORY: The rumors claimed that the LDS Church, many years ago, wisely invested its tithing or other funds into money-making business ventures including huge purchases of Coca-Cola or Pepsi Cola stock. The irony was that the Church supposedly was reaping huge financial rewards from enterprises that ran contrary to Church teachings. The rumors grew to the point that people were claiming the Church had majority ownership of one or the other cola companies.

TRUTH: These companies are so large, no singular group or alliance owns a majority ownership, and the Church doesn't own any stock. LDS individuals might, but not the Church. Both Coca-Cola and Pepsi Cola companies are publicly traded. About 15 percent of Coca-Cola's shares are owned by current or former executives, descendants of the founders, and other retirees. SunTrust Bank owns 9 percent. The remainder is owned by other investors. Stock genius Warren Buffett is the largest individual owner, holding 200 million shares, or about 8 percent, through his company, Berkshire Hathaway. What's that worth? About $11 billion. Trying to buy, say, one percent of Coca-Cola today would require about $1.375 billion, and who among the Saints has that kind of change?

CLAIM: Mormons have horns

STATUS: Only in the wind section

STORY: This rumor surprisingly still has legs in some parts of the world. This old rumor got its start during the early polygamy days of the Church. Cynical non-LDS probably

---

Canon (canonized), is a Hebrew-Greek word that means a cane or measuring rod.

expected at least one of an elder's multiple wives to be unfaithful and "cuckold" him. Therefore, most Mormon men must have large horns on their heads. What's the connection?

ORIGINS: In medieval and Elizabethan literature, if a woman cheated on her husband, it was said that she "cuckolded" him. Cuckoldry is a corruption of the words *cuckoo bird*, a mischievous bird that laid her eggs in other birds' nests so she wouldn't have to do the nesting work. The ancient belief held that the cuckolded man would sprout horns because his wife's indiscretions lowered the husband's place in her life to that of a beast of the field, or of no real value. For example, in the play *Othello*, one man taps himself on the temple and says to Desdemona, "I have a pain upon my forehead here." That is, he believes himself to have been cuckolded and horns are sprouting. It's possible that the connection to Mormons sprouting horns came from this ancient belief of cuckoldry.

CLAIM: Atheists are petitioning the FCC to ban all religious broadcasting

STATUS: False

STORY: Every few years, a new version of an old e-mail pops into thousands of in-boxes around the world with the same threatening word of warning: Atheist leader Madalyn Murray O'Hair is petitioning the FCC (Federal Communications Commission) to ban all religious broadcasting, including the weekly broadcasts by the Mormon Tabernacle Choir, and other religious broadcasting.

TRUTH: Ms. O'Hair is dead. Over the years, the FCC has regularly issued statements denying that any such effort by O'Hair or her former organization to ban religious broadcasting was in the works. On some days during the 1980s, as many as 8,500 pieces of mail poured into the offices of the FCC, and with the advent of e-mail, hundreds of thousands of messages bombed their web site. The myth continues to generate volumes of messages to the FCC. The most recent e-mails claim all Christian broadcasting and evangelical programming are in O'Hair's crosshairs. Not true.

For more Mormon Myth Busting, see Part II on page 142.

The first pioneers who entered into the Salt Lake Valley included 3 black men.

STAYING AWAKE FOR CAFFEINE

*A lot has been said about the Word of Wisdom, can
there be any more? Brother Paul thinks so.*

HOT DRINKS? How did we get "coffee and tea" from the term "hot drinks"? A good, faithful Saint of yesteryear, Joel H. Johnson, the very man who penned the words to the famous LDS hymn "High on the Mountain Top," gives us the answer. He writes that he was present when the Prophet Joseph Smith received the Word of Wisdom, today's Doctrine & Covenants 89.

I'LL TAKE MY CAFFEINE COLD, PLEASE

At age 31, Brother Johnson had been an avid user of tobacco, strong drink, tea, and coffee for several years, as had many other converts. But when the Prophet delivered the Lord's word that this stuff was bad for everybody, Brother Johnson was fast obedient and "laid them all aside."

But that didn't stop some members from continuing to use coffee and tea. "I well remember," he wrote almost 50 years later in 1882, "that soon after the publication of the Word of Wisdom, the same excuse was made, by some of the people, for drinking tea and coffee that is now made—that hot drinks did not mean tea and coffee."

DON'T MESS WITH THE PROPHET

Five months after the Word of Wisdom revelation, Brother Johnson attended Sabbath services on a hot July day when Joseph and Hyrum Smith were on the stand to address the Saints. Joseph stood, and in Johnson's recorded version of the speech, gave clarification: "I understand that some of the people are excusing themselves in using tea and coffee, because the Lord only said 'hot drinks' in the revelation of the Word of Wisdom. The Lord was showing us what was good for man to eat and drink. Now, what do we drink when we take our meals?

Tea and coffee. Is it not? Yes; tea and coffee. Then, they are what the Lord meant when He said 'hot drinks.'" Brother Johnson adds, "Brother Hyrum Smith spoke to the same effect."

MAKING THE CONNECTION TO CAFFEINE

Then why do "hot drinks" equal caffeine? Those who have labored to break down all of the parts and chemicals in coffee and tea have posted a list of naturally and artificially occurring compounds that are ominously toxic to humans and lab rats. Take them in slightly larger degrees of concentration and they're poison. So, why keep all the focus on caffeine? Because it's the caffeine content more than any other chemical or compound in these beverages that has the power to stimulate and give momentary energy. And that's where the addicting power comes from that keeps us asking for more.

BRIGHAM SUGGESTS FORGET THE COKE AND ...

Brigham Young lumped the stimulative power of hot drinks with narcotics. When addressing the Saints about proper rest following rigorous labor, he pointed out that "some argue that they need stimulants in the shape of tea, coffee, spirituous liquors, tobacco, or some of those narcotic substances which are often taken to goad on the lagging powers to greater exertions. But instead of these kind of stimulants they should recruit by rest."

Good idea, Brigham. I could use a nap just about now.

****

Baptisms for the dead were first performed in the river at Nauvoo. This changed when Joseph Smith declared at a Church conference on Oct. 5, 1841: "There shall be no more baptisms for the dead until the ordinance can be attended to in the Lord's house and the Church shall not hold another general conference until they can meet in said house for thus saith the Lord." At this time, progress on the Nauvoo Temple had reached the point that the font in the basement could be used. From then on, no more proxy baptisms in a river.

Coconuts kill about 150 people each year—more than those killed by sharks.

WHAT WERE THEY THINKING?

BOTCHED TRY: Bomb threat
WHERE: At an airport in Canada
THE STORY

It all began with a pair of missionaries in Canada. The one was fighting discouragement and had decided to return to his home in California. His Utah-born companion was very distressed at this situation and begged his companion to stay just long enough to talk to the mission president. The elder refused and proceeded to board the plane.

Meanwhile, the Utah elder called the mission president. "Hurry up, the plane is going to leave." The president was on his way to the airport, but he wouldn't make it before take off. The Utah elder decides, "Hey, why not force a flight delay? I know, I'll call in a bomb threat." And that's exactly what he did.

When the mission president arrived, he discovered that indeed the plane had been delayed. But now he had two problems. First, an elder who absolutely refused to reconsider staying on his mission and who remained adamant about heading back to California. And second, a well-meaning but misguided Utah companion who waited at airport security, under arrest, and watched over by some not very amused Canadian security guards.

After some explaining, the authorities put the Utah elder in the slammer for a day and fined him $2,000. That was $2,000 in American dollars, not Canadian.

BOTCHED TRY: Enforcing the dress code at BYU
WHERE: BYU's testing center
THE STORY

Brigham Young University is known for its strict dress code. In 1979, enforcement of that code sort of backfired.

A coed named A. Lavon Bryan had braved the wintry cold that day in December to take a test at the testing center. She had dressed warm for the trek across campus and was wearing

---

The average number of minutes between new member baptisms is 2.

jeans, an obvious violation of dress standards.

When confronted by personnel about her breach of etiquette, Ms. Bryan was incensed. How dare they force her to walk all that way back to her apartment just to change into a dress? That's when she got an idea.

Slipping into the women's restroom, she removed her pants and buttoned her winter coat all the way down to her knees, then returned to the testing center.

Approving student administrators admitted her into the testing center where she took her test and returned home.

That week, she fired off a letter to the student newspaper, *The Daily Universe*, expressing her frustration that legs were mandatory on campus, especially in those trying circumstances, and how ridiculous and embarrassed she felt.

Her letter was printed. And then the Associated Press picked up on it. And then Paul Harvey News, and across the country the tale trailed until everybody in North America knew about BYU's dress code.

The code has since been relaxed, and nobody has to remove their pants to pass a test at the BYU testing center.

****

In 1988, Elders Jesus Cabinar and Patrick Shen, serving their missions in the Philippines, were ready to baptize 210 new converts. Unfortunately, their only water source, a semi-dry river, was good for just 12 baptisms before it was too muddy to use. The elders and their converts had to wait months until the rainy season brought clean water to baptize the other 198.

****

President Jeffrey Morrow of the New York New York South Mission suddenly noticed an amazing pairing of missionaries in 2005. In fact, it was probably a new Mormon World Record for the most same-named missionary companions in one mission: Elder Choi with Elder Choi, Elder Kim with Elder Kim, Elder Nelson with Elder Nelson, and Elder Chan with Elder Chan!

In 2002, the Tabernacle Choir performed live before an estimated 3 billion people.

THE MOST CORRECT BOOK

JUST AFTER the third edition of the Book of Mormon came off the press in October 1840, Joseph Smith Jr. wrote,

"I TOLD THE BRETHREN that the Book of Mormon was the most correct of any book on earth, and the keystone of our religion, and a man would get nearer to God by abiding by its precepts, than by any other book." (see DHC 4:461)

- What did he mean, "the most correct of any book on earth"?

BROTHER PAUL'S FREE ONLINE DICTIONARY:
Correct: free from error and conforming to fact or truth
Perfect: being complete of its kind and without defect or blemish

BACKGROUND

Some people misread Joseph's wording and insert *perfect* where *correct* was written. They attack the prophet's comment because of subsequent typographical errors, grammar problems, and other perceived contradictions and flaws. Some of these were real, most were not, and those that existed were later corrected. Critics of the Prophet use these human flaws injected in the writing and printing process as fuel to degrade the book to less than "perfect."

The record reveals that with minor corrections made at each printing, Joseph was well aware the book wasn't perfect, yet he was fully willing to declare it "the most correct."

CONCLUSION

Joseph Smith's simple declaration that the Book of Mormon is the most correct book means it contains the most correct doctrine and teachings of Jesus Christ on earth today.

DOES THIS CORRECT BOOK contain all truth? No. But as Elder Hartman Rector Jr., and other brethren teach, the Book of Mormon most certainly embraces all truth.

- It does not explain principles of physics, such as gravity (although it strongly endorses the fall of Adam).
- It does not talk in detail about medicine or cardiovascular surgery. (Despite encouragement to have bowels of mercy and an open heart!)
- And it does not technically address western versus European horse-riding styles (despite reference to Nephi's horse named Be Unto You—"Wo, be unto you!").

ALL RIGHT THEN, CAN THIS CORRECT BOOK lead readers to "all truth"? The concepts taught within its pages open a conduit to divine inspiration to help all people in all walks of life to become their best—and contribute their most.

- **IT PREPARES YOU.** "The world would mold men by changing their environment. Christ changes men, who then change their environment."—*President Ezra Taft Benson*

- **IT REFINES YOU.** "The study of the doctrines of the gospel will improve behavior quicker than a study of behavior will improve behavior."—*Elder Boyd K. Packer*

- **IT REINFORCES YOU.** "Teach the people correct principles and they will govern themselves."—*Joseph Smith*

- **IT IMPROVES YOU.** "Our whole objective is to make bad men good and good men better, to improve people, to give them an understanding of their godly inheritance and of what they may become."—*President Gordon B. Hinckley*

AND WITH THAT, any of life's pursuits will be more productive, enjoyable, and of greater value if carried forward in harmony with the principles beautifully taught by the Book of Mormon. And for that grand and gracious gift we can thank the most correct of any book on earth and those who brought it to us.

Ants make up 1/10 of the total world animal tissue.

'KILLER' DESERET!

*For several decades, so-called killer bees have been invading
Northern America. What's the story beehind these bees?
Should Utah change its beehive emblem to a
skull and crossbones?*

KILLER BEES are honeybees from Africa. They are worrisome because they're more aggressive, but also less disciplined when it comes to maintaining home and hive.

APPEARANCE: They are slightly smaller than our own Northern European honeybees, but only an expert can really tell the difference.

STORY: In 1956, somebody imported African honeybees into Brazil planning to breed them with the local brood to increase honey production. The next year, 26 African queens escaped, taking with them swarms of local European worker bees. The traits of the African version have combined with European traits to give us the so-called killer bees.

SPREAD: The Africanized bees have been moving north at about 100-200 miles a year, creating hybrid populations (produced by crossbreeding) of bees as they move north. In 1990, Africanized honeybees reached southern Texas, and three years later they were in Arizona. By 1995, they were in California.

ANGRY: Africanized bees are called killer bees because they've killed people and animals who have wandered into their territory. Though the numbers are usually exaggerated, some 14 Americans have died from attacks by Africanized bees since the bees first arrived more than 25 years ago. One U.S. rancher survived 1,000 stings, another died from 40. The impact varies. About 90-100 Americans die from regular bee stings each year but usually because it compounds other medical problems.

VENOM: The killer bees' stinger venom is no different than regular honeybee stings, but they attack in greater numbers, usually ten times as many.

A bee could fly 4 million miles at 7 mph on the energy of 1 gallon of nectar

GROUCHY: Africanized bees react to noises and invaders ten times faster than regular bees and will chase a person at least a quarter mile. They can launch 10,000 to 20,000 bees from the hive in 15 seconds! Bee keepers don't like to raise Africanized bees because they work much harder to attack the man in the white bee suit! (Brother Paul has raised bees, and it's creepy to have all these bees stinging at your clothes if they're mad!)

POLLINATION: Africanized bees don't work as hard or efficiently to pollinate field and orchard crops. They don't survive the winter as well either, meaning they don't swarm back to the home hive to keep the queen warm like our locals do.

CONTROL: Drone-flooding is an effort to prevent the spread of Africanized bees in America. The theory is to release thousands of male bees in areas where European queen bees mate (at bee farms), and reduce the chances of her mating with the wild African variety. The other way is to replace the queen of an Africanized colony with a European queen already impregnated, so all baby bees are European.

HOPE: Our friendly European bees were once as aggressive as their African cousins, but centuries of breeding have rendered them more gentle, less grouchy, and better at producing honey. While the Africanized version is more closely aligned with how nature intended, their infestation will probably impact the honey industry more than people's safety out-of-doors.

SAFETY TIPS
- If attacked, RUN! And run FAST.
- Cover face and head with your shirt.
- Don't head to water—bees will hover until you emerge for air.
- Remove stingers by scraping instead of picking ... you can squeeze more venom into your skin if you pick at them.
- See the doctor if you're stung more than 12-15 times.
- If allergic, keep bee venom & a friend with you when outdoors.
- Don't destroy a hive yourself; call the agriculture department.
- Be alert when moving junk in the yard; Africanized bees are less selective about nesting sites (tires, junk piles, etc.).
- Outdoors: wear light colors, avoid using perfumes/deodorants.

Hello, Texas! A 10-gallon hat actually only holds about 3/4 gallon.

J. GOLDEN KIMBALL

J. Golden Kimball was loved and enjoyed by Saints far and wide for his sage advice and his salty cowboy sermons. Here are some favorite quotes, actual or legendary, in three parts. See page 113 for Part II. Caution: salty words ahead!

WHEN A NEPHEW asked Brother Kimball if he wanted to hear the latest story about him, he responded, "Hell, no! It seems that all the stories told these days are either about me or Mae West!"

"CUT ME OFF FROM THE CHURCH? They can't do that! I repent too damn fast."

"SOME PEOPLE SAY a person receives a position in this Church through revelation, and others say they get it through inspiration, but I say they get it through relation. If I hadn't been related to Heber C. Kimball, I wouldn't have been a damn thing in this church."

AFTER GIVING A BLESSING to a woman whose pregnancy was at risk, she was so touched she began to cry. "Now stop your crying, Louise. You're going to be all right. The Lord has never let me down and He won't start now!"

"THERE ARE NOT ENOUGH general authorities to do all the thinking for the membership of the Church."

TO CURB J. Golden's occasional use of cuss words, the Brethren prepared a speech for him to read in general conference. Growing frustrated at the podium, he stopped halfway and said, "Hell, Heber, I can't read this damn thing!"

"YOUNG MEN, always marry a woman from Sanpete County. No matter what hard times you experience together, she has seen worse."

MEET BROTHER LEHI

Here is a really great man! Lehi of the Book of Mormon was not only a prophet, but he was a great husband, dad, grandpa, and leader. Here's what the book says of him.

LEHI WAS WEALTHY, with a lot of gold, silver and "all manner of riches." He owned his home in Jerusalem, but the land he inherited from his dad lay outside of the city, possibly at a recently discovered site some 20 miles from town.

HE CAME from an old, cultured and distinguished family.

HE WAS OF MANASSEH, a tribe known for retaining their old desert ways and who were active in the caravan trade.

HE HAD STRONG TIES TO SIDON, a name repeated often in the Book of Mormon, and the name of a busy port through which Israel did a lot of trade with Egypt and the west.

HE KNEW Egyptian and insisted that his sons learn it.

HE KEPT meticulous records, and apparently was known for giving long tirades to local youth on morals and good living.

HE HAD a great knowledge of many things that he passed on to his boys. He was something of an expert in wine, the cultivation of olives, figs and honey, fashioning things with gold and silver, and making weapons, armor, plates, and engravings.

LEHI WAS A MERCHANT and blazed his own trails and made his own markets. Only the best swordsman and fighters became traders. And based on his successes, Lehi was one of the best traders around, with plenty of reputation to prove it.

HE WAS COURTEOUS and firm, gentle and tough, cautious and daring. All of these traits, skills and demonstrations of faith proved him the ideal man to take on an errand from the Lord.

NAMES FROM THE BOOK OF MORMON

Key characters in the opening chapters of the Book of Mormon have names deeply embedded in ancient history.

LEHI: This is a Hebrew name used as both a personal name and a place name. It means "cheek" or "jaw bone" and many believe it refers to the weapon (jaw bone of an ass) used by Samson to slay thousands.

SARIAH: This name comes from the same Babylonian root word as Sarai, the wife of Abraham. It means "princess of the Lord Jehovah."

LAMAN: It appears this name is the same as Laban, with the "b" and "m" interchangeable. It means "white."

LEMUEL: This name is thought to be taken from Proverbs 31:1,4, where it is poetically used as another name for Solomon. It means "Godward," or "God is bright."

SAM: This name is not a shortened form of Samuel as many have supposed. It is a pure Egyptian name of great dignity. It is the Egyptian word for Shem, the son of the prophet Noah. Among the Egyptians, their highest order of Priesthood was the "holy priesthood" after the order of Sam (Shem). Even Rameses himself claimed lineage through the order of Sam.

NEPHI: This is an Egyptian name, usually given as Knephi, and in Hebrew we get Nebi. It means "prophet" or one who speaks with God. The Egyptian god Osiris was called Nephi or Knephi, and the city in his honor was "N-ph," the city we know today as Memphis across the Nile from Cairo. Its original use as "Noph" is found in the writings of Hosea, Isaiah and Jeremiah.

THE CAVE OF LEHI

Did the sons of Lehi hang out in a known cave after killing Laban? One Israeli archeologist says, "Sure looks like it!"

IN 1961, A BULLDOZER cutting a road at a site known locally as Beith Lehi or the "House of Lehi," about 20 miles southwest of Jerusalem, broke into the roof of a tiny man-made cave. Ancient inscriptions of sailing boats and some old Hebrew on the cave's walls were discovered. Plaster casts were made and the words translated: "I am Yahweh thy God. I shall accept the cities of Judah and will redeem Jerusalem."

• **AN ARCHEOLOGICAL EXAMINATION** of the cave and area concluded that Beith Lehi was once a village destroyed by the Assyrian king Senacherib in 701 B.C., forcing the inhabitants to flee. Experts speculate the tiny cave's inhabitants might have belonged to the family that once owned Beith Lehi, and returned there for refuge around 600 B.C. Other caves existing close by that are larger and easier to live in were *not* lived in at that time, leading experts to conclude this served more as a hideout.

• **LOCAL BEDOUINS** herding their flocks at the Beith Lehi site say the place takes its name after an ancient Israeli prophet named Lehi who once judged his people while sitting under an oak tree. A stone fence surrounds a descendent of that oak, and the bedouin consider it a sacred tree and keep clear of it.

• **DR. JOSEPH GINAT,** the archeologist who first examined the tiny cave, stumbled on the Book of Mormon while in Salt Lake City in 1970-71. Ginat was fascinated that so much detail about Beith Lehi and the cave is explained in 1 Nephi. (1) Bedouin tradition sets Beith Lehi apart as the ancient homestead of a religious leader. Later excavations also unearthed a church. (2) The cave was a perfect prolonged hiding place easily familiar to Lehi's sons, if this was their home, to serve as shelter while dodging the manhunt after Laban's death. (3) Why the boat carvings? Did these people anticipate a future trip as they did indeed later make?

Be polite in Church: Gorillas stick out their tongues when angry.

PIONEER CURES

As recorded in pioneer woman Patty Bartlett Sessions' diary:

• **SALVE FOR OLD SORES:** Bark of indigo weed root, boiled down beeswax, mutton tallow, a very little rosin.

• **FOR JAUNDICE:** Take one tablespoonful of castile soap shavings, mixed with sugar, for three mornings; then miss three until it has been taken nine mornings—a sure cure.

• **FOR BOWEL COMPLAINT:** Take one teaspoonful rhubarb, one-fourth carbonate soda, one tablespoon brandy, one teaspoon peppermint essence, half-teacupful warm water; take tablespoonful once an hour until it operates.

• **FOR VOMITING:** Six drops laudanum, the size of a pea of soda, two teaspoons of peppermint essence, four cups water; take a tablespoonful at a time until it stops it; if the first does, don't repeat it.

• **HEARTBURN:** Laudanum, carbonate soda, ammonia, sweet oil, camphor. Also for milk leg inflammation or sweating.

• **FOR DROPSY AND FOR FITS:** Indian hemp root.

• **FOR GRAVEL:** Wild rose berries boiled long. Drink the tea.

• **EYE WATER CURE:** Wrap two eggs in a wet cloth and roast them till quite hard, then grate or grind them fine, add half-ounce white vitriol, mix it well together. Add one pint of warm rain or snow water and keep it warm for three hours, after stirring or shaking it. Strain it through a fine thick flannel, and bottle it up for use.

****

AFTER THE CIVIL WAR, Brigham Young wanted to be able to communicate with each settlement and organized the Deseret Telegraphy Company. Each ward collected donations and the priesthood and Relief Society contributed labor in the construction of the line. In less than two years, more than 500 miles of regional lines were erected. Each settlement was asked to send two young men or women to a school of telegraphy in Salt Lake City. These young people regarded this assignment as a Church mission and were supported with food and clothing by their parents or local communities. The line was also of some value to the U.S. Army. The first news of Gen. Custer's defeat by the Souix reached the world through the Deseret Telegraphy Company.— *Rod Reed, Latter Day Sentinel, 1988*

Now you know: elephants are not afraid of a mouse.

UTAH FRIED CHICKEN?

One of the most successful fast food chains in the world had its roots right in the middle of Mormondom.

When Colonel Harland Sanders went looking for a way to promote his special chicken recipe that included 11 herbs and spices, he encountered a friend who would make all the difference. Leon "Pete" Harmon had been looking for something new for the menu at his Do Drop Inn on State Street in Salt Lake City.

PROOF IS IN THE GIBLETS
When he tasted Sanders' chicken, prepared with his secret recipe in a pressure-cooker, Harmon raced out the very next day to buy several pressure cookers and hire a sign painter. He had found his new specialty.

A COMBO-PLATE BY ANY OTHER NAME IS ...
But what would he call this new chicken delight? 'Utah Fried Chicken' just didn't sound right, so Harmon named it Kentucky Fried Chicken because Kentucky was Col. Sanders' southern home, and it gave the idea of fried chicken a nice southern feel. From this small beginning, the KFC empire began to grow.

A BILLION CHICKENS CAN'T BE WRONG
Today, Harmon owns 300 franchises himself, but there are almost 12,000 others spread over 80 countries that serve eight million people a day. The finger-licking good empire has $10 billion in annual sales, staying neck-and-neck with McDonald's as the fast food leader.

In the 1830s, ketchup sold as medicine: Dr. Miles's Compound Extract of Tomatoes.

NEAL A. MAXWELL ONE-LINERS

"Disengagement from the world is best followed by being anxiously engaged in the Lord's work."

"Discouragement is not the absence of adequacy but the absence of courage."

"If we entertain temptations, soon they begin entertaining us!"

"Gospel guard rails."

"Mother lode of learning."

"Don't fear, just live right."

"There is no democracy of facts."

"Celestial criteria measures service, not status."

"All crosses are easier to carry when we keep moving."

"It is our job to lift others up, not to size them up."

"It is not the years but the changes that make us grow."

"Letting off steam always produces more heat than light."

"The 'new' in us is bound to notice the 'old' that remains."

"How could there be refining fires without our enduring some heat?"

"You must not mistake passing local cloud cover for general darkness."

"We must endure the contempt of others without reciprocating that contempt."

"A patient willingness to defer dividends is a hallmark of individual maturity."

"Patience stoutly resists pulling up the daisies to see how the roots are doing!"

"We should not assume, however, that just because something is unexplainable by us, it is unexplainable."

If only? The brethren considered moving the Church west as early as 1842.

MEDICAL MILESTONES

DIALYSIS
Replacing the kidneys with a machine had but one major roadblock: how to access a patient's blood without medical intervention. By 1943, a kidney machine was invented, but doctors couldn't hook patients to it with much comfort or convenience. By 1963, Wayne E. Quinton, Seattle 1st Ward, Seattle Washington Stake, brought to life the Schribner Shunt. This special U-shaped tubing was permanently installed between a patient's vein and an artery, protruding from the skin for easy hook up to the kidney machine. Millions have lived because of it.

ARTIFICIAL HEART
The first successful and permanent artificial heart was invented by Dr. Robert K. Jarvik and implanted by Dr. William DeVries into the chest of Dr. Barney Clark, all three men good members of the Church. Dr. Clark lived 112 days on the machine, giving him and his sweetheart, Una Loy, almost four more months together that they otherwise would have lost.

HEART TO HEART
The first exchange of hearts in the world between two immediate family members took place in 1987 when a young LDS priest, Jonathan Simper, 16, was killed in an accident and his heart went into the chest of his grandpa who was on a waiting list. Albert Nielson was 63 when his grandson's heart brought him more years of loving gratitude and productivity.

RINSE AND SPIT
Okay, this is dental, but that's medical, too! If you're a baby boomer or older, you'll remember visits to the dentist where you sat upright and periodically got a squirt in the mouth and was told to spit into a bowl. (Note: this hasn't changed in many

---

Now you know: 1/3 of people with alarm clocks hit the snooze button every morning.

places, by the way!) Thanks to Utah dentist Elbert O. Thompson, this procedure is no longer necessary. He invented the washed field technique that lets the dentist sit upright and work over a reclining patient while an assistant vacuums out fluid as work proceeds.

PRENATAL SURGERY

In 1986, Dr. Steven Clark, Orem Utah 27th Ward, operated on little Amy Spencer who was still in her mother's womb and 17 weeks away from her expected delivery date. Dr. Clark made careful incisions, gently treated little Amy with some sedation and inserted a tube in her chest that would drain away fluid so her little heart and lungs could properly form. After delivery, he removed the shunt. The surgery saved her life. The fantastic procedure drew attention from doctors all around the world. The grateful parents of healthy Amy were Darwin and Susan Spencer, Pleasant Grove Utah 3rd Ward.

****

Is today "the longest day of your life"?

WE'VE ALL HAD THEM, those long days that drag on forever and ever with no happy end in sight. If you're having one of those today, and you feel like it's the longest day of your life, well ... you're right! Blame the moon.

Our earth's satellite is a relatively large chunk of rock, large compared to most moons orbiting other planets. The moon's gravity is strong enough that it plays havoc with our oceans. Lunar gravity pulls at us all the time and creates tidal bulges. This process gradually transfers momentum from the earth's rotation to the moon's orbit, and our rotation is gradually slowed at the rate of 0.02 seconds per century, making each day a tiny fraction longer than the previous day.

So, is today the longest day in your life? Absolutely. And tomorrow will be even longer. Oh, what joy! That gives you more time to read *Brother Paul's Mormon Bathroom Reader*! We are lucky, indeed.

The beaver is America's largest rodent and can remain underwater for 20 minutes.

OH, MY HECK!

Swearing up a blue streak takes on a whole new vocabulary among Mormons. While our angry alternatives are usually not derivatives of the actual bad word, Brother Paul observes that some are at least kiss 'n cuss 'ins.

FLIP—A common term used by missionaries of the baby-boomer era to express shock, dismay, excitement, frustration, or reacting strongly. First recorded in 1594, it gained its "get excited" or "lose one's head" meaning around 1950. Usage: "Oh, flip!"

FETCH—Thought to have been coined in the movie, *Mean Girls*, it means cool and trendy. Probably comes from "fetching,"—meaning crafty back in 1581, but changed to attractive and alluring by 1880. Usage: "That new shopping mall is so fetch!" (Expect this word to unfetch pretty soon.)

HECK—Used as a mild oath and first recorded in 1865, it is a euphemistic alteration of hell. The word *heck* comes from the old English hatch, a half-door or the bolt or latch of a door. Usage: "Oh, my heck!"

DARN—Aside from the obvious reference to repairing holey socks, darn is a pretty mild curse word—an euphemism for damn that dates to about 1780. Swearing was a punishable offense in early America, so this alternative probably kept many a cussing cad out of trouble. Similar in sound, the word *'tarnal*, a shortened version of *Eternal* (Eternal God) probably helped spread *darn* around the whole *darn 'tarnal* town. Usage: "Oh, darn!"

DANG – Used to express annoyance or dissatisfaction, it is another euphemism for damn and dates to at least 1793. Its roots stem from words meaning to beat down, knock, or hammer. Usage: "He ate the whole dang thing."

Caffeine is on the International Olympic Committee's list of controlled substances.

FREAKING – From Old English meaning "to dance" or "a sudden turn of mind," this word dates to 1563. After evolving 200 years, it came to mean an "unusual thing," such as a freak of nature, by 1850. In the 1900s, it started out meaning "to distort," such as health freak, and by the 1960s, it meant a drug abuser who "freaked out." Usage: "You're such a freak!"

GOSH – Another attempt to use God in the vernacular, *gosh* showed up in the mid 1700s. It probably was influenced by the old English word for God of 200 years earlier: gosse. Usage: "Oh my gosh!"

CRAP – From the Middle Ages English crappe, this word originally meant chaff or grain trodden underfoot (wasted). It applies to things cast off or thrown away. Contrary to popular lore, it has no connection to Thomas Crapper, inventor of an early design of the flush toilet (Crapper is a form of Cropper, a reference to farming). Usage: "That's just a bunch of crap."

JERK – A putdown of another as foolish or rude, jerk might come from jerkwater town, a slang reference to places where steam locomotives of the 1870s had to take on water from a creek or cattle trough because there was no water tower. It now means an inferior person. Usage: "Give it back, you jerk!"

FUDGE—A Captain Fudge of the late 1700s had a reputation for bringing home from long voyages a large cargo of lies. He became known as Lying Fudge. The meaning evolved to "nonsense" or to "create without the necessary ingredients." By 1896, Americans were using it as an exclamation about something bad or disappointing. Usage: "Oh, fudge."

OH, MY HECK, THERE'S MORE

The list of our alternative cuss words is long, including such strange usages and creations as crud, geez, golly, gawl, sweet, kick your trash, and others that Brother Paul's kids were not willing to confess. These will have to be dealt with at a future time, dang it.

Camels have three eyelids to protect themselves from blowing sand.

A FACE-OFF WITH FACE CARDS

Brother Paul grew up in a home where face cards were banned in accordance with the Brethren's counsel. Be they called playing cards or face cards, the question remains, what brought about the banishment of this brainial banter? Brother Paul takes a closer look. First up, the origins of playing cards.

ORIGIN: Nobody knows when playing cards were invented, but they are mentioned in surviving documents that date to 1100-1200 A.D. Some credit the crusaders with spreading the popular pastime after their contact with the Eastern empire, and others point to the Moors who brought the game from Africa to Spain. The leaps and crossovers include Egypt, China, Germany, the Netherlands, and beyond. Some scholars believe the game has roots extending back 2-3000 years before Christ, but the proof of all claims has long since disintegrated with the passage of time.

OLDEST

The oldest preserved cards that we can find come from India. They were round and hand-painted on ivory, and date to around 1100 A.D. Some scholars think the Chinese might have introduced the idea to the Brahman Priests in India.

INSTANT TROUBLE MAKERS!

A century after Marco Polo, cards were a common place nuisance in European society. Johannes, a German monk, notes in 1377 that folks were objecting to playing cards' distracting influence on laborers, including John of Castile, who decreed that cards not be played at all. His edict was followed by similar banishments in the cities of Basle, Florence, Regensburg, and the Duchy of Belgium. The provost in Paris posted a warning to workers in 1397 that playing cards on a work day was forbidden. And our friend St. Bernardino of Sienna gave a famous

Big hand: The world's largest playing cards measure 37 inches by 26.5 inches.

speech in 1423 denouncing cards as an invention of the devil.

In those days, cards were hand painted or printed with woodcut engravings on cloth, parchment, paper tortoise shell, ivory, and mother of pearl, and sometimes decorated with precious metals or gems to impress guests of royalty or elitists who were invited to indulge. When Gutenberg's movable type printing press came along, playing cards became cheap to reproduce and exploded in popularity and variations.

WHY CARDS?

Scholars speculate that face cards might be an off-shoot of chess. Chess is also an ancient game and was used to entertain concubines in China (so they say), as well as to teach strategy to young soldiers and commanders. Its roots go back thousands of years, and at one time chess was called the game of four kings, with each court protected by the four parts of the army: the elephant, horse, chariot, and foot soldier. Over time the game changed from four kings to two, and the playing pieces took on the shapes of figures and animals with varying degrees of power and agency. The similarities between chess and face cards are too close to discount, but speculation is all that remains to explain it.

For a look at how our modern playing cards came about, see Chapter 2: A Face Off with Face Cards, page 180.

****

After the Nauvoo Temple was burned on Oct. 9, 1848, a French communistic group called the Icarians tried to save the building. They bought the walls of the edifice with a plan to rebuild a new roof, and then use the building as a seminary. The Icarians had planned to rebuild the whole city and bought a great deal of property at ridiculously low prices. But on May 25, 1850, a powerful wind sighed across the Mississippi River and blew down the walls. The Icarians couldn't make a success of their plans to rebuild Nauvoo, and they disbanded shortly there after.

Q: Why are there no Mormon vampires? A: Too many stakes in Zion. (*Joe Skousen*)

THE BRETHREN SAID IT!

PART II

The wit is thick during general conference, but you gotta keep an ear out or you'll miss it. For more, see page 82.

"Look, for instance, at Adam. Supposing that Adam was formed actually out of clay, out of the same kind of material from which bricks are formed; that with this matter God made the pattern of a man, and breathed into it the breath of life, and left it there, in that state of supposed perfection, he would have been an adobe to this day."—*Brigham Young*

SHORTEST SERMON in general conference, given by President Ezra Taft Benson upon receiving the Boy Scouts' high honor, the Bronze Wolf, from an official representative. Said the prophet while shaking the man's hand at the podium, "May the Lord bless you and the devil miss you!" And then the prophet sat down.—*General Conference, 1989*

"THE PRINCIPAL CHARGE made against the elders was that of inducing young women to go to Utah for polygamous purposes. The only evidence adduced in support of this charge was a quotation from one of our Articles of Faith—an adaptation of the well-known words of St. Paul: 'If there is anything virtuous, lovely, or of good report or praiseworthy, we seek after these things."—*Orson F. Whitney, 1924*

"IT IS A GOOD THING to look wise, especially when not overburdened with information."—*J. Golden Kimball, 1906*

"I IMAGINE that when we get to the spirit world, spirits will be there doing various things and we shall walk up to them and say, 'I am a missionary of The Church of Jesus Christ of Latter-day Saints.' Perhaps they will slam the door in our faces there. Of course, it won't slam as loud, but it will slam."—*S. Dilworth Young, 1969*

"THERE is no law against doing good."—*Brigham Young*

Only modern temples destroyed and rebuilt: Nauvoo and Apia Samoa temples.

ELVIS PRESLEY AND THE LDS CHURCH

ENCOUNTER: Elvis' first copy of the Book of Mormon
WHERE: Graceland
STORY: A young LDS woman handed Elvis a copy of the Book of Mormon through the gate at Graceland. After Elvis' death, the book was returned to the owner, who gave it to Alan Osmond who turned it over to the Church. Within its pages, Elvis had written "Priscilla needs to read this," and "There is only one King." Elvis didn't like being called "the King," because he always viewed Jesus Christ as "the King." That copy of the Book of Mormon remains at Church headquarters.

ENCOUNTER: *The First 2000 Years* by W. Cleon Skousen
WHERE: In the limo en route from Las Vegas to Los Angeles
STORY: Ed Parker, who was LDS and a martial arts expert, trained Elvis in self defense and became Elvis' body guard for concerts. During long limo drives from Vegas to Los Angeles, the conversation often drifted to religion and history. Parker gave Elvis a copy of Skousen's book, plus other LDS books. Did he read them? "Oh yes," Parker said. "He had all kinds of questions that we'd discuss on our way home from a concert." Skousen's book is on display at Elvis' Graceland home.

ENCOUNTER: Elvis attends early morning seminary
WHERE: Los Angeles
STORY: After a concert in Las Vegas, Elvis presented Ed Parker with a new Cadillac, and the two drove it to Parker's home in Pasadena. They arrived at 6:30 AM, and Parker invited Elvis to meet his daughters, who were attending early morning seminary. They met outside the seminary building where Elvis embraced the girls. He asked to speak to their whole class and was invited in where he witnessed his belief in Jesus Christ and complimented the kids on learning of Him. Rumors that Elvis would return resulted in 100 percent attendance for years.

The largest animal ever seen alive was a 113.5-foot, 170-ton female blue whale.

ELDER NELSON HAS HEART

When talking heart surgery, Latter-day Saints and grateful patients around the world look up to Quorum of the Twelve member Russell M. Nelson with heart felt thanks.

The difficulty in open-heart surgery is keeping the patient alive while the blood flow is taken off-line so repairs can be made to the pump (the heart). The old way was to induce hypothermia in heart patients by packing their bodies in ice to lower their body temperatures and reduce the need for oxygen. Another approach was to hook up the blood flow to another living person and let his or her set of lungs and heart do the work for both bodies while the other was repaired. Both processes were risky and not very successful solutions.

A GRANT IN TIME SAVES NINE

The idea of a heart-lung machine had been in the works for years before Elder Nelson came along. In 1948, just as he was starting advanced surgical training at the University of Minnesota Hospitals, a large grant was issued to the hospital to develop a heart-lung machine. The goal—invent a way to keep blood circulating and oxygenated without the heart and lungs. Elder Nelson heard of the work and arranged to be part of the heart-lung machine team.

DO IT YOURSELFERS

The doctors literally designed and built the machine themselves. Said Elder Nelson, "We had glass-blowing equipment, a lathe, a drill press, and a machine shop. Every part of the machine was built by one of us." The doctors had to figure out what they wanted and then figure out how to build it with the tools at hand.

COAGULATION: One problem that took months to solve was preventing the blood from coagulating inside the heart-lung machine but still allowing for it to coagulate normally when the test animal's heart was started up again.

Two states added: It was a 15-star, 15-stripe flag that inspired "Star Spangled Banner."

EARLY EFFORTS GO TO THE DOGS

The first heart-lung machine kept dogs alive for a few minutes, but the animals succumbed because something mysterious kept killing them. The doctors couldn't figure out what. When the lead doctor left town for a while, he put Elder Nelson in charge of the lab, and during his absence, Elder Nelson solved the problem. Their heart-lung machine was not removing all of the bacterial toxins as thought, and this was killing the dogs.

With the lead doctor's return, they corrected the cleaning process, and the dogs started to survive a long time on the heart-lung machine. In 1951, the first open-heart surgery was attempted on a human, and the new heart-lung machine functioned as planned. History had been made.

ELIMINATING THE FOAM

A few years later, Elder Nelson continued to pour research into an improved heart-lung machine, also called a pump-oxygenator. Elder Nelson was trying to figure out how to introduce a tiny column of oxygen bubbles gently enough to oxygenate the blood without excessive bubbling and foaming of the blood.

INVADING THE HOUSEHOLD SUPPLIES

With an idea in mind, Elder Nelson invited his wife, Dantzel, to assist, and they raided the kitchen for workable parts. They cut off the end of a rubber nursing nipple, attached the small end to an oxygen tube, and glued the larger end to a rubber diaphragm punched with 100 holes by Sister Nelson's sewing needle. Using copper, Chore-girl scrubbing pads coated with a silicon anti-foaming agent, they passed the blood through the tubing and over the copper pad where the foam was broken down and the blood was pooled until it was safe to return to the body.

PUTTING UTAH ON THE MAP

The new procedure was used successfully on a patient in Salt Lake City, putting Utah on the map in 1955 as only the third state in the country to perform open-heart surgery with a heart-lung machine.

MORMONS AND COMPUTERS

INVENTION: Personal Computer
INVENTOR: Alan C. Kay, Salt Lake City, Utah
STORY: In 2004, Brother Kay was honored for "creating the concept of personal computing and contributing to its realization" with the $450,000 Kyoto Prize. Back in 1971, he declared, "The best way to predict the future is to invent it." It was his leadership and invention that gave us GUI (graphical user interface) icons on our computers—little emblems that represent computing functions such as folders, menus, and overlapping windows—that make personal computers usable by the common person. He also visualized the first laptop that he called Dynabook.

INVENTION: Digital Animation
INVENTOR: Ed Catmull, Salt Lake City, Utah
STORY: The co-founder and president of Pixar Animation studios developed the first computer animation software in the world. Brother Catmull's ingenious ideas gave birth to the software used in *Toy Story* films and *A Bug's Life*, *Jurassic Park*, *Titanic*, and *Gladiator*. He received Scientific and Technical Engineering Awards in 1992 and 1995, and shared an Oscar in 2001 for his inventiveness and its contribution to the motion picture industry.

INVENTION: Flatbed Scanner
CO-INVENTOR: Dexter Francis
STORY: Brother Francis was employed by Apple Computer when he worked with a contractor to design and create Apple's first flatbed scanner. The tool snaps an electronic photograph of something and translates it for a computer user to save, print, change, and e-mail. The scanner became one of the most important tools for the budding desktop publishing revolution.

INVENTION: Internet
CO-INVENTOR: Alan C. Kay and numerous others
STORY: The first effort to make an Internet began with a government-sponsored project called ARPANET, or Advanced Research Projects Agency Network. Utah had a powerful cluster of computer genius at the time and early on was invited to help. Computers were wired together from MIT and Chicaco to the University of Utah, UCLA, Stanford, and Berkeley. Utahn Alan C. Kay was an integral link in the discovery of how to send packets of information between computers and can lay claim to helping create the technology that gave birth to the amazing and world-wide Internet.

INVENTION: Video Games
INVENTOR: Nolan Bushnell, Salt Lake City
STORY: In 1971-72, Bushnell set up a computer lab in his daughter's bedroom and began inventing the first computer game that he called Computer Space. It was too complicated for the average person so he dumbed it down to a game he called Pong. That same year he founded Atari, and developed the Atari 2600 home-video game system. Today, computer video games are a multi-billion dollar industry.

INVENTION: Computer Simulation
INVENTOR: David Evans, Salt Lake City
STORY: David Evans' creative genius helped invent the world of computer simulation. With Ivan Sutherland he formed Evans & Sutherland, that today is the world leader for computer graphics, aircraft flight simulators, and other virtual reality products. His early inventions also led to the development of Macintosh computers.

ACHIEVEMENT: First Software Patent
ACHIEVER: S. Pal Asija, Richardson, Texas
STORY: Brother Asija was inducted into the Hall of Fame for Engineering Science and Technology in 1991 for obtaining the first software patent ever issued. Asija's software enabled novice computer users to communicate with computers in a human-like manner.

INVENTION: Digital Movies and Sound
CO-INVENTOR: Robert B. Ingebretsen, Salt Lake City, Utah
STORY: Brother Ingebretsen received an Oscar in 1999 for his work to develop digital sound in the early 1970s. As a masters project at the University of Utah, he developed a way of sampling music at 30,000 times a second and storing the information on a computer. This process gave birth to the digital world we know today. Next time you play a music CD, you're using Brother Ingbretson's decoder idea! He also created the world's first digital movie with the help of Brother Ed Catmull. The movie was a 20-second portrait of a human hand. Ingebretsen's ultimate gift to the world—CDs, DVDs, digital music & movies!

INVENTION: Word-Processing Software
CO-INVENTOR: Alan Ashton, Orem, Utah
STORY: Once the most popular word-processing software in the world, the various versions of WordPerfect commanded anywhere from a 30 percent share in its smallest market to 92 percent of the DOS market in North America. The company was founded by Alan Ashton and Bruce Bastian in a basement and grew into the largest privately held software company in the world. In the 1980s, it was worth more than $2 billion. With the advent of the Microsoft Windows operating environment, WordPerfect eventually lost popularity and was later sold.

ACHIEVEMENT: World's Best Nintendo Player
ACHIEVER: Jeff Hansen, Murray, Utah
STORY: For scoring 2,009,950 points in 6 minutes 21 seconds, 10-year-old Jeff Hansen became the 1991 world champion Nintendo player for his age group. Jeff not only scored highest for anyone in his age group (11 and under) but also scored higher than the winner of the 18-and-over championship.

****

"I went to my toolhouse, where I save things for two years before throwing them away."—*Gordon B. Hinckley*

I never would have thought: The symbol on the pound key (#) is called an octothorpe.

ANCIENT APOSTATES

*Okay, maybe some of these people were
as passionate as they were apostate about their
beliefs, but for a long time after Jesus arrived on the
scene, the Sadducees and Pharisees had him in their cross hairs.*

The Sadducees and Pharisees were the most influential of the various sects that existed during the time of Jesus. And they were usually in opposition to each other.

SADDUCEES: Generally speaking, Sadducees is a conglomeration of words. The root probably comes from one of King Solomon's early priestly leaders, and the rest from words meaning wealthy and powerful, fiscal officials, or administrators of justice. In the days of Jesus, Sadducees were bureaucrats in the guise of religious leaders. The sect existed from 200 B.C. until Jerusalem fell in 70 A.D. Their alliance with the Roman rulers gave them political power among the people. They clung to the teachings of the Pentateuch (the first five books of the Old Testament), and rejected anything not specifically outlined in those books. And, they played the major role in the trial and execution of Jesus.

REJECTED: Eternal soul, resurrection, angels, spirit world, God's rewards and punishments, divine guidance, & intervention.

PHARISEES: The seeds for this sect were planted during the Jews' captivity in Babylon during the mid-500s B.C. and became a group to be dealt with during the Maccabee revolt about 200 B.C. They disbanded around 200 A.D. The name is thought to mean "those separated" from impurity and defilement. Once heavily involved in politics, they withdrew from policy making around 40 B.C. They believed in the written word of the Torah but also the oral traditions. They were extremely letter of the law, and viewed Jesus as a political threat and a religious rival. They were fanatically precise pertaining to the Law of Moses, priding themselves in living it exactly, and self-righteously snaring those who were not.

ACCEPTED: Eternal soul, resurrection, angels, spirit world, God's rewards and punishments, divine guidance, & intervention.

They're good for you: The only food cockroaches won't eat are cucumbers.

WHOSE PRAYERS?

Here is a heartwarming event witnessed by
Brother Paul and his family at Bear Lake, Utah.

President Spencer W. Kimball once wrote, "Would all prayers be immediately answered according to our selfish desires and our limited understanding, then there would be little or no suffering, sorrow, disappointment, or even death, and if these were not, there would also be no joy, success, resurrection, nor eternal life and godhood."

IT WAS THE SUMMER OF 2003, and the terrible drought in Utah was at its worst. For the prior few years, temperatures crept past 100 degrees on far too many days leaving reservoirs dried up, streams and creeks bone dry, rivers slack, and water-conservation mandates in panic mode all across the state.

For the Saints, the drought had long been an issue of fervent prayer and fasting. But this particular year, the mild winter, early spring, and hot sunny days added up to trouble. The drought was on everyone's mind. Our prayers had been constant: "Please, more snow. Please, more rain. Please, more water."

What strikes visitors to Bear Lake's Laketown Ward each Sunday is their powerful faith, simple testimony, and the members' sincere fulfillment of the their callings. Their faces wear the stress and strain of hardship wrought by the unpredictability of ranching and farming, but their pioneer spirit shows in those well-worked and well-groomed pastures and hillsides that provide their sustanance. And come Sunday, the western attire, the sometimes out-of-style clothing, the cowboy boots, the worn and calloused hands, and sun-wrinkled smiles greet the "city folk" visitors with a surprisingly warmhearted and loving embrace.

It was fast Sunday at Laketown Ward in July 2003. The congregation was filled to overflowing as is common during the vacation months.

After opening exercises and the serving of the sacrament, a weather-worn rancher and high priest stood to bear his testimony of the power of prayer regarding the ongoing drought.

"Brothers and sisters," he began, "we have witnessed a wonderful miracle that stands as a testimony that the Lord hears and answers our prayers. As we all know, this drought has had a ter-

Just after Brigham Young died, lightning struck the St. George Temple, burning its tower.

rible impact on our crops and livestock and threatens our liveli-
hood. When the brethren asked us to make it a matter of prayer,
all of us here know that's exactly what we did."

At this point, most of us vistors from the city knew exactly
where this brother was headed. He'd admonish us to continue in
fasting and prayer because there had been weeks and weeks of no
rain—only hot, record-high temperatures. He would encourage
us to continue petitioning Father. We all shifted position and got
comfortable on the soft, cushioned benches. After all, there was
still 35 minutes left in the meeting.

But then came the surprise as he concluded:

"And Father answered those prayers. We prayed for more
hot, sunny days. We prayed that He would stay the cooler
weather. And the Lord heard our plea. He brought us more hot
days and the snows in the higher Uintas melted and sent life-sav-
ing water down our streams and rivers to save our cattle, irrigate
our crops, and end the suffering. For this generous blessing by
our Father who heard our petition in this time of desperate
need, may we all be so very grateful that God answers prayers."

****

AN INCIDENT that was later reported in the *Reader's
Digest*, happened in the Phoenix Camelback Arizona
Stake where a ward magazine representative got up in
Sacrament Meeting to announce: "Please, brothers and sisters,
start your subscriptions this month, so that we can all expire
together."

UTAH'S ALICE THE ELEPHANT was supposedly the first
elephant to calve in North America. She first arrived in Salt
Lake City around 1918 and resided in the Liberty Park Zoo.
When the new Hogle Zoo was opened, Alice was moved
there ... after she packed her trunk, of course.

"ON ONE OCCASION, when Dr. Wilkinson showed concern
for President Kimball's health and the increasing demands he
was making on his body, President Kimball responded in a
kindly way, 'Your job, Brother Wilkinson, is to keep me going
at the pace I am going to go.'"—*Elder J. Richard Clarke*

A cheetah can run at 70 miles per hour, a squirrel at 12, and a snail at .03.

POLYGAMY PRECEDENTS

Say the "P" word, and most folks think Mormons. In truth, polygamy has been around forever and just about everywhere. Here are some real record holders in the difficult field of procuring and supporting multiple spouses.

FOR the record, Brigham Young had 56 children by his 27 wives. And people were shocked with this? They didn't know their history!

• **KING MONGUT OF SIAM,** he who was made famous in the musical *The King and I,* had 9,000 wives and concubines. He fathered 82 children by 39 of his wives.

• **KING SOLOMON** of Old Testament fame was "ratted on" by scribes in I Kings 11:3 when they revealed he had 700 wives and 300 concubines, a total of 1,000—earning him the Lord's wrath.

• **AUGUSTUS THE STRONG OF SAXONY** allegedly had more than 200 wives and supposedly fathered 364 children. After his death, Friedrich Augustus I acknowledged eight wives, and historians came up with 13. Whatever the truth, it will be a difficult genealogy project for somebody.

• **GIOVANNI VIGLIOTTO,** a rather recent polygamist, married 104 times from 1949 to 1981. His marriages took place in 27 states and 14 countries. The law caught up with him in Arizona, and in 1983, he was sentenced to 28 years for fraud and 6 years for bigamy, and fined $336,000.

• **FON OF BIKOM,** Cameroon, is noted for having 100 wives. Somebody even wrote a book about him.

• **MRS. THERESA VAUGHAN** (or Vaughn), aged 24, while on trial in Sheffield, Yorkshire, England, in 1922 admitted

There are 400 million cars and light trucks in the world. In 1950, there were 50 million.

under oath that in the prior 5 years she had married 61 husbands in 50 cities throughout England, Germany, and South Africa.

• **GLYNN WOLFE** of Blythe, California, married 27 women, taking his first bride in 1927.

• **WANT HER PHONE NUMBER?** Linda Essex of Anderson, Indiana, married and divorced 15 men beginning in 1957. Her most recent marriage ended in divorce in 1991.

• **IBN SAUD** of Saudi Arabia had 52 children by his 16 wives.

MEANWHILE, THE INTERNET IS the latest recruitment tool for polygamists who are looking for that (those) special somebody(s) to join all of their other special somebodies. "Poly Matchmaker" declares, "The Perfect Place to Find Your Poly Mate(s)!", and "2Wives" boldly invites, "Where Good Pro-Polygamy Families Find More Wives." Oh, whoopee.

FROM THE CHURCH'S WEB SITE, "In this dispensation, the Lord commanded some of the early Saints to practice plural marriage. The Prophet Joseph Smith and those closest to him, including Brigham Young and Heber C. Kimball, were challenged by this command, but they obeyed it. Church leaders regulated the practice. Those entering into it had to be authorized to do so, and the marriages had to be performed through the sealing power of the priesthood. In 1890, President Wilford Woodruff received a revelation that the leaders of the Church should cease teaching the practice of plural marriage."

IN 1998, President Gordon B. Hinckley left no question: "This Church has nothing whatever to do with those practicing polygamy. They are not members of this Church ... If any of our members are found to be practicing plural marriage, they are excommunicated, the most serious penalty the Church can impose. Not only are those so involved in direct violation of the civil law, they are in violation of the law of this Church."

PANCHO VILLA

*The Mormon Colonies in northern Mexico were the scenes for
some amazing events in modern Church history. Even
Pancho Villa was amazed. Here's his story.*

KEY PLAYERS

PANCHO VILLA: bandit, soldier, rebel, and famous revolutionary general. His real name: **Francisco Doroteo**
FELIPE ANGELES: Mexico's most capable leader, a favorite general, trained at West Point, sent to France by the U.S. as an artillery expert during WWI.
JAMES R. WHETTEN: Called as mission president to start up the interrupted missionary work in northern Mexico in 1918.
JOSEPH C. BENTLEY: President of the Juarez Stake in Colonia Juarez.

STORY

The decade of revolution in Mexico in the early 1900s was dangerous to any Americans living there. The Mormon Colonies had been spared attack during the time, but the missionaries had been withdrawn. By 1918, the brethren decided to try proselyting again and called James Whetten to start up the mission.

In March 1919, President Whetten took a trip to visit his missionaries and bring supplies. He was joined by his younger brother-in-law and Colonia Juarez stake president, Joseph Bentley.

BANDITS ABOUT!

Fears and rumors of Pancho Villa in the region seemed to spring up everywhere. President Whetten was about 50 miles south of Colonia Dublan when locals warned Villa was in the region. Should the brethren abandon their mission and turn back? They talked it over and agreed to press on.

Traveling up a long flat, about 15 miles toward a canyon, they were suddenly stopped by armed men. They were escorted to a larger group of 50 and were told they had to stay there, by orders of the general. President Whetten protested their innocence and insisted on seeing the general. Permission was refused.

Expecting the worst but hoping for the best, they hobbled their mules and took shelter from the dry wind behind a large 8-foot tall boulder. About midnight, a dozen men arrived on horseback to escort the trio to Pancho Villa's camp.

PRISON

With Villa off on a raid, the brethren were taken to the main camp and locked in a 10-foot x 10-foot room with no windows. President Bentley's asthma would endanger his life in such cramped quarters, so Brother Whetten kept his foot in the door of the cell—allowing in fresh air—and talked gospel to the guards for all of that next day.

The next morning, Felipe Angeles stopped by and took Whetten and Bentley to breakfast. Afterwards, he escorted them into a room with another man and asked who they were and what they were up to. President Whetten was the only one fluent in Spanish and explained that they were Mormon missionaries. He gave Angeles a tract and a copy of the Book of Mormon.

THE POWER OF TESTIMONY

Angeles took a deep interest in the presentation and asked many questions. President Whetten opened the scriptures and taught him. The questions kept coming, and the conversation continued into its second hour. Finally, President Bentley asked again if they could meet with Pancho Villa and secure their release. Angeles then turned to the other man who had been standing there the entire time and said, "They want to talk to you." It was Pancho Villa himself.

BY EXAMPLE AND GOOD WORKS

By this time, a warm spirit of trust filled the room as Villa and Angeles realized they were among Americans whose best interests were also Mexico's. President Whetten wrote that Angeles then turned to Villa: "The Mormons have established by teaching people what you are trying to do with a rifle ... If I ever get out of this alive, I'm going to join your Church."

Villa responded, "I've always respected the Mormons. I don't know much except that they minded their own business. Now I can only blame you for not telling me sooner ... You go on and tell the people what you are doing. Tell those who have fled to the hills for safety to go back to their homes. They are free to come and go anytime. I will give my soldiers strict orders not to molest people. How about this religion, is there any chance for me?" President Whetten says, "I told him there was always a chance for a man to quit what he was doing and do better, but that I didn't know about him."

Villa replied, "No doubt you have heard a lot about me. Take all you have heard and cut it in half twice and it will probably be true."

The men parted as friends. Villa gave President Whetten an *abrazo* (hug) and sent them on to see their elders.

EXECUTED

Shortly after the visit by the three Mormons, Angeles left Villa's camp and headed to Mexico City. He had told President Whetten that he was sent by the U.S. to convince Villa to step down and stop the violence. But the Mexican government thought Angeles was a traitor and executed him in November 1919.

And then Villa stopped his raids and surrendered his weapons. His only request was that his men be given farm land.

On June 5, 1923, Pancho Villa drove into Durango for supplies and on his way home he was ambushed. His bullet-riddled car remained in the possession of his wife as late as 1966.

UNFINISHED BUSINESS

After a number of decades passed, President Whetten had an amazing experience. In 1965, he related a dream in which Pancho Villa came to him asking for his temple work to be done. He researched Villa's genealogy and even visited Mrs. Villa to confirm the names and dates. With all the information in hand, and a letter of permission from the First Presidency, President Whetten joyfully wrote in his journal, "On March 1, 1966, almost 47 years to the day that they had first heard of the gospel, I did the temple work for my friends Felipe Angeles and Francisco Doroteo—Pancho Villa."

To learn about Villa's first encounter with Mormons at Colonia Dublan, see page 229.

Seagulls beware: Hard to believe, but hamsters love to eat crickets.

TV AND MOVIE QUIZ

Some of the following movies and television series were created, written, or screen written by creative Latter-day Saints. Can you guess which, based on content or title alone? Answers are at the bottom.

1. *The Absent-Minded Professor* (1961 movie)

2. *Son of Flubber* (1963 movie)

3. *Flubber* (1997 movie)

4. *Divine Secrets of the Ya-Ya Sisterhood* (2002 movie)

5. *As Good As It Gets* (1997 movie)

6. *The Santa Clause 2: The Mrs. Clause* (2002 movie)

7. *Galaxy Quest* (1999 movie)

8. *The Exorcist* (1973 movie)

9. *Sky King* (TV series, 1951)

10. *McCloud* (TV series, 1970-77)

11. *The Virginian* (TV series, 1962-71)

12. *Six Million Dollar Man* (TV series, 1974-78)

13. *Buck Rogers in the 25th Century* (TV series, 1979-81)

14. *Magnum P.I.* (TV series, 1980-88)

15. *The Fugitive* (TV series, 1963-67)

16. *It Takes A Thief* (TV series, 1968-70)

17. *Baywatch* (TV Series, 1989-2001)

18. *Eight Is Enough* (TV series, 1977-1981)

19. *The Waltons* (TV series, 1972-1981)

20. *The Texas Chainsaw Massacre* (Movie, 1974)

Everyone but 8 and 20 were written, screen-written, or created by Latter-day Sentinal 1, 2, 3 by Samuel W. Taylor; 4, 5 by Mark Andrus; 6 by Ken Durio and Cinco Paul; 7. David Howard; 8. Are you kidding me? No way, man! 9. Sloan Nibley, Hugh Nibley's brother; 10-16, Glen Larson; 17-19, Claire Whitaker; 20. Oh, heavens, not this one either!

JOHN DEWEY

Often people can attack serious problems by tracing them to their roots. Here's a serious problem we can trace to Mr. John Dewey.

JOHN DEWEY: 1859-1952
CLAIM TO FAME: Sometimes called The Father of Education in America
IMPACT: Is blamed/credited with driving out the traditional God-centered education system in the United States and replacing it with a humanist or God-less education system.
DON'T CONFUSE WITH: Melvil Dewey (not closely related) who invented the Dewey Decimal System in 1876.

STORY:

John Dewey had an early fascination with Darwin's theories on evolution. He liked Darwin's explanation that creatures could survive their changing world by adapting and evolving.

Dewey believed this principle should apply to education.

- **HE TAUGHT** that the only real truth in the universe was what mankind said it was.
- **IT IS BAD**, he said, to simply perpetuate our own beliefs from generation to generation. Our understanding should be evolving just like the "creature" (us!).
- **PASSING ALONG INFORMATION** from one generation to the next doesn't let intellectual evolution take place. He advocated that we break free from the foolish traditions of our fathers that weigh us down.
- **HE KNEW THAT CHILDREN** become what their environment teaches, and said, "Any education given by a group tends to socialize its members, but the quality and value of the socialization depends upon the habits and aims of the group."
- **WHAT WERE DEWEY'S** "habits and aims" for the future education system in America? Remove God and let scientific truths lead the way.

A MISSIONARY FOR MIS-INFORMATION

In the 1920s-1930s, Dewey gained a huge reputation and following as the leading "idea guy" when it came to theories on how to educate and teach. He wrote articles that appeared in

---

Dominique Larrey, Napoleon's chief surgeon, could amputate a leg in 13 seconds.

The New Republic and Nation magazines. He was active in political causes such as women's suffrage (right to vote) and unionizing teachers. He was invited to speak at public and academic settings where he shared his views with the rising generation of educators and decision makers in America.

FRONTAL ASSAULT ON GOD

A pivotal document called the "Humanist Manifesto" was published in 1933. Many believe Dewey was the primary author, and it was signed by him and 33 other leading philosophers, educators, and leaders. Among its 15 conclusions are:

- **"RELIGIOUS HUMANISTS** regard the universe as self-existing and not created."
- **"HUMANISM BELIEVES** that man is a part of nature and that he has emerged as a result of a continuous process."
- **"HUMANISM ASSERTS** that the nature of the universe depicted by modern science makes unacceptable any supernatural or cosmic guarantees of human values."
- **"MAN WILL LEARN** to face the crises of life in terms of his knowledge of their naturalness and probability. Reasonable and manly attitudes will be fostered by education and supported by custom. We assume that humanism will take the path of social and mental hygiene and discourage sentimental and unreal hopes and wishful thinking."
- **"THOUGH WE CONSIDER THE RELIGIOUS FORMS** and ideas of our fathers no longer adequate, the quest for the good life is still the central task for mankind. Man is at last becoming aware that he alone is responsible for the realization of the world of his dreams, that he has within himself the power for its achievement. He must set intelligence and will to the task."

FORCING A PARADIGM SHIFT? *(Paradigm means a set of beliefs that governs all thoughts and actions)* It is no wonder then, with this dark power at work, that only a generation was needed to make prayer, God, and the Bible illegal in public schools. Fortunately, the "evolution" in thought that Dewey so anxiously anticipated is materializing in a much different way. Increasing numbers of disgusted parents, educators, and leaders are taking back the philosophical high ground and adapting to meet this God-less trend in America in a battle that ultimately will be won. How do we know? Because we've read the book—and in the end, we win.

Information in the human DNA written down would fill a 1,000-volume encyclopedia.

H... E... DOUBLE TOOTHPICKS!

Latter-day Saints have a much different concept of the afterlife and hell than do most other religions thanks to modern prophets and scripture. What follows is a cliff-notes version of LDS beliefs.

TRADITIONAL CHRISTIAN VIEW

Hell is understood by most Christians as a place of eternal punishment, a pit or hole where doom, anguish, and never-ending torment lasts forever. There are lakes of eternal burning and everything else the human imagination has contrived—from pointy-eared Satan and his legions of pitchfork-wielding ghouls to centuries of all other horrible human concoctions and fantasies that have been brought to life in art, novels, movies, jokes, and long-winded, pulpit-pounding Sunday sermons.

LDS VIEW

Hell is not a good description of how things are actually set up. That word describes a very real state of mind and anguish meant to be a long-lasting teacher for each of us, but it doesn't describe Father's plan of justice and mercy. There are multiple kingdoms prepared wherein His repentant children find everlasting joy according to Father's judgments and the laws they are willing to obey.

OUTER DARKNESS

The great storehouse of raw materials from which all things are organized is beyond the realm of the organized universe. This is outer darkness. When a little intelligence is scooped up and brought into Father's kingdom, it is given opportunity to grow based on the laws it is willing to follow. It can qualify for a spirit body, a physical body, and a resurrected body. And progression continues from there based on the kingdom for which he or she qualifies.

BACK TO OUTER DARKNESS

For a select few who fully rebel and disobey all of Father's laws, it's back to the rubble heap for them—back to outer darkness where they are stripped of their resurrected, physical and spirit bodies. Now that sure sounds like hell to Brother Paul.

MORMON METEOR!

What Latter-day Saint comes to mind when you hear "land speed records"? There was a day when Ab had them all.

AB JENKINS—born David Abbott "Ab" Jenkins II, in Spanish Fork, Utah, in 1883.

CLAIM TO FAME: At one time, Ab held more records than anybody in the history of sports!

STORY: It was 1925 when a highway was built through the 100-square mile Bonneville Salt Flats, and Ab Jenkins was asked by a friend to help inaugurate the newly completed project. The task, he was told, was to race a train whose tracks ran parallel to the new highway. Ab accepted the challenge and beat the train by five minutes!

That wasn't Ab's first victory, though. He embarked on his racing career at age 15 (in 1898) when he began racing on his bicycle. He started racing automobiles in 1912 and just kept going.

In 1927, he set a world record by driving from New York to San Francisco in 76 hours. Eleven times he drove a race car for 24 hours straight without getting out of a sitting position. One of his most memorable races was in 1940 when he was mayor of Salt Lake City. Driving his newly designed Mormon Meteor III, he broke all of the world circular records from one to 3,868.14 miles in a 24-hour race. His record for driving one hour was 182.51 mph, and for the 24-hour period he averaged 161.18 mph. The rest of the world's car makers took more than 50 years to break Brother Jenkins' 24-hour average record.

On Labor Day 1950, Jenkins lapped a circular track at 199 miles an hour, breaking 34 more American and world records. The records Jenkins set covered distances from ten to 10,000 miles. By age 73, Jenkins had broken every American unlimited and Class C endurance record up to 24 hours. Jenkins' Duesenberg cars were built especially for him. Mormon Meteor I set records with its original engine. Mormon Meteor II had a Curtis Conqueror airplane engine for more record-breaking performance. In 1938, Augie Duesenberg designed the Mormon

Meteor III, the last car built by the famous auto engineer. The airplane engine was moved to this car, and it went on to become one of the most successful race cars ever. Its last record run was in 1950.

As for Ab, he was in Elkhart, Wisconsin to drive the pace car for the Road American Auto Races when he died. It was August 9, 1956, when Ab finished life's greatest race of all.

WHAT HAPPENED TO THE CAR?

After Ab retired, he wanted his Mormon Meteor III to inspire rising generations of children, so he "sold" it to the State of Utah for $1. The simple contract stated that Utah would keep it on display at the capitol and keep it well maintained. If the state ever failed in this task, the contract would be void and the car would be returned to Jenkins. The state agreed, and it stood for years in various displays. In 1992, *Motor Trend* magazine listed it as the fourth most valuable car ever built, priced at more than $5 million. To Utahns, it was invaluable.

Many years after Ab's death, his son Marv, who was living in Texas at the time, received a phone call. A friend said the Mormon Meteor III was no longer on display in the Utah capitol. Marv grabbed a flight and raced to the capitol. After some searching, he found it sitting in a truck wash, abandoned, vandalized and sadly neglected. "It was enough to make you want to cry," Marv said.

Turns out the car had been in a parade in 1971, and the state forgot to pick it up. A towing company had hauled it to a storage yard where it sat for years.

Marv tried three times to get the state to take responsibility and repair the damage, but to no avail. Marv ended up pouring 7,000 hours into restoring the car back to its former glory.

Would it sell? Most certainly. The original Mormon Meteor was sold by Ab back in 1943, and on August 15, 2004, it sold for $4,445,000 at Gooding & Company's Pebble Beach auction. Version III would do much better, but Marv isn't selling. Nowadays, he takes it on tour and displays it for an admiring public that is very aware of its fabled past. They can touch its smooth finish and feel the days of roaring glory when a clean-living, milk-drinking Mormon set the racing world's records and reputation upside down as "the world's safest speedster."

CAN YOU STUMP KEN JENNINGS?

The best television during the summer of 2004 and spring of 2005 was Sony Pictures television hit, Jeopardy! *Latter-day Saint Ken Jennings set all the records with the most games won (74 in a row), and most money ever won ($2,520,700), and spawned a huge following, fan clubs, appearances on national programs and more. Afterwards he was on television ads, and sponsored a board game and another TV game show. Can you stump Ken? Here are a few of the questions he answered correctly. Find the answers to these* Jeopardy! *questions on the pages that follow.*

1. **NOT EVEN** the president of Belarus spoke Belorussian, so Belarus made this a state language too.
2. **UNLIKE** the other cadets at this school, Shannon Faulkner was not required to get her head shaved.
3. **HIS SONG** "Hello Muddah, Hello Faddah!" may have been based on the letters his son Robert sent from Camp Champlain.
4. **WAGNER, HOLMES, COURIC**
5. **EXPLORER SCOUTS** form units; Boy Scouts form troops & Cub Scouts form these.
6. **THE MOST COMMON** one used by artists is probably the X-acto.
7. **THIS QUESTION** about grocery bags could also apply to how you're paying for those groceries
8. **PROVERBIALLY**, necessity is its mother.
9. **FOR ITS 20TH** Anniversary edition in 1997, Christian Crawford added 100 pages to this memoir.
10. **THE FIELD** of this in which Holden Caulfield imagined himself could have been grown for feed.
11. **PLACE A BET** and name this classic heard here.
12. **THIS FUNKY GUY** was "born in Arizona, moved to Babylonia" and "got a condo made a stone-a."

13. **AMONG PLANTS** whose seeds are found in these, peas are human food while vetch is fed to animals.
14. **FROM THE ITALIAN** for *bell*, it's a type of bell tower
15. **IN** *The conduct of Life*, this transcendentalist reminded us, "men are what their mothers made them."
16. **THIS LEGUME** that probably originated in Asia is the main source of protein supplements in livestock feed.
17. **IF YOU KNOW** that El Castillo del Morro looms over this city's harbor, have a cigar.
18. **SIP SOME PORT** while lounging on the port side of a ship in one of these chairs named for part of a ship.
19. **BABIES' BOTTOMS** can rest a little easier with Balmex, a diaper rash ointment made by JNJ, this company.
20. **IN 1804** Rhode Island College was renamed this.
21. **ON THE ROAD AGAIN,** he donated a blue bandana & a pair of sneakers to the hall.
22. **A 2004 BIOGRAPHY** of this president born November 23, 1804 is subtitled *New Hampshire's Favorite Son*.
23. **THE COUNTRY MUSIC** Hall of Fame has a dress made & worn by this Kentucky-born singer as a 14-year-old newlywed.
24. **IT'S DIFFICULT**, but try picturing George Bernard Shaw as a baby when you visit his birthplace in this world capital.
25. **THIS BRITISH CHEMIST** took his last breath of oxygen Feb. 6, 1804.
26. **COBALAMIN OR** Pyridoxine or Riboflavin
27. **"THE TENDER LAND"** is a 1954 opera by this "Appalachian Spring" composer
28. **JACK THE RIPPER** is Cockney rhyming slang for this breakfast favorite.
29. **SUBATOMIC PARTICLE** referred to as an intermediate vector boson.
30. **HE SUPERVISED** a 1907 phonograph recording of his own "Pagliacci"

Had enough? Turn the page for Ken's questions.

STUMP KEN JENNINGS ANSWERS!

1. What is Russian?
2. What is The Citadel?
3. Who is Bobby Sherman?
4. Who is Katie?
5. What are packs?
6. What is knife?
7. What is paper or plastic?
8. What is invention?
9. What is Mommie Dearest?
10. What is rye?
11. What is Camptown Races?
12. Who is King tut?
13. What are pods?
14. What is campanile?
15. Who is Ralph Waldo Emerson?
16. What is the soybean?
17. What is Havana?
18. What is a deck chair?
19. What is Johnson & Johnson
20. What is Brown?
21. Who is Willie Nelson?
22. Who is Franklin Pierce
23. Who is Loretta Lynn?
24. What is Dublin?
25. Who is Joseph Priestly?
26. What is Vitamin B?
27. Who is Aaron Copeland?
28. What are kippers?
29. What is a W boson?
30. Who is Leoncavallo?

Myth: spot exercising will remove fat from that place. ONLY weight loss will do the trick.

TIE ONE ON!

*When the railroads finally came to the tops of the mountains,
they also brought an appetite for thousands of wooden
ties to hold the rails in place. Here's how the
early Saints met the challenge.*

IT WAS EARLY 1869 when the Transcontinental Railroad finally reached Utah, and the competition between companies to complete the most track grew stiff. When Central Pacific crews heard that Union Pacific crews were making rapid progress, they decided to prove a point. On April 28, 1869, with their supervisors pushing the workers to their limits, they worked sunrise till sunset and laid a record ten miles of track across the Utah desert. The Irish and Chinese crews did their job in 12 hours and consumed 25,800 ties, 3,520 rails, 55,000 spikes, and 7,040 fishplates. It is said such a feat in railroad construction by human beings has never been duplicated since.

THE RAPID CONSUMPTION of wooden railroad ties was difficult to replenish. In Utah, suitable wood had to be hauled in from the Wasatch and Uinta mountains and canyons. Hauling heavy loads from these remote places, especially in the winter time, was dangerous and dozens of serious accidents resulted when horses or ox teams slipped or lost control. How to solve the problem? Float the ties down rivers in "tie drives."

- Tie drives went like this: The Saints cut trees, hauled them to the rivers, cut them into the correct size and length, branded them using a series of unique hack marks, and piled them up. When the heavy water flow started in the spring, they'd float the ties downtream to a rail line.
- The trips down the Bear, Provo and Weber rivers sometimes were 100 miles long and moving an entire load could take from a few weeks to two months. The Saints had to fix the rivers in some places by building up the banks or dredging to keep the ties from wandering into flooded meadows or getting snagged on the trip down.

The energy from one hurricane could power the entire U.S. for 3 years.

- If all the ties didn't make it down river before the high water period ended, they'd be stranded until irrigation season was over, and then the river flow went back to normal.
- In one season, Samuel Stephen Jones of Provo floated 140,000 ties down Provo River. Horse riders would escort the ties downriver, and sometimes the men would have to dismount and enter water up to their armpits to undo jams. They had long poles with iron hooks to do the job. Once in a while the jams could grow so huge and so tight, a man could walk on them for a mile or more without stepping into the water.
- The largest tie drive was in the mid-1880s when 350,000 ties were floated down various Utah rivers to the hungry line layers.
- At one point, the Saints created a large raft of ties, stacked about four feet high, and surrounded by longer ties pinned together. It was floated 30 miles across the Great Salt Lake. About 20 men with long poles propelled the raft by pushing into the silty lake bottom and walking a runway. It took them three days and nights to make the journey.

LOCAL TREATMENT

With the railway headed for Utah, Brigham Young wanted spurs constructed to all major Mormon towns in the Utah area. He and others formed the Utah Central Railroad company on March 8, 1869. Land was bought in Ogden for a depot and a 36.3-mile line was laid from there to Salt Lake City.

SELF-SUFFICIENT

Bringing the train to the rest of Utah became a great Church project. Each community downline was responsible for preparing the grade and procuring more railroad ties.

On Feb. 7, 1870, two brand-new locomotive engines arrived in the territory, No. 3 and No. 4, ready for the new Utah Central Railroad. It was an exciting time to finally be "in business."

As pointed out a few years later, the 36.6 miles of the Utah Central Railroad were perhaps the most miles of track ever laid west of the Mississippi without some form of federal government help. That project was financed, built and improved by private money and people. But that was nothing new or really that unusual for the Saints to tackle—they were hardworking, driven, and knew how to stay on track.

Weather erosion: A mountain erodes away at about 3.5 inches every 1,000 years.

BEYOND THE MOON

Why do you suppose the Lord put that moon out there? Just for decoration or something to light up the night? Hardly!

IF THERE WAS never a moon orbiting our earth, the consequences would have been huge.

- The moon stabilized the 23.5 degree tilt in the earth's axis.
- Without the tilt, there would be no seasons—always very hot at the equator, always frozen solid towards the poles.
- High and low tides would be half their size, affected only by the sun.
- The earth would spin much faster, about ten hours in a day, instead of 24.
- Extreme temperatures, strong and constant winds, awkward circulation, no seasons, short days—all these things would make life unsuitable for us were the moon not here.

MEANWHILE, ABOUT THE MOON . . .
- The moon orbits the earth in the same direction as the earth turns, just slightly slower.
- Therefore, it rises 52 minutes later each night.
- It orbits the earth every 27.3 days.
- The moon's drag on the earth increases our 24-hour day by 0.02 seconds per century.
- Billions of years from now, our day will be about 50 hours.

THROUGH SPACE AND BEYOND!
- Our earth spins at 1,000 miles an hour.
- It moves through the solar system at 66,000 miles an hour.
- Our sun drags us on its journey around the galaxy at 540,000 miles an hour.

SIZE MATTERS?
- Jupiter is the largest of all the planets. Over 1,000 earths could fit inside.
- Our sun weighs 2.2 billion billion billion tons, and a million earths could fit inside of it.
- The sun burns some 4 million tons of nuclear fuel every second to produce the energy that allows for life on our earth.

Diesel engines endure: A 1957 Mercedes 180D drove 1 million miles in 21 years.

- The largest star yet discovered is Mu Cephi. It is in our Milky Way Galaxy but is thousands of light years away. Put it in the middle of our solar system and it would reach to Saturn's orbit—making this mammoth star more than 1 billion miles in diameter.
- Mu Cephi is so big it could hold a billion of our suns!

SIZE STILL MATTERS!
- The size of a printed letter on this page is about ten billion times smaller than the earth.
- The same printed letter is ten billion times larger than an atom.
- If we enlarged a hydrogen atom to the size of the earth, its very core, the nucleus, would be the size of a normal basketball. And this represents only a trillionth of the atom's total volume. Its electron would be orbiting the core at about 4,000 miles away.
- So, atoms are almost completely empty space, and billions of these can fit in the space of a single printed letter.

WHAT DO WE LEARN from this adventure beyond the moon and back again, all the way to the smallest of known particles in the universe? Let this exchange between Moses and the Lord declare it (from Moses 1 in the Pearl of Great Price):

"**AND, BEHOLD,** thou art my son; wherefore look, and I will show thee the workmanship of mine hands; but not all, for my works are without end, and also my words, for they never cease. Wherefore, no man can behold all my works, except he behold all my glory; and no man can behold all my glory, and afterwards remain in the flesh on the earth... And now, behold, this one thing I show unto thee, Moses, my son ... And it came to pass that Moses ... beheld the world upon which he was created; and Moses beheld the world and the ends thereof, and all the children of men which are, and which were created; of the same he greatly marveled and wondered. And the presence of God withdrew from Moses, that his glory was not upon Moses; and Moses was left unto himself. And as he was left unto himself, he fell unto the earth. And it came to pass that it was for the space of many hours before Moses did again receive his natural strength like unto man; and he said unto himself:

"**NOW, FOR THIS CAUSE** I know that man is nothing, which thing I never had supposed."

One inch of rainfall on one acre weighs 113 tons!

ALL WORTHY MALES

What an astonishing announcement! Where were you when it was made? As word spread that all worthy males, including blacks, could now hold the priesthood, it was headline news around the world. Somebody was doing something good and except for a grumbling few, everybody loved it.

FOR A GOOD TWO DECADES, the Church had grown far and wide in Brazil, where most converts had so-called "Negro blood." They were faithful members who donated money and labor to build their new temple even though the no-priesthood policy would prevent them from using it.

GROWING NEEDS

This concerned President Spencer W. Kimball. He spent long hours in prayer in the upper room of the Salt Lake Temple, and he asked the Twelve to pray about it as well. The goal? To receive the will of the Lord on this problem.

CHECKING IN

Said President Kimball, "Day after day I went alone and with great solemnity and seriousness in the upper rooms of the temple, and there I offered my soul and offered my efforts to go forward with the program. I wanted to do what he wanted. I talked about it to him and said, 'Lord, I want only what is right. We are not making any plans to be spectacularly moving. We want only the thing that thou dost want, and we want it when you want it and not until.'"

CAREFUL, CAUTIOUS CONSIDERATION

President Kimball was so intent on working with a unified Quorum, he invited each member of the Twelve individually into his office to discuss the matter. He asked each of them to research all of the scriptures and commentary on the subject, both for and against giving the blacks the priesthood. It became an important discussion topic at their weekly Thursday temple meetings. They prayed about it, and prayed again. This continued as weeks grew into months.

The North Pole is not land, just a large raft of floating ice. In 1958, ...

THE TIME IS NOW

Finally, on June 1, 1978, the brethren met for their regular monthly fast and testimony meeting. Three hours later, the members of the Seventy and the Presiding Bishopric were excused, and President Kimball made an unusual request of the remaining brethren: Could he please lead them in prayer? Before proceeding, he asked each man there to present his views on the issue of blacks and the priesthood. For two hours, they took turns sharing their heartfelt feelings, and then he prayed.

ELDER DAVID B. HAIGHT: "As each responded, we witnessed an outpouring of the Spirit which bonded our souls together in perfect unity—a glorious experience."

ELDER BRUCE R. MCCONKIE: "It was during this prayer that the revelation came. The Spirit of the Lord rested mightily upon us all; we felt something akin to what happened on the day of Pentecost and at the dedication of the Kirtland Temple. From the midst of eternity, the voice of God, conveyed by the power of the Spirit, spoke to his prophet ... And we all heard the same voice, received the same message, and became personal witnesses that the word received was the mind and will and voice of the Lord."

PRESIDENT GORDON B. HINCKLEY: "There was a hallowed and sanctified atmosphere in the room. For me, it felt as if a conduit opened between the heavenly throne and the kneeling, pleading prophet of God who was joined by his brethren."

ELDER HAIGHT: "President Kimball arose from the altar. (We surrounded it according to seniority, I being number twelve.) ... He turned to his right, and I was the first member of the circle he encountered. He put his arms around me, and as I embraced him I felt the beating of his heart and the intense emotion that filled him. He then continued around the circle, embracing each of the brethren. No one spoke. Overcome with emotion, we simply shook hands and quietly went to our dressing rooms."

PRESIDENT GORDON B. HINCKLEY, reflecting on the event ten years later: "Every man in that circle, by the power of the Holy Ghost, knew the same thing ... No voice audible to our physical ears was heard. But the voice of the Spirit whispered with certainty into our minds and our very souls. No one of us who was present on that occasion was ever quite the same after that, nor has the Church been quite the same."

FROM THE MOUTHS OF 2 OR 3 WITNESSES ...

As for why the revelation came to the entire Twelve and First Presidency was due to its significance in light of past policies and the future eternities to come. Elder McConkie said, "The Lord wanted independent witnesses who could bear record that the thing had happened."

OFFICIAL DECLARATION 2

The First Presidency had a document prepared, a very brief announcement, and asked the Twelve how they felt about it. Elder Mark Petersen was in South America at the time, but President Ezra Taft Benson had arranged for immediate contact by telephone should the need arise. The need had arisen, and President Kimball read the announcement to Elder Petersen who voiced his approval.

SUPPORT AT ALL LEVELS

Next, President Kimball wanted the other leading Church authorities to be aware of the announcement. The next morning, Friday, all of the General Authorities were called—the Seventies' Quorum, the Patriarch, and the Presiding Bishopric, and they all approved the message. Those presiding over missions were contacted individually by members of the Twelve. They also voiced their joyful support.

A SPECIAL PRESS CONFERENCE

On June 9, 1978, a press conference was called at the Church Administration Building in Salt Lake City, Utah, where the announcement was given to the world. It was the same announcement that each of the brethren had been shown beforehand.

WORLD REACTION

- *Time* magazine planned to give it a cover story.
- President Jimmy Carter: "I welcome today your announcement ... I commend you for your compassionate prayerfulness and courage in receiving a new doctrine. This announcement brings a healing spirit to the world and reminds all men and women that they are truly brothers and sisters."
- Major newspapers across the country and around the world—New York Times, Washington Post, Los Angeles Times, and more—all gave the story headline news. In a world filled with trouble and inflation and difficulty, something good had just happened!

SUPPORT FROM THE SAINTS

On September 30, 1978, at the 148th Semiannual General Conference of The Church of Jesus Christ of Latter-day Saints, President N. Eldon Tanner (first counselor to President Kimball) read the announcement to the body of the Church. It was accepted with a unanimous vote in the affirmative.

EMBRACED IN THE BOOK

Today, the 1978 announcement, in the form of a letter to the brethren, and President N. Eldon Tanner's preliminary remarks, are included at the end of the Doctrine and Covenants as Official Declaration 2. And the kingdom continues to grow.

****

ARE YOU SIFTED?

IN SEVERAL SCRIPTURES the Lord warns choice people that Satan desires to sift them as wheat. What does that mean?

Sift means to pass something through a sieve. Metaphorically, it means to "look carefully through" something.

While Satan probably desires to "look carefully through" the most valiant for some advantage, a more alarming interpretation is this: When wheat is ground to flour and then sifted, it isn't so much that pure flour then emerges from this process, but rather that total and complete control was surrendered to the miller so he could thoroughly emulsify and reduce the grain for his purposes.

GETTING STONED IN THE ROCK OF AGES

An intriguing part of the debate about the earth's age surrounds petrified wood and fossilized animals, insects, and plants. Here's a good question to throw in the mud: Does it really take a million years to turn a tree into rock?

The Petrifying Stream is a cascade from the River Nidd at Knaresborough, Yorkshire, England. The cascade flows at 15 feet high and about 30 feet across, and creates a watery curtain over the mouth of Mother Shipton's Cave. The water of this spring begins with an underground lake and is pushed up through porous rock acquifers and emerges above ground with extremely high mineral content—calcium, sodium, magnesium, and a little lead, zinc, iron, manganese, and aluminum. Its flow has been measured at about 700 gallons an hour, 24 hours a day, year-round.

We are interested in this water because in its path things petrify in just a matter of days or weeks. Is there anything mysterious about this place in England? No, it's been a tourist trap since at least 1538!

BROTHER PAUL'S NO-CHARGE WORD DEFINITIONS
   Fossil: Latin for "to be dug up"
   Petrify: Latin for "rock" (petra) and "to form," (-ficare),
      that is, "to make rock or stone"

WHAT IS PETRIFACTION?
   This amazing process is also called fossilization. It's really quite a rare event because living things typically decay and recycle through natural processes. But trap the living thing in sediment, deprive it of oxygen, and a nice little copy is created.
   Without oxygen, the decay process is slowed. Minerals are carried into and around the object by seeping water and are deposited to replace molecules, one at a time, making a stone copy of what once was living. If that doesn't work, compression

of the sediment can make a mold of a plant or animal, and long after it has rotted or washed away, minerals fill the cavity and you have a nice little stone statue. Or, the thing might have left an imprint, footprint, or a dragging tail line in the mud. If covered over quickly enough, these "trace fossils" can often be preserved in the same way, with mineral deposits filling the depressions with something harder or softer than the surrounding rock, making it stand out when uncovered.

STONE TEDDY BEAR

Meanwhile, back in England at the Petrifying Stream, for centuries, people have hung objects in the water flow to turn them to stone. Today, a visitor can see a Teddy Bear turned to stone in only three months. Or visit the gift shop and see common everyday objects—a hat, toys, a doll, even a dead bird turned to stone.

RECENTLY IN AMERICA ...

An interesting property about some petrified rocks is that they are porous and can filter or absorb chemicals and pollutants.

The Pacific Northwest National Laboratory in 2005 published their efforts to make petrified wood for that very purpose (filtering and absorbing). Scientists took half-inch cubes of pine and poplar, gave them an acid bath, and then soaked them in a silica solution for several days. The wood cubes were dried and cooked in an argon-filled furnace at 1,400 degrees. Why argon? Because it helps silica crystals grow while other gas elements inhibit or prevent crystal growth.

The result was a square rock, petrified wood, a new silicon carbide that acted just like the real nature-made stuff.

ROCK AND ROLL

So, what can we conclude? If we can see items petrify in weeks by the Petrifying Stream or in days in a 1,400-degree oven, it looks like turning something to stone doesn't necessarily have to take "a million years." While it may well indeed have taken that long in some instances, in others, maybe not. Throw that into your next age of the earth debate and see what rocks!

In 1790, 36 percent of U.S. families had 7 people; by 2003, 33% had only 2 people.

NAPOLEON DYNAMITE

For those who missed it, the smash comedy hit Napoleon Dynamite *(written, produced, and starring several LDS) swept the country in 2004 and was the best-selling DVD in the U.S. for one week during Christmas 2004. Some viewers didn't "get it": others laughed till they cried. Here is Idaho's House Concurrent Resolution 029, honoring the movie and its creators. (If you haven't seen the movie, this will make no freakin' sense, gosh.)*

IN THE HOUSE OF REPRESENTATIVES HOUSE CONCURRENT RESOLUTION NO. 29

A CONCURRENT RESOLUTION STATING LEGISLATIVE FINDINGS AND COMMENDING JARED AND JERUSHA HESS AND THE CITY OF PRESTON FOR THE PRODUCTION OF THE MOVIE "NAPOLEON DYNAMITE."

BE IT RESOLVED by the Legislature of the State of Idaho:

WHEREAS, the State of Idaho recognizes the vision, talent and creativity of Jared and Jerusha Hess in the writing and production of "Napoleon Dynamite"; and

WHEREAS, the scenic and beautiful City of Preston, County of Franklin and the State of Idaho are experiencing increased tourism and economic growth; and

WHEREAS, film maker Jared Hess is a native Idahoan who was educated in the Idaho public school system; and

WHEREAS, the Preston High School administration and staff, particularly the cafeteria staff, have enjoyed notoriety and worldwide attention; and

WHEREAS, tater tots figure prominently in this film thus promoting Idaho's most famous export; and

WHEREAS, the friendship between Napoleon and Pedro has furthered multiethnic relationships; and

WHEREAS, Uncle Rico's football skills are a testament to Idaho athletics; and

WHEREAS, Napoleon's bicycle and Kip's skateboard promote

The Apostle Paul wrote 14 of the New Testament books—over half.

better air quality and carpooling as alternatives to fuel-dependent methods of transportation; and

WHEREAS, Grandma's trip to the St. Anthony Sand Dunes highlights a long-honored Idaho vacation destination; and

WHEREAS, Rico and Kip's Tupperware sales and Deb's key chains and glamour shots promote entrepreneurism and self-sufficiency in Idaho's small towns; and

WHEREAS, Napoleon's artistic rendition of Trisha is an example of the importance of the visual arts in K-12 education; and

WHEREAS, the school wide Preston High School student body elections foster an awareness in Idaho's youth of public service and civic duty; and

WHEREAS, the "Happy Hands" club and the requirement that candidates for school president present a skit is an example of the importance of theater arts in K-12 education; and

WHEREAS, Pedro's efforts to bake a cake for Summer illustrate the positive connection between culinary skills to lifelong relationships; and

WHEREAS, Kip's relationship with LaFawnduh is a tribute to e-commerce and Idaho's technology-driven industry; and

WHEREAS, Kip and LaFawnduh's wedding shows Idaho's commitment to healthy marriages; and

WHEREAS, the prevalence of cooked steak as a primary food group pays tribute to Idaho's beef industry; and

WHEREAS, Napoleon's tetherball dexterity emphasizes the importance of physical education in Idaho public schools; and

WHEREAS, Tina the llama, the chickens with large talons, the 4-H milk cows, and the Honeymoon Stallion showcase Idaho's animal husbandry; and

WHEREAS, any members of the House of Representatives or the Senate of the Legislature of the State of Idaho who choose to vote "Nay" on this concurrent resolution are "FREAKIN' IDIOTS!" and run the risk of having the "Worst Day of Their Lives!"

NOW, THEREFORE, BE IT RESOLVED by the members of the First Regular Session of the Fifty-eighth Idaho Legislature, the House of Representatives and the Senate concurring therein, that we commend Jared and Jerusha Hess and the City of Preston for showcasing the positive aspects of Idaho's youth,

Most scholars believe Job is the oldest book of the Bible, written before 1500 B.C.

rural culture, education system, athletics, economic prosperity and diversity.

BE IT FURTHER RESOLVED that we, the members of the House of Representatives and the Senate of the State of Idaho, advocate always following your heart, and thus we eagerly await the next cinematic undertaking of Idaho's Hess family.

BE IT FURTHER RESOLVED that the Chief Clerk of the House of Representatives be, and she is hereby authorized and directed to forward a copy of this resolution to Jared and Jerusha Hess, the Mayor of the City of Preston and the Principal of Preston High School.

PASSED by the Idaho State Legislature on April 6, 2005.

YEA votes: 69
NAY votes: 0
ABSENT: 1

****

IN 1989, BYU ETHNOBOTANY PROFESSOR Paul A. Cox returned from "chatting" with Sweden's king and queen and 300 other dignitaries about rain forest preservation. The annual event features one scientist from around the world to speak on subjects of interest to the royal couple. The only uncomfortable moment: When they rose to toast the queen, Brother Cox had just been given a glass of wine, but quickly grabbed his water glass instead. Responded the queen: "You are very wise."

"A YOUNG MAN APPROACHED DIOSTHEMES and asked him to be his tutor and to teach him what he knew. Diosthemes took the young man to the seaside and out into the water. Then he pushed his head under the water for almost too long. The young man struggled, came up gasping for air and demanded the meaning of such unwarranted action. The great Diosthemes responded, 'When you want to learn as badly as you wanted a breath of air, then only can I teach you what you want to know.'" —*Elder Royden G. Derrick*

THE BRETHREN SAID IT!

PART III

All is not always sober and somber at the podium, as evidenced
by these humorous anecdotes from the brethren.
For more, see page 140.

For more, see page 140.

" **I**f I am ever so foolish as to quarrel with a woman, I ought to be whipped; for you may always calculate they will have the last word."—*Heber C. Kimball*

Elder J. Golden Kimball was visiting a Church-owned woolen mill, on assignment from the First Presidency. He was wearing a long-tailed coat, which unfortunately got caught in a piece of machinery that proceeded to drag him around in a circular fashion. Unable to keep up with the rapid revolutions, he lost his balance and was swept wildly around the floor until the manager of the mill shut off the machine. Rushing to the dazed man's side, the manager shouted, 'Brother Kimball, speak to me!' Looking him straight in the eye, Golden retorted, 'I don't know why I should. I just passed you twelve times and you didn't speak to me once!'

"It is said that during courtship we should keep our eyes wide open, but after marriage keep them half shut. What I mean may be illustrated by the remark of a young woman who said to her husband, 'I know my cooking isn't good. I hate it as much as you do; but do you find me sitting around griping about it?'"
—*David O. McKay*

"I am grateful to be here again and to look at this very impressive sight. I guess my favorite and appropriate story is the one about the man who suffered a beating at someone's hands, and when the police asked him about it, trying to get the details, they said, 'Could you describe the man who hit you?' And he said, 'That's what I was doing when he hit me.'"—*Marion D. Hanks*

World Record: LDS K.C. Williams (Utah) can inflate 661 balloons in one hour.

RATINGS OR CONTENT?

Brother Paul asks, Is there any Latter-day Saint who really needs
to be told to avoid R-rated movies? Hopefully not! Then
what should a Saint do when historical realities or
even the Atonement are graphically portrayed
in a film that receives an R rating?

THE R BASICALLY MEANS PORNOGRAPHY

Pornography is just about as old as the dinosaurs. The word is of Greek origin and means the literal writing about or drawings of harlots. With improved communications during the past few centuries, pornography has moved from paintings and sketches to printing, color printing, movies, and today's Internet. The spread of this spiritual virus is global and available in almost every home connected to the electronic world.

IT DOESN'T TAKE A ROCKET SCIENTIST

The negative impact of pornography on society is unquestionable. Said one FBI agent who was a Latter-day Saint, "At the root of every crime where I'm given access to the personal belongings of the accused, I am shocked at how many times I find pornography in the deepest recesses of their private lives. That's not what the search warrants entitle me to go after, but that's what I find." According to that special agent, a corrupted personal life was always part of a corrupted business life, community life, or church life.

CAUTION: BRIDGE OUT AHEAD

Because pornography has such a personal impact, it puts personal choice right out in front of everything. Given a chance to see it, most men do, while most women do not. Why? Because it's a visual thing, and men are designed by God to respond to things visual. But visual isn't the whole package, and it can as easily destroy as it can empower to create. Hence, the

For 5 years, Webster's had a definintion of "dord," a word that never really existed...

need for cautionary signs when porn lies ahead. That's why there are movie ratings.

WHO RATES THE MOVIES?

In 1968, Hollywood film producers voluntarily set up a ratings system for one purpose: to give parents information about a movie's content so they could make a judgment whether or not to allow their children to view the film. That's it. The entire foundation of the ratings system rests on the responsibility of the parents. If the parents don't care, the ratings system is useless.

The full-time rating board is located in Los Angeles and has 8-13 members serving for varying periods of time. It is funded by fees received from movie producers and distributors for the rating service given their films. The chairman of the rating board and its members are all insulated from pressure by movie producers so that decisions are based on standards and not "under the table" payoffs.

There are no particular requirements to be on the rating board except to share a parenthood experience, have reasonable intelligent maturity, and be able to fill the role of the average American mom or dad and place a rating that most parents would find reasonable.

THE PROCESS

No one is forced to submit their film to the rating board. It is voluntary. Each movie is viewed by those on the board, and each member estimates what the average American would give as a rating. They fill out a form specifying their thoughts, a discussion ensues, and they vote. Majority rules.

The rating is broken down into these categories: theme, violence, language, nudity, sensuality, drug abuse, and other elements. The rating board considers each element separately and can therefore give, for example, an R rating to a movie that has no nudity but contains too much adult sensuality.

I OBJECT!

If a production company wants a less severe rating, they may re-edit the film to remove offensive material and submit it again for review. If they are still not satisfied, the production company may go to the Appeals Board. This group of 14-18 men and women are from the film industry organizations that support the rating system.

Both sides are heard—the production company, and the chairman of the rating board. After questioning and rebuttal, the two sides are excused and the Appeals Board votes by secret ballot. A 2/3rds majority is needed to override the rating board.

ALPHABET STANDARDS

Today's ratings have undergone a lot of evolution since 1968. Those on the board readily admit the system isn't perfect, but still, it is intended as a guide for parents, nothing more.

G stands for General Audiences–All Ages Admitted. What the G does NOT stand for is a certificate of approval or that it's a children's movie. It simply means there is nothing in the seven major categories that the panel views as damaging for younger children.

PG: Parental Guidance Suggested. Some Material May Not Be Suitable for Children. This rating is the first line of defense. The rating board hopes parents won't assume content is only lightly sprinkled with little things; the board warns parents to look carefully before allowing children to attend such films unseen.

PG-13: Adding the 13 is a sterner warning that this film has elements not suitable for under-teenage-aged children. A single use of the harshest sexually-derived word earns an automatic PG-13 rating, and multiple use is an automatic R rating. Brief nudity is an automatic PG-13, but when presented in a sexual manner (not just exposure), it's an automatic R.

R: Restricted, Under 17 Requires Accompanying Parent Or Adult Guardian means the rating board has declared the movie definitely contains adult materials not suited for children and the R is an urgent call to parents to preview first.

NC-17 No One 17 and Under Admitted means just that. It's an adult movie. An NC-17 does not automatically mean a film is boiling over with porn. It could be violence, aberrational behavior, drug abuse, and/or sex.

The Gunlock Ward in St. George, Utah, had 100 percent home teaching for 8 years!

WHO SETS THE STANDARD?

The rating board founders and members all agree that the question of what is "too much" is always up for debate. Nobody gets it right. Their emphasis then remains with the parents. If the parents don't take responsibility to check things out themselves, then the debate about too tight or too loose is meaningless.

Steps are taken to insulate the rating board from outside economic pressure to change the standard, but personal standards of the individual members still play a role. That's why an advisory committee made up of representatives in the motion picture industry, the theater owners, and others help set standards to keep the rating board somewhere in America's midstream of standards. And as that midstream vacillates between extremes, or slouches in one direction, so go the movie ratings.

THE BRETHREN SPEAK

At general conference in April 1997, Elder L. Tom Perry stated, "We do not need man-made rating systems to determine what we should read, what we should watch, what we should listen to, or how we should conduct our lives. What we do need to do is to live worthy of the continued companionship of the Sprit and have the courage to follow the promptings that come into our lives."

This guiding counsel is echoed by countless others before and since: keep our minds and hearts pure. The Spirit will dictate, and for those incapable of following the spirit to that degree, follow the Brethren who do stay close to the Spirit, whose counsel supports parents, teachers, and other leaders who have our best interests at heart.

R MEANS PORNOGRAPHY

Of the seven elements the rating board considers in each film, only one cannot be faked: pornography, with offensive language a close cousin. Some would elevate the seriousness of the other elements as an effort to dilute the destructiveness of porn.

And is death, destruction, and violence of the R variety, therefore acceptable because it's not pornography? Naturally not. The counsel is consistent: avoid all things that darken the spirit.

The first LDS martyr was Philo Dibble, killed by mobsters in 1833.

WHY AN EXPLICIT "DON'T DO R" IS DIFFICULT

The problem with any standard not based on the Lord's program is that it can't be trusted.

The rating board in Los Angeles is not a group that was duly called by inspiration, set apart by the laying on of hands, and sustained as the Church's entertainment cop, but they're certainly a valuable asset to LDS moviegoers.

To flatly state that movies rated R is the Church's boundary line for entertainment creates an uncomfortable displacement where the promptings of the Holy Ghost are set aside in favor of the rating board's ruling. And that is obviously not what the council is intended to imply. That is why the Brethren always lump R-rated movies with "other spiritually destructive" elements no matter what their ratings.

ARE SOME R-RATED MOVIES OKAY?

Justification is easy in all things once the Spirit is gone. And this brings us back to the beginning. It is the sole responsibility of parents and adults to serve as a righteous filter for their children. When R-rated material does not offend them, and is deemed acceptable for whatever reason given, that doesn't make that material suitable for others. In most cases, a person will discover that rationalization has replaced inspiration, and it's time to be sure that choices are made slowly, prayerfully, carefully.

A RECENT EXAMPLE

Mel Gibson's *The Passion of the Christ* (rated R) illustrates the dilemma. To some viewers, it was a powerful, life-altering ratification of their deepest belief in what Jesus endured for the atonement. Many were moved to tears of understanding and gratitude.

For others, it was a cheapening of His experience because it wasn't scripturally correct to the letter. Or the Catholic elements added to the story were too far removed from a personal set of beliefs.

And to others, it was just too gory. Or, it was branded a tempting deviation from the truth because it was rated R, and "you know what the Brethren say about R."

But for the good it did in the lives of millions, it had its

Since his "birth," two LDS artists have drawn Superman for D.C. Comics.

place, even among members of the Church who exited the theaters stating they felt a good spirit of testimony while viewing the film. Once again, R means parents be cautious.

IS IT RATINGS OR CONTENT?

Brother Paul's opinion:

RATINGS: When in doubt or in a hurry, let the ratings be the guide, and stay away from all movies violating clear-cut Church standards that active Latter-day Saints strive to uphold.

CONTENT: When willing to judge something first hand, either preview the content or seek out commentary from trusted reviewers before inviting others to participate.

FAIL SAFE: Follow the Brethren. In all cases avoid any offenses to the Spirit by listening to it. If the Spirit is in a person's heart, it will offer guidance regardless of what conclusions the good people on the rating board have voted on. After all, the ratings are nothing more than red flags of caution meant to attract our attention: slow down, the bridge might be out.

****

ELDER BIGFOOT

The first sighting by early LDS pioneers of anything resembling Bigfoot is tied up in the legend and lore of "The Bear Lake Monster." Joseph C. Rich reported spotting something near Bear Lake in 1868 that was huge, charged people, and had no description. Wilford Woodruff and John Taylor also recorded seeing the Bear Lake Monster. Its ultimate fate was never discovered. And then David W. Patton reported seeing a strange man approach him one day as he was out riding. The man was very tall, standing even with Brother Patton's shoulders, who was sitting on his horse at the time. The man was dark, covered with hair, and according to the journal entry, identified himself as Cain, son of Adam, who killed Abel. Patton used his priesthood to send the creature away. Fact, fiction, lore, or legend? Maybe a little of everything!

Abraham Lincoln read the Book of Mormon in 1861.

SUCCESS FORMULA!

Typical of the teachings of Jesus, here are the best ideas for personal refinement and a balanced life while trying to make "a go of it" on this planet. By the way, Brother Paul loves this kind of stuff.

DO UNTO OTHERS as you would have them do unto you.

- Blessed are the peacemakers.

- It is better to give than receive.

- Do not hate your enemies but do good unto them.

- Be as humble and teachable as a little child.

- Be wise, aggressive, and alert to promote good and preserve peace.

- Perfect yourself by overcoming personal weaknesses.

- Follow the commandments of God to increase the value of your life and blot out the scars of past mistakes.

- The greatest happiness comes through the greatest service.

- Do good secretly and God—who seeth in secret—will reward you openly.

FRANCIS BACON SAID, "It is not what you eat, but what you digest that makes you strong. It is not what you earn, but what you save that makes you rich. It is not what you preach, but what you practice that makes you a Christian!"

Of the 70,000 pioneers who trekked on foot to Utah, 6,000 were buried along the way.

THE SIXTH OF APRIL

What significant events took place on the Church's most important day?

648 B.C. – APRIL 6: The earliest recorded total eclipse is seen by the ancient Greeks.

0 – APRIL 6: Jesus is born in Bethlehem.

33 – APRIL 6: Jesus is resurrected.

610 – APRIL 6: The first passages of the Muslim holy book, *The Koran*, are delivered to Muhammad.

1759 – APRIL 6: George Friedrich Handel gives his last performance of *"The Messiah,"* dying 7 days later.

1789 – APRIL 6: George Washington is elected President of the United States, the only president ever to be elected unanimously.

1830 – APRIL 6: The Church of Jesus Christ of Latter-day Saints is formally organized.

1889 – APRIL 6: George Eastman introduces the first Kodak camera.

1893 – APRIL 6: The Church dedicates the Salt Lake City Temple after 40 years of construction.

1896 – APRIL 6: The modern Olympic Games are inaugurated in Athens.

1909 – APRIL 6: Americans Robert Peary and Matthew Henson become the first men to reach the North Pole.

1930 – APRIL 6: An important event in Brother Paul's life—the first Hostess Twinkie is invented by James Dewar, a baking executive. A billion of these are eaten every year.

1954 – APRIL 6: Another important event for Brother Paul—Swansons introduce the first heat-and-eat TV dinners.

1965 – APRIL 6: The world's first commercial communications satellite, *Early Bird I,* is launched into orbit.

IN THE LAST 300 YEARS: Easter Sunday has fallen on April 6 eleven times: 1738, 1749, 1760, 1806, 1817, 1828, 1890, 1947, 1958, 1969, and 1980. Easter will next occur on April 6 in 2042.

They say the horned owl is the only mammal stupid enough to attack a skunk!

SURVIVING THE LONG SEA VOYAGE

Venturing beyond familiar shores in sailing ships was not for the faint of heart. The Jaredites, Lehi and early LDS immigrants suffered for it—but survived. What was their trip like? Let's look at Christopher Columbus. Here's how it went for the most part.

DEPARTURE: August 3, 1492, from Palos de la Frontera; stopped at the Canary Islands on Sept. 6, 1492, for supplies before heading west. Three ships, the *Nina* and *Pinta* (each held 18 men) and the *Santa Maria* (52 men).

NAVIGATION: Celestial navigation is looking to the sun, moon and stars for guidance. Columbus used dead reckoning. With a compass pointing the way, he checked his speeds by dropping flotsam into the water and timing how long it passed between two marks on the ship's railing. Once an hour, they'd drop flotsam and calculate miles per hour.

DRINK: They had to bring everything in casks—water and wine—red wine was used because its high alcohol content was an excellent preservative.

FOOD: On their first voyage, Columbus packed Gomera goat cheese, vinegar, olive oil, molasses, honey, raisins, rice, garlic, almonds, sea biscuits (hardtack), dry legumes (chickpeas, lentils, beans), salted and barreled sardines, anchovies, dry salt cod, pickled or salted meats (beef and pork), and salted flour.

STORAGE: Earthenware jugs for olive oil, wooden casks for all else. Sometimes large casks of wine were put in the keel of the ship to keep it bottom heavy. If poorly manufactured casks were on board, they typically leaked out brine so fish, meats and vegetables would rot—a dangerous discovery when far out to sea.

COOKING: Food was mostly boiled and served in a large, wooden communal bowl. Sailors picked at the meat with fingers as they had no forks or spoons. Larger pieces were cut with knives that each man carried. Meats were usually prepared as a

Ocean water is 96% pure water, 3% salt, and 1% containing at least 80 elements.

stew with peas, rice, or other legumes. Fish was more easily available and used more often. On calm days, the sailors could catch fish and eat them.

FIRE: An open firebox called a fogon had a back to screen it from the wind. Sand was spread on the bottom of the box, and a fire built atop the sand for cooking. In rough seas, water usually doused these dinner fires in a flash of foamy surprise.

COLUMBIAN EXCHANGE
With the New World a reality in 1492, an amazing exchange of goods, animals, and disease began. Here's a sampling:

DISCOVERED IN THE NEW WORLD
- dog
- fowl (a few species)
- llama
- alpaca
- guinea pig
- cotton
- maize (corn)
- potato
- sweet potato
- manioc
- peanut
- tomato
- squash (incl. pumpkin)
- pineapple
- tobacco
- papaya
- avocado
- chocolate
- rubber
- disease similar to syphilis
- tuberculosis (a form of it)
- Chagas' disease

BROUGHT FROM THE OLD WORLD
- dog
- fowl (several species)
- camel
- horse (they think!)
- donkey
- pig
- cattle
- goat
- sheep
- honeybee
- cotton
- rice
- wheat
- barley
- oats
- rye
- turnip
- onion
- cabbage
- lettuce
- peach
- pear
- sugar
- diseases including syphilis, tuberculosis, smallpox, malaria, yellow fever, measles, cholera, typhoid, bubonic plague.

Almost 1 million earthquakes occur each year, and 1 undersea about every 2 weeks.

CHOOSE THE RIGHT

Brother Paul is left-handed. Nevertheless, he is confident nothing untoward was intended by the Church's declaration that all its members "Choose the Right." But on the other hand, Brother Paul still wonders, why the right hand?

ABOUT 90 PERCENT ARE RIGHT HANDED
This hand business is nothing to shake your fist at. The Bible uses the word *hand* at least 1,000 times. Our hands are important for interaction with others to help, hurt, promise, commit, or reject. The Bible compliments the right hand and usually uses it to denote power and strength, or a place where one can be protected and loved, such as at God's right hand.

SINISTER MEANS LEFT-HANDED!
On the other hand, the left hand is often associated with mischief, weakness, rejection, or being sinister. Eastern cultures associate the left side of the body with femaleness or weakness. Looking at Middle Ages' coats of arms, a bar slanting to the left meant the person or family traced their lineage through their mother's line because they didn't know who the father was.

The old Saxon word *lyft* means "worthless," and the French used *gauche*, for left, a word meaning clumsy. The Latin "sinister" means left-handed, while *dexter* means right-handed. So who gets the accolades if you use both with equal skill? Not the lefties! Ambidextrous means "right handed on both sides." Even the modern keyboard favors the right, the number of words typed solely with the left hand is around 3,400, and those typed solely with the right is 450 or so. The right gets to rest!

The favoritism shown the right hand appears in nearly all cultures. The ancient Egyptians' devil god was named The Left Eye of the Sun, while the good god was The Right Eye of the Sun. The Buddhists point at two paths to Nirvana (enlightenment and salvation), but the left-hand-side is the wrong path. People should choose the right! And the Mayan and Aztec civilizations had a ritual where they used the

On average, Americans eat 18 acres of pizza in one day.

middle fingers of the right hand to touch the soil and then their lips to bring blessings. American Indians extended the left hand to show that not only was there no weapon in the right, but no shield in the left (not defensive)—let us be trusting friends.

DAILY WASHINGS

The most direct impact on our right-handed culture might have roots in ancient Israel and, much later, Islam. In the ancient Arabic countries, for example, where there was a shortage of double-ply, extra-soft toilet paper, the left hand was used for nature's duty. Naturally, that hand became a very nasty thing to have around come meal time, greeting strangers, or having prayers. The right hand was exalted and protected. Oblations, or washings prior to prayer or eating, involved washing the right hand first, and then it served to cleanse the rest of the body in a ritualistic pattern.

When Jesus walked the earth, he identified the righteous heirs to God's kingdom as standing on His right. The sheep on His right, the goats on His left, the believing thief on His right, the scorning, mocking man on His left. The right seems to be the right way to go.

SACRAMENT

The pattern continues today. Our right hand is designated as our covenant hand. Partake of the sacrament with the right hand, swear to tell the truth with the left hand on the Bible, the right hand to the square; sustain, welcome, thank and release by raising the right hand; priesthood blessings are ordered such that we bless the sick with right hand on the head or supporting an infant, and left hands on shoulders.

NOTHING AGAINST LEFTIES!

When we choose the right, it isn't a conspiracy against the lefties—it's a pattern that has roots as old as humanity itself.
Brother Paul says, "Right on."

During the Nauvoo exodus, nine babies were born on the banks of the Mississippi.

MORMON PRIMER ON MASONS

PART I

Some Latter-day Saints have heard about loose connections between Mormons and the Masons. What's the real story, here? There are several pieces. Together, they make for an interesting finished puzzle.

MASON: From the Latin *maceria* meaning a wall, or the French *masson* meaning a bricklayer or stone cutter.

FREE MASON: This term first shows up in the late 1300s and was formalized in 1717 in England as a distinct group of masons. The reason for "free-" falls into three camps of thinking (take your pick!): (1) the French *frère* meaning "brother mason;" (2) a reference to free-standing stones; (3) and free from the union-like control of local masonic guilds.

THREE DEGREES: The three levels of advancement and opportunity are: Entered Apprentice, Fellow Craft, and Master Mason or Master Mahan (see Moses 5:31,49 where this title is identified with Satan's secret combination and blood oath).

RELIGION: While it is very God-centered, it is not Christ-centered and people of all religions are invited to join. (Thanks, but no thanks.)

WHAT IS IT?

No one really knows what Masonry or Freemasonry is, or at least nobody can prove a definitive answer. The problem is that there is no central authority to declare or correct histories, legends, lore, practices and teachings. What one passionate historian cites as truth will be disputed by another equally passionate historian. Anybody pretty much can do or say anything, and for lack of investigation or follow up, nobody steps forward to correct error or undo change.

Black or white? The human eye can distinguish between 500 shades of gray.

MYTH-STORY: The art and craft of masonry (stone cutting) is as old as civilization itself. From ancient monuments such as the pyramids and the Sphinx to the Salt Lake Temple, working the stone has never been a backyard hobby. The most ancient of legends is that the mason's unionized their artistry back in the days of Solomon's Temple around 900 B.C. Some speculate that several fragments of the temple ceremony were learned by these early stone workers and were adopted as rites of passage and brotherhood among fellow masons.

KNIGHTS TEMPLAR
* Jump ahead 2,000 years (wow, that's one BIG jump): By 1095 A.D., the Holy Land of Jesus was locked up by the Muslims. Pilgrims who once freely visited the place of Jesus's birth and death were forbidden or at least at risk to enter the Muslim's holy land. The European Christians organized several crusades to free the land. The Crusade of 1095 did indeed free Jerusalem (temporarily), but fighting continued.
* In 1118 A.D., a group of nine knights were sent to escort pilgrims around Jerusalem and environs. Though terribly out-numbered, they stayed the course and did their duty. They were housed in an apartment near the Dome of the Rock. Because it was the site of Solomon's Temple, these knights became known as Knights of the Temple, or Knights Templar. They took a vow of service to Christ, refused pay, lived as paupers, were chaste, and only accepted alms from visiting pilgrims.
* Over the years, their numbers, wealth, and power grew.

THREE STRIKES AND YOU'RE ...
* **STRIKE ONE:** Connecting masons with secret ceremonies and codes can be traced to the Knights Templar. They had fre-quent contact with Coptic Christians in Egypt, and it appears they picked up a few fragments of the temple rites and cere-monies as practiced by early Christians and possibly back to the days of Solomon. The Knights Templar embraced these secret rites as membership ceremonies, though original meanings were completely lost at this point.

* **STRIKE TWO:** In the 1200s, a large building boom started in Europe—cathedrals and castles were going up everywhere.

Masons and stone cutters were in high demand and decided to solidify their hold on the various contracts, skilled labor, and trade secrets by organizing themselves into guilds.

• **STRIKE THREE:** After 200 years, the Knights Templar had grown powerful and rich. Their vows of poverty and chastity, along with their acts of valor and piety, won them grants of lands and wealth. With the crusades over (for now), the Knights Templar disbanded, returned to Europe, and became money-lenders to the landowners.

France's King Philip in the early 1300s was waging war with England and really needed a lot of money. On Oct. 13, 1307, he sent troops to arrest the templars and confiscate their land and money. He used their secret rites and anti-Christian practice of loaning money for interest (usury) as proof the templars were guilty of heresy. Under guidelines of the Inquisition, he tortured them for confessions of other crimes of heresy against the Church, for which he imprisoned and killed hundreds. He went laughing all the way to the bank ... and war.

With the passage of the Knights Templar, their secret rites were handed off to the masonic guilds, who adopted them for membership rituals.

A BIG BUDDY NETWORK

With the decline in castle and cathedral building, the masonic guilds had less work to do and began accepting non-masons into their orders before the 1600s. The money they gathered went to help widows and orphans, and to maintain their society of "You scratch my back, I'll scratch yours." These were called Free and Accepted masons. In 1717, four masonic lodges met at the Apple Tree Tavern in London and established the first Grand Lodge. Three degrees of membership were also established, a practice continued to this day. Some believe this is when the masons as we know them today, with temples and secret ceremonies, actually started.

THEY'RE COMING TO AMERICA!

Known by the early 1700s as Freemasons, Masonry became a highly respected and popular socializing club for the well connected to connect with others. In the U.S., Freemasonry began

A jumbo jet burns 4,000 pounds of fuel to take off.

when the first American Lodge was organized in Philadelphia in 1730, and three years later in Boston. Membership rolls eventually included such luminaries as George Washington, Benjamin Franklin, John Hancock, the 13 signers of the U.S. Constitution, and many others. Even the Boston Tea Party is thought to have been primarily a Freemason freedom job!

To read about Joseph Smith joining the Masons, and how false accusations erupted over the origins of the Temple Endowment, see page 194.

****

"YEARS AGO WHEN OUR daughters were little girls who wanted to be big girls, the style of the day was to wear multiple petticoats. A little contention could have crept in as the girls soon learned that the one to get dressed first was the best dressed. In a large family of boys, those with the longest reach were the best fed. In order to avoid the obvious contention, they adopted a rule that required them at meal-time to leave at least one foot on the floor." —*Russell M. Nelson, 1989*

"OCCASIONALLY WE NEED to step back and look at ourselves from a nonmember's perspective. Really now, to them, aren't we just a little bit strange? Imagine yourself coming into a Mormon community for the first time and hearing talk about gold plates, an angel named Moroni, and baptisms for the dead. Imagine seeing, for the first time, nine children and two beleaguered parents in a beat-up station wagon with a bumper sticker reading, Families are Forever. The poor nonmember doesn't know if this is a boast or a complaint." —*Glenn L. Pace, 1989*

"ONE DAY you will cope with teenage children of your own. That will serve you right." —*Boyd K. Packer, 1989*

"MAY the Lord bless you ... and the Devil miss you." —*Ezra Taft Benson, 1989*

A large swarm of locusts can eat 80,000 tons of corn in one day.

WHERE WE GOT 'EM: THE JOURNAL OF DISCOURSES

Wow, almost 11,000 pages of speeches by the brethren, and each loaded with great stuff. Let's take a look.

TOTAL VOLUMES: 26
LEADERS QUOTED: More than 100
TOTAL SPEECHES: 1,438
TIME FRAME: 1854-1886

STORY

Our top hats off to good brother George D. Watt, a man baptized by Heber C. Kimball in 1837 in England. This faithful soul learned Pitman shorthand, and for many years, he faithfully recorded the speeches at the various conferences of the Church. He was also called upon to record the trial of those who murdered the Prophet Joseph Smith.

SPREAD THE WORD

After Brother Watt's immigration to the U.S., and subsequent venture out west, he began recording the Church conferences for the *Deseret News*. There was a problem here because the newspaper wasn't distributed outside of Utah. So, Brother Watt came up with an idea. He would print the speeches onto 16-page issues of a publication he named the *Journal of Discourses* and would publish a new set every two weeks.

MAKING A LIVING FOR THE LIVING

Brigham Young encouraged the project and asked the Saints to support it by purchasing issues so Brother Watt could make a living from his shorthand. This would help the Church serve the Saints abroad so they could stay abreast with the latest from Salt Lake City. It was a good mix, and the project went forward.

Utah is 70% LDS, Idaho is 30%; after Catholics, LDS is the largest sect in 10 states.

- The earliest volumes of the discourses focused mostly on speeches by the First Presidency and the Twelve.
- Later volumes included other general authorities, and outstanding missionaries, teachers, writers, and others.
- Most of the speeches were delivered in Salt Lake City, and quite a few were delivered in towns around Utah and Idaho. A few of Joseph Smith's sermons are included.
- Most of the talks apparently were extemporaneous without notes.
- It also sounds like many speakers had no advance notice they were going to speak.
- Many talks relied on the Holy Ghost, others reflected a unified position deeply discussed among the brethren at the time.
- Other talks were very temporal, slanted to the newly arrived immigrants and the needs of the audience.
- Brigham Young has the most talks: 390; John Taylor is second with 162.
- Twelve people, including one of Brigham Young's daughters recorded, speeches by the brethren, .
- The original Discourses were printed in Liverpool, England. In 1966, an exact photo reprint of the original edition was lithographed in the U.S., and made available to everybody.

COOL STUFF!
These books give a wonderful insight into the major trends in the Church's thinking on all sorts of topics. Here is a sampling of a few of Brother Paul's favorite sections:

- How many Earths are there? They are continually coming into existence. See Brother Brigham speaking in Vol. 14, pg. 71.

- How many Redeemers and Tempters are there? Brigham says one of each for every planet. See Vol. 14, pg. 71.

- Do resurrected people give birth to physical babies or spirit babies? Only spirits! See Vol. 6, pg. 275.

- And how are physical bodies created for the first time? An Adam and his Eve dwell in a new Earth and partake of the fruits of the corporeal world until the grosser matter is diffused in them so they can produce mortal tabernacles. See Vol. 6, pg. 275.

• Who brought plants and animals to this Earth, and from where? Adam did, from other places where they were already flourishing. Makes sense to Brother Paul! See Vol. 3, pg 319.

• The famous Adam-God discussion offers a glimpse into the logical uniting of eternal families of many generations to further our Eternal Father's work. Take a look in Vol. 1, pg. 50.

• Brigham worries he might have said too much about Heavenly Father and how his kingdom runs. If he has grossly erred on anything, he said, this is probably it. Vol. 8, pg. 58.

• Brigham sheds light on how the atonement works, that it is through mercy that justice is satisfied, and therefore anyone breaking their Temple covenants with God must personally atone for it—the Savior's atonement won't work in those instances. Vol. 3, pg. 247.

• The power of the priesthood is the power to organize matter. Christ "spoke to the native elements and brought forth bread ... Is that a mystery to you?" See Vol. 1, starting on page 264.

AND THERE ARE a lot more from where these came from! Read one volume a month, and you can finish off the whole set in a couple of years. But you won't because you'll be stopping all the time to go, "Oh my goodness, that is so way amazing!" or words to that effect. And then you'll want to write it down in your "Stuff I should remember" file. Brother Paul just loves these great records. He has been stuck in Vol. 7 for about a year, now. So much to learn, so little time.

****

... but "word" authorities claim "Sesquippedalophobia" is the real name. I'm afraid of both.

MORMON INVENTIONS

INVENTION: Disposable diapers' absorbency material
INVENTOR: Carlyle Harmon (roots in Utah)
STORY: Billions of babies owe him thanks—4-5 times a day.
Brother Harmon was on to something great when he took a
close look at the single-cell amoeba. He noticed that the little
critter could absorb an amazing quantity of liquids. Exploring
the processes involved started him down the path of developing
the world's first commercially successful synthetic absorbency
material that launched several billion-dollar corporations.
Disposable diapers, feminine hygiene products, disposable hospital and surgery products, and more, are used around the
world, thanks to Brother Harmon's discovery. His day job was
heading up the fabrics research at Johnson and Johnson. He
went on to discover a whole bunch more, from nonwoven fiber
fabrics used for wipes, gowns, and sheets used in hospitals, to a
tanning material, a disbursing agent for deep well drilling, and
even vanilla extract from lignin. In total, he had 39 patents to
his name. He taught at BYU and founded the Eyring Research
Institute. He died in 1997 at age 92.

INVENTION: World's best guns
INVENTOR: John Moses Browning (Utah)
STORY: John Moses Browning, son of the talented gunsmith
Jonathan Browning of Nauvoo fame, is the greatest inventor
and designer of firearms ever. His skill and inventiveness
changed the world forever. Although the Browning name isn't
on many of his most famous designs, they nevertheless are his
patented creations. He sold manufacturing rights to such nota-
bles as Winchester, Fabrique Nationale, Remington, Colt, and
Savage. Some of his early masterpieces include the first lever-
action repeater. In 1883, Winchester bought Browning's newly
invented rifle that facilitated easy ejection of a used cartridge
with one flip of a lever and the loading a new one with another

---

Goodyear Rubber reports: right shoes wear out faster than left shoes. Now you know.

flip. This began Winchester's 50-year domination of the firearms industry. Models 1886 and 1894 won worldwide acclaim.

• Browning sold more than 40 gun designs to Winchester, including pump-action rifles and shotguns, a lever-action shotgun and a bolt-action rifle. The Remington Model 11 Automatic and Browning Automatic-5 were the most popular shotguns for 50 years.

• Shortly after Brother Browning's mission, he devised a way to harness the expanding gas from a firing bullet to push out the used cartridge and load another—the world's first automatic. In 1890, he offered his invention to Colt Firearms. It was developed as the famous Colt Model 95 and could unleash 1,800 rounds in three minutes. This gun made the famous Gatling gun obsolete in six years and gained the nickname, The Peacemaker.

• Browning's inventions changed the way armies fought each other. Instead of the cavalry charge or the open-field standoff of gunfire exchange, warring troops moved to trench fighting during World War I, where they could find protection from the more deadly and accurate weapons. The new Browning Automatic Rifle (known by millions as the B.A.R.) was an 18-pound automatic that could shoot 500 rounds per minute at a range of 600 yards. Soldiers from World War I to Vietnam all benefitted from this, the most effective infantry weapon of all times.

INVENTION: Roadometer (an odometer for wagons)
INVENTOR: William Clayton and Appleton Harmon
STORY: The idea of an odometer dates back to at least 15 B.C. when a Roman architect invented a crude machine that helped measure short distances. Built like a wheelbarrow, as it was pushed by hand along the ground, the turning wheel would deposit a stone into a container after each revolution.

The Roadometer invented by the early Mormon pioneers is considered a "first" because nothing like this had been tried before for a wagon train crossing the American plains. Even Lewis and Clark's famous expedition was without an odometer of any kind, and their distance estimates were by sight and guess, often being way off.

A car traveling 100 mph would take 29 million years to reach the nearest star.

William Clayton had discovered that 360 revolutions of a wagon wheel equaled one mile. He tied a rag to a spoke and counted the revolutions that way. And then came his idea:

• "I walked some this afternoon in company with Orson Pratt and suggested to him the idea of fixing a set of wooden cog wheels to the hub of a wagon wheel, in such order as to tell the exact number of miles we travel each day. He seemed to agree with me that it could be easily done at a trifling expense."

"Brother Appleton Harmon is working at the machinery for the wagon to tell the distance we travel and expects to have it in operation tomorrow, which will save me the trouble of counting, as I have done, during the last four days."

"About noon today Brother Appleton Harmon completed the machinery on the wagon called a 'roadometer' by adding a wheel to revolve once in ten miles, showing each mile and also each quarter mile we travel, and then casing the whole over so as to secure it from the weather." The date was May 12, 1847.

****

WHAT HAPPENED TO MORONI?

In 1897, Charles D. Evans wrote in his journal:

At a meeting at Spanish Fork, Utah County, in the winter of 1896, Brother Higginson stated in my presence that Thomas B. Marsh told him that the Prophet Joseph Smith told him (Thomas B. Marsh, he being then president of the Twelve) that he became very anxious to know something of the fate of Moroni, and in answer to prayer, the Lord gave Joseph a vision, in which appeared a wild country and on the scene was Moroni, after whom were six Indians in pursuit; he stopped and one of the Indians stepped forward and measured swords with him. Moroni smote him, and he fell dead; another Indian advanced and contended with him; this Indian also fell by the sword; a third Indian then stepped forth and met the same fate; a fourth afterwards contended with him, but in the struggle with the fourth, Moroni, being exhausted, was killed. Thus ended the life of Moroni."

MORONI'S QUOTE

Is Brother Paul the only one who ever wondered what Angel Moroni was talking about when he visited young Joseph Smith during the night of September 21, 1823? Thanks to Brother Sidney B. Sperry, who gave this insight at BYU back in 1956, we have some solid understanding.

MOST LATTER-DAY SAINTS are familiar with the events of Moroni's visit to Joseph Smith the night of 1823. Joseph wrote that Moroni called him by name, identified himself, and said that God had a work for Joseph to do. He spoke of a book written on gold plates telling of the former people on the American continent and about a visit to them by the Savior. He told of the Urim and Thummim, a breastplate, and their function.

And then Moroni quoted scripture that varied only slightly from Joseph's own King James version. Here's the list:

QUOTE 1: PART OF MALACHI 3 AND MALACHI 4

Joseph didn't say exactly which parts of the Malachi scriptures Moroni quoted, but those in chapters 3 and 4 talk about the restoration of the gospel, preparations for the Millennium, and the importance of the sons of Levi. Moroni made slight additions to three verses (emphasis added to each).

Note: Brother Sperry observes that Moroni was paraphrasing Malachi 4:5-6 for Joseph's understanding because the resurrected Jesus Christ quoted the verses exactly to the Nephites.

• Malachi 4:1 was changed to, "For behold, the day cometh that shall burn as an oven, and all the proud, yea, and all that do wickedly shall <u>burn as</u> stubble; <u>for they that come</u> shall burn them, saith the Lord of Hosts, that it shall leave them neither root nor branch."

• Malachi 4:5 was changed to "Behold, <u>I will reveal unto you the Priesthood, by the hand of</u> Elijah the prophet, before the coming of the great and dreadful day of the Lord." (Restoration of the priesthood came a few years later).

Cliff diving, anyone? Hawaii has sea cliffs 3,300 feet high (same as a 275-story building)!

- Malachi 4:6 was changed to: "And he shall <u>plant in the</u> <u>hearts of the children the promises made to the fathers, and the</u> <u>hearts of the children shall turn to their fathers. If it were not</u> <u>so, the whole earth would be utterly wasted at his coming.</u>" (Doing work for the dead was set up later).

QUOTE 2: ISAIAH 11

The Isaiah quote explains the Millennium and the part Joseph is to play in preparing for it. In the first part of this chapter, the stem of Jesse is mentioned, and we know that to be Christ (see D&C 113). As for the root and rod, the root describes Joseph Smith's earthly mission and the rod dessribes his mission after the resurrection when huge responsibility is placed on him that is much greater than that given to him during his lifetime. Of Isaiah 11, Moroni said, "It was about to be fulfilled."

QUOTE 3: ACTS 3:22-23

Moroni then quoted, "For Moses truly said unto the fathers, A prophet shall the Lord your God raise up unto you of your brethren, like unto me; him shall ye hear in all things whatsoever he shall say unto you.

"And it shall come to pass, that every soul, which will not hear that prophet, shall be destroyed from among the people.

Explained Moroni, "That prophet was Christ, the day had not yet come when 'they who would not hear his voice should be cut off from among the people,' but soon would come."

QUOTE 4: JOEL 2:28-32

- The quotes from Joel talk about things just before the "great and terrible day of the Lord." Moroni said "This was not yet fulfilled, but was soon to be," answering once and for all the debate whether or not Joel was speaking of his own day. He wasn't!

STAY TUNED FOR MORE!

Joseph concluded with this enticing thought: Moroni also quoted many other scriptures with explanations that "cannot be mentioned here."

'Can't be mentioned'? That always is an intriguing invitation to explore for more. But as with all prophecy, we'll find out soon enough.

Sound moves through water at 4,945 feet a second and air at 1,087 feet a second.

FREQUENTLY FORGOTTEN
FIGURES OF SPEECH

These strange words have passed across Brother Paul's desk and memory for many years, and he is so tired of trying to remember their differences and meanings. This list is provided as a personal reference page so he won't have to go hunting every time somebody says, "A simile is like a metaphor without all the hyperbole ..." Oh heavens, what does all that mean?

SYNONYMS Words that have a similar meaning: brave, courageous.

ANTONYMS Words that mean the opposite: brave, cowardly.

PSEUDONYM A made-up name used in place of one's real name: Brother Paul.

ALLONYM A famous or authentic name hijacked to give authenticity to a work he or she did not create: Brother Paul's *Mormon Bathroom Reader* was ghostwritten by Elder B.H. Roberts!

HOMONYMS Pronounced the same, but spelled differently, and having different meanings: past, passed.

METAPHOR An implied comparison of dissimilar things: breaking news, caged emotions, stubborn stains!

SIMILE When you use the terms *as* or *like* in a comparison: As busy as a bee. Like a breath of fresh air.

ANALOGY Comparison of similar traits between dissimilar things. An analogy can carry on for several sentences or pages: Reading Brother Paul's bathroom reader is like rolling your brain down the creaky, glass-strewn basement stairs of an abandoned house and when you get to the bottom, you know it was a bumpy ride and you think you've really been somewhere!

HYPERBOLE Exaggerated for effect: I'd sell my first-born son into slavery to publish a book. (Hey, wait a second, I already did!)

ONE NATION UNDER GOD

America's Pledge of Allegiance has come under attack in recent years. Where did we get it, and what do people want to change?

The celebration of the 400th anniversary of Christopher Columbus in 1892 was going to be a really big deal according to Francis Bellamy (1855-1931), who chaired the committee in charge of the festivities for America's school children. His committee decided to have every school in America open that day with a flag ceremony and a flag salute. What would the flag salute consist of? Bellamy wrote a pledge.

THE VERY FIRST PLEDGE written in August 1892 read: "I pledge allegiance to my Flag and the Republic for which it stands, one nation, indivisible, with liberty and justice for all."

Bellamy envisioned a great patriotic swell across America. Said he, "Let the flag float over every school-house in the land and the exercise be such as shall impress upon our youth the patriotic duty of citizenship."

Bellamy almost put the word "equality" in the pledge, but he had on his committee some state school superintendents of education who were opposed to equality for women and blacks, so to keep the peace on the committee, he left the word out.

• **ON SEPT. 8, 1892,** the most popular family magazine, *The Youth's Companion*, published Bellamy's Pledge. By Columbus Day of that year 12 million American children were reciting the pledge as part of their daily ritual.

• **IN 1923,** the American Legion and the Daughters of the American Revolution changed "my Flag" to "the Flag of the United States." The following year they added "of America."

• **ON JUNE 22, 1942,** with World War II in full blaze and children all across America reciting the pledge, Congress gave it official sanction by including it in the United States flag code, including the practice of placing the right hand over the heart.

John Wycliffe and John Purvey completed the first English Bible in 1388.

A year later the U.S. Supreme Court ruled that school children could not be forced to recite the pledge as part of their daily school activities.

• **IN 1954,** after a popular push started by numerous religious groups, the Knights of Columbus and the Hearst Newspapers, the words "under God" were added by Congress. The 31-word pledge was now an oath and a prayer. Said President Dwight Eisenhower: "In this way we are reaffirming the transcendence of religious faith in America's heritage and future; in this way we shall constantly strengthen those spiritual weapons which forever will be our country's most powerful resource in peace and war."

• **THE PRECEDENT** for using the words "under God" was set when President Lincoln ad-libbed during his Gettysburg address—"This nation, under God, shall have a new birth of freedom." The "under God" words were spontaneous and not part of his written text.

• **THE NEXT TIME YOU RECITE THE PLEDGE,** remember that there is no comma between the words, "one nation under God." You shouldn't pause when saying these words.

• **FAMOUS COMEDIAN** and performer Red Skelton talked about the change in the pledge during his lifetime: "Since I was a small boy, two states have been added to our country, and two words have been added to the Pledge of Allegiance: Under God. Wouldn't it be a pity if someone said that is a prayer, and that would be eliminated from schools, too?"

• **IN JUNE 2002,** the 9th U.S. Circuit Court of Appeals ruled "under God" rendered the pledge unconstitutional as a government endorsement of religion. On Nov. 13, 2002, President George Bush signed a bill reaffirming "under God" and "In God We Trust." The bill was approved by Congress unanimously in the Senate and by 430 'yea' votes to 5 'nay' votes in the House.

Holy days begin for Hindus at sunrise, Jews at sunset, & Christians at midnight.

JAMES E. TALMAGE

Brother Talmage is one of the Church's great early scholars. He was a scientist by training, and he loved the Lord.

BROTHER TALMAGE WAS BORN in Hungerford, England, in 1862 and was baptized in 1873. And without a doubt, this guy was smart from the start, becoming an Oxford diocesan prize scholar in 1874. His inquisitive mind clung to chemistry and geology, and that's what launched him into a great life filled with scholarship, travel, adventure, and even some controversy.

- **AGE 20:** In 1882-83, he took selected courses in chemistry and geology at Lehigh University, Bethlehem, Pennsylvania. In one year he passed nearly all of the examinations required for the four-year course, even though he was a special student and not enrolled for a 4-year degree.
- **AGE 21:** In 1883, he was steeped in work at Johns Hopkins University, Baltimore, MD.
- **AGE 22:** Taught geology and chemistry at Brigham Young Academy—1884-88.
- **AGE 24:** In 1888, he was called as president of Latter-day Saints College. That service ended in 1893 when he became a professor of geology at the University of Utah from 1894-97.
- Married Mary May Booth in 1888, and they had eight children.
- **AGE 28:** Honorary doctor of Science and Didactics awarded by the LDS Church in 1890.
- **AGE 34:** Doctor of philosophy from Illinois Wesleyan University in 1896.
- **AGE 37:** A great thinker is never without controversy. A little of Brother Talmage's early controversy came when he published *The Articles of Faith* in 1899. Some Church leaders accused him of apostasy and he narrowly escaped Church sanction.
- **AGE 49:** When it was discovered in 1911 that the interior of the Salt Lake Temple had been photographed, and blackmailers were demanding $100,000 to prevent the photos from going

Tree of life: One acre of trees produces enough oxygen for 18 people every day.

public, Brother Talmage suggested the Church circumvent the attempted sabotage by taking its own photos and publishing them in a book. This was the foundation for his book, *House of the Lord*.

• Ordained an apostle and member of the Twelve in 1911.

• **AGE 50:** Honorary doctor of science degree from Lehigh University in 1912.

• He was known worldwide as one of the finest mining geologists and engineers, and was a fellow, delegate or member of dozens of scientific groups. His speaking expertise was widely admired, and he drew large crowds as a guest lecturer.

• His expertise was used by the Church to advise regarding underground ventilation options for the Salt Lake Tabernacle, and for his opinion on an official Church position on the scientific evidence for organic evolution.

• **AGE 52:** Another brush with controversy happened in 1914 when Brother Talmage stood in general conference and shared some advance text from his yet to be finished *Jesus the Christ*. Some Church leaders didn't like portions of his doctrine, and they had those particular comments stricken from the official published version of conference speeches.

• **AGE 53:** Wrote *Jesus the Christ* in 1915. This book reflected the thinking of his day and relied quite a bit on the view of Christ as developed in Frederick Farrar's *Life of Christ*. Is there any significance to the fact that he wrote it in the Temple? That undisturbed setting helped him work very fast, completing the document in longhand in seven months. Finishing the book on April 19, 1915, Elder Talmage wrote, "Had it not been that I was privileged to do this work in the Temple it would be at present far from completion. I have felt the inspiration of the place and have appreciated the privacy and quietness incident thereto. I hope to proceed with the work of revision without delay."

• **AMONG HIS OTHER WRITINGS** are included *First Book of Nature* (1888); *Domestic Science* (1891); *Tables for Blowpipe Determination of Minerals* (1899); *The Great Salt Lake, Present and Past* (1900) ; *The Articles of Faith* (1899), an exhaustive look at the doctrines of the Church; *The Great Apostasy* (1909); *The House of the Lord* (1912), mentioned above that looked at both modern and ancient places of holy sanctuary; *The Story of Mormonism* (1907); dozens of lectures delivered at Michigan, Cornell and other universities; *The Philosophical Basis of Mormonism* (1915); *Jesus the Christ* (1915); *The Vitality of Mormonism* (1919), and dozens of pamphlets and contributions to periodicals.

- **AGE 70:** He died in 1933 in Salt Lake City, Utah.

Brother Paul loves this great man who gave so much of himself to help build the kingdom. Despite any flaws and warts and whatever caused some stirrings or controversy, Brother Paul would be pleased to have 1/100th of Brother Talmage's smarts and understanding. Read more about him in Brother James P. Harris' *The Essential James E. Talmage*, which annotates and brings to life Brother Talmage's great contributions as summarized here.

****

“The mission president said, 'I want you to go down there and learn how to speak Maori.' He didn't say anything to the branch president, but the branch president had assigned all the Primary children to teach me how to speak Maori. I was helping to build a small chapel. While we were up there hammering nails, these Primary children would sit down on the grass and jabber Maori to me all day. They wouldn't speak any English. They knew how to speak English too—they knew more languages than I did. But, they wouldn't answer me if I spoke to them in English. I had to speak Maori to them. They were forcing me to learn this language, that I might be a more effective missionary.

“I remember they taught me a little song. Oh, how grateful I was to them! I thought to myself as I was learning this little ditty, 'Here I am, learning the great chants of the old Maoris passed down through hundreds of years. I have just been in New Zealand a few weeks and already I can sing this old time song.' I didn't know at the time what it meant, but I will never forget it as long as I live. Imagine my surprise when I found out it was 'Hey diddle diddle, the cat and the fiddle, the cow jumped over the moon!'”—*Robert L. Simpson, 1965*

J. GOLDEN KIMBALL
Part II

*We continue our three part journey through the wonderful world
of J. Golden Kimball quotes. Part I begins on page 32. To read
Part III, see page 175. Caution: salty words ahead!*

I MAY NOT WALK the straight and the narrow, but I sure
as hell try to cross it as often as I can!"

"THIS CITY (BRIGHAM CITY) looks like hell. You need to
clean things up, mow the grass, paint your houses and barns.
And you sisters, you could stand a little paint yourselves."

"I AM A LITTLE LIKE FATHER. When he used to quote
scripture, he would say, 'Well, if that isn't in the Bible, it ought
to be in it.'"

"I UNDERSTAND you brethren can't go on missions because
you swear too much. You can overcome it. Hell, I did."

SOME DIFFICULTY in the J. Golden Kimball household
apparently had become public, and a passerby caught up with
J. Golden with the obvious intent to rub it in his face. "Brother
Kimball, I understand you're having some problems with one of
your children." And J. Golden replied, "Yes, and the Lord is
having some problems with some of his, too."

"I FEEL aroused sometimes and the palms of my hands just
itch to take hold of the jaw-bone of an ass and beat these things
into dull men's skulls; I would do it, too, if I only had the jaw-
bone."

"WHY, BROTHER KIMBALL, you needn't be afraid, you'll
get Justice. Well," J. Golden said, "that is what I am afraid of."

The longest military march in U.S. history is 2,000 miles by the Mormon Battalion in 1847.

LOAD THE WAGON!

Pioneers to Utah in the 1850s were told to pack their wagons so as to "not encumber themselves with any other items than those just enumerated; as it is impracticable for them to take all the luxuries to which they have been accustomed."

THE RECOMMENDED LIST OF WHAT TO BRING:

- 1 good strong wagon, well covered with a light box
- 2 or 3 good yoke of oxen between the ages of 4 and ten years
- 2 or more milk cows
- 1 or more good beeves
- 3 sheep if they can be obtained
- 1000 lbs. of flour or other bread or bread stuffs in good sacks
- 1 doz. nutmegs
- 25 lbs salt
- 5 lbs. saleratus
- 10 lbs. dried apples
- ½ bushel of beans
- A few pounds of dried beef or bacon
- 5 lbs. dried peaches
- 20 lbs. dried pumpkin
- 25 lbs. seed grain
- 1 good musket or gun to each man over age of 12 years
- 1 lb. powder
- 4 lbs. lead
- 1 lb. tea
- 5 lbs. coffee
- 100 lbs. sugar
- 1 lb. cayenne pepper
- 2 lbs. black pepper
- ½ lb. mustard
- 10 lbs. rice for each family
- ½ lb. cloves
- 1 lb. cinnamon
- Cooking utensils to consist of a bake kettle, frying pan, coffeepot, and tea kettle
- Tin cups, plates, knives, forks, spoons, and pack as few as will do
- A good tent and furniture for each 2 families
- 20 lbs. of soap
- 4 or 5 fishhooks and line
- 15 lbs. iron and steel
- a few lbs. of wrought nails
- one or more sets of saw or grist mill irons to each company of 100 families
- 2 sets of pulley blocks and ropes to each company for crossing rivers
- 1 good seine and hook for each company
- From 20 to 100 lbs. of farming and mechanical tools
- Clothing and bedding to each family not to exceed 500 lbs.
- Ten extra teams for each company of 100 families.

Homosexuality was on the American Psychiatric Assoc.'s list of mental illnesses until 1973.

NIGH UNTO KOLOB?

Are we nigh unto Kolob? Until you look up on a cloudless night at the immensity of outer space, our home planet seems like the biggest place around!

EXPLORING: In 1977, NASA sent two Explorer probes on a tour of Jupiter, Saturn, Uranus, and Neptune, and their 48 moons. From there, the probes were aimed at the edge of the solar system. They're traveling at 37,000 miles an hour, or 330,000,000 miles a year, and as of 2005, Voyager I is "only" 7 billion miles from the sun. Its radio messages take ten hours to reach earth.

WHERE ARE WE? Our planet is the third of nine known orbiting planets around a medium-sized star that shares the galaxy with more than 200-400 billion other stars.

MEASURING STICK: Because space is so vast and limitless, we need some measuring sticks so we can talk intelligently about distance and size. One such measuring stick is the light-year—the distance light travels in the vacuum of space in one year. Light moves pretty fast, about 186,000 miles in a second, that's seven times around the earth in one second. In one year it travels 5,865,696,000,000 miles (round that to 6 trillion!)

DISTANCE: Memorize these three—earth is 93,000,000 miles from the sun; the sun is 27,700 light-years from the center of our Milky Way galaxy; and our galaxy is 100,000 light-years in diameter. That light-year thing means that if you pointed your flashlight to the center of the galaxy, it would take somebody out there 27,700 years before they saw it, and another 27,700 years for you to see them wave back.

NEIGHBORS: The galaxy closest to our Milky Way is Andromeda. It is 2.9 million light-years away, or the distance of 29 Milky Way Galaxies lined up edge to edge. That's not far away because Andromeda is approaching us at 87 miles per sec-

Thunderheads packed with rain or snow are called cumulonimbus clouds.

ond, and in only 3 billion years, we're going to collide! The result will probably be one giant combined elliptical galaxy.

OUR GALAXY is part of a local group of 30 galaxies. Our Local Group is ten million light-years in diameter—or 100 diameters of our galaxy across. The gravitational center of that group is between us and Andromeda.

OUR LOCAL GROUP is a member of the Virgo Super Cluster. This monster-sized group is shaped like a disk, and it's about 200 million light-years in diameter, (the distance of 2,000 Milky Ways lined up edge to edge!). The super cluster is a family of 5,000 other galaxies all moving, circling, and orbiting in an amazing harmony of light-speckled behemoths.

THE GREAT WALL: The largest known superstructure in the universe is called the Great Wall. It is a mass of thousands of galaxies grouped together in a band 300 million light-years away, and it measures 600 million light-years long, 300 million light-years wide, and 15 million light-years thick. It may be longer than we think, but our own Milky Way Galaxy prevents us from seeing how far into the universe it actually reaches.

THE GREAT ATTRACTOR: Now for a mystery! Way out there in the universe is a group of galaxies so dense and heavy that the group's combined gravitational force is pulling in galaxies from hundreds of millions of light years away. We call it the Great Attractor. From what we can see, there's an old cluster of many thousands of galaxies clumped at its center. Dust and dark matter in our Milky Way and prevent us from taking a closer look, but its powerful presence is obvious from the direction surrounding galaxies are moving—TOWARDS it!! (There's another good puzzle to ask the Lord about when the time comes.)

SO, ARE WE NIGH UNTO KOLOB? Compared to the immensity of outer space, we're probably pretty close to Kolob in galactic terms, but more likely we're still many light years away. But that doesn't stop the Lord—he probably offers shuttle service: "Nigh unto Kolob, next stop, tickets please?"

"SECRET" COUNCILS

*Three temporary organizations in the early Church continue to
generate more myth than truth. Here are their stories.*

NAME: Council of Fifty
LEGEND OR FACT: Fact.
EXISTENCE: Formed March 11, 1844, disbanded
1850; leaned upon in the 1880s for a brief period.
STORY: The Council of Fifty was organized by Joseph Smith
to help the brethren with the temporal affairs of the Church.

The Council of Fifty included members of the Twelve, and
met in secret until Joseph Smith died. Under Brigham Young
and John Taylor, the group met openly. They helped with
Joseph's presidential campaign, explored places and possibilities
for relocating the Saints, including a look at western Iowa,
Oregon, California, and Texas. They helped plan the exodus of
Nauvoo, and performed scouting duties for Brigham Young during the trek west. They served as the legislature in the new
Utah territory, but when the government replaced them over
concerns of separation of church and state, the Council of Fifty
dwindled in importance. John Taylor called a similar group
together to help him with polygamy issues in the 1880s. The
last minutes of the Council of Fifty were recorded in 1884.

NAME: Danites
LEGEND OR FACT: Both.
EXISTENCE: Formed 1838, disbanded 1838
STORY: With rising discord among early Church members in
Kirtland over Joseph Smith's failed bank, and murmuring
among the Missouri Saints, a Brother Sampson Avard took it
upon himself to organize a secret society that was armed, united
by secret oath, and bent on protecting the Church and avenging
its losses. When fellow Danites realized how Avard was abusing
their trust to terrorize and commit crime, they brought it to the
attention of Joseph Smith. Shortly afterwards, Avard was arrested for crimes and he "confessed" that Joseph was behind it all
with plans to overrun the state of Missouri. For this plea bar-

gain, Avard was released and Joseph Smith, and others, were thrown into Liberty Jail for six months. Avard was excommunicated and the Danites were immediately disbanded.

However, so zealous was Avard in his criminal activities and secrecy that a legend grew that secret Danite avengers remained active. This soon ignited the imaginations of writers and the idea of a murderous band of secret Danites was accepted as fact. The Danites had been the subject of at least 50 novels by 1900. Zane Grey (western writer), Robert Louis Stevenson (adventure writer), Arthur Conan Doyle (Sherlock Holmes fame) were among those who loved the Danite image for their murder mysteries, and their books perpetuated the myth.

NAME: 70 Destroying Angels
LEGEND OR FACT: Legend.
EXISTENCE: After the Saints arrived in the Salt Lake Valley
STORY: With no lawmen to police the behavior of the early Saints in Utah, Brigham Young appointed several trusted, gun-toting brethren to patrol the new settlements. These men were good shots and knew about life on the frontier. They responded to emergencies ranging from conflicts with Indians to stealing, cattle rustling and murder that increased as California gold-seekers and other immigrants passed through the valleys of Utah.

These makeshift sheriffs became part of a rumor mill that mixed the infamy of the secret Danites with a new mystery group called Brigham's "70 Destroying Angels." The number "70" apparently was borrowed from the Church's well-known Quorum of Seventy.

Newspapers in the east even identified five Danites who might be "avenging angels"—William Adams "Bill" Hickman, Orrin Porter Rockwell, Ephe Hanks, Robert Burton, and Lot Smith. The truth was that these good brethren stood by Brigham as defenders of the faith and the Saints during troubled times and the later conflicts with the U.S. Army in the so-called Utah War. There were no "70 Destroying Angels," the rumors and legends notwithstanding.

Don't like big bugs? Then don't grab a stick insect, they grow to 15 inches long.

WILFORD WOODRUFF'S EMINENT PEOPLE, Part I

An amazing event in the early decades of the restoration took place in 1877 involving Wilford Woodruff. In this three part spread, Brother Paul offers the story and the names.

STORY: Wilford Woodruff, then president of the St. George Temple in 1877, had an astonishing experience. He reported that spirits of the dead, primarily the key founders of the United States, came to him asking why their baptism and temple work had not yet been done.

Two public references to this experience and official temple records provide the names of close to 200 eminent men and women for whom temple work was performed. It is not clear how many people actually appeared to President Woodruff, but recorded below are his words about the others, as written in the *Journal of Discourses* and *The Discourses of Wilford Woodruff*.

EXACT NUMBER IS UNKNOWN

How many people actually visited President Woodruff, and how many others were only on "the list"? This is a tough question to answer. From the records we learn this much:

• Baptizing began on Aug. 21, 1877, when 100 individuals including 54 signers of the Declaration of Independence and other founders were baptized by proxy. President Woodruff was proxy and John D.T. McAllister did the baptizing.

• Also on Aug. 21, President Woodruff baptized Elder McAllister for 21 other men.

• Sister Lucy Bigelow Young was baptized for Martha Washington, nine members of her family, and 47 others (according to temple records). At least 196 names have been mentioned.

• High Priests ordained: George Washington, John Wesley, Benjamin Franklin, Christopher Columbus, Admiral Horatio Nelson. All other men were ordained elders.

• Wilford's journal entries and Temple records don't agree and some of the Temple records are gone, so the exact list is unknown.

WILFORD WOODRUFF, SPEAKING TO THE SAINTS ....

"I will here say, before closing, that two weeks before I left St. George, the spirits of the dead gathered around me, wanting to know why we did not redeem them. Said they, "You have had the use of the Endowment House for a number of years, and yet nothing has ever been done for us. We laid the foundation of the government you now enjoy, and we never apostatized from it, but we remained true to it and were faithful to God." These were the signers of the Declaration of Independence, and they waited on me for two days and two nights. I thought it very singular, that notwithstanding so much work had been done, and yet nothing had been done for them. The thought never entered my heart, from the fact, I suppose, that heretofore our minds were reaching after our more immediate friends and relatives. I straightway went into the baptismal font and called upon brother McCallister to baptize me for the signers of the Declaration of Independence, and fifty other eminent men, making one hundred in all, including John Wesley, Columbus, and others; I then baptized him for every President of the United States, except three; and when their cause is just, somebody will do the work for them." (*The Discourses of Wilford Woodruff,* p. 160-61).

AND AGAIN

"I am going to bear my testimony to this assembly, if I never do it again in my life, that those men who laid the foundation of this American government and signed the Declaration of Independence were the best spirits the God of Heaven could find on the face of the Earth. They were choice spirits, not wicked men. General Washington and all the men that labored for the purpose were inspired of the Lord.

"Another thing I am going to say here, because I have a right to say it. Every one of those men that signed the Declaration of Independence with General Washington, called upon me as an Apostle of the Lord Jesus Christ, in the Temple at St. George, two consecutive nights, and demanded at my hands that I should go forth and attend to the ordinances of the House of God for them. Men are here, I believe, that know of this, Brother J. D. T. McAllister, David H. Cannon and James S. Bleak. Brother McAllister baptized me for all those men, and then I told these brethren that it was their duty to go into the temple and labor until they had got endowments for all of them. They did it. Would those spirits have called upon me as an elder of Israel, to perform that work, if they had not been noble spirits before God? They would not. I bear this testimony because it is true. The Spirit of God bore record to myself and the brethren while we were laboring in that way." (*Journal of Discourses*, Vol.19, pp. 229-31; September 16, 1877)

JAMES GODSON BLEAK, CLERK TO BRIGHAM YOUNG: "I was also present in the St. George Temple and witnessed the appearance of the Spirits of the Signers of the Declaration of Independence. And also the spirits of the Presidents of the U.S. up to that time. And also others, such as Martin Luther and John Wesley, who came to Wilford Woodruff and demanded that their baptism and endowments be done. Wilford Woodruff was baptized for all of them. While I and Brothers J.D.T. McAllister and David H. Cannon (who were witnesses to the request) were endowed for them. These men that we did work for, were choice Spirits, not wicked men. They laid the foundation of this American Gov., and signed the Declaration of Independence and were the best spirits that the God of Heaven could find on the face of the Earth to perform this work. Martin Luther and John Wesley helped to release the people from religious bondage that held them during the dark ages. They also prepared the people's hearts so long as they would be ready to receive the restored gospel when the Lord sent it again to men on Earth."

For the list of eminent men who were part of this amazing experience, see page 319.

For the list of eminent women, see page 367.

****

WHERE WE GOT 'EM

Some practices and ideas in the Church that seem ancient are actually relatively new. Brother Paul observes a few.

NO MORE CLAPPING
In 1954, as dozens of new chapels were being completed each year, the question of applause and whether it is appropriate in the chapel was posed to the Brethren. Their counsel: "There shall be no applause on the Sabbath Day, but it may be permitted on other days of the week. ... Shouting, whistling, and stamping of feet should never be permitted in chapels or in the amusement hall."

TITHING SETTLEMENT IS A FAMILY AFFAIR
For a long while, heads of families went to the Bishop at the end of the year to reconcile an honest and fair tithing for the prior 12 months. In 1955, the Brethren changed that with this announcement in the *Church News*, "Church authorities have requested that not only heads of families and those earning incomes, report for tithing settlement but the entire families—mom, dad, sisters and brothers—that all might get into the habit of 'setting their ledgers with the Lord.'"

FAMILY HOME EVENING I n 1915, the First Presidency under the leadership of President Joseph F. Smith, instituted a "Home Evening" to draw families closer together.

WARD TEACHERS NOT TO BE SET APART
In 1955, the Brethren clarified the setting apart question. "Because all who bear the Priesthood have the authority and the responsibility of a ward teacher, it is not necessary that they be set apart for this work."

OH MISTER, WHERE ART THOU?
In 1949, the *Church News* made it clear that "brother" was the best and proper salutation for all males in the Church. No more "Mr." Members of the Twelve were to be "Elder" not "Apostle."

Roll the dice? The numbers on opposite sides of a die always add up to 7.

INFAMOUS MORMONS

As they say on The Three Amigos, *'Infamous means he's MORE famous!' Actually, infamous means famous for a bad reason. Here are some names of the past that have gone down into Brother Paul's* Annals of Infamy.

NAME: Sonia Johnson
REASON WE REMEMBER: She led a fight against the LDS Church and its stand opposing the Equal Rights Movement.
STORY: In the late 1970s, Sister Johnson became a huge supporter of the weakly crafted Equal Rights Amendment, and when the Church came out against it, she came out against the Church. In 1977, she started down the path of becoming a radical feminist activist and co-founded "Mormons for ERA." The following year, she spoke at the U.S. Senate's Constitutional Rights Subcommittee and got in a big fight with Utah Senator Orrin Hatch over the ERA. That's when she became the nationally recognized figurehead for women's rights, anti-Mormonism, and pro-ERA activism.

In 1979 she was excommunicated and divorced from her husband. ERA died shortly afterwards. Ms. Johnson went on to write *Housewife to Heretic* (1981), *Going Out of Our Minds: The Metaphysics of Liberation* (1987), *Wildfire: Igniting the She/Volution* (1989), *The Ship that Sailed Into the Living Room: Sex and Intimacy Reconsidered* (1991), and others. She later became a lesbian separatist and founded a short-lived commune for women called Wildfire. It was disbanded in 1993.

NAME: Cody Judy
REASON WE REMEMBER: He briefly held Elder Hunter hostage with a fake bomb at BYU.
STORY: It was February 7, 1993, when President Howard W. Hunter, then President of the Quorum of the Twelve Apostles, stood at BYU's Marriott Center podium to give a fireside speech to 17,000 students. Cody Judy stormed the podium holding up what he claimed to be a bomb, and demanded President

Hunter read a three-page statement that proclaimed Judy to be the prophet of the Church. Judy was arrested, found guilty and thrown in prison for 15 years. In 2000, he was released on parole and ran unsuccessfully for Congress. He's been unheard of since.

NAME: Ervil Morel LeBaron
REASON WE REMEMBER: He instigated murders among large polygamist families beginning in the 1950s.
STORY: In the 1950s, several "Church of the First Born" organizations were started by LaBaron family members. Ervil LaBaron's was called "The Church of the Firstborn of the Lamb of God." He had 13 wives and 50 children, and believed that anyone who crossed him was worthy of death. Drawing his authority from D&C 85:7, he viewed himself as the prophet and the "one mighty and strong." A glimpse into the dark mind of LeBaron came when Salt Lake County investigator Dick Forbes asked him in 1979, "Ervil, what would you do if someone doesn't pay their tithing?" LeBaron replied, "You kill them."

Having had a hand in eliminating family members so he could be in charge, LeBaron had his "soldiers" murder his rival polygamist Rulon Allred in Murray, Utah, in 1978. This continued the revenge and avenge murders that carried on for years and took the lives of at least 20 in Utah, Mexico and Texas.

The ugly saga ended with the murder conviction in 1993 of three clan members for murdering four siblings in Texas in 1988. As for Ervil himself, he died much earlier of a heart attack at the Utah State Prison in 1981.

Various family members, disgusted with who they called "Evil Ervil" have since broken free of the terror, many have joined the LDS Church and served honorable missions, and have started building a productive and positive heritage for which their descendants may reflect upon with pride.

****

"THERE'S MANY A BESTSELLER that could have been prevented by a good teacher."—Flannery O'Connor (1925-1964)

THE LESSON BEHIND BIOSPHERE II

There's an amazing truth to be learned from an amazing place.

ERECTED OF STEEL AND GLASS, and spread out over three acres in central Arizona is the world's largest outdoor sealed enclosure called Biosphere II. This giant greenhouse lab was first created to test the ability of science to recreate mother nature (the original Biosphere I) on a much smaller scale to support a manned mission to Mars.

MAN-MADE GARDEN OF EDEN

In this amazing air-tight structure is a 900,000 gallon saltwater ocean, a rain forest with trees approaching 80 feet tall, a desert, fruit trees, shrubs, a 15 foot mountain, a sprinkling system, animals, insects, birds, in all about 3,800 species of flora and fauna, and habitation for eight humans.

CAN'T TAKE IT WITH YOU

The goal was to see if Biosphere II, once established with mature plant life, could support humans, recycle waste, produce needed energy, and bear fruit and oxygen for a long, 2-year mission to Mars. Sunshine enters Biosphere II through 8,000 double-pane sheets of glass, and the space-bound version would absorb sunshine in the same way.

For several years the trees inside Biosphere II grew, the flowers bloomed, the cycles of nature unfolded with regularity, and the insects pollinated the various blossoms. It seemed like a paradise on Earth—the genius of Biosphere II was working.

TOO BIG FOR ITS BIRCHES

But early into the experiment, an interesting problem began to grow. One morning, the people living inside noticed a strange occurrence. One of the tall trees in the rain forest was behaving oddly. Its upper branches were spreading out far too wide and too thick for its trunk to support them. The overgrowth didn't

---

Frustrated with weight loss? Banging your head against a wall uses 150 calories an hour.

create too much of a stir as there were plenty of other issues to deal with. But it was taken note of and watched.

IF A TREE FALLS IN A FOREST ...

And then one morning during a routine inspection, there on the ground they discovered a broken limb, snapped off from this oddly growing tree due to the limb's own sheer weight.

Specialists were called to Biosphere to examine the problem. Was it a bad strain of tree, a bad seed, a problem with the fertilizer or insects or the roots? Why the strange growth?

IT'S NOT NICE TO FOOL MOTHER NATURE

After extensive examination, no one could solve the puzzle—until one day when a young man was on the scene, passively examining the anomaly. He looked at the tree, looked at the surrounding interior of this huge and costly miniature Earth, and suddenly he knew exactly what was wrong.

LEHI KNEW ALL ABOUT TREES AND SUCH

The answer came from father Lehi in 2 Nephi 2:11-15: "For it must needs be, that there is an opposition in all things ... And now, my sons, I speak unto you these things for your profit and learning; for there is a God, and he hath created all things, both the heavens and the Earth, and all things that in them are, both things to act and things to be acted upon."

THE ANSWER IS BLOWING IN THE ...

What was needed? In a word, opposition. The multi-million dollar Biosphere II had no wind.

When a new seedling first pokes its head above the soil, God does not stop the winds, the rains or the storms. That opposition beats against the seedling from its first day till its last.

OPPOSITION IS HARD BUT NEEDFUL

As the seedling grows and matures, it begins to grow stress bark. This material allows the seedling to bend in the wind without breaking. The stronger the wind, the more stress bark it will grow. When the seedling becomes a mature tree, its many branches and leaves stand in the way of tons of force applied when the wind blows. And yet the tree holds strong, swaying in the breeze, giving just enough to take the pressure without snapping its branches or trunk, or becoming uprooted.

REFUSING TO YIELD CAN BE DEADLY

As a tree grows older, it can lose its ability to flex and bend. Eventually a storm strong enough comes along and snaps off its branches and leaves. The roots suffer and the tree dies. In another storm, it topples and becomes food for the bark beetles, termites and vermin of the forest floor.

ATOP CALIFORNIA'S WHITE MOUNTAINS

Old Methuselah—a bristle cone pine tree, is the oldest living thing on Earth, and now estimated to be just a few decades shy of 5,000 years old.

Methuselah is a massive, sturdy old tree about 36 feet around and just 30-40 feet tall. A few inches of bark connect the few remaining live branches to its roots. Short growing seasons give this tree a very dense, insect- and fungi-resistant wood.

Methuselah's home is a wind-swept, barren wasteland at about 10,000 feet. Little water, terrible winter temperatures, and lashing winds are customary for this very inhospitable place. But Methuselah is not alone. An entire mountain side is included in this 28,000 acre national park where the daring visitor can stare at dozens of these ancient witnesses whose existence on the gravely slopes precede the coming of Christ, the brilliance of Rome and perhaps the building of the great pyramids.

And yet for these trees, it is exactly the harsh home in which they live that extends their lives these many thousands of years.

EDEN ISN'T HEAVEN

The tree in Biosphere II had no opposition to help it grow strong to meet adversities, to learn to yield when yielding was important to survival. It was pampered and unchallenged, and as a result, it out grew itself, suffered for it, and died.

We are all as the trees. Our roots, our limbs, our lives, are burdened and strengthened to survive—if we'll take it. It is the winds of opposition that make us strong. Like Methuselah.

Don't blink! Fastest moving human muscle are those that open and close the eyelid.

SPEEDY DELIVERY!

The Saints are fast. We're not talking once a month going without two meals, we're talking speedy fast. See if you can catch up with these!

FASTEST TIME TO EAT A RAW ONION (2004 World Record). Trevor Reilly, 16, Valley Center California Stake, shattered the old world record of 2 minutes, 45 seconds by eating a 7.5 ounce raw onion in 1 minute, 35 seconds.

FASTEST TYPIST. In 1985, Von E. Christensen, Sandy 37th Ward, Sandy Utah East Stake, typed 124 words per minute to win a Utah speed contest.

FASTEST SOAP BOX CAR. In 1969, Steve Souter, 12, Midland Ward, Texas, West Stake, won the 32nd All-American Soap Box Derby in Akron, Ohio, finishing the 974.5-foot course in 27.34 seconds.

FASTEST CIVILIAN FLIER. In 1990, John Goddard, La Canada California Stake, flew an F111 fighter-bomber to a new civilian air-speed record in that class at 1,500 mph.

FASTEST KNOT TYING. In 1974, Kenneth Purnell, 12, Calgary 3rd Ward, Alberta, Canada, set a new Canadian national record for tying six different knots in 10.9 seconds. The old record set in 1957 was 12.5 seconds.

FASTEST GROCERIES BAGGER. Micah Crapo, 17, Bluffdale 2nd Ward, Bluffdale, Utah, Stake, was crowned, er, bagged as Best Bagger 2001 by the National Grocers Association at its annual contest in Dallas. He won $2,000 and an appearance on "The Late Show with David Letterman."

FASTEST READER. In 1966, 11-year-old Tanya McBride, Dunn Branch, Raleigh North Carolina Stake, was clocked at reading 100,000 words a minute with comprehension above 90

The U.S. flag's blue star field was to represent "a new constellation" in the sky.

percent. Her father, the local branch president, was a teacher of speed reading along with English courses in Methodist College in Fayetteville.

FASTEST 100-METER DASH. In 1971, Canagasabai Kunalan, Singapore Branch in the Southeast Asia Mission, ran the 100-meter in 10.3 seconds, just 4/10ths of a second off the world record at that time.

FASTEST UNDER-FOUR-MINUTE-MILE. On May 6, 1989, Doug Padilla set the Church's best mile time at 3:54.2. In 1996, Jason Pyrah set a new personal best in the mile during a track meet at Eugene, Oregon, when he ran a 3:55.14 mile.

FASTEST WALK ACROSS THE UNITED STATES (1968 World Record). In 1968, Bryon D. Young walked across the United States in 64 days 14 hours, a new world record. But considering he had rested on Sundays, his trip actually took the equivalent of 55 days 14 hours.

FASTEST BICYCLE TRIP AROUND THE WORLD (1984 World Record). In 1984, Matt DeWaal and Jay Aldous, both of Salt Lake City, pedaled 14,290 miles around the world in 106 days to set a new record.

FASTEST SPEED CLIMBER (1999 World Record). In 1999, Aaron Shamy, Holladay 24th Ward, Holladay, Utah, North Stake, shattered the world record in the 60-foot World Extreme Speed Climbing Championship in San Francisco with a time of 12.61 seconds.

****

"I HOPE all you single adult brethren will follow our Prophet's admonition to marry at the proper time and will not procrastinate your opportunity to be a husband and father. That is the order of the gospel. President Benson meant when he said: 'Understand that temple marriage is essential to your salvation and exaltation.' I would add: Better late than never."
—Elder Joseph B. Wirthlin

In 2001, a high school graduate earned an average $34,723; a PhD. earned $86,965.

MORONI'S PROMISE!

PART II

*More famous people who received a copy of
the Book of Mormon.*

READER: Queen Victoria (1819-1901)
DATE: 1841
CIRCUMSTANCE: Lorenzo Snow, a newly baptized convert serving as president of the London Conference as part of his mission to England, had an opportunity to meet Queen Victoria by appointment and presented her with a copy of the Book of Mormon.

READER: Pope John Paul II (1920-2005)
DATE: 1981
CIRCUMSTANCE: Famed LDS Polish pianist Vladimir Jan Kochanski met the Pope after a concert and presented him a copy of the Book of Mormon. Upon receiving the book, the Pope responded: "This is a Mormon publication ... Ah, yes. Beautiful young prophet."

READER: Pope Pius XII (1876-1958)
DATE: 1945
CIRCUMSTANCE: Anthony I. Johnson, Blythe California, had help from a friend in the U.S. Embassy to meet the Pope in the summer of 1945. He gave the Pope his GI version of the Book of Mormon, and in good English and with great cordiality, the Pope thanked him for the gift.

READER: Thailand Queen Sirikit
DATE: 1981
CIRCUMSTANCE: As a guest of the Church in 1981, Queen Sirikit was given a brief tour of Temple Square and taken to meet Church leaders. During her visit, she was given a beautifully-bound set of the four standard works.

To read more about Moroni's Promise, see page 201.

Malachi is the "youngest" book of the Old Testament, written about 400 B.C.

WHICH FIRST VISION?

The Prophet Joseph Smith left behind three renditions of his First Vision. Because there are differences in the accounts, critics of the Church like to cite these as evidence of a history and doctrine that evolved with each retelling. The allegations couldn't be further from the truth.

CLAIM: The Prophet Joseph Smith Jr.'s three versions of his vision differ enough to prove they were embellished as time passed.

EVENT: Joseph Smith is visited by the Father and the Son while in prayer in a grove of trees not far from his home in western New York state, in the spring of 1820.

JOSEPH'S JOURNAL NOTE: "I soon found, however, that my telling the story had excited a great deal of prejudice against me among professors of religion ... and though I was an obscure boy, only between fourteen and fifteen years of age ... yet men of high standing would take notice sufficient to excite the public mind against me." (JSH 1:22-28)

FIRST DRAFT: The 1832 version of the First Vision was written in both the hand of Joseph Smith and his scribe Frederick G. Williams. This version does not mention God the Father appearing with his son Jesus Christ.
• Joseph says he was told to join no other Church.
• The 1832 draft is loaded with insertions, corrections and mistakes, with more than 70 misspellings and run-on sentences.
• It lacked the polished smoothness of the Book of Mormon and other revelations recorded in the Doctrine and Covenants written 2-3 years earlier.
• No effort was taken to prepare this version for publication.

1835 VERSION: Joseph divulges in the second version that there were two individuals but does not identify them. "A pillar of fire appeared above my head, it presently rested down and filled me with joy unspeakable, a personage appeared in the midst of this pillar of flame which was spread all around ... another personage soon appeared like unto the first ... he testified unto me that Jesus Christ is the Son of God, and I saw many angels in this vision."

1838 VERSION: Joseph makes it clear in the official version: "When the light rested upon me I saw two personages, whose brightness and glory defy all description, standing above me in the air. One of them spake unto me, calling me by name and said, pointing to the other—This is My Beloved Son. Hear Him!"

APOSTLE PAUL SETS THE PRECEDENT

Ezra Taft Benson points out that Paul's First Vision reporting technique closely parallels that of Joseph Smith's.

PAUL'S FIRST VISION VERSION

In Acts 9, Paul says he was surrounded by a bright light, fell to the ground, and heard a voice ask him, "Saul, Saul, why persecutest thou me?" He says fellow travelers "stood speechless, hearing a voice," but saw no man.

PAUL'S SECOND VERSION

In Acts 22, Paul makes a second report on his experience. Still no mention of seeing Jesus, but he says he fell to the ground when he heard the voice. However, we know he was blinded by a light because he went to Ananias to have his sight restored. Ananias assures Paul he was chosen to "see that Just One" to receive instructions, indicating Paul saw the Savior.
• A change from the first report: Paul said his friends "heard not the voice" but they saw "the light and were afraid."

PAUL'S THIRD VERSION

Finally, in Acts 26, Paul records that the Lord told him he appeared so Paul could be a witness "of both these things which thou has seen, and for those things in the which I will appear unto thee."
• Another change from the other version: yes, his friends did indeed fall to the ground, they didn't just stand there.

WHICH FIRST VISION?

The Apostle Paul's first vision and Joseph Smith's first vision are not diminished or weakened just because more detail was reported or corrections made with each written version. Their experiences are made stronger because the essential messages remain consistent throughout.

• Everyone who reads the amazing experience these brethren shared should be grateful that they or their scribes took the time to provide the last and most correct versions. Nevertheless, an honest skeptic rejecting Joseph Smith's three renditions must also reject the Apostle Paul's for the same reason.

****

Secret Retirement Location?

IF YOU tried scanning the local phone directory in the Phoenix metropolitan area a few years ago, you would stumble on the secret retirement location for many of the famous names in the Church!

• **JOSEPH SMITH:** There were two with no middle initials, one from Scottsdale and the other from Phoenix. Some 15 additional Joseph Smiths with various middle initials lived in the area.
• **JOHN TAYLOR:** Five of them live there with no middle initial, and 17 others with a middle name.
• **JOSEPH F. SMITH:** Lives in Glendale.
• **GEORGE A. SMITH:** Three of them are out there enjoying the hot Arizona sunshine.
• **HAROLD B. LEE:** Find him living in Sun City.
• **THOMAS MONSON:** There's a Thomas A. and a Thomas J. but no Thomas S.
• **PAUL DUNN:** Paul D. and Paul N. both live in Phoenix.
• **MORMON:** Yes, there's even a Mormon, Naomi Mormon of Phoenix. She's not LDS but she fields plenty of phone calls from people looking for more information about the Church. "We used to live in Chicago," she said, "and we were the only Mormons in the phone book there, too."

****

... William B. Burt received the first U.S. patent for a typing machine.

MORONI'S CODE

*Captain Moroni was a tremendous leader—large in stature, intel-
ligent, honest, merciful, stalwart, passionate, devoted and understanding. What made this righteous commander tick? Here
is how this military man of honor viewed his job.*

"**S**urely God shall not suffer that we, who are despised
because we take upon us the name of Christ, shall be trodden down and destroyed, until we bring it upon us by our
own transgressions."

"**CAN YOU THINK TO SIT** upon your thrones in a state of
thoughtless stupor, while your enemies are spreading the work
of death around you?"

"**FOR THE LORD SUFFERETH** the righteous to be slain
that his justice and judgment may come upon the wicked."

"**WE DO NOT DESIRE** to be men of blood. Ye know that ye
are in our hands, yet we do not desire to slay you."

"**DO YE SUPPOSE** that the Lord will still deliver us, while we
sit upon our thrones and do not make use of the means which
the Lord has provided for us?"

"**REMEMBER THAT GOD** has said that the inward vessel
shall be cleansed first, and then shall the outer vessel be
cleansed also."

"**BEHOLD I WILL STIR** up insurrection among you, even
until those who have desires to usurp power and authority shall
become extinct."

"**I DO NOT FEAR** your power nor your authority, but it is
my God whom I fear."

"**I SEEK NOT** for power, but to pull it down."

"**I SEEK NOT FOR HONOR** of the world, but for the glory
of my God, and the freedom and welfare of my country."

"**IN THE MEMORY OF** our God, our religion, and freedom,
and our peace, our wives, and our children." (Title of Liberty)

CONVERTING COMMUNISTS?

Most of the middle-aged to aging members of the Church are well familiar with cold-war Soviet leader Nikita Khrushchev. He once pounded his shoe on a table at the U.N. to get his own way. He was also famous for saying his empire would bury the United States. But guess what happened when he visited the U.S.?

NIKITA KHRUSHCHEV
BORN: 1894
ACTIVIST: In his teens he became politically active and organized strikes for better treatment of employees.

POLITICS: Joined the Bolshevik forces of the Red Army in 1917 and served as a political commissar. He supported Stalin and became a full member of the Politburo in 1939.

BLOODY HANDS: Khrushchev helped during Stalin's bloody purges of the 1930s, and denounced friends and co-workers in the process. He also took part in the murderous extermination of the Ukrainian intelligentsia.

TOP POST: At Stalin's death in 1953, Khrushchev rose to became head of the Communist Party and Premier. He encouraged more independence for Soviet satellite nations, made political hay over the U2/Francis Gary Powers spy plane incident, had the Berlin Wall built, and triggered the Cuban Missile crisis.

DEMISE: He was ousted in 1964 by conservative Communists and died in retirement in a rural Russian dacha in 1971.

CHURCH CONTACT: During his visit to the United States in September 1959, Khrushchev and his family were given a tour of Washington, D.C. Ezra Taft Benson was serving as the Secretary of Agriculture at the time, and he hosted Khrushchev

---

The Seven Deadly Sins: pride, greed, lust, envy, gluttony, anger, and sloth.

for part of the visit. While Elder Benson and Khrushchev were visiting the Beltsville Department of Agriculture research facility outside of Washington, Khrushchev's wife and family were hosted by Benson's son, Reed.

STOKING THE HOME FIRES ....

Reed had a great time with the Khrushchev family. When the conversation turned to Utah and the Mormon Tabernacle Choir, Reed took the opportunity to spend some 45 minutes telling Mrs. Khrushchev, and her daughter and husband (Adzhubei, then editor of Izvestia) all about the Church and offered the family copies of the Book of Mormon in Russian. Adzhubei gave Reed the family's address where six copies of the book could be delivered. Mrs. Khrushchev said, "I give you a five (Russian for an "A") for doing a great job teaching us ... you must do more in our country." As they departed, Adzhubei took Reed aside and suggested, "Come to Russia and do some missionary work for your Church!"

WHEN EZRA TAFT BENSON next went to Russia, he delivered the promised books to the family of the most powerful Communist, athiest, and anti-American in the world.

Did somebody say Elder Khrushchev? No, but it has a nice Slavic ring to it.

****

CAN YOU NAME all the presidents of the Church in order (as of 2005)? That was the question asked at BYU-Hawaii. Of the 100 asked, 40 couldn't name the prophets in correct order past Brigham Young. Only four named all 15 prophets with no mistake.

1._____	2._____	3._____	4._____
5._____	6._____	7._____	8._____
9._____	10._____	11._____	12._____
13._____	14._____	15._____	

Joseph Smith, Brigham Young, John Taylor, Wilford Woodruff, Lorenzo Snow, Joseph F. Smith, Heber J. Grant, George Albert Smith, David O. McKay, Joseph Fielding Smith, Harold B. Lee, Spencer W. Kimball, Ezra Taft Benson, Howard W. Hunter, Gordon B. Hinckley.

NOTORIOUS MORMONS

Brother Paul observes that there are some well known—and not so well known—names that every now and then become associated with the Church in some huge headliner scandal. Most certainly, such were Mormons by name only.

CLAIM TO INFAMY: Serial killer
PERSON: Ted Bundy
STORY: During 1973-79, Ted Bundy murdered dozens of young women, and left a string of terror that stretched across the Western U.S. and Florida. Some put the number of victims at 100 or more. Most of the details of his atrocities went with him to his grave, although prior to his execution, he dropped a few clues as to the whereabouts of some of the bodies he buried. In the middle of his murder spree, he moved to Utah and enrolled at the University of Utah's Law School. He apparently joined the Church, or at least attended with other LDS associates. He impressed his LDS friends and leaders as a quiet but sociable person. "All my memories of him are quite positive," said Mel Thayne, former branch president. Another branch president, Michael Preece, said, "While I knew him, I didn't really see him as but a kind of lonely sort of a socially graceful guy who was pretty well ordered. People are always kidding me about my lack of perception in the matter." In fact, no one had "perception" of the killer, until he was finally caught. He was found guilty of three murders, confessed to many others, and was electrocuted by the State of Florida in 1989.

CLAIM TO INFAMY: Treason
PERSON: Richard Miller
STORY: In 1984, FBI agent and apparent Church member Richard Miller engaged in a four-month affair with his Soviet lover, Svetlana Ogorodnikova. The affair was his "own stupidity," he said later, but what was unforgivable was giving her secret U.S. documents including FBI training manuals. For the documents, Miller demanded $50,000 in gold, $15,000 in cash,

---

The Salt Lake Tabernacle organ has more than 11,000 individual pipes.

and apparently became sexually involved with Svetlana. The FBI was widely scorned for mismanagement for failing to "skunk out" Miller's activities. Critics pointed out the obvious disconnects in Miller's behavior: his work was substandard, he had no people skills, supervisors reported he made stupid mistakes, he had abysmal personal hygiene, and he sold Amway products from the trunk of his official FBI vehicle. After three trials he was sent to prison where he served 13 years of a 20 year sentence before being released on May 6, 1994.

CLAIM TO INFAMY: Robbery
PERSON: Butch Cassidy
STORY: "Butch" was born Robert LeRoy Parker in Beaver, Utah on April 13, 1866. He was the first of 13 children from convert parents who had emigrated from England. Taking the name of Butch Cassidy, possibly from his childhood hero Mike Cassidy, Butch left his boyhood home of Circleville, Utah, and began his career of crime at age 18. Butch gained a reputation as a sort of Robin Hood by stealing from the large cattle outfits that were hurting the small ranchers, and from other similarly placed wealthy institutions. Robbing banks and trains, and traveling along the Outlaw Trail or restocking at Robber's Roost or the Hole-In-The-Wall, Butch's legacy with his Wild Bunch and the Sundance Kid runs deep in western lore. Thought to have been killed in a shootout in Argentina in 1909, new research points to a faked death. Some now believe he changed his name to William Phillips, a businessman who died of cancer in Spokane, Washington, on July 20, 1937.

CLAIM TO INFAMY: Ransom
PERSON: D.B. Cooper
STORY: In 1971, a man identifying himself as D.B. Cooper boarded a Northwest Orient 727 in Portland, Oregon, for a 30-minute hop to Seattle. When on board, Cooper notified a stewardess that he carried a bomb in his briefcase (he showed her), and demanded two parachutes with reserve chutes, and $200,000 in random twenty-dollar bills. The plane landed in Seattle where all hostages except for the flight crew and one stewardess were released. When airborne, Cooper ordered the

plane on a route towards Reno, Nevada, at 10,000 feet altitude, and no faster than 150 knots. About 25 miles north of Portland, the plane's pilot noted a change in aircraft attitude and guessed that Cooper must have opened the rear stairs and jumped. He was never heard of again. The Mormon connection comes with a copycat hijacker who performed a nearly identical hijacking on April 7, 1972. The man, using the alias James Johnson, bailed out over central Utah with $500,000. About this time, Richard F. McCoy bragged to a friend about a foolproof ransom scheme. The friend reported it to the police, and the Mormon Sunday School teacher, married father of two, and BYU law enforcement student was arrested. A jumpsuit and $499,970 in cash was found at his house. He was convicted, later escaped, and died in a shootout with the FBI. The shooting agent believes to this day that when he shot McCoy, he also shot D.B. Cooper.

CLAIM TO INFAMY: Texas Chainsaw Murder
PERSON: Robert Kleasen
STORY: He was the kind of Church investigator of the worst kind—psychopath. Robert Kleasen lived with his wife in a trailer in Travis County, Texas. Two local missionaries had been working with him in 1973. The Bishop of the local Austin Ward cautioned the elders to cease contact as the starving hunter's behavior was combative towards other ward members and his wife. But the elders chose to part ways with Kleasen after this one final dinner appointment.

As it turned out, it was a fatally bad decision. The missionaries were reported missing several days later. Police went to their last known appointment, and knocked on Kleasen's door. They found Kleasen's chain saw with the elder's blood, tissue and hair on it. Kleasen was convicted of the elder's murders, but an improper search warrant helped acquit Kleasen. Before new DNA evidence could be brought forward for a new trial, he died. *The Texas Chainsaw Massacre* movie claims it is based on the true stories of the Kleasen murders and another nut case named Edward Gein of Wisconsin (not LDS), who murdered people and used their skin and body parts in various ways.

Isn't this a cheery subject? "By name only," says Brother Paul.

California's Frank Epperson invented the Popsicle in 1905 when he was 11-years-old.

THE BRETHREN SAID IT!

PART IV

All is not always sober and somber at the podium!
For more, see page 191.

"There is nothing else annoys me so much as for a man to run on to me with one of those great, powerful machines, and just before hitting me, honk his horn ... I got that the other night on First North Street ... Here came two machines around that corner, with these cars all packed right up to the corner, and they tried to beat each other through and caught me in the center. The only thing that saved my life was being thin."—*J. Golden Kimball*

"There was a minister who once made a speech about hell and afterward somebody commented that he was certainly full of his subject."—*Sterling W. Sill*

"It is something of a matter of pride with me that I never yet preached the Gospel in a manner that it resulted in mob violence."—*B. H. Roberts*

"I told him that he reminded me of a young bride who said to her mother on her wedding day, 'I am the happiest girl in all the world because I have come to the end of all my troubles,' and the wise old mother answered, 'Yes, my dear, but you don't know which end.'"—*Hugh B. Brown*

"I sometimes confess men's sins for them, and they will get up and parry off. I confessed a man's sins here lately, and he supposed that I did not know what I was talking about. If he had corrected me a little further, I would have told all his sins."
—*Jedediah M. Grant*

A toast given by Jedediah M. Grant: "To Martin Van Buren and all mobocrats: May they be winked at by blind men, kicked across lots by cripples, nibbled to death by ducks, and carried to hell through the keyhole by bumblebees."—*Jedediah M. Grant*

Contrary to legend, the bee-sized airfoil of the bumblebee wing is perfect for flight.

UTAH OR DROWN!

Pioneers to Utah were not necessarily just those in covered wagons. Some took that dangerous journey by way of the sea, the longest ocean voyage for civilians ever up to that time.

On Christmas Day, 1845, Elder Samuel Brannan chartered the ship *Brooklyn*, 450 tons in size, to carry Latter-day Saints from New York to California. It would cost them $1,200 a month, plus any additional port charges that came along. The adults had to pay $50 each, and the children between 5 and 14 had to pay $25 each. On top of the ticket price was another $25 for provisions.

A GOOD DAY TO LEAVE
The ship pulled out of port on Feb. 4, 1846, coincidentally the very same day that the Saints in Nauvoo began their exodus from their beloved "city beautiful." A total of 238 passengers signed up for the long sea voyage—70 men, 68 women, and 100 children.

A LONG WAY TO SALT LAKE!
It was an amazing journey of 20,000 miles around South America's dangerous Cape Horn, with stops at Robinson Caruso's island, and Hawaii. Along the way, the crowded vessel provided few comforts. There was just 2 square feet of space for each person, and amidst the crowding, infested food and finally no food at all, suffocating heat, stink and sickness, some perished and the Saints had to bury at sea ten of their friends and family. This sadness was offset with the joyful birth of two babies during the voyage. Huge storms threatened the ship, forcing passengers to remain cramped inside as the waves crashed over them outside.

JULY 29, 1846
When the *Brooklyn* ended its 5-month 27-day voyage in July, the Saints had anticipated landing in Mexican territory, free from persecution. But things had changed. The Mexican-American war started while they were at sea, and California had fallen into American hands. The ship's landing place was the old Mexican whaling village Yerba Buena. The Saints pitched tents for housing and put 16 families in the Old Spanish Barracks. With so many new settlers suddenly on the scene, the city was pretty much a Mormon town until they left. And just where was Yerba Buena? It was later renamed San Francisco.

The New York phone book listed 11 Hitlers before WWII ... and none after.

MORMON MYTH BUSTERS, PART II

Brother Paul continues his debunking of popular LDS legend and lore. To read Part I, see page 22.

CLAIM: Howard Hughes left his fortune to LDS member Melvin DuMar

STATUS: Legally resolved, but otherwise the truth is unknown

STORY: The fortune that almost was would have made a millionaire out of Brother Melvin DuMar, Gabbs, Nevada, and provided millions for the Church. A handwritten document that was purported to be the last will and testament of billionaire Howard R. Hughes, was found in the Church Office Building in Salt Lake City on April 27, 1976. The will gave 1/16th of the Hughes fortune to the Church and another 1/16th to Melvin DuMar who claimed he gave an old, sick man a ride into Las Vegas; the man identified himself as Howard Hughes. An envelope containing the will was discovered in the Church's Public Communications Office addressed to President Spencer W. Kimball. Inside, there was another envelope with these words: "This was found by Joseph F. Smith's house in 1972—thought you would be interested." And inside was the will with a note supposedly written by Howard Hughes to President David O. McKay. The legal battle to determine the validity of the will raged on for years, resulting in a finding that the will was a forgery. To this day, the debate continues as not everyone is convinced the will was a phony.

CLAIM: There was only one tree in the Salt Lake Valley when the pioneers first arrived

STATUS: Myth long since disproved.

STORY: In an earlier day, young primary children and adults alike were told that the Salt Lake Valley was so desolate and barren that there was but one tree standing to offer shade to the travel-weary pioneers. According to research by BYU geology

---

The number 111,111,111 multiplied by itself results in 12,345,678,987,654,321.

professor Richard H. Jackson, pioneer diaries show the Salt Lake Valley was actually quite a pleasant place. For a desert, it offered a river, mountain streams, tall grasses, and plenty of trees. The "one tree" myth is perpetuated by the "Lone Cedar Tree" monument in Salt Lake City that protects a stump—all that remains of a once well-known landmark that was frequently called a "friend to the pioneers."

CLAIM: Hawaii Temple Bomber
STATUS: False
STORY: There are more variations and general kinds of "knowledge" about the Japanese bomber who tried to bomb the Hawaiian Temple, than any other Mormon myth. As the story goes, during the Japanese bomb attack on Pearl Harbor on December 7, 1941, a plane sent to conduct a "demoralizing" attack against the Hawaiian Temple couldn't release its bomb, even after the pilot made three dives at the Temple.

So deeply imbedded in the Mormon grapevine is this myth, it just won't die. People continue to hotly dispute the findings of those who have researched the story and found it false. Comments received by a privately-owned LDS newspaper ranged from, "My father worked at that Temple, and met the man who witnessed it, and my father wouldn't lie," to "the bomber has since joined to the Church," to "I know in my heart it is true."

CLAIM: People who reject the missionaries suffer terrible fates
STATUS: False
STORY: Don't throw out the missionaries! In the early 1880s, Cedar Key was one of the fastest growing towns in Florida. By 1895, Mormon missionaries had reportedly arrived to teach, but were thrown out by the townspeople. The following year, a combination hurricane, tidal wave and fire destroyed nearly all of the town. About the same time, the railroad moved south to Tampa, the oyster beds dried up and the forests were over-cut bringing an end to Cedar Key's lumber industry. The rumors spread among the Church members that it wasn't just coincidence, but rather divine retribution for maltreatment of the missionaries.

For more Mormon Myth Busting, see Part III on page 249.

For more Mormon Myth Busting, see Part III on page 249.

The Olympic was the sister ship of the Titanic—she provided 25 years of service.

THE MAN WHO KNEW DARWIN

*A long-forgotten clash of two mental Titans is remembered here
with admiration for their curiosity and
strength of character.*

It was an amazing battle of wits between two of history's
mightiest intellects. On the one hand was Charles Darwin—
the highly intelligent entrepreneur of the natural sciences,
"captain" of the adventures aboard the Beagle that carried him
to the Galapagos Islands, and the father of a new theory about
the origins of life that carried his own name: Darwinism.

And on the other hand was Louis Agassiz of Switzerland—a
keen observer of nature's unified presence on the Earth, father
of the Ice Age, discoverer of the eternal and mighty power of
glacial movement, founder of the world-renowned natural history museum at Harvard, and chief proponent of divine intervention in the process of creation.

STAKING OUT THEIR CLAIMS

It was 1859 when the greatest contribution of each man was
held up for all the world to see. Darwin published his first edition of *Origin of Species*, and Agassiz published his crowning work,
Essay on Classification. Each in his own way was trying to accomplish the same thing: give order and purpose to life on Earth.

FAME AND INFAMY

What followed that year was a watershed event for both
men. As the discoverer of a grand explanation for the origin of
all life on Earth, Darwin's reputation soared beyond imagination. People loved his book and his theory. But for Agassiz,
many of his biographers cite this as a tragic turning point when
he publically rejected Darwinism. Agassiz was respected for his
insight, clear-thinking and meticulous method, but his refusal to
sign on to evolution, as were all the world's greatest scientists,
was shocking to the intellectual elite. Agassiz denounced
Darwin's theory as incomplete thinking based on flawed logic

and research. The best evidence of all, Agassiz insisted, was in nature itself where the brush strokes of the Great Master could be seen at all levels of creation. Yes, all levels including the fossil record itself.

TAKING SIDES

But that old time religion, as popular as it was, couldn't retain the loyalties of the scientific community. With too few answers to combat Darwinism, the Biblical basis for creation was finally and comfortably abandoned by the greatest scientific minds around. Agassiz was left alone, adrift in a sea of cast-off notions.

And he held to this belief until the day he died. Some speculate he wanted to join the Darwin bandwagon in his later years, but Agassiz's life and writings reveal a man slow to yield on evolution. His works exposed flawed reasoning in the theory of Darwinism, giving so much more evidence to the contrary.

A GIANT PASSED THIS WAY

Agassiz's death in 1873 was mourned around the world—by scientists, politicians and theologians alike. After the ceremonious adulations quieted and the posthumous recognitions were awarded, there was no doubt—Louis Agassiz's mark on the world was large and permanent. He was a great and widely admired man, thought never to be forgotten.

But today, the name doesn't ring a bell, and is usually only a footnote in natural science and ichthyology textbooks.

MEANWHILE, BACK IN UTAH ...

Four years after Agassiz's death, Wilford Woodruff, then president of the St. George Temple, recorded in his journal an amazing and curious event. He wrote that in a single evening, he beheld the visages of the Founding Fathers, the signers of the Declaration of Independence, and other historical figures who asked directly why their Temple work had not yet been performed. While the rest of Brother Woodruff's list reads like an honorable Who's Who in the world, there is one name unfamiliar to most, but nonetheless a sterling standout in the great battle of wits between man's way and God's way—the name of an old Swiss scientist named Mr. Louis Agassiz.

IS IT REALLY 666? Part I

Let's not get too disappointed over this recent discovery, but if it's true, all of our doomsday "mark of the beast" ruminating will need to be reworked. Why? Because Satan's phone number may not be 666 ... it could be 616.

AMAZING FIND: An ancient fragment stating the mark of the beast is 616.

WHERE: An ancient garbage dump just outside of Egypt's city of Oxyrhynchus (City of the Sharp-nosed fish).

WHEN: Found in 1895; translation has come slowly.

WHO: BYU scholars and new ultraviolet & imaging technology.

WHO, PART II: For clarification of the "666/616" fragment, Dr. Daniel B. Wallace of the Center for the Study of New Testament Manuscripts in Frisco, Texas, offers some information not contained in the newspaper reports (see Part II).

STORY: In 1895, the largest cache of ancient papyri ever discovered—more than 400,000 fragments—was found at an excavated garbage heap in Oxyrhynchus, Egypt, about 100 miles south of Cairo. And that location, thankfully, was sufficiently above the flood-plain of the Nile so the dump's contents were preserved in the hot desert climate.

This ancient Greek-Roman city did not become important until after Alexander the Great in about 332 B.C. It was lived in until 641 A.D. when it was abandoned, covered over by desert sand, and lost to time. For its 1,000 years of existence, the people tossed all kinds of documents into their dump including tax receipts, plays, poetry, philosophy and personal letters.

READING THROUGH A GLASS DARKLY

The problem with deciphering the retrieved papyri fragments has been damage that rendered them unreadable. Some described the documents as "like burned newspaper." Most fragments were coated with an opaque film, possibly dried plaster or mud. When restoration experts tried to remove the film, the ancient writing ink came off with it. Other fragments were

---

Japanese research: peeling apples stimulates the frontal lobe (logic, judgment, imagination).

charred or otherwise ruined to the point that early scholars thought them unusable and unfortunately tossed them into a more modern trash heap. From the fragments that could be read came these unbelievably valuable and ancient written treasures:

- Plays by Menander (342-291 B.C.), a gifted Greek comedy writer who wrote at least 100 major works.
- Poems by Pindar (522-443 B.C.), the greatest lyric poet of ancient Greece (at least 17 books known to exist long ago).
- Fragments of writings by Sappho (630-581 B.C., a woman and lyric poet) and her lover, Alcaeus (620-5?? B.C., lyric poet).
- The oldest and most complete diagrams from Euclid's Elements (13 pivotal books on math written in 300 B.C.).
- Fragments of the Gospel of Thomas, probably dating from the 2nd or 3rd century A.D.
- Gospel according to the Hebrews (3rd century A.D.).
- The Shepherd of Hermas, a Christian writing (2nd century) recommended for inclusion in the New Testament.
- And a work of Irenaeus (approx. A.D. 120-200).

TECHNOLOGY TO THE RESCUE!

Thanks to NASA's Jet Propulsion Laboratory, a new technology for outer space is helping discover outer history. Multispectral imaging (MSI) was created to analyze surfaces of planets and moons in our solar system. Dr. Greg Bearman, one of those who developed the technology, wondered if the same technology could be applied to ancient texts.

That's when BYU's Dr. Gene Ware, now professor emeritus of engineering at BYU, carried the idea into practical use by creating the first multispectral imaging system for use on texts.

IMAGE(ING) IS EVERYTHING ...

In 2005, Dr. Ware visited Oxford to create MSI images in all ranges of the light band, of papyri in Oxford libraries. Dr. Ware's efforts worked, and didn't work. It was a test of the system in several applications. But where it worked, WOW! Peering beneath the sooty film on some papyri fragments uncovered a potential treasure trove of lost history, including:

- Writings by literary giants of the ancient world whose works were lost for millennia, including a long-lost tragedy by Sophocles (about 496-406 B.C.), a general and a priest who wrote more than 120 plays of which only 7 survived;
- Part of a lost novel by Lucian (about 200 B.C.), a Syrian satirist who wrote in Greek in a witty and scoffing style;
- Writings by Euripedes (480-406 B.C.), one of the three great tragedians of classical Athens;
- And poetic writings by Hesiod (about 700 B.C.).
- A 30-line passage from the poet Archilochos (about 600 B.C.), from whom only 500 lines survive in total, who preceded Homer and described events leading up to the Trojan war— (Described as "invaluable" by Dr. Peter Jones, author and co-founder of the Friends of Classics campaign).

To read Part II where we learn about "666" and "616," see page 390.

****

SOMETHING FISHY ABOUT the Word of Wisdom? In 1999, thousands of fish in France were killed when heavy rains washed into a nearby river the residue of the pressing of champagne grapes. For about 20 miles down stream of the Marne River, the dead fish were scooped out and piled up in stacks six feet high. The residue polluting the river consumed most of the oxygen and allowed a bacteria to grow that killed the fish. The residue was particularly heavy that year because the champagne industry was making extra supplies in anticipation of the world-wide celebrations that were coming to celebrate the new millennium.

****

CHURCH MARQUEES

"If you don't want to reap the fruits of sin stay out of the devil's orchard."

"Don't give up. Moses was once a basket case."

"Prevent truth decay. Brush up on your Bible."

"The best vitamin for a Christian is B1."

"A clear conscience makes a soft pillow."

"God answers kneemail."

"Under same management for over 2,000 years."

"Soul food served here."

"Tithe if you love Jesus! Anyone can honk!"

"Beat the Christmas rush, come to church this Sunday!"

"Life has many choices, Eternity has two. What's yours?"

"Worry is interest paid on trouble before it is due."

"Preach the gospel at all times. Use words if necessary."

"It's hard to stumble when you're down on your knees."

"What part of 'THOU SHALT NOT' don't you understand?"

"Don't wait for the hearse to take you to church."

"The wages of sin is death. Repent before payday."

"Never give the devil a ride. He will always want to drive."

"Can't sleep? Try counting your blessings."

"Forbidden fruit creates many jams."

"Christians, keep the faith...but not from others!"

"Satan subtracts and divides. God adds and multiplies."

"To belittle is to be little."

"Don't let the littleness in others bring out the littleness in you."

"Wal-Mart isn't the only saving place!"

"Try Jesus. If you don't like Him, the devil will always take you back."

Puritans banned young men from hunting to prevent weapons from falling into Indian hands.

THE SUPERNACLE!

*The Church's new Conference Center is a beautiful and magnificant
meeting place. But that's only half the story. Here's a
look at the old and the new.*

SALT LAKE TABERNACLE	CONFERENCE CENTER
DEDICATED: October 1875	**DEDICATED:** October 2000
EXTERIOR MATERIALS: Sandstone pillars supporting wooden frame roof.	**EXTERIOR MATERIALS:** 1-½"-thick panels of granite (quartzite) and ashlar granite, both stone types from Little Cottonwood Canyon.
FLOOR SPACE: About 37,000 square feet.	**FLOOR SPACE:** More than 1.4 million square feet.
SEATING CAPACITY: 6,500 in main auditorium.	**SEATING CAPACITY:** 21,333 in main auditorium.
ROOF: Trusses are ten feet in thickness and are held together with wooden pegs and rawhide. At first it had 400,000 shingles until replaced with aluminum roofing.	**ROOF:** The King Truss—the main support beam for the building—weighs about 621 tons. Atop this is 4 acres of landscaped roof with fountains, waterfalls, trees, planters, flowers, and a 3-acre meadow complete with irrigation systems.
OTHER: The acoustics are so perfect, a dropped pin at the podium can be heard at the opposite end of the Tabernacle; the Tabernacle Choir has performed thousands of times during its record streak of 75+ years of broadcasting from this location.	**OTHER:** The Center has 50,000 miles of wire, 13 passenger elevators, 750,000 cubic yards of dirt excavated, 23.5 million gallons of cement, and 15,000 tons of cement rebar. A 747 could fit in the main auditorium with room to spare.

A FISH STORY

*Here's one that didn't get away, and Nate
has the stuffed prize to prove it.*

The alarm roused 12-year-old Nate Anderson and his brother at 5 a.m. on June 30, 1988 for what they thought would be a routine mid-week fishing expedition. The two quietly dressed, grabbed their gear, and headed for the back door.

The Anderson home, located within the boundaries of the Soldotna Alaska Ward, was nicely located for fishing trips such as this. Built almost next to the Kenai River, known for its huge salmon, the boys had some of the best fishing in all of Alaska just 57 steps outside their back door.

GOTTA KNOW THE RIVER

Nate and his brothers had that river just about memorized. They knew all about the family secret, that perfect spot where they could catch a month's worth of salmon in a single bite.

Their favorite lower-river hole was nicknamed "Big Eddy," and seemed to be a preferred feeding place for the biggest salmon. Nate thought the record for the largest salmon caught with 80 pound test line was within his reach, and on that particular morning, he was ready. He had spooled up the necessary Trilene monofilament on a big halibut reel the night before, and had it attached to a good stiff rod that his dad helped him pick from the collection in the garage.

WHERE THE GIANTS LIVE

Motoring to their favorite spot by Big Eddy, they started "back-bouncing," their term for powering the boat into the current and then letting it slowly drift with the current down stream. Nate had a 3-pound 6-ounce weight on his line that lifted up and down off the river bottom with the movement of the boat. For bait, he had a green spin-n-glo and cured salmon eggs. It was a combination too irresistible for a big king salmon that happened to be feeding there that morning.

STRIKE!

After two hours of teasing the fish, he suddenly felt a firm strike at the shallow end of the hole. A problem for Nate was feeling the fish hit because the heavy fishing line required that extra heavy weight to hold it down. But this bite was hard and strong.

He set the hook and immediately the fish exploded out of the water. "How big a fish do you need?" his brother shouted in excitement. "45. You got it."

FRIENDLY PERSUASION

Nate did careful battle for the next 15 minutes. He had to remind himself that although he had 80 pound test line, his leader was only 40-pound test.

At long last, the tired fish nudged up to the boat at the end of the taught line and surrendered to capture in the net. With jubilation the boys heaved the slippery champion over the side and into their boat and sped away to the nearest bank-side scale. The monstrous copper-pink fish weighed just a hair under 76 pounds. Unfortunately, they cut a gill while weighing it and by the time they reached an official scale, it had lost a lot of blood. The official weight came in at 71 pounds 4 ounces.

LARGEST KING SALMON IN ITS CLASS

Nate narrowly defeated the old 80 pound class record of 67 pounds and was awarded $1,000 from Berkely Trilene. Half the money went to mounting the fish.

Since then, Nate has come close to another record. In 1993, he fought a 70-pound salmon for 2 hours and 30 minutes, using only 8-pound test line, but lost it at the net.

And that's the one that got away.

****

Two bike-riding Mormon missionaries found themselves motionless and speechless when two scantily dressed female joggers passed them at Sego Lily Lane and 1300 East in Sandy. They were so absorbed they didn't notice a Sandy City police car behind them, until the officer advised over his loudspeaker, "Think of a hymn, elders."

The Union's ironclad *Monitor* was the first U.S. ship to have a flush toilet.

TOP TEN LDS BOOKS

Brother Paul speculates: Given the choice, what top ten books would you say are of greatest value to a Latter-day Saint?

I**T'S TOUGH PICKING THE TOP TEN** because every Latter-day Saint will value certain writings above others for an assortment of personal reasons—loyalty, research, friends, book marketing, counsel, etc. But given the passage of time, what books might make a great top-ten list that are most beneficial during the average member's lifetime? Here is one such list to inspire contemplation and consideration. How would your list be different? What would you add or subtract?

BOOK: The Book of Mormon
RANKING: 1
YOUR RANKING? _____
REASON: This one is easy. The Book of Mormon is just about everything a religious book should be--inspirational, educational, historical, prophetic, entertaining, exciting, and very re-readable!

BOOK: The New Testament
RANKING: 2
YOUR RANKING? _____
REASON: The narrations and gospels that tell of Jesus Christ and his teachings are some of the best road maps for surviving this life than any other. Personal power grows from this book.

BOOK: *A Marvelous Work and a Wonder*
RANKING: 3
YOUR RANKING? _____
REASON: Why a non-scripture book here? This book sums up the restoration and our roles in that, and gives reason, hope and direction for faithful membership in words that are quickly understood. This presentation is easy to embrace and it is very positive and encouraging. Read it over and over, and you'll find it still teaches and inspires, encourages and reminds. There's a great spirit of positive growth within its pages.

BOOK: *The Miracle of Forgiveness*
RANKING: 4
YOUR RANKING? _____
REASON: Another non-scripture masterpiece, President Kimball's outline for perfecting the flawed human soul is presented with simplicity. It softly carries the important messages of self-improvement into a person's heart for quick understanding, with a step-by-step route to correction and repentance. Such personal refinement must be high on everybody's to-do list.

BOOK: The Old Testament
RANKING: 5
YOUR RANKING? _____
REASON: The first time Brother Paul read this book he was shocked at how much he had missed out on by not studying it earlier. For the hungry brain looking for patterns, history, a testimony of the Lord's winning formula, and a foundation for all other scripture, this sweet-sour glimpse of Earth's history as seen from a Mediterranean perspective is irreplaceable.

BOOK: *The Journal of Discourses*
RANKING: 6
YOUR RANKING? _____
REASON: This collection of 26 volumes is a gem field of clarity, explanation, understanding and powerful declarations. Where else could so much fodder for deep discussion be mined than from these great speeches and testimonies by leaders many of whom who were taught at the feet of Joseph Smith?

BOOK: *My personal journal*
RANKING: 7
YOUR RANKING? _____
REASON: Brother Paul isn't joking here. Tracking the passage of time on this planet, recording the insights and lessons, pouring out frustration and grief, and then lightly penning the joyfelt illumination that comes from a spiritual experience can be some of the very best writing for anyone to re-read and hopefully share, as their own book of personal scripture and testimony, with generations to come.

BOOK: Doctrine and Covenants
RANKING: 8
YOUR RANKING? _____
REASON: This is a great treatise on the early laws and gospel understandings of the restoration. Perusing its sections is a huge plus for personal and Church-wide understanding of how to apply the Lord's laws, ordinances and principles for this life and the eternities that follow.

BOOK: *Teachings of the Prophet Joseph Smith* or *The Discourses of Brigham Young*
RANKING: 9
YOUR RANKING? _____
REASON: As Nephi brought clarification to Isaiah, so do Joseph Smith and Brigham Young bring clarification to the good meaty concepts of the gospel that are sometimes not well understood. These good brethren's analysis and commentary help bring passages of scripture to life like none other!

BOOK: Various histories of the Church
RANKING: 10
YOUR RANKING? _____
REASON: Catching the spirit of the restoration is sometimes the last grasp some members have on the Church when passing through rough times. Seeing the common ground of faith during times of struggle, uncertainty and doubt as revealed in a good Church history book can prevent a tragic falling away. Or, encourage more strength among the membership still firmly in the path. Histories are valuable because they wrap understanding around out-of-context events that sometimes don't make sense. And, historical knowledge fends off doubts and criticisms—though some would argue exactly the opposite!

Brother B.H. Roberts, Brother Arrington, modern writers, early writers, all of them give Latter-day Saints a lifetime of wonderful analysis, faith-promoting adventures, experiences and revelations that teach and edify. They're all a great read, and worthy of an important place on every Latter-day Saints' book shelf. Do you have yours?

LIST OF LISTS

*Some arbitrary scrapings from the bottom of
Brother Paul's Pile O' Stuff.*

Eight Saints who fathered 40 or more children:
1. Heber C. Kimball, 65
2. Christopher Layton, 64
3. John D. Lee, 60
4. Brigham Young, 56
5. Orson Pratt, 45
6. Joseph F. Smith 43
7. Marriner W. Merrill, 45
8. Lorenzo Snow, 42

Former professions of eight General Authorities:
1. nuclear engineer
2. newspaper editor
3. seminary teacher
4. pharmacist
5. dentist 6. heart surgeon
7. CPA 8. military officer

13 Sins of omission according to Spencer W. Kimball—failing to: 1. home teach
2. pay tithing
3. observe Sabbath
4. get married
5. have children
6. be an example
7. be a missionary
8. fast   9. love God
10. have reverence
11. honor parents
12. be pure 13. love others

Eight animals mentioned in the Bible:
1. Ape   2. Unicorn
3. Mouse   4. Hornet
5. Ostrich   6. Stork
7. Leopard   8. Pelican

Eight children born because of prayer:
1. Isaac   2. Esau   3. Jacob
4. Dan   5. Joseph   6. Samuel
7. John the Baptist   8. Dinah

Contemporaries of Lehi:
1. Aesop 2. Pythagoras
3. Confucius 4. Zarathustra
5. Cyrus the Great
6. Nebuchadnezzar
7. Daniel 8. Jeremiah

Four curious names of creatures mentioned in the Book of Mormon:
1. Deseret   2. Cureloms
3. Cumoms   4. Dragon

Eight weapons in the Book of Mormon:
1. ax 2. cimeter 3. javelin
4. spear 5. sword
6. bow and arrow
7. sling 8. dart

The first Allied bomb dropped on Germany in WWII killed Berlin's only elephant.

SCRIPTURES IN CONTEXT: TURKEY

This is a really cool, or hot, connection to a famous scripture passage and its original setting in Turkey.

SCRIPTURE: Revelations 3:14-16 (quoted below)
PLACE: Laodicea, a once popular and thriving city about 250 miles south of today's Istanbul.

BROTHER PAUL'S NO-CHARGE WORD GUIDE:
Laodicea = Lay-od'ih-SEE-uh
Colosse = Kuh-LOS-ee (modern Honas)—10 miles east of Laodicea
Hierapolis = Hi 'uh-RAP-uh-lis (modern Pamukkale)—4.7 miles north of Laodicea

STORY: There are several cities named Laodicea in southwestern Asia. The specific city of Laodicea that Jesus was talking about in Revelations was the one in today's Turkey on the banks of the Lycus River in the fertile Lycus Valley.
• Anciently, Laodicea had other names but around 250 B.C., it received its name after the wife (Laodice) of Antiochus II. Nothing special about Syria's king, Antiochus, except that he later divorced Laodice and married the daughter of an Egyptian king to restore peace in the region. How did ex-wife Laodice take this? She poisoned her hubby and murdered the second wife (this is why many brethren stay single).
• Laodicea was the largest of three cities that included Colosse (to where Apostle Paul sent his mail) and Hierapolis, famous for its hot mineral baths. These two cities, by the way, are what bring us here talking about this interesting reference in Revelations 3:14-16.

PARTY CENTRAL

Laodicea was a very popular place. From its vantage point on the Lycus River, it controlled all the trade flowing down the river. It was also the hub of three well-traveled highways on which rich trading caravans constantly stopped by for rest and recreation. It was wealthy and it controlled much of the banking activity for Asia Minor. Its significance wasn't realized until Rome established it as a part of a new province in 190 B.C. Afterwards, it grew rapidly into the center of Greek and Roman culture.

• **IT ALSO HAD** two commodities that were in high demand. The soft, glossy deep-purple wool produced by Laodicean sheep herders was in huge demand all over the area. In fact, clothing made of Laodicean wool was the foundation of their famous weaving and textile industry, a popular money-maker that continued for centuries up until the 1800s A.D.

• **LAODICEA'S** other famous product was its Phrygian eye ointment made of the dried mud from the nearby thermal springs in Hierapolis. A school of medicine was set up outside the city a dozen miles away. Their doctors discovered the healing power of the powdered thermal mud, and developed a poultice that helped people's weak and failing eyes, and reduced inflammation.

HIERAPOLIS AND COLOSSE

The mineral water at Hierapolis rose from the ground nearly boiling hot. From some collection place, the steaming water was piped about 4 miles to Laodicea, and en route, cooled down. Likewise, fresh water runoff from the mountains was piped in from Colosse. When the tepid water entered Laodicea, it was still warmish and still loaded with enough minerals to make people vomit. But they wanted it anyway for health reasons.

• And now, the verse. Revelation 3:14-16: "And unto the angel of the church of the Laodiceans write ... I know thy works, that thou art neither cold nor hot; I would thou wert cold or hot. So then because thou art lukewarm, and neither cold nor hot, I will spue thee out of my mouth."

• Brother Paul loves this connection. The slothful, sluggish church members of Laodicea were just like their water—neither cold nor hot, neither doing good nor doing terribly bad. Good for nothing, but good for something: vomiting.

In other words, they made the Lord *sick*.

At the height of its power, ancient Sparta had 25,000 citizens and 500,000 slaves.

WHERE WE GOT 'EM: DOCTRINE AND COVENANTS

THIS IS A REALLY COOL BOOK. It has been refined and added to over the years, but those improvements were to complete the history, fix unpolished text, or add new revelations worthy of general distribution among the Saints.

In general, the Doctrine and Covenants is the official and amazing constitution of the Church, laying out its government, operations and justifications. Energetic commentary, explanations of concepts long misunderstood or lost, and direct commandments on how to survive the crazy chaos that grips our world, the Doctrine and Covenants gives readers a map by which the great messages of the restored Gospel can be enjoyed, shared and sustained.

JOSEPH'S REVELATIONS: The problem with being a prophet is that you get a lot of instruction. And the work to restore the actual complete and magnificent gospel program took a lot of instructions. But not all of this information was relevant to everybody—some was quite particular and applicable to only Joseph Smith and a handful of other individuals. Find many of these recorded in the *History of the Church*. That's why we don't have all of his revelations assembled into a single canonized book. But what we do have promises a lifetime of study, enlightenment, and enjoyment.

FIRST TRY: The restored church had been around for about a year and a half when the brethren decided it was time to publish a collection of Joseph's revelations. He had received more than 70 by the fall of 1831, and at a November conference in Ohio, the Saints voted to go forward with the book publishing project. Joseph received an additional revelation on that very day, now included as Section 1, and this is probably where they got the book's title, *Book of Commandments*.

BOOK OF COMMANDMENTS: The work of editing and refining the hand-written revelations proceeded with haste, and after 18 months, the first collection was ready for the printer.

A tragic but thrilling story took place when a mob attacked the Church's printing press in Independence in 1833, just as the Saints started printing the Book of Commandments. Five signatures with 32 pages on each, had just come off the press when a mob busted into the place and scattered everything. With the signature pages flying out a window and into the street, two young sisters retrieved as many of the pages as they could and escaped the enraged mob by ducking through a gap in a fence into a large cornfield. They ran far into the tall green maze and threw down the pages, lay on top, and prayed. Two mobsters hunted around but failed to find them. From these pages only a few copies of the Book of Commandments could be created. For collectors, a complete copy of these hand-bound books are worth close to a quarter million dollars apiece!

SECOND TRY: The next year, Joseph and the Brethren worked to clean up some printing and scribal errors in the Book of Commandments collection, and added some more revelations before going to a printer again. In 1835, the first large version of the book, now named *Doctrine and Covenants of the Church of the Latter Day Saints* came off the press. It had 103 sections plus the *Lectures on Faith* (See page 268).

LATER EDITIONS: Five years later, the first edition was sold out. Time to do another. The new edition included eight more revelations and was ready for the press in 1844, but the Prophet never saw it finished because he was killed that year. This didn't stop the work from moving forward. Wilford Woodruff saw that additional printings were done in Liverpool, England, long after the Church was moved to Salt Lake Valley, to meet the needs of the saints at home and abroad.

CHAPTER AND VERSE: Finally, things started to settle down for the Church's book publishing endeavors in the mid-1800s. Numerous printings of the Doctrine and Covenants were ordered over the decades, many from England, others domestically. Almost 30 years after arriving in the valley, it was time for a new edition. The 1876 edition was published in Salt Lake City and included Orson Pratt's diligent work to divide the revelations into verses. The brethren added twenty-six more revelations.

POLYGAMY ABANDONED: Starting with the 1908 version, Wilford Woodruff's "Manifesto," also called the Official Declaration 1, was included to make it clear the Church had ended its support of plural marriage.

OUT WITH THE OLD: The 1921 edition was neatly divided into double columns on each page, with improved footnotes, and the *Lectures on Faith* were removed. This was the version familiar to just about all members of the Church until the administration of President Spencer W. Kimball.

IN WITH THE NEW: The 1981 edition had two new sections added, 137 and 138, plus the Official Declaration 2 announcing that all worthy male members of the Church could now hold the priesthood.

Brother Paul cannot say enough good about this wonderful book. It gives purpose, understanding, challenge and wonderful hope to all those seeking truth and answers. Put it high on your reading list, and take it slow—it's a great exploration.

****

"WHEN I WAS IN THE MISSION FIELD, I said to the elders: Whenever you are moved upon by the Spirit of God, and the spirit of testimony, you are to testify that Joseph Smith is a prophet of God, and I promise you it will make all the trouble you can bear."—*J. Golden Kimball*

Joseph Smith used a wax seal of his own likeness to authenticate all Church business.

HENRY EYRING

Some of the world's greatest innovators have stood head and shoulders above others because they lay claim to enlightenment from the gospel, a credo from Dr. Eyring himself.

THE SCIENTIST Dr. Eyring was a smart guy whose expertise in molecules and math charted the course for more than a dozen branches of chemistry ranging from cancer to explosives and metals to anesthesia. He served as president of the two most prestigious chemistry and science associations, won 18 top chemistry prizes—all but the Nobel Prize—was awarded 15 honorary doctorate degrees, wrote 600 papers and half a dozen books, and worked at the University of Utah in a building named after him.

THE MAN Dr. Eyring was a funny guy. He liked to challenge distinguished visitors to a table hop—from the floor to the table. Dr. Eyring always won. For 21 years, he sponsored an annual 50-yard dash with his students, an event he regularly lost. His personal friendship with Albert Einstein spawned this favorite joke: walking in a Princeton garden one day, Dr. Eyring asked Einstein to identify a green plant. Einstein could not. Dr. Eyring told him it was soybean, and from that time forward he bragged that Einstein didn't know beans.

THE MORMON Dr. Eyring's pursuit of scientific truth was the same as pursuing gospel truth, he said, "because the gospel is truth where ever you find it." He served on the Sunday School General Board for 25 years, and authored the popular *Faith of a Scientist* that was widely read. "True religion was never a narrow thing," Dr. Eyring said. "True religion concerns man and the entire universe in which he lives. It concerns his relationships with himself and his fellow men, with his environment, and with God his creator. It is therefore limitless, and as boundless as that eternity which it teaches lies ahead of every son of God ... Here is the spirit of true religion, an honest seeking after knowledge of all things of heaven and Earth."

The Pine Valley, Utah, pioneer-built chapel has a ship's keel for a roof!

HOOK DATES

Hook dates are powerful mental organizers perfect for connecting world events to a familiar date already seared into our memories. For example, in what year did the Spanish drive out the Muslims and Jews from Spain? It was the same year Leonardo da Vinci sketched out his famous Universal Man, or in 1492 when Columbus sailed for America. Commit to memory these hook dates that Lehi's contemporaries would have known and then see how well you do with the Hook Date Quiz (next page)!

4000 B.C.—Adam and the beginning of human history.

3200 B.C.—The approximate time when Enoch enters the Earth and builds a city of righteousness.

2344 B.C.—The year of the great universal flood. Remember the drowning sinner coming up for air, "TWO!," he says, and goes down again. Then "THREE," then "FOUR—burp—FOUR!"

2000 B.C.—The century of Abraham (2022-1847 B.C.).

1900 B.C.—The century belonging to Isaac (1922-1742 B.C.).

1800 B.C.—The century belonging to Jacob (1862-1715 B.C.).

1700 B.C.—The century that belonged to Joseph and Israel in Egypt (1771-1661 B.C.).

1500 B.C.—The century belonging to Moses (1597-1477 B.C.).

1400 B.C.—The beginning of Israel's great dark ages when apostasy engulfed the people for several centuries.

1100 B.C.—The century belonging to Samuel and king Saul.

1000 B.C.—The century belonging to David (1032-962 B.C.) and Solomon (987-922 B.C.)—the great golden age of Israel.

922 B.C.—The year the ten northern tribes separated from the tribes of Judah and Levi.

900 B.C.—The century that belonged to Elijah.

800 B.C.—The century that belonged to Elisha.

721 B.C.—The year the northern Ten Tribes were conquered and carried off by the Assyrians.

700 B.C.—The century that ended with the great prophet Isaiah at the height of his ministry.

600 B.C.—The century that belonged to Jeremiah, Daniel, Ezekiel, Lehi and Nephi.

The safety pin was patented in 1849 by Walter Hunt. He sold the patent rights for $400.

HOOK DATE QUIZ

Okay, now that you've memorized those 16 hook dates, test your-self with this Hook Date Quiz. Cover up the prior page, promise no cheating, and see how you do!

1. What is a "hook" date? Must it be memorized? Who is hooked to the date of 2,344 B.C.? 1,500 B.C.? 600 B.C.?

2. Name three world-famous men who were contemporaries of Jeremiah and Lehi in the sixth century.

3. Three other great prophets were raised up about the time of Jeremiah. Who were they?

4. Who came first, Elisha or Elijah? What hook date belongs to each?

5. While Daniel was making history by surviving a trip to the lion's den, who was making history by departing on a trip to somewhere else?

6. Jared is remembered primarily because of his famous son, Enoch. When Adam was 460, Jared was born. What year was that?

7. When Adam was 622, Enoch was born. What year was that?

8. The City of Enoch was translated 604 years before the Great Flood. What year was that?

9. Approximately when did Isaiah live? Abraham?

10. What year did the northern ten tribes separate from Judah and Levi? How many years transpired before they were conquered and carried off by the Assyrians?

The first copy of the Book of Mormon launched into space took off in 1985.

THE JEWS' LOST TUNNEL

Some prophecies have exciting "pointers" that let people know they're being fulfilled. One of those pointers is the rebuilding of the Jews' temple in Jerusalem. Here's a progress report.

PROPHECY: A temple will be built in Jerusalem wherein the Jews will make an offering in righteousness (see Micah 4:1, Ezekiel 40-47, Isaiah 2:1, D&C 13)

LOCATION: Tradition puts the temple site atop Mount Moriah where the Muslim's Dome of the Rock currently stands.

PROBLEM: Destroying the Dome of the Rock to build a Jewish temple would ignite a bloody holy war in Israel.

QUESTION: Is Mount Moriah really the right place where Solomon's Temple once stood?

STORY: After the 1967 war in the Middle East, Israel took control of their ancient and historical cities and landmarks. On their list of things to get busy with was their temple. They knew that a prophecy and commandment from God appointed them the task of rebuilding the temple according to plans laid out in detail in the Bible.

•   In the 1970s, a group of Levite priests established a school in old Jerusalem to prepare everything necessary for the new temple.

•   This same group has created architectural drawings of their new temple (according to Old Testament descriptions).

•   They have built a model of what that temple will look like.

•   They have designed ceremonial robes and are teaching other Levites the ordinances to be performed once the temple is built.

•   The state of Israel has been accumulating building materials for the temple.

•   And wisely enough, Israel posts guards around the Dome of the Rock to prevent terrorists from destroying that sacred shrine.

IS THIS THE PLACE?

The one major obstacle to the temple was location. Mount Moriah was traditionally the place where their ancient temple stood, and had been twice destroyed. But was tradition enough reason to destroy an existing ancient shrine and risk bloody warfare and condemnation from the world? What if the temple stood at some other location?

SECRET EXCAVATION

When the Jews' second temple was destroyed by the Romans in 70 A.D., the building materials were thrown over the western wall in a mighty heap dozens of feet deep and a thousand feet long. Over the centuries, the mound was filled in and eventually Arabs built homes and schools on top.

In 1968, ten Jerusalem Rabbis began a project that would help the Jews with their important assignment to rebuild their temple. The Rabbis were looking for something. They thought it lay somewhere along the ancient western wall and began tunneling beneath the Arab structures. Their digging was done secretly. They removed debris in buckets so as not to attract attention. They pulled out stones and dirt, and as the tunnel enlarged, they reinforced the ceiling and sides with reinforced cement.

What were they so anxious to find?

EMERGENCY EXIT

The Jews ancient temple had a Holy of Holies (most sacred part) in the middle of the building surrounded by temple courts. A problem for priests working in the Holy of Holies was the natural consequence of being human, and that was doing something to violate the sanctity of the place by becoming unclean. Everybody knew about the two sons of Aaron, struck down instantly for violating God's direct commandments—nobody wanted to reap the wrath of God when it came to His holy house, so they made an accommodation.

The Jews created an emergency exit through which a priest who became ceremonially unclean by touching a dead fly, spider, or worm, or becoming unclean in some other prescribed way, could flee the presence of the Lord. The emergency exit was a tunnel, and a priest could leave from there, race to the outer walls of the temple square, and find a priest from whom he could receive the rituals to become "clean" again.

If this emergency tunnel exit could be found, people could follow it underground and it should lead them to the temple's original Holy of Holies. That would settle once and for all the debate about where the Jew's temple had to be built.

AUGUST 1981

As excavators passed the half-way point along the foundation stones of the ancient western wall, they stumbled on something astonishing. It was an arched doorway, about eight feet tall, 4 feet across, and sealed off with ancient brick and mortar. They immediately opened the seal and found a tunnel with about 150 feet of clean passage. It appeared to extend another 50 feet where it terminated at another sealed entrance. When the Rabbis excavated further, and reached about 35 feet from the end of their dig, they knew what lay beyond—the tunnel pointed directly and without question to a terminal point beneath the Dome of the Rock. The place of the new temple had at last been found.

At this point, the noise of excavation alerted the Muslims above ground who filed an official protest, and the Israeli government stopped the dig. The tunnel's entrance was sealed up.

THAT'S WHOSE PROBLEM?

Today the tunnel extends the full 1,250-foot length of the ancient temple wall. Shortly after the 1967 war, a reporter for *Life Magazine* asked an old rabbi about the new temple they planned to build. "Tradition says you must rebuild your ancient temple where the Dome of the Rock now stands, right?" "That is correct," the old Rabbi replied. "And the Dome of the Rock will need to be destroyed, then." "We will not destroy anyone's sacred place," the Rabbi said. "But where the Dome of the Rock stands is where you will build your temple." "Correct." "Then how will you build your temple without destroying the Dome of the Rock?" "That," said the Rabbi with a shrug, "is God's problem."

Emma Smith was baptized in a Colesville, New York creek.

HOW TO MARK SCRIPTURES

W. Cleon Skousen taught his students at BYU a great way to extract the most from scripture study and to remember it for future reference. Here is his presentation.

THREE LEVELS: Latter-day Saints typically have three levels of scriptural literacy: The Testimony Level is a heartfelt belief that the scriptures are the word of God. This person my never really read them, but will accept them as truth. The Listening Level is a willingness to read scriptures in class or by assignment, and accept what other speakers or students tell them is good and true. The Organized Knowledge Level is where the Brethren want the Church to be. As Peter said, "Be ready always to give an answer to every man that asketh you a reason for the hope that is in you." (1 Peter 3:15)

ORGANIZING KNOWLEDGE: To achieve the highest level, students need a marked set of scriptures, a card index file, and a basic gospel reference library. The card index file is where you write everything new that you learn, and organize it accordingly by topic. A good library should include a concordance for each standard work, any of the commentaries now available, and a pronouncing guide.

MARK THE KEY WORDS: Read a verse through once, and go back again and underline no more than four key words, usually nouns and verbs, that identify that verse. Read eight pages a day, and you can finish all four standard works in one year.

WHAT HAPPENS? Key words identify each verse in your mind. You may not recall chapter and verse, but you will remember generally where something is. And once in the general location, it will take less than a minute to scan a two-page spread with 100 or so key words underlined. After some practice, underlining becomes an easy habit—and indispensable.

The farthest south LDS group meets at McMurdo Station in Antartica.

WHERE ARE THEY NOW?

Johnny Lingo, a Church-BYU production released in 1968, was drilled into the head of every Latter-day Saint youth for decades. Its most famous line? "Mahana, you ugly!"

JOHNNY LINGO: Makee K. Blaisdell
KOOL DEED: Buying Mahana for the oustanding though unheard-of price of eight whole cows (not 1%).
CAREER: Blaisdell was a native of Honolulu, Hawaii, and began his acting career at BYU where he was honored as actor of the year in the late 1950s. Afterwards, he went to Hollywood to star in several movies and television shows—he starred in original episodes of Star Trek, and had small roles in the movies, *Paradise, Hawaiian Style,* (1966) and *The Last of the Secret Agents?* (1966). He had parts in "Wild, Wild West," "Big Valley," "Hawaiian Eye," "Ironsides," and "F-Troop," among others. Most of these jobs were before he was cast as Johnny Lingo. He died of heart failure in Oxnard California, in 1988.

MAHANA: Naomi Kahoilua
KOOL DEED: Delightfully filled Johnny Lingo's gift of a handheld looking glass with her beautiful countenance.
STORY: Sister Kahoilua was attending the church College of Hawaii as a drama and theater arts major when she was cast at age 19 as Mahana. After filming, she graduated and went to work for Hawaiian Airlines. It is her image, the profile of a Polynesian girl, that has adorned those jets for decades since. In 1971, she married Brent Wilson in the Hawaii Temple and they moved to Washington State. Brother and Sister Wilson now live in the Indian Ward, Spokane Washington North Stake, and their three children are all grown. Sister Wilson stays busy in the arts, teaching concert piano, performing and encouraging others with a message about positive self-esteem.

TRADER HARRIS: Francis L. Urry
KOOL DEED: Enthusiastically ordered that looking glass for Johnny Lingo in plenty of time before the movie ended.

Saved millions and millions: In 1929, Alexender Flemming invented penicillin.

STORY: Brother Urry was a performer all his life, beginning in 1937 as a private voice teacher. He worked for KSL radio, and was on network radio and television for decades as a prominent radio, stage and film actor. He starred in numerous films for the Church including the role as President Lorenzo Snow in *Windows of Heaven* (1963). After *Johnny Lingo*, Brother Urry had parts in numerous other LDS films, and was the main male voice for the Mormon Miracle Pageant, a part he performed for the rest of his life. He became a major force for professionalism and encouragement to the Pageant's staff and cast. He starred in numerous other BYU films during the 1970s, and performed for the audio book, *Smiles on Smoking*, an anti-smoking production. He passed away in 1985.

To read more "Where are they now?" see page 376.

****

SPEAKING OF COWS ...

The case of a 1983 accident involving a "Mormon cow" remained very much alive in the courts for half-a-dozen years while attorneys tried to prove that LDS jurors in a negligence lawsuit may have been prejudiced.

On March 30, 1983, James Hornsby was riding his motorcycle down the road when suddenly a runaway cow, from a nearby LDS welfare farm, lumbered across the road.

Hornsby swerved to miss the cow but crashed.

He was udderly distraught, and sued the Church for injuries sustained in the accident. The jury was not mooooved by his argument and found him negligent in failing to heed the warning wave of a welfare worker who was chasing the cow.

Hornsby appealed and tried milking the system one more time.

The Utah Appeals Court remanded the case back to the 3rd District for a new trial after agreeing that Hornsby should have been allowed to determine prejudice by asking prospective jurors if they were LDS, held positions in the Church, and if Church membership would in any way impair their judgement. But the udder nonsense was all for naught, as the case finally landed in the pasture with a cud.

RICHARD JONES

*Feats of courage. They come in all sizes. But here's one
that surpasses most—the story of a man who wanted
to row across an ocean. And he did.*

On Oct. 10, 2000, Richard Jones, a 57-year-old high priest from Sandy, Utah, embarked on the almost impossible goal of rowing solo across the Atlantic Ocean. His amazing trip of 4,579 miles took him 133 days, an average of almost 35 miles a day, and landed him in the world record books.

Beginning at Los Gigantes, Tenerife (among the Canary Islands, off the west coast of northern Africa), he tried to follow the same route Columbus took in 1492.

THE BOAT

Brother Jones' home-made, high-tech rowboat was a sleek yellow torpedo aptly named *Brother of Jared*. Jones had three sets of oars, the best food-storage supply money could buy, and a desalinator to provide fresh water. Communication included a laptop computer with a satellite link for guidance and e-mail correspondence, and an emergency Coast Guard satellite beacon that could bring help from anyone in the vicinity.

THE TRIP

The first few weeks quickly grew routine—row hardest in the morning hours before sunup when the ocean was calm, take frequent breaks, take pictures and chart the day's progress, and stay in touch with home base.

At night, he bundled inside his watertight compartment with a 500-pound seawater ballast that he hand-pumped in each night and pumped out again in the morning to prevent his boat from rolling as he slept.

SHIPS PASSING IN THE NIGHT ...

One night, when he was about 2,000 miles into the journey, his collision-proximity alarm jarred him from sleep. He inched his

---

Cat gut used for tennis rackets and stringed instruments actually comes from sheep.

way to the door of his sleeping compartment and popped the hatch. He silenced the alarm and scanned the horizon. It was then he noticed that out towards the west the stars were blinking out. A giant black hole seemed to be swallowing them up from the horizon. Suddenly, he realized in a sickening panic that the growing black shadow was a ship plying directly towards him in stealthy silence. He quickly buckled the oars into the locks and rowed in a panic this way and then that, unable to tell exactly what direction the ship was moving. With the 500-pound ballast anchoring his progress, his pull on the oars was that much harder. He moved his craft far enough that when the massive ocean freighter finally churned by 60 feet away, he could almost feel the froth kicked in the air. "Had it hit, they would have never known. I would have been just a mysterious yellow streak on the bow," Jones said.

U.S. NAVY TAKES A LOOK

Another close encounter took place as Jones neared the western part of the Atlantic. Suddenly merging into view on his left was a huge U.S. Navy ship. He immediately grabbed for his radio and made contact. "Do you require assistance?" they radioed back. "No! Just don't hit me!" Jones called. In astonished respect he watched the seven-ship convoy of the USS *John F. Kennedy* aircraft-carrier battle group change course in a mighty arc to avoid *The Brother of Jared*. His presence in the middle of nowhere drew the respect of sailors who lined the rails of the various ships passing by, watching with binoculars in utter amazement.

HOME AT LAST

Jones' trip ended a few hundred miles early when equipment failure and a storm forced him to call for help near Ragged Island, one of about 700 islands in the Bahamas, about 60 miles off the southern tip of Florida. A local fisherman miraculously heard his emergency call for help and came to tow him in. A mishap during the tow nearly drowned Jones as his boat flipped over and flooded, ruining supplies, film, computers, and much more. Nevertheless, his trip put him in the record books as the oldest man (57) ever to row an ocean.

CHRIST IN AMERICA?

The Book of Mormon makes it clear that Christ visited the Americas after his resurrection. But are there any independent sources to validate this claim? Wayne May, writing in "Ancient American" magazine, points out the conclusions of numerous researchers looking into the legends of ancient America.

The traditions of a bearded visitor who was also a great religious leader, robed and light skinned, are beliefs that lived on among the lore and legends of numerous pre-Columbian natives in North and South America.

MANY NAMES
In Central and South America, this person was known as the East Star Man, Peace Maker, Pale One, Dawn Star, Sea Foam, Feathered Serpent, Kukulcan, and Quetzalcoatl.

THIS SURE SOUNDS FAMILIAR
Various stele reliefs and oral traditions tell of his arrival with the rising sun, setting up a Priesthood, healing the sick and giving them new laws.

FEATHERED SERPENT
Quetzalcoatl is nearly always portrayed as the main god among many other lower-ranking gods, but sometimes joining allegiances with them. He is credited with naming all things on Earth, giving to the Earth the blessing of maize (corn), fire, music, dance, and domesticated animals for the use, entertainment and work needs of man.

WHERE CAN I READ MORE?
The Visitor also commanded there be no blood sacrifice, ordering instead that tobacco be used, hence the importance of tobacco in all native ceremonies. Read a more complete and interesting account of this bearded visitor and his amazing works in the Book of Mormon, particularly III Nephi.

The Mona Lisa, now hanging in Paris's Louvre museum, is valued at $100,000,000.

JAMES BROWN

Another of the great converts to the early Church whose contributions are revered, but whose name is by and large forgotten.

Brother James Brown's Church roots stretch back to Illinois where he was living in 1838 with his wife, Martha. Here, they met the missionaries and were baptized. They moved to Nauvoo in 1840, and worked hard to help build the Nauvoo Temple. When Joseph Smith was killed, Brother Brown followed President Brigham Young and the Saints west. He was with the first company to arrive at Council Bluffs in the middle of June 1846.

About this time, volunteers were called to fight the war with Mexico, and Brown was one of the first to enlist. He was captain of Company C, and was allowed to bring his wife and children along. After a very difficult journey to Santa Fe, about 80 fellow soldiers could not continue and were sent under Brother Brown's leadership to Colorado to spend the winter of 1846-47. They were known as the "sick detachment."

The following spring, Captain Brown heard that Brigham Young and a group of pioneers had passed Fort Laramie, Wyoming, on their way to the Salt Lake Valley. He was thrilled. He rallied the strength of the "sick detachment" and followed. They arrived in Salt Lake just five days after the first pioneers, on July 29, 1847.

A month passed, and Brother Brown headed to California to collect pay for himself and the solders of the "sick detachment." He returned in November with $3,000 in gold. The brethren advised Brown that he should use some of his pay to buy out a claim by Miles Goodyear, a trapper who built a fort near the junction of the Ogden and Weber Rivers.

Brother Brown negotiated a deal and bought Goodyear's 14 square miles of land, a small log house, 75 cattle, 75 goats, 12 sheep and six horses for the amazing deal of $1,950.

The Miles Goodyear cabin still stands on the Tabernacle Square in Ogden, Utah, and is the oldest house in Utah.

In the spring of 1848, Brother Brown moved two of his sons and several other families to the new homestead, fondly named "Brownsville." Two years later, the name was changed to "Ogden" after Peter Skeene Ogden. Brother Brown went on to serve a mission and died in 1863 after an accident at a sorghum mill.

Sing me a lullaby: The national anthem of Greece has 158 verses.

J. GOLDEN KIMBALL,
Part III

*We conclude here our favorite quotes from J. Golden Kimball.
To begin with Part I, turn to page 32. Or, read Part II on page
113. Caution: salty words ahead!*

I DON'T KNOW HOW the people of St. George can stand
the heat, the Indians, the snakes and the flooding Virgin
River. If I had a house in St. George and a house in Hell, I'd
rent out the one in St. George and move straight to Hell."

PARTWAY THROUGH A FUNERAL SPEECH, he noticed
the man he thought had died seated in the front row. He
stopped and blurted, "Hey, who the hell is dead around here
anyway?"

AS HE SET APART a brother called to be a Seventy, J. Golden
did not know the man was earlier that day handed a cigar by a
co-worker to celebrate a newborn baby. With the offending evil
stogie forgotten but still in the jacket, and in full view of
Brother Kimball as he stood behind the brother, he began, "By
all the power invested in me, I ordain you a Seventy in the
Church of Jesus Christ of Latter-day Saints—cigar and all."

"I LOVE all of the brethren, but I love some a hell of a lot
more than I do others."

ASKED BY A BISHOP to deal with young ruffians in his
ward, J. Golden stood at the podium and glared down at them:
"And by the way, I've been hearing that some of you are carrying six shooters around in your hip pockets. Be careful—they
might go off and blow your brains out."

AT A FUNERAL in San Francisco, J. Golden said the dead
man was a good man because he read the Church-owned
Deseret News—"And it takes a damn good man to do that."

In 2003, the oldest living Boy Scout was Latter-day Saint George Freestone.

PORTER ROCKWELL

*Nicknamed the Lord's Destroying Angel, Brother Rockwell helped
the early brethren protect the Saints, tame the west, and
defend the truth. There's plenty of myth and lore mixed
with truth about this good brother's life.*

BORN: June 28, 1813 in Belchertown, Massachusetts
HEIGHT: 6 feet
HAIR: Charcoal black
EYES: grey/blue
BAPTIZED INTO THE LDS CHURCH: April 6, 1830
MARRIED: Feb. 2, 1832 to Luana Beebee; married two other
women and had 19 children.
DEACON: Ordained July 6, 1838
ELDER: Ordained in 1846
SEVENTY: Ordained in 1847
DEPUTY MARSHALL of the State of Deseret: 1849

SWORN PROTECTOR OF JOSEPH SMITH

As a young man, Porter learned early about Joseph Smith
and came to love, admire and respect him. When help was needed
to print the Book of Mormon, Porter gathered wood and picked
berries at night to earn money and gave it to Joseph. As turmoil
and persecution grew up around the prophet, Porter swore he'd
protect his friend from his many enemies. He was away on an
official assignment when the mob murdered the prophet, and
Porter turned his sworn devotions to Brigham Young.

A LEGEND IN HIS OWN TIME

Porter has been described by historians and biographers as
tough, humble, faithful, loyal, noble, a scout, pioneer, a rough-
and-ready frontiersman, rancher, iron willed, level headed,
straight-shootin' talker and, well, straight-shootin' shooter. He
was a dead-on straight shot. He became known as one of the
west's best known lawmen, a man sought out by journalists,
celebrity seekers and myth-making authors. He was one of the
fastest draws around, and it was rumored he gunned down more
than 150 outlaws. "But only those who deserved it," he once said.

In 1912, Pres. Taft ordered that stars on the U.S. flag be arranged in horizontal rows.

LIKE SAMSON OF OLD

In 1843, Joseph Smith blessed Porter that if he would remain true and faithful to the Church, and "cut not thy hair and no bullet or blade can harm thee!" When he died at 65 years old, a wealthy and faithful man, Porter's flowing long hair that hung from his bald crown had become a symbol of true devotion and faith to that promise, and the cause he believed in.

FASTEST DRAW IN THESE PARTS, MISTER

Porter's reputation drew assassins from hundreds of miles around for the honor of killing him. One day a rider intercepted Porter near his Skull Valley Ranch and pointed his gun in his face. "Rockwell, I come all the way from California just to kill you." It was a cap-and-ball pistol that needed a cap to fire, and sometimes those come loose. "Can't shoot me without a cap on yer gun," Porter drawled. The shooter was stunned and stole a quick glance to check his gun. It was the wrong move. Porter drew and fired, blowing the outlaw clean off his horse.

BOGG'S ASSASSINATION ATTEMPT

After Governor Lilburn W. Boggs issued his infamous extermination order against the Saints in Missouri, there was an assassination attempt on May 6, 1842. A gunman shot four large balls from a handgun through a window during a rainstorm at night as Boggs sat reading the paper. Two balls lodged in his skull, one in his neck and a fourth broke into his throat and he swallowed it. He barely survived. The sheriff found the pistol outside, loaded with more shot, but an owner was never found.

ROCKWELL NOT INVOLVED

Rockwell was fingered immediately and labeled a Danite avenger sent to kill the governor. He was arrested on suspicion. However, Boggs was running for reelection against several violent men, any one of them capable of committing the deed. The case against Rockwell fell apart for lack of evidence and reason. Rockwell's attitude about the accusation: "Well he ain't dead is he?" For lack of evidence, he was released after spending months in jail.

DON'T MESS WITH "PORT"

As the Saints were hurrying out of Nauvoo following

Joseph Smith's death, Hancock County Sheriff Jacob
Backenstos was being menaced by a man named Frank A.
Worrell. Rockwell was quickly deputized to help, and just
moments after taking the badge, the problem exploded in gun-
shots. When the smoke cleared, Rockwell had shot Worrell
dead. The story became sensational when it was learned that
Worrell was the militia lieutenant placed in charge of protecting
Joseph Smith when he was assassinated the year before.

EVEN THE INDIANS!

Another account tells of how the Indians respected him
because they couldn't kill him. "Indians tried to shoot at him,"
according to Susan Trane of Lehi, Utah. "But they couldn't hit
him because he was promised in that blessing that a bullet
would never strike him ... So the Indians tried to shoot him but
they couldn't do it and he'd shoot those Indians." After a while,
they just left him alone, she said.

NOW THERE'S A DISGUISE!

Another time, Porter was being chased by four gunmen and
he took safety in the farmhouse of a family who knew him.
The women put him in one of those long pioneer-style dresses
and sent him out back on a fresh horse. The other women then
went out front and watered the gunmen's horses and the men
stayed up all night waiting for Porter to emerge from that house.

GOOD OLD BUFFALO HIDE!

People liked to test the blessing given Porter regarding his
long hair and protection. Other times, they just wanted to
avenge a killing. One day Porter was facing down a whole gang
of outlaws who had ambushed him and in a hail of gunfire he
didn't fall. The astonished killers galloped off in a huge fright.
With them out of sight, Porter shook his buffalo robe, and the
bullets fell to the ground like a lot of loose change. Nothing
short of a rifle gets through buffalo skin, or so the story goes!

AND SO GOES the legend and lore of a great western saint,
hero, lawman and marksman. Read hundreds of similar stories
in any of his biographies. True to the prophet's promise, Orrin
Porter Rockwell passed away on June 9, 1878 of natural causes in
Salt Lake City—with neither a bullet nor knife wound to show.

Marriage helps? Of the 3,557 on death row in 2002, all but 709 were divorced or never married

PRESSED FOR TIME?

When it comes to printing, the Church does not mess around with make-do solutions. It owns some of the finest presses in the world, and look at what they can do!

IN ONE YEAR, it can print 5 million copies of the Book of Mormon in all languages. Stacking these books one atop the other for 8 hours a day would take 4-1/2 years and the resulting stack would be as tall as 164 Empire State buildings!

INSTEAD, LET'S STACK 'EM on pallets, but where do we store them? The storage area is five stories high and can hold 15,000 pallets.

THE PLANT encompasses 281,000 square feet—about the same as 5 football fields or 69 basketball courts.

THE NEXT TIME you use a tithing envelope, remember the Church's press can pump out 20,000 per hour or 22.3 million in a year.

CHURCH MAGAZINES roll off the presses at the rate of 18 million every year, in 42 languages.

IN 2002, the press received and delivered 5,844 print jobs that required 23,744 new plates.

READING IS FOR THE SIGHTED? The press also delivers 1,270,000 pages of Braille impressions per year—more if needed.

THE PRESSES RUN 24 hours a day, 6 days a week, and at full speed the web presses can deliver 34,000 impressions every hour. There are other presses and equipment that are always busy: sheet-fed, perfect binders, forms press, and more.

HOW MANY TREES to create the 14,000,000 pounds of paper the presses process in a year? At least 7,000 tons worth!

A mummy is an Egyptian pressed for time.

A FACE-OFF WITH FACE CARDS, PART II

Brother Paul continues his exploration into the banishment of face cards in the LDS home. To read this story from the beginning, turn to page 43.

MODERN CARDS TAKE SHAPE Early card designs reflected a style of art that wasn't in cards alone. Such images were in paintings and other art work of that medieval period.

The Italian decks were most popular in the 1400s with 56 cards and four courts each with a king, queen, knight and knave. The courts were represented by realities of those hard days. The Church was depicted by the chalice or cup, representing the Holy Grail, or the cup of the Last Supper. The military of the day was represented by the sword. The merchants were those taking the common man's money for goods, so they are alluded to with images of coins. The peasantry couldn't afford swords, so they were represented with clubs or batons. Some Europeans didn't like a queen in their deck. The Spanish took away the queen and replaced her with a mounted knight. The Germans replaced her with an "upper man." The German courts used bells (hawk bells were used for falcon training by the nobility), hearts (the Church), leaves (the middle class) and acorns (the peasantry).

THE FROGS LEAP AHEAD

But the French version is the one that finally took off. They liked the queen and returned her to her royal place in the deck. For the aristocracy card, they used the spade because it was shaped like the spearhead used by knights. The heart represented the Church (bleeding heart of Christ), and diamonds were a sign of the wealthy—no, not gem-quality diamonds, but the diamond shape of the paving stones in churches where only the well-to-do were buried. For the peasantry, the clover was used because that's the food the peasant's fed to their swine.

The French version was a lot easier to stencil, and because they were more simple to re-create, this version caught on. The French also created a better mass production process, and German card makers couldn't compete. The French design soon became the standard in Europe.

NAMING THE COURTS Do the kings and queens represent real people? They did for a time. In the mid-1400s, the French began naming their kings and actually printed the name on the cards. But the naming nomenclature varied according to maker. For 350 years, popular names appeared on cards such as Solomon, Augustus, Clovis, Constantine, Charlemagne, David, Caesar, and Alexander.

YOU KNAVE, YOU!
A similar evolution with the queens and knaves took place. Judith (hearts), Pallas (spades), Rachel (diamonds), and Argine (clubs) are harder to identify in history, but they represented lesser known wives, mistresses, in-laws, or mythological heroines.

As for the knaves, they too received names but usually of famous or honorable men serving in a knightly capacity.

After the French revolution in 1800, the naming of court cards was abandoned. Today, the figures on the cards have no more identity than the kings and queens in a chess set. There circulates the occasional myth that the figures have always represented known individuals. However, for the past 200 years, the generic face card represents no one.

What about fortune-telling tarot cards the Joker? Our discussion continues on page 271.

****

A young missionary was walking down the street with the Book of Mormon in his coat pocket when he was shot by an armed robber. Fortunately, the bullet lodged part way in the book and saved him. "See," the missionary said to his companion, pointing out where the bullet actually stopped, "NOTHING can get through Second Nephi!"

First Mormon immigrants from England, a group of 40, left for the U.S. in 1840.

TWO SEAS

Two bodies of water dominate the geography of modern-day Israel. To the north is the Sea of Galilee, and 65 miles south, the Dead Sea. Together, these great seas embody an amazing parable about the teachings of the Savior and life's amazing purpose.

The Dead Sea is the lowest point on the earth's surface at 1,292 feet below sea level. Rivers flow into it, but nothing flows out. It is surrounded by steep, rocky cliffs 2,500-4,000 feet high. Its deepest point is 1,300 feet, and possibly covers the ancient cities of Sodom and Gomorrah. Its close neighbors include Jericho, Masada and En Gedi. From caves along its western shore came the Dead Sea Scrolls, and its coastline is dotted with tourist hotels, spas, and parched beaches. The salt and mineral content is so thick, a person can float without touching bottom in water only a foot deep. It has 12 minerals found in no other lake or sea in the world. And no lake matches its 35% salinity!

The Sea of Galilee is the lowest fresh water lake in the world at 575 feet below sea level. It is fed by underground streams and the Jordan River flows into it at the north and flows out at the south. It is vulnerable to sudden and violent storms but its serenity is unmatched, and is rich in aquatic life. It has served untold thousands—villagers, fishermen, traders, merchants, and settlers. Jesus recruited four of his apostles here; he walked on the water, calmed the sea, fed the 5,000, taught the Sermon on the Mount from a hill that overlooks the sea, and other miracles. And Galilee is vital as the main source for modern Israel's fresh water supply—the whole country benefits.

- **THE DEAD SEA IS LIKE** a selfish man hoarding, taking all, giving back nothing. Its reward? Briny, poisonous death. No life can survive in its waters or shores—it takes and gives nothing.
- **THE SEA OF GALILEE IS LIKE** a giving man, returning generously from what is given, sharing everything for the benefit of others. Its reward? Fresh, cooling waters teeming with life, its shores giving rest to the weary traveler and the tired birds.

Be it a body of water or the body of man, he who hoards is dead, but he who gives with pure intent has life everlasting.

Now what do we do? The word *Sunday* is not in the King James Bible!

HALF GOD, HALF MAN?

THE MYTH: Jesus was half god and half man.
SUPPOSITION: No mortal could do all that Jesus did.
BACKGROUND: Christians for centuries have defined
Jesus as being part god and having godly powers born into him
because of who His father was. A few Latter-day Saints embrace
the same idea to explain how Jesus could atone for the sins of
the world, something they believe that no mortal could otherwise do.

GREEK ORIGINS: The half-god, half-man myth is borrowed
from Greek mythology. The story goes: One day, the head god
Zeus had relations with a mortal woman named Alcmene. The
resulting pregnancy produced Hercules who was half god and
half man, with amazing and super-hero godly powers. When
Hercules matured and ultimately asked to be a god his mother
gave him 12 impossible tasks to perform, which he did.

CORRECTIONS: This myth is tough to expunge from some
people's understanding because it appears to offer simple
answers and solutions to the difficult task laid before Jesus.
Atoning for the sins of the world is at a minimum fantastically
daunting and it's impossible to imagine that a mere mortal
could execute the assignment with any degree of adequacy.

FACTS:
• Jesus never taught He was endowed with godly powers, nor
did He exercise any miraculous power on any other basis than
what He said all people have access to—humble faith and obedience to Heavenly Father's wishes and commands from which
comes priesthood authorization to do Father's work in the
earth.

• Jesus never claimed He was more than a mortal while in the
flesh, though He openly declared his lineage. To link special
powers to lineage is like saying the son born to a bishop arrives

on Earth as part bishop. There's a lineage of father to son, but no inherited power, responsibility or keys. The same is true of Jesus, although He came with an important assignment.

• Joseph Smith and Brigham Young never taught that Jesus skirted this mortal existence with a body gifted with supernatural powers. His was the same priesthood power given all worthy men; He had no supernatural advantage for the atonement.

• Brigham Young dedicated the largest portion of a lecture on christiandom's notion of half-god/half-man, and dismissed it with the analogy of the mule, it being half horse and half ass, a non-specie that was, he opined, "The most hateful creature that was ever made." Said he, "The Savior was begotten by the Father of His spirit, by the same Being who is the Father of our spirits, and that is all the organic difference between Jesus Christ and you and me." (J of D, vol. 4, pg. 216-218)

• Jesus came to conquer death and conquer the flesh. He lived a sinless life. His eternal token of honor is that He did what no other person could do—make it through the second estate unscathed by sin and corruption.

• Jesus took on His tabernacle of clay, just as we did, and conquered it, something He says we can all do if we'll but try. Bottom line: Jesus couldn't conquer the flesh unless He was flesh.

****

SHAKE THE HABIT! Addicted to caffeine? Kicking the habit abruptly can bring on a host of problems including headaches, tremors, lethargy, and symptoms of depression. In the U.S., more than 90 percent of Americans consume caffeine on a regular basis, most of it coming from coffee. Those who try to break free should do it gradually, over a period of days or weeks. Studies show that the "cold turkey" approach of stopping caffeine all at once can result in withdrawal symptoms of fatigue and "the blahs" that are just about the same for everybody, regardless of how much caffeine they use each day.

Pain travels along our nerves at 50 feet per second.

A TON O' WHEAT

The Saints are counseled to have food storage so they can live for a year independent of the world. Impossible? No. But most worrisome to Brother Paul is what the heck is a "legume"?

LET US SING TOGETHER, "The big red letters stand for the storage fam-i-leeee—G-L-O-W-S-M: Grains, Legumes, Oil, Water, Sugar, and Milk (Powdered)." Poundage per person per year can vary depending on your appetite. It makes sense, then, that very few lima beans will be stored for anyone but the family horse. Poor horse.

• **GRAINS:** These are any of the foods that break your teeth unless you prepare them, such as wheat, rice, corn, rolled oats, spaghetti. When most good Mormons die, they leave behind about 400 pounds of wheat for every year they expected to eat it. That's about right.

• **LEGUMES:** Those mysterious colorful things that either smell bad or work well for craft projects include dry beans, peas, lentils. About 60 pounds a person should do you in after a year.

• **POWDERED MILK:** Awful tasting on a bowl of Corn Flakes. But if you store a lot of Corn Flakes, be sure to include at least 16 lbs. of powdered milk. Or, save money by scorching some cardboard, pulverizing it to powder and mixing with white glue and water until you have a nice milk-like consistency. Tastes just about the same as the expensive stuff—more fiber, too.

• **SUGAR OR HONEY:** The universal condiment that goes with all things edible or not. Also good for attracting ants for that added protein snack. Sixty pounds will attract all the ants you want for a year.

• **COOKING OIL:** Important for french fries and popcorn. If you store a lot of popcorn, make sure you have ten quarts of oil per adult. I'd store some good movies, too.

Ordained ministers: TV's "Mr. Rogers" and Leave it to Beaver's dad, Hugh Beaumont.

- **WATER:** Better served cold and mixed with powdered lemonade. For a full year, a swimming pool is the answer here, but you run the risk of kids swimming in it ... especially the little kids. Better to keep 14 gallons on hand to get yourself through a good two weeks. The kids will need to find their own.

NOW THAT YOU have your stuff, what do you do with it?

- **ALL THINGS NEED FUEL.** That means you better hope the utilities are working during your year-long crisis. If not, better re-think your food supplies. Another solution is to store cigarettes and beer and exchange them for use of your neighbor's portable generator. Or, I suppose you could get one yourself.

So, not only do you store food, but you should think about how to use that food. At a minimum, wheat can be softened by boiling it. Oh yum. Cracked Wheat 38 times a week. That'll clean out the old pipes for sure.

- **SO, LOOK AT STORING** a hand wheat grinder to make flour. Include some yeast so you can make bread. Boiling water will take a lot of the wood from your deck, so think about storing coal under the swing set, or plant more apricot trees so you'll have plenty of dead, seasoned wood to pluck should the need arise.

- **BROTHER PAUL HAS A 6-FOOT TV SATELLITE DISH** out back. He coated it with aluminum foil and mounted a couple of forks to hold various containers. He aims this at the sun and the rays focus on the containers and ... instant boiling water, baked bread or potatoes, and even fried guinea pigs (they love 'em in Peru). He can make 3-4 loaves of bread on a good sunny day.

- **THERE ARE A ZILLION COOKBOOKS** available, but the bottom line for every survivalist is this: Own a pickup so you can loot the grocery store. No, no, that's not it, as Brother Paul's eternal companion reminds him with "that look." It's to store what you eat and eat what you store. That's the ticket. And when it comes to surviving, always remember this from Brother Paul: A three-legged dog means somebody just had dinner.

Scholars speculate: Aramaic had no simple word for "many," so they used "40."

THE CROSS

With Christianity now the largest religious group in the world
numbering more than 2 billion, the cross has come to
mean many things. Brother Paul takes a closer look.

CROSS, from the Latin "crux" meaning stake or cross. As a torture device it was originally a tall, round pole, and it's been in use, unfortunately, for thousands of years.

VOCABULARY ENHANCERS:
- **1500s:** The word "cross" took on the meaning of contrary, as in contrary winds for sailing ships.
- **1639:** Took on the meaning of rude or ill-tempered.
- **1664:** Cross-examine was first used.
- **1710:** Cross stitch was first recorded.
- **1826:** Cross-eye first used.
- **1860:** Cross-fire first used.
- **1914:** First crossword puzzle; it was originally called word-cross.

ANCIENT ORIGINS

Variations of the cross have been used as religious symbols and ornaments as far back as recorded history can show. All over the world, cross symbols have been found that predate the Romans and Christ by thousands of years. From the stone age forward, in Egypt, India, Syria, Persia and elsewhere, the cross is everywhere in all times of history.

FIRST CROSSES

The so-called tau cross is one of the most ancient. Its name comes from the Greek letter tau which looks like a capital T. The other ancient cross is the swastika, infamous because of Hitler and Nazism. The swastika was also known as the Gammadian cross because it was formed by placing together, tail to tail, four Greek capital forms of the letter gamma. By 1000 B.C. the swastika was being used as a religious symbol in India and China. Crosses inside of circles of many variations predate the Savior, and examples can be found in museums all over the world.

AS A TORTURE DEVICE

The torture device used in crucifixion took many shapes. Sometimes it was a single pole for impaling or holding a person inescapably upright. A tree trunk served this purpose, or for more efficient torture and killing, timbers were placed in the form of a T or an X. The ancient civilizations punished people with crucifixion, as did the Greeks, Carthaginians, Macedonians and the earliest Romans.

TOO MUCH INFORMATION

In Roman times, the victims were typically stripped naked and tied to a stake. A whip was fashioned with several long leather strings tied to the end of a wooden handle. At the end of the leather strings were pieces of sharp iron or bone. The executioner's job was to rip open flesh and in some cases, the internal organs were exposed or came out. Whipped and scourged, the person was reclothed, and if still physically able, was forced to drag the pole or cross to a place of execution where he was fastened to it with ropes or spikes, or impaled, and left to die.

THE CROSS OF JESUS

Tradition says that Jesus's cross was the Latin Cross, or the four-pointed cross shaped like a lower-case "t." However, with the task of carrying one's own cross to the place of execution, hauling 300-400 pounds of wood was probably impossible, especially after being scourged.

The more likely cross was the St. Anthony Cross which is shaped like a capital "T." Carrying the 100-pound cross member (estimated weight) was probably the most that a person could do who had just been pulverized with a cat-o-nine tails. The cross-member rested snugly on top of the upright into a notch or groove and could be hoisted up and lowered down easier than uprooting an entire cross assembly. This fits better the Savior's statement in John 3:14: "Even so must the Son of man be lifted up." Once in position, a hanging or slouching Jesus left plenty of room above his head for the sign that was nailed above him: "This is Jesus King of the Jews."

RELIGIOUS SYMBOL

Jesus's death focused a lot of attention to this ancient symbol. After Christ's death, the use of the cross in religious ceremony was kept secret at least after 100 A.D. But two centuries later, Constantine made it the official symbol of Christianity starting in the early 300s A.D. Over the centuries the cross as a symbol evolved to reflect various groups or causes.

- **Latin Cross:** Shaped like a lower-case "t"
- **St. Anthony's Cross:** Shaped like a capital "T"
- **Greek:** Four equal arms similar to that used by the Red Cross.
- **Maltese:** Four equal-sized arms except each is flared out like a dove's tail or an arrowhead pointed inwards.
- **St. Andrew's:** Shaped like an "X" and often used by knights on their breastplates or shields during the crusades.
- **Calvary:** A Latin cross on a foundation of three stepping stones or platforms.
- **Patriarchal:** A Latin cross with an additional though smaller cross member near the top.

SIGN OF THE CROSS

Many Christian groups remind themselves of what Jesus went through on the cross by ascribing the image of the cross on their bodies. In any instance of prayer or worship, they make the sign of the cross by touching their fingers to the forehead, breast, left shoulder, and right shoulder. The Russian and Greek churches touch the right shoulder first.

LATTER-DAY SAINTS AND THE CROSS

President Gordon B. Hinckley said, "For us, the cross is the symbol of the dying Christ, while our message is a declaration of the living Christ... the lives of our people must become the only meaningful expression of our faith and, in fact, therefore, the symbol of our worship ... On Calvary he was the dying Jesus. From the tomb he emerged the living Christ. The cross had been the bitter fruit of Judas' betrayal, the summary of Peter's denial. The empty tomb now became the testimony of His divinity, the assurance of eternal life, the answer to Job's unanswered question: 'If a man die, shall he live again?' (Job 14: 14)."

The Shroud of Turin, thought to be Jesus' burial shroud, was carbon dated to the A.D. 1300s.

WHY WOMEN ARE JUST HAPPIER PEOPLE

Brethren of the Church, are not women just difficult, sometimes? This list has been floating around the Internet for years, in various forms. Its origin is unknown to Brother Paul. Nevertheless, his wife insists he share this version because it feels so right ...

It's great to be a woman because:

Free drinks, free dinners, free movies!

Speeding ticket? What's that?

New lipstick gives you a whole new lease on life.

If you have to be home in time for *Melrose Place*, you can say so, out loud.

If you're not making enough money, you can blame the glass ceiling.

You can sue the President for sexual harassment.

No fashion faux pas you make could rival The Speedo.

Brad Pitt.

You know why it's good to have 5 pairs of black shoes.

Discovering a designer dress on the clearance rack can be considered a peak life experience.

You understand why a phone call between 2 women never lasts under ten minutes.

You understand the inaccuracy of every bathroom scale ever made.

A salad, diet drink, and a hot fudge sundae make a balanced lunch.

At times, chocolate really can solve all your problems.

You know the difference between cream, ivory, and off-white.

You always get to choose the movie.

You don't make fools of men. Most of them are do-it-your-self types.

No one passes out when you take off your shoes.

Excitement is as close as the nearest beauty-supply store.

If you forget to shave, no one has to know.

If you're dumb, some people will find it cute.

You have the ability to dress yourself.

You can quickly end any fight by crying.

You've never had a goatee.

You can fully assess a person just by looking at their shoes.

You know which glass was yours by the lipstick mark.

The remote control is not an extension of yourself.

You get to hate Kathie Lee in the way only another woman truly can.

Your conversations generally consist of more than just "uh huh, yep, ok, then bye."

There are more coffee drug addicts in the U.S. than drug addicts of any other kind.

THE BRETHREN SAID IT!

PART V

All is not always sober and somber at the podium.
For more, see page 256.

"If a man worships a cow or a crocodile, he can gain any reward that cows and crocodiles happen to be passing out this season."—*Bruce R. McConkie*

John Taylor writing to George Q. Cannon about the local judge's drinking addiction: "It is said, notwithstanding his high position, that the posts in the streets sometimes run against him and that the houses rush irreverently against his honor's body, and that not infrequently the sidewalks fly up and hit his honor on the forehead. That is really too bad and ought to be inquired into."—*John Taylor*

"I was standing one day between Picadilly Circus and Leicestier Square talking to an American officer during the first world war. We saw a man coming down the sidewalk with his hat on one side, swinging a swagger stick, a Charlie Chaplin moustache, and a monocle. I said to the officer, 'I wonder why those fellows wear a one-eye glass instead of two.' 'Well,' he said, 'I'll tell you. A guy like that can see more with one eye than he can comprehend.'"—*Hugh B. Brown*

"I discovered in reading the genealogical history of one line of my heritage, that it was carried back to the Norsemen who came into England such a long, long time ago. Now, I admit that this student in carrying it back had to use ten-league boots over some of the stretches, but I hope it is true, nevertheless."
—*Antoine R. Ivins*

"I also heard about a mother and her young daughter who were listening to a public speaker when the child said to her mother, 'Isn't that man happy?' The mother replied, 'I guess so.' To which the girl remarked, 'Why doesn't he tell his face?'"
—*Paul H. Dunn*

Grin and bear it: routine smiling takes 12 primary muscles, frowning takes 11.

DIGGING UP THE REAL BIBLE STUFF

Did those people and events described in the Old and New Testaments really exist, or are the books just collections of ancient legend and folklore?

REFERENCE: Golden calf
ARTIFACT: In 1990, Harvard researchers working near the Gaza Strip found a small silver-plated, bronze calf figurine that dated back to 500-1000 B.C., that was reminiscent of the huge golden calf described in Exodus.

REFERENCE: Books predating 200 B.C.
ARTIFACT: In 1986, archaeologists found the earliest known text of the Bible, dated to about 600 B.C., suggesting that at least part of the Old Testament was written shortly after some of the events it describes.

REFERENCE: Manner of preserving the ancient texts
ARTIFACT: In 1979, Israeli archaeologists found two tiny silver scrolls dated to around 600 B.C. with a benediction from the Book of Numbers etched into their surface, making it clear that parts of the Old Testament were being copied long before people believed it had been written.

REFERENCE: Jeremiah's scribe, Baruch
ARTIFACT: In 1986, lumps of clay used to mark documents were found depicting the seal of Baruch, son of Neriah, the scribe who recorded Jeremiah's doomsday prophecies.

REFERENCE: Did Israel exist prior to 200 B.C.?
ARTIFACT: In 1990, hieroglyphic clues helped identify figures in a Luxor wall relief as ancient Israelites. The stele, dated to 1207 B.C., tells of a victory by Pharaoh: "Israel is laid waste," it reads, suggesting that Israel was a distinct population 3,000 years ago.

Two copies of the Book of Mormon sank on the Titanic.

REFERENCE: King David
ARTIFACT: In 1993, Jewish researchers found an inscription bearing the phrase, "House of David" and "King of Israel," dating to 900 B.C., only a century after David's reign. It describes a victory by a neighboring king over the Israelites. In 1994, a French scholar studying the Moabite Stone, which was discovered in 1868 at the ruins of Dibon, found on the stone the phrase, "The House of David." The surrounding commentary was also from an enemy to Israel, King Mesha of Moab, boasting of his victory.

REFERENCE: City of Jericho
ARTIFACT: Researchers at Jericho say the city was uninhabited from 1400 to 1100 B.C. and determined the Battle of Jericho was fought sometime during this period. Modern estimates place Joshua in the period shortly after Moses died around 1500 B.C.

REFERENCE: Pontius Pilate
ARTIFACT: In 1961, diggers in Caesarea found the fragment of a plaque indicating that a building had been dedicated by Pontius Pilatus, Prefect of Judea. Now Pilate is a real person.

REFERENCE: Fishing boats as described in the New Testament
ARTIFACT: There are some 45 references in the New Testament about boats and fishing as they related to Jesus. In 1986, two members of a Galilean kibbutz came across the remains of a 26-foot wooden dory buried in the mud. Carbon dating placed it at the first century A.D.

REFERENCE: Money changers
ARTIFACT: Discovery of an astonishing variety of 1st century coins helps explain why money changers were needed in Jerusalem, and that for whatever reason he had, an angry Jesus drove them from the temple.

Missionary handshakes: anciently men shook hands to prove they were unarmed.

MORMON PRIMER ON MASONS

PART II

To read this article from the beginning, see page 95. We've been discussing the origins of the Masons and their alleged connection to the LDS Temple Ceremony. Read on for the conclusion to this puzzling pursuit.

JOSEPH SMITH BECOMES A MASON
In 1842, the Prophet Joseph joined the Masonic Order hoping to increase the acceptance of the Church by the Masons in Nauvoo and elsewhere. This was great news for the local Grand Master in Illinois! "To get a guy this famous into our Order? This calls for a personal visit." So he rushed to Nauvoo and pushed Joseph through all three degrees of Masonry.

NOT A THREAT

Joseph did not see Masonry as a threat and did not discourage or forbid members from becoming Masons. He seems to have appreciated the bleak remnants of the ancient endowment given to Adam that were then barely hinted at by the Masonic order and all those intermediary parties that preceded and inadvertently preserved a little of it.

THE ENDOWMENT RESTORED

Four months after Joseph became a Mason, he was visited by an angel around May 1, 1842. He was taught the temple endowment verbally (no written notes) over a period of 2-3 days.
• On May 4 and 5, 1842, he had the upper floor of his red brick store divided into several rooms and furnished, as instructed, and began using the same memorization process to teach nine brethren who likewise had to commit the ceremony to memory. In his journal he wrote,

"IN THIS COUNCIL [of nine men] was instituted the ancient

A manned rocket can reach the moon in less time than a stagecoach can cross England.

order of things for the first time in these last days ... setting forth the order pertaining to the Ancient of Days, and all those plans and principles by which anyone is enabled to secure the fullness of those blessings which have been prepared for the Church of the First Born, and come up and abide in the presence of the Eloheim in the eternal worlds."

APOSTATES ATTACK

When disenchanted converts left the Church, they helped lead the fallacious claim that Joseph Smith copied or otherwise borrowed the Masonic ceremonies for his own.

MODERN ANALYSIS

On going research has uncovered amazing and interesting comparisons between the endowment and the Masonic ceremonies. Symbols and markings used by the Masons are not unique to them. American Indians carried some of them for centuries if not longer in their ancient ceremony and lore. The ancient Chinese martial arts and military had several of them as part of their sacred temple rites.

Of the 700 distinct elements of the LDS ritual, about 690 are completely different from the Masonic ceremony, and ten or so are very similar. But similarity aside, they have no meaning to the Masons. Their version has *nothing* to do with temple ordinances, dispensations of the gospel, ordinances of washings and anointings, or the relationship between the priesthood powers and covenants, or the design, purpose and significance of priesthood robes, signs, tokens, the creation, purpose and nature of the fall, true order of prayer, consecration, celestial marriage, and the list goes on and on and on.

MASONIC TERMS AND DEFINITIONS

• **APRON** Part of the Masonic ceremony is elaborately decorated or embroidered aprons as a symbolic connection to the medieval stone cutters from where they believe their Masonic traditions originated.
• **DEGREES OF MASONRY** Membership and knowledge of the principles of Freemasonry are indicated by three basic

degrees: Entered Apprentice, Fellowcraft, and Master Mason.
• **FREEMASON** The word free was added to mason during
the Middle Ages (see Part I).
• **GRAND LODGE** The administrative body in charge of
Freemasonry in a specific geographic area. The United States
has Grand Lodges in all 50 states and the District of Columbia.
• **GRAND MASTER** The elected leader of the Grand Lodge.
• **LODGE** This refers to both a unit of Masons as well as the
room or building in which they meet. There are more than
13,000 lodges in the U.S.
• **MASON** A member of the Masonic fraternity.
• **MASTER** The elected leader of the local lodge; also the title
a Mason acquires once he has completed the third degree of
membership.
• **TEMPLE** Another name for a Masonic building. The word
is used in the same sense that Justice Wendell Holmes called the
Supreme Court a "Temple of Justice."
• **YOUTH GROUPS** Masonic organizations for young people
include *DeMolay International* for boys ages 12-21, *Rainbow for
Girls* for girls ages 11-20, and *Job's Daughters* for young women
ages 11-20.

AN OPINION

Brother Paul is of the opinion that the restored gospel of
Jesus Christ and the ever-expanding needs of His Church in these
latter days leaves the converted member with no time to spare on
membership with any secretive fraternity, including the Masons.
There is more than enough in our local wards, branches and
neighborhoods that need our full and undivided attention.

TO LEARN MORE

Much of this article's information comes from the two-vol-
ume work on Joseph Smith titled, *Brother Joseph* by Richard
Skousen and W. Cleon Skousen, as well as private research,
encyclopedias, and more of the usual (there are MOUNDS to be
read, if you want to). It's a big, complex story, and one day,
Brother Paul hopes somebody will write the definitive book
that will weave it all together. It's an amazing and often over-
looked part of the entire restoration story.

A panagram is a sentence that contains all 26 letters of the alphabet.

ELDER JEREMIAH BENJAMIN SEAGULL MEETS SISTER CRICKET

The lonely gull gained eternal fame and glory when it became part of Utah's story. Just who is this scavenger of our local trash heaps and farmer's fields?

CALIFORNIA SEAGULL (*L. californicus*, or when targeting you for droppings, it is also known as *L. aggrieved dumpacuss*)

- **LENGTH**: Up to 17 inches
- **WINGSPAN**: Up to 52 inches
- **HEAD**: Rounded forehead with a more gentle appearance than other gulls. The head is typically white, black, gray or brown during mating season, and streaked or smudgy in winter.
- **HABITAT**: All over the United States. It loves water. Those nesting inland usually go to the coasts in the winter, unless they pass a Utah dump on the way, and that makes for a great layover.
- **COLORS**: Mainly grey and white.
- **FOOD**: Gulls are valuable scavengers of food, taking insects, mollusks, and crustaceans on beaches; worms and grubs in plowed fields; and fish and garbage from ships and along shores. Some of the larger gulls go after the eggs of other birds, including fellow (or sister) gulls.
- **CLAIM TO FAME**: Credited with saving Utah's first pioneer crops in 1848 from the voracious eating habits of the Mormon cricket. Wrote Orson F. Whitney, "When it seemed that nothing could stay the devastation, great flocks of gulls appeared, filling the air with their white wings and plaintive cries, and settled down upon the half-ruined fields. All day long they gorged themselves, and when full, disgorged and feasted again, the white gulls upon the black crickets, list hosts of heaven and hell contending, until the pests were vanquished and the people were saved." After devouring the crickets, the gulls returned "to the lake islands whence they came."

TOP 100 SCRIPTURES!

*Thanks to some amazing software available at scriptures.byu.edu,
a scan of all general conference talks from 1942 to 2004
reveals this list of top 100 scriptures quoted most often.
The number of times they were used is in brackets.
The first 20 are spelled out.*

1 **MOSES 1:39 [264]** "For behold, this is my work and my glory—to bring to pass the immortality and eternal life of man."

2 **JS-H 1:17 [173]** "It no sooner appeared than I found myself delivered from the enemy which held me bound. When the light rested upon me I saw two Personages, whose brightness and glory defy all description, standing above me in the air. One of them spake unto me, calling me by name and said, pointing to the other—This is My Beloved Son. Hear Him!"

3 **JOHN 17:3 [138]** "And this is life eternal, that they might know thee the only true God, and Jesus Christ, whom thou hast sent."

4 **MATTHEW 6:33 [119]** "But seek ye first the kingdom of God, and his righteousness; and all these things shall be added unto you."

5 **ARTICLES OF FAITH 1:13 [110]** "We believe in being honest, true, chaste, benevolent, virtuous, and in doing good to all men; indeed, we may say that we follow the admonition of Paul—We believe all things, we hope all things, we have endured many things, and hope to be able to endure all things. If there is anything virtuous, lovely, or of good report or praiseworthy, we seek after these things."

6 **2 NE. 2:25 [96]** "Adam fell that men might be; and men are, that they might have joy."

7 **MATTHEW. 5:48 [92]** "Be ye therefore perfect, even as your Father which is in heaven is perfect."

8 **ROMANS. 1:16 [88]** "For I am not ashamed of the gospel of Christ: for it is the power of God unto salvation to every one that believeth; to the Jew first, and also to the Greek."

9 **JOHN 14:27 [85]** "Peace I leave with you, my peace I give unto you: not as the world giveth, give I unto you. Let not your heart be troubled, neither let it be afraid."

A person will die from total lack of sleep sooner than from starvation.

10 JOHN 14:6 [84] "Jesus saith unto him, I am the way, the truth, and the life: no man cometh unto the Father, but by me."

11 JOHN 3:16 [82] "For God so loved the world, that he gave his only begotten Son, that whosoever believeth in him should not perish, but have everlasting life."

12 D&C 14:7 [81] "And, if you keep my commandments and endure to the end you shall have eternal life, which gift is the greatest of all the gifts of God."

13 MATT. 25:40 [80] "And the King shall answer and say unto them, Verily I say unto you, Inasmuch as ye have done it unto one of the least of these my brethren, ye have done it unto me."

14 LUKE 23:34 [79] "Then said Jesus, Father, forgive them; for they know not what they do. And they parted his raiment, and cast lots."

15 D&C 59:23 [79] "But learn that he who doeth the works of righteousness shall receive his reward, even peace in this world, and eternal life in the world to come."

16 MOSIAH 3:19 [78] "For the natural man is an enemy to God, and has been from the fall of Adam, and will be, forever and ever, unless he yields to the enticings of the Holy Spirit, and putteth off the natural man and becometh a saint through the atonement of Christ the Lord, and becometh as a child, submissive, meek, humble, patient, full of love, willing to submit to all things which the Lord seeth fit to inflict upon him, even as a child doth submit to his father."

17 JAMES 1:5 [77] "If any of you lack wisdom, let him ask of God, that giveth to all men liberally, and upbraideth not; and it shall be given him. "

18 1 NEPHI 3:7 [76] "And it came to pass that I, Nephi, said unto my father: I will go and do the things which the Lord hath commanded, for I know that the Lord giveth no commandments unto the children of men, save he shall prepare a way for them that they may accomplish the thing which he commandeth them."

19 AMOS 3:7 [73] "Surely the Lord GOD will do nothing, but he revealeth his secret unto his servants the prophets. "

20 ACTS 4:12 [72] "Neither is there salvation in any other: for there is none other name under heaven given among men, whereby we must be saved."

21	D&C 93:36 [71]	61	D&C 68:28 [49]
22	Matt. 7:12 [66]	62	D&C 38:27 [49]
23	Ex. 20:12 [65]	63	D&C 101:80 [49]
24	Josh. 24:15 [65]	64	Gen. 1:28 [48]
25	1 Pet. 2:9 [65]	65	Luke 22:42 [48]
26	John 14:15 [64]	66	Acts 3:21 [48]
27	Matt. 5:16 [63]	67	BM Title Page [48]
28	3 Ne. 27:27 [63]	68	Matt. 11:28-30 [47]
29	Matt. 24:14 [62]	69	Matt. 3:17 [47]
30	D&C 1:30 [62]	70	John 14:26 [47]
31	D&C 68:25 [60]	71	Ether 2:12 [47]
32	D&C 82:10 [60]	72	D&C 59:9 [47]
33	Matt. 22:39 [59]	73	John 16:33 [46]
34	Alma 41:10 [59]	74	Isa. 9:6 [45]
35	A of F 1:1 [59]	75	John 3:5 [45]
36	James 1:27 [57]	76	John 8:12 [45]
37	A of F 1:9 [57]	77	Eph. 2:20 [45]
38	Mal. 3:10 [56]	78	D&C 121:45 [45]
39	D&C 130:20-21 [56]	79	2 Ne. 2:27 [44]
40	John 7:17 [55]	80	Moro. 10:32 [44]
41	D&C 88:118 [55]	81	D&C 84:38 [44]
42	John 5:39 [53]	82	JS-H 1:19 [43]
43	D&C 20:77 [53]	83	Isa. 29:14 [42]
44	A of F 1:3 [53]	84	Matt. 4:4 [42]
45	A of F 1:4 [53]	85	Matt. 25:21 [42]
46	Dan. 2:44 [52]	86	1 Tim. 4:12 [42]
47	Matt. 28:19-20 [52]	87	Rev. 14:6-7 [42]
48	1 Cor. 15:22 [52]	88	A of F 1:12 [42]
49	2 Ne. 31:20 [52]	89	A of F 1:8 [42]
50	Mosiah 18:9 [52]	90	Matt. 26:39 [41]
51	D&C 38:30 [52]	91	Mark 16:15 [41]
52	Moro. 10:4 [51]	92	A of F 1:5 [41]
53	D&C 1:38 [51]	93	Gen. 1:27 [40]
54	Gen. 3:19 [50]	94	Ex. 20:8 [40]
55	Philip. 4:7 [50]	95	Prov. 22:6 [40]
56	Moro. 7:47 [50]	96	Eph. 1:10 [40]
57	Moro. 10:4-5 [50]	97	D&C 76:22-24 [40]
58	D&C 13:1 [50]	98	Matt. 4:19 [39]
59	Ex. 20:14 [49]	99	Matt. 7:21 [39]
60	Rev. 14:6 [49]	100	D&C 4:2 [39]

Makes sense to me! Men tend to crave fat and salt; women tend to crave chocolate.

MORONI'S PROMISE!

PART III

*More famous people who received a copy
of the Book of Mormon.*

READER: John F. Kennedy (1917-1963)
DATE: August 1962
CIRCUMSTANCE: When Mrs. Kennedy announced plans for a White House library of first editions, Congressman Ralph R. Harding (Idaho) and his wife decided their cherished 1830 first-edition copy of the Book of Mormon they bought in 1949 would make an excellent addition to this library. Rep. Harding made arrangements to meet with Kennedy in August 1962, and in the sunshine of the Rose Garden he presented the gift, giving also a brief history of the book and the Church.

READER: Oldest living person (1887-2004)
DATE: 2003
CIRCUMSTANCE: When Russian citizen Afanasy Ivanovich Tarasov turned 116 and became the world's oldest living human, local LDS members presented him with a blanket and a Russian translation of the Book of Mormon. Though not LDS, Tarasov attributed his longevity to clean living, no alcohol or tobacco, and politeness at home. "I know a lot about Jesus Christ," he was quoted as saying in the *Church News*. "He was the greatest revolutionary."

READER: Boxing Great Muhammad Ali
DATE: 1986
CIRCUMSTANCE: Bob Wilke of Chandler, Arizona happened to intercept The Champ at the airport in Dallas Texas. After striking up a brief conversation, Wilke presented Ali with a personalized copy of the Book of Mormon. Ali in turn autographed a "What is Islam?" pamphlet and returned the favor saying, "I'll read your book if you'll read mine."

To read more about Moroni's Promise, see page 273.

The Book of James is the "oldest" New Testament book written about 45 A.D.

ATOMIC MORMONS!

*Many LDS helped develop the first atomic bomb. Here are
a few of the challenges some of them faced.*

SECRET LDS BRANCH

When work on the bomb began at Oak Ridge Tennessee,
this sleepy, small community suddenly popped into a huge
city of 23,000 houses, apartments, and dormitory spaces, with
5,000 trailers and 16,000 barracks spaces, all to house more than
75,000 people. Eldred G. Smith was the first branch president
and invited members to his home. As converts and membership
swelled their ranks, they overflowed into the Elm Grove School.

TESTING

Early A-bomb tests at sea took place at Bikini Island. On hand
to support the project were 150 ships and 40,000 sailors. Latter-
day Saints who were spread out on those ships tried hard to
gather on one ship for Sunday services. Their first Sunday meeting in 1946 consisted of only six members. Within months,
more than 30 could fly, boat, or paddle to make the meetings.

PHOTOGRAPHING THE FIRST

Latter-day Saint George Marquardt piloted the B-29 Super-
fortress assigned to photograph the atomic blast over Hiroshima
on Aug. 6, 1945. His plane was an escort to Paul Tibbets'
Enola Gay when the bomb was dropped. Unfortunately, the
excited government photographer aboard Marquardt's plane forgot to remove the lens cap of his camera, but another crewman
had smuggled a camera on board to catch the historic photos.

RELOCATION PLAN

Only in Utah would residents be evacuated to safety according
to LDS stake boundaries. The Federal Emergency Management
Agency said the Church's efficient organization allows for the
state's major population areas to be evacuated in less than three
days. BYU wasn't included in the plan because students would
be sent home far in advance of hostilities.

More than 120 million copies of the Book of Mormon have been printed.

POPCORN POPPIN'!

Guinness is known for its fine Irish Stout; Brother Paul is known for his excellent buttered popcorn. This Mormon treat has roots older than our genealogy.

MOM AND POP CORN

Dig beneath Mexico City a good 200 feet and you'll find corn pollen that researchers have dated at more than 80,000 years old. This isn't our Family Home Evening popping variety, but it is an early type of maize that after thousands of years of cultivation eventually gave birth to today's assorted forms of corn.

LEND ME YOUR EARS

The oldest ears of popping corn date to at least 5,600 years ago and were discovered in the Bat Cave (no, not THAT Bat Cave) in New Mexico in 1948. These ears range in size from a ½ inch long to 2 inches long, and are the oldest ears of popcorn discovered so far. Evidence of popping corn has been dated back at least 2,000 years

NO POT O' POPCORN

Early popcorn lovers had a variety of ways to cook it. Sand was heated over a fire and popcorn kernels were stirred in that eventually popped out—probably giving this particular brand a rather unique gritty texture. Hot stones around a roaring fire, carefully watched over, offered a fun game when kernels were placed there and would pop in just about any direction. Whoever could catch the flying popped corn won the privilege of eating it. Ancient kernels still work: seeds dating back 1,000 years were so well preserved in Peru, they still pop.

EARLY POPPERS NOT BIG SELLERS

Poppers were few in the early days. Clay pots followed by metal pots or wire baskets made popping corn easier to control. When Columbus and Cortez first encountered popcorn-loving natives, they made note of the decorations of strings of popped corn and ears of corn with popped kernels still attached.

The human body has enough fat to make 7 bars of soap.

FAMILY HOME EVENING MAINSTAY!

By 1880, popcorn in America was finally ready to go prime time. Catalog companies began selling the seeds to farmers across the country. Street vendors were selling popcorn by the 1890s, and when the Great Depression hit, popcorn sales thrived while so many other businesses failed. Poor families could afford the 5 or 10 cents for a sack of freshly popped corn —a cheap luxury and pleasant pastime during those hard years.

Today, Americans eat about 17.3 billion quarts of popcorn each year, or an average of about 68 quarts per person.

****

WHO EATS THE MOST CRACKER JACKS? For several years the Cracker Jack consumption capital of the world has been Utah. Studies show that this popcorn treat is particularly popular among youth ages 3 to 11. About 37 percent of the state's population is under 18, compared to the 26 percent national average, the study showed, giving more reason for the high consumption rate of Cracker Jacks.

• Lay all the Cracker Jack boxes ever produced end to end, and they would circle the Earth 70 times.

• Cracker Jack is the largest distributor of toys in the world, having given out 23 billion "peanuts and a prize!" since 1912.

• Some Cracker Jack toys are extremely valuable. A complete set of 1915 baseball cards in excellent condition was valued at more than $60,000.

• *Cracker Jack* was first a slang term that meant something was really great, similar to the word *awesome*!

• The Inventers: In 1896, the two Rueckheim brothers discovered a way to coat popcorn with molasses in a way so the pieces wouldn't stick together. Their special process and formula continues to be used and remains a secret to this very day.

Will it never end? The sign for infinity (an 8 on its side) is called a lemniscate.

HOW MANY ON LEHI'S SHIP?!

Brother Paul is continually amazed at how the most improbable declarations in the Book of Mormon find scientific "coincidences" somewhere, somehow, sometime in the course of further research and examination. Here's a recent one.

SOURCE: *PLoS Biology* magazine, June 2005
RESEARCHER: Jody Hey, geneticist at Rutgers University
CLAIM: According to genetic studies, it appears that North America was originally settled by only a few dozen people.

STORY: With the discovery of DNA and genetic coding, researchers have been looking for patterns and relations among humans and their origins. One such study many years ago tried to discover how the New World was first settled. It focused on one gene and assumed population sizes were constant over time.

Their conclusions? They postulated that an unknown large number of humans crossed the Bering land bridge some 14,000 years ago to fill North and South America with people.

NEW STUDY: Professor Jody Hey's study focused on one of the three primary language groups that had ties back to what is believed to be some of the earliest settlers in this hemisphere. Hey explained that for his study he didn't make large assumptions and estimates as done before, and he used actual DNA sequence from Asian and American Indian people.

NEW CONCLUSIONS: Looking at nine genomic regions to hunt for variations in single genes, Professor Hey told the media, "The estimated effective size of the founding population for the New World is about 70 individuals"—a claim also consistent with other archaeological evidence putting the first people here at an estimated 12,000 to 14,000 years ago.

LEHI'S COLONY, when it arrived in uninhabited America in 589 B.C., is estimated by some at 62 people, by others at 60-80.

Cover up! 90% of skin cancer develops on the face, neck, ears, forearms, and hands.

THE JEWS' LATTER-DAY JOSEPH

Ancient Jewish tradition speaks of a Joseph who precedes the coming of their Messiah. Has he already come?

CURIOSITY: Is Joseph Smith the "Joseph" of ancient Jewish tradition?
SCHOLARLY SOURCE: Dr. Joseph Klausner (deceased), professor of Hebrew literature and Jewish history at Hebrew University in Jerusalem
HIS BOOK: *The Messianic Idea in Israel*

IN 1955, THE MACMILLAN COMPANY of New York published an English version of Klausner's book. It caught the attention of LDS scholar W. Cleon Skousen who presents this interesting list of highlights from Klausner's book:
• Klausner devotes one entire chapter (chapter 9) to the ancient Jewish tradition that a future Joseph would be raised up in the last days to prepare the way for the Messiah.
• This tradition is highly respected, is mentioned in the Talmud, and is recognized by Christian scholars.
• Tradition says the future Joseph would be killed fighting the "anti-Christ."
• Joseph would be a descendant of Joseph who was sold into Egypt.
• Joseph would descend through Ephraim (Joseph's heir).
• Klausner was puzzled why the tradition was so firmly established among Jewish scholars, but there was no reference in the Hebrew scriptures; it is mentioned in the Talmud, and that's all.

WE HAVE A JOSEPH, TOO!
Klausner also cited Samaritan sources supporting the same tradition of a latter-day Joseph. The Samaritans said of him,
• He would be a descendent of the patriarch Joseph through Ephraim, a "son of Ephraim."
• They called him Teal, meaning "The Restorer, he who returns," or "he who causes to return."

Coconut milk can be used as a human blood plasma substitute.

• They said he would call the world to repentance and bring back better days for Israel.

• They said he would "restore everywhere the true Law to its former validity and convert all peoples, especially the Jews, to the Samaritan (Ephraimite) religion."

BROTHER SKOUSEN CONCLUDES: "It is unfortunate that Dr. Klausner is no longer with us. If he were, it would be a pleasant task to share with him the exciting news that the great 'Joseph' promised in Jewish-Samaritan tradition has come."

THE LORD'S POINT OF VIEW

The work of Joseph Smith is talked about all through the ancient scriptures and modern. From Adam and Enoch, to the Brother of Jared and on down, prophets saw the last days when the earth's great last scene would begin to wrap up, commencing with the religious awakening of a young man named Joseph.

SAID JOSEPH OF OLD, the modern Joseph would be a chosen seer with authority to receive revelations from God. He would be esteemed highly and great like unto Moses, with an important mission from God. His name would be Joseph, and his father's name would be Joseph. He would help teach the Jews, confound false doctrine, put down contention, and establish peace.

ISAIAH SAW the work of the restoration in the Western Hemisphere, the coming of the Gentiles, the mission of Joseph Smith, Martin Harris, Professor Charles Anthon, the coming forth of the Book of Mormon, the fact that part of the plates were sealed, and that Joseph Smith would be "unlearned."

17 PROPHETS TESTIFY: Be sure to add to the above prophets the names of Moses, David, Nephi, Lehi, Jacob, Jeremiah, Ezekiel, Daniel, Malachi, John the Revelator, Moroni, and Jesus Christ who all spoke of Joseph Smith, his work to unite the sticks of Judah and Joseph, and his role as the Lord's messenger. Indeed, Dr. Klausner, Messiah ben Joseph has come!

"THAT'S NOT CRICKET!"

*Seagulls eating crickets—it was an amazing miracle that contin-
ues to teach and inspire generations of Latter-day Saints,
even today. But is that the end of the story?*

THE MIRACLE OF THE GULLS in 1848 wasn't the
end-all of bug invasions in Utah. Turns out there were
cycles of infestations that had gone on for centuries
prior. In fact, a human dwelling that dated back 2,000 years pre-
viously was discovered near a cave in Wyoming that had hundreds of roasted Mormon crickets in its roasting pit.

After the miracle of 1848, the Saints were revisited by the
crickets in 1855, 1860, and 1864-66. But these minor invasions
were not severe. Turns out the pioneers' biggest problem wasn't
the Mormon cricket at all—it was the Rocky Mountain Locust,
the common grasshopper.

WE CAN FLY!

Grasshoppers were amazing but devastating. They
approached the Saints in huge swarms described in journals as a
"heavy snowstorm" that "filled the sky for three miles deep, or
as far as they could be seen without the aid of Telescopes."
While the Mormon crickets could only hop, grasshoppers took
wing and came with a loud buzzing. Any wash left out was
pelted with "tobacco juice" stains, as the children called it, that
even the best homemade soap could not totally remove.

The grasshoppers lingered for weeks, even in bad weather
when they would bunch up on tree trunks and fence posts.

GREEN WITH ENVY

As it turns out, the color green is what "did everybody in."
Not just green crops were eaten, but clothing, paint, window
blinds—*anything* green. Said one settler, "It would not take them
long to eat up a fellow's pantaloons when the color suited them."

Grasshoppers caused more damage to Utah crops than did
the more famous crickets. They'd hatch in the spring and feed
on the unharvested crops all summer long and go after the second and third sowings as well.

After Columbia's 1998 flight, there had been more crickets in space than humans.

EVERYTHING WAS ON THE MENU

Grasshoppers loved the wheat, but they also devoured corn, oats, barley, and even grass. Most garden crops were wiped out: potatoes, onions, peppers, rhubarb, beets, cabbages, radishes, turnips, and tomatoes.

They cleaned out orchards and vineyards, doing permanent damage by eating bark. "Even shawls or sheets thrown over plants or trees to protect them would be quickly destroyed," said William Jennings. "They would be found among the skirts, under a muslin dress, eating and destroying everything."

WHIRLS WITHOUT NUMBER

The pioneers tried to describe the magnitude of the infestations with terms such as "intense swarms," "by the millions," and "myriads."

And then came the bushel. Skimming six bushels of dead grasshoppers in an hour from the streams was considered average. Other more scientific calculations estimated that some areas had 100 bushels of grasshoppers per acre. Thanks to winds or the green-colored water, an estimated 1-1/2 million grasshoppers perished in the Great Salt Lake and washed up on shore for miles in 2-feet high stacks, smelling just like dead fish.

EARTH'S CREATURES DO THEIR PART

Hoping for another miracle as they had in 1848, the Saints petitioned heaven for help. The gulls did come, but not as numerous or frequent, as before. Seagulls worked on the grasshoppers in the severe outbreak of 1855, and returned to eating Mormon crickets again in 1860. They came back for grasshoppers in Huntsville in 1866.

Pigeons were eating grasshoppers in Payson in 1855. Chickens helped keep gardens clean, and sheep did a good job out in the fields. Others reported some hoppers were killed by gnats, maggots, grubs, and a parasite that would hollow them out.

HEAPING HOPPERS BY HAND

With the Saints trying everything they could from scooping up the grasshoppers with sheets and dumping them in the water to burning them in straw or burying bags of them, it still

George Washington declared the first national Thanksgiving day on Nov. 26, 1789.

seemed hopeless. In some areas, 90-100 percent of the crops were destroyed, and replanting seemed a waste of time. Some farmers tried coating tree trunks with axle grease, or sprinkling whisky and water on trees and plants. Adults would fan out in squads of 3-4 each with willow bushes and sweep grasshoppers in creeks, or catch them in sheets and drive them to water or fire, or flood farmland to catch grasshoppers on the ground. It was a fierce battle between man and insect—it was the "grasshopper war."

THE PROPHET SPEAKS

It was very discouraging. Said Brigham Young, "The only remedy that we know for them out here is to exercise faith and pray the Lord to bless our land and our crops and not suffer them to fall a prey to the devourer."

President Young used the experiences to teach the Saints. He admonished them to plant more than the insects could eat. The *Deseret News* gave this interpretation: "Better sow a large crop and save half of it, than a small crop and lose it all." Young also pointed out that it is better to entice the grasshoppers to an easily replanted crop such as grain for their voracious appetite than to force them to look towards the orchards where they could quickly destroy tree bark and vines that take years to establish.

PROMISES FULFILLED

William Moore Allred wrote in his journal that he remembered Joseph F. Smith visiting his settlement in 1872 or 1873, and prophesying "that the grasshoppers would leave us if we would do right." With the grasshopper invasion subsiding with the passing seasons in the latter 1800s, Brother Allred concluded, "And we have had none since, altho I presume we have not done everything right."

Thanks to Davis Bitton (University of Utah) and Linda P. Wilcox (historical researcher) for this amazing and well-researched information.

****

SPEAKING OF BOOKS ...

Some of Brother Paul's favorite commentators comment on books.

"I find television very educating. Every time somebody turns on the set, I go into the other room and read a book."—*Groucho Marx*

"The best way to become acquainted with a subject is to write a book about it."
—*Benjamin Disraeli*

"Where is human nature so weak as in the bookstore?"
—*Henry Ward Beecher*

"The man who does not read good books has no advantage over the man who cannot read them."—*Mark Twain*

"What we become depends on what we read after all of the professors have finished with us. The greatest university of all is a collection of books."
—*Thomas Carlyle*

"A bookstore is one of the only pieces of evidence we have that people are still thinking."—*Jerry Seinfeld*

"I'm all in favor of keeping dangerous weapons out of the hands of fools. Let's start with typewriters."
—*Frank Lloyd Wright*

"A book tightly shut is but a block of paper."
—*Chinese Proverb*

"There are two motives for reading a book: one, that you enjoy it; the other, that you can boast about it."—*Bertrand Russell*

"Do give books—religious or otherwise—for Christmas. They're never fattening, seldom sinful, and permanently personal."—*Lenore Hershey*

"In the highest civilization, the book is still the highest delight. He who has once known its satisfactions is provided with a resource against calamity."—*Ralph Waldo Emerson*

"From the moment I picked your book up until I laid it down I was convulsed with laughter. Some day I intend reading it."—*Groucho Marx*

"Most new books are forgotten within a year, especially by those who borrow them."
—*Evan Esar*

"This book fills a much-needed gap."—*Moses Hadas*

Puritans banned smoking to force farmers to grow badly needed food instead of tobacco.

ANOTHER LOOK AT ETERNITY

The infinite, or more simpl, eternity, is a really hard concept to grasp. Brother Paul stumbled on this fascinating Cosmic Calendar that helps a little. Never mind its lack of orthodoxy—let it give you an idea of how long "less than eternity" actually is.

FIRST, LET'S REDUCE the past 15 billion years (science's guess at the age of the universe) to one year. If the theoretical big bang took place way back then, how long did it take things to settle in and be as they appear, based on astronomical and earthly observations? Our units are: one second = 475 years, and one day = 41 million years.

- Origin of the universe—Jan. 1
- Origin of our galaxy—May 1
- Origin of our Solar System—Early September
- Formation of the earth—Mid-September
- Life on earth—Late September
- Sexual reproduction by microorganisms—November 1
- Oxygen atmosphere—December 1
- Cambrian Explosion—600 million years ago when most complex organisms appear—fish, trilobites [brace yourself, here comes all of that evolution stuff]—Mid-December
- Land plants & first insects (millipedes)—Dec. 19, 20
- First amphibians—December 22
- First reptiles and trees—December 23
- First dinosaurs—December 25
- Dinosaur extinction, rise of mammals, first birds, flowers—December 28
- First primates (monkey-like creatures)—December 30
- Australopithicenes (Lucy, etc.)—10:00 p.m., Dec. 31
- Homo Habilis—11:00 p.m., December 31
- Homo Erectus—11:15 p.m., December 31
- Early Homo Sapiens—11:53 p.m., December 31
- Neanderthals—11:56 p.m., December 31
- Homo Sapiens—11:56:30 p.m., December 31
- Adam and Eve—11:59:47 p.m., December 31
- Ancient Greeks to present—last five seconds
- Average human life span—a little over one-tenth of a second.

Every day, the heart pumps 2,000 gallons of blood through 60,000 miles of veins.

STAR OF DAVID

It sparks questions among some who visit Salt Lake City's Temple Square and see the Assembly Building. "Why is there a Star of David up there?" some ask. It's a good question.

In the beautiful mosaic glass windows above the entrances of the Assembly Building can be seen what appears to be a six-pointed star like unto the Jewish Star of David. First of all, this has nothing to do with the Jews. But here is an interesting theory worth considering.

SECLUSION FROM THE WORLD

When the Saints arrived in the valley, it appears their mind-set was one of "free at last!" And thinking that the world was now pushed far away, some of their sacred symbols that would turn their minds and hearts to the Lord were not to be hidden away but placed openly as reminders of God's greatness and glory. That may explain why the older temples have more external emblems and representations than do newer temples.

FOR EXAMPLE

The five-pointed star, as seen on every U.S. flag, has another symbolic use besides that of another state on our national flag. The star has also been used to symbolize man.

UNSPORTSMAN-LIKE CONDUCT

Imagine a guy just knocked down at a Church ballgame. He is sprawled out on the gym floor with arms outstretched, feet spread apart, and birds singing around his head. Before teammates haul him off the floor, you could make a chalk outline of his body in the shape of a star. Head at the top, two points at the outreach of his arms, the other two points for each leg.

SYMBOLIC OF "IN THE GAME" OR FOULED OUT

With the star pointed upwards, it could represent the living human being. Point it down and it could represent the dead. Stars positioned in this way can be found on the outside of the

Salt Lake Temple. Brother Paul's interpretation, though certainly unofficial, is that they could represent sacred work for the living (pointed up) and sacred proxy work for the dead (pointed down) being performed inside the building. They might also represent man's need to beseech Father for help in all things (pointing up) and God's dispensation of help and love down to man (pointing down).

TRYING TRIANGLES

A shorthand way of depicting a five-pointed star is with the more simply shaped triangle. Triangles pointed up could represent the living or present, and pointed down, they could indicate the dead or the past. Some have speculated that the two crystals talked about in the Urim and Thummim were like lenses of eyeglasses shaped like triangles. The one pointing up symbolized that the user would receive revelation of the present and future. The lens pointing down symbolized the user would receive revelation or knowledge about the past.

AND WHAT WILL THEY THINK OF NEXT?

Inside the user's mind and heart, the representations of what the triangular lenses of the Urim and Thummim signify are then overlapped in the mind, one atop the other, symbolic of the user receiving knowledge of all things past, present, and future, and thereby receiving truth. Hence, two triangles overlapped forming what appears to be the Jewish Star of David.

IT GIVES ONE PAUSE

This theory isn't official, of course. This is speculative. Brother Paul doesn't like to dwell in the world of speculation, even with his meager and undernourished savings account. The real answer as to why there are stained-glass windows on the Assembly Hall with a shape similar to the Star of David is probably far different from what is presented here, but the aforementioned does give one pause. And giving pause is, after all, the full intent and strategic mission of this very important and time-consuming Mormon bathoorm reader.

THE BEET-ATTITUDES

In the early 1890s, the Utah Sugar Company in Lehi, Utah, became the first sugar beet factory in the Mountain West, the first to use beets grown by irrigation, the first to grow its own beet seed, and the first to use machines made in the U.S.

PREHISTORY: Cane sugar was developed in Polynesia and spread to India.

510 B.C.: Emperor Darius invaded India and found "the reed which gives honey without bees."

642 A.D.: Muslim invaders to Persia found sugar cane growing and learned how sugar was made.

1095: Christian crusaders returning from the east bragged about a new spice and how pleasant it was. By 1099, the first use of sugar in England is mentioned.

1319: Sugar sells in London for about $100 per kilo.

1493: Columbus took sugar cane to the Caribbean where it flourished.

1747: The sugar beet is identified as a source of sugar.

1750: Britain boasts more than 120 sugar-cane refineries with an output of 30,000 tons a year.

1880: The sugar beet replaces cane sugar as the main source of sugar in Europe.

THE EARLY SAINTS IN UTAH were always on the lookout for cash crops. They found that sugar beets grew well in Utah's soil, and in the 1850s, the brethren sent a party to France to learn how their sugar beet industry worked.

SWEET AND SOUR

Embracing the sweet smell of sugary success, the traveling elders formed a company and imported 500 bushels of sugar-beet seed. They also bought the required machinery from Liverpool and had it shipped to New Orleans. The trip to Utah required 52 ox teams pulling wagons loaded with all the parts. The manufacturing plant was assembled at Sugar House in Salt Lake City.

A strand of spider web may be stronger than an equal diameter of steel.

Beets grew well in Utah and were dutifully sent through the imported machinery—but there was a problem. Beets raised in Utah's alkali soil wouldn't convert correctly, and the effort to magnify the European's sugar-beet process was abandoned.

UTAH'S GROWING SWEET TOOTH

By the 1880s, sugar was in high demand. Arthur Stayner, a horticulturist from England, tried to resurrect the sweet dream. With the full financial backing of the Church, and the alkali problem solved, Stayner formed the Utah Sugar Company in 1889. It took two years and a lot of work, but in 1891, a $400,000 sugar-beet factory, with a 350-ton capacity, was built in Lehi, Utah. It was the first sugar-beet factory in the U.S. built with U.S. machinery.

The plant was a success! With plenty of adults to run the plant and youth to thin, weed, and harvest the crop, sugar manufacturing became a good income for the Saints. Another 14 sugar factories were built over the next two decades under the direction of the new Utah-Idaho Sugar Company that was organized in 1907.

SHALL SUGAR LOSE ITS SAVOR?

All looked wonderful until World War I ended. That's when the bottom fell out of the agricultural industry, thanks to the U.S. Federal government's failure to prevent that post-war agricultural depression. And then came the white fly that caused a blight, or curly top, on Utah's beets. As producers consolidated operations and moved out of state, high demand and expensive labor was met with improved mechanization—and that took a lot of money, something the Saints didn't have at the time. So, their factories left town. As they dismantled, the Utah sugar industry dismantled. By the 1980s, the last sugar-beet factory had left Utah.

HOW TO MAKE SUGAR FROM SUGAR BEETS

• **HARVESTING:** Beets are planted in huge crops covering many acres. Plenty of pioneer stories exist that tell of the toil to hoe, thin, and irrigate the rows of crops in hopes of a good har-

A teaspoon of a neutron star's material weighs 110 million tons!

vest. By late autumn, the beets are dug from the ground, washed, and separated from leaves, stones, and trash.

• **EXTRACTION**: The beets are then sliced into thin chips to increase the surface area from which to extract the sugar. The beet chips are soaked in hot, circulating water for an hour. This "juice" becomes loaded with sugar, but also with other chemicals from the beet's flesh.

• **PRESSING**: The water-soaked chips still have sugar in them, so screw presses squeeze out every drop of water. This is added to the sugar water from the first process. The beet pulp is dried and turned into animal feed. The pioneers also gave the exhausted beet remains to their animals or plowed it back into the soil.

• **CARBONATATION**: The juice (sugar water) is cleaned with small clumps of chalk. As the chalk clumps grow, they take out the non-sugars and are then strained out. Afterwards, the juice is ready for evaporation. Evaporation takes place in 2-3 stages, making the juice thicker at each stage until it becomes a syrup.

• **BOILING**: A modern sugar-beet factory will put 60 tons or more of the syrup in a large container and boil off more water. When conditions are right, sugar dust is thrown in the syrup to trigger formation of sugar crystals. The resulting mixture of crystals and "mother liquor" goes to the centrifuges where the two are separated out. The crystals are dried with hot air before being packed.

• **BEAUTIFUL SUGAR!** The final sugar product is raw, clean and white. As for the "mother liquor" that was left over, this byproduct is more appropriately called beet molasses which goes to another process to make cattle food. It isn't suitable to make rum as is cane sugar molasses when it reaches this part of the process, but the Saints would have no use for rum, anyway. They firmly believed that beets were able to beat cane—or was it cane that beet able? Brother Paul is so confused. Where's a cookie when he needs one?

*Thanks to Leonard J. Arrington and others for
this fascinating information!*

A typical lightning bolt is 2-4 inches wide and two miles long.

THE BROTHER OF JARED'S REAL NAME

*Talk about writer's cramp! With a name like his, it's no wonder
the inscribers always used 'the brother of Jared'!*

The brother of Jared lived about 2200 B.C., and is talked about in the Book of Mormon (Ether). He was a great man—strong, very faithful, and loved by the Lord. In fact, the Lord granted the brother of Jared's plea that his family not lose their language at the Tower of Babel.

The brother of Jared was shown a vision of the earth's history and of all its inhabitants. The Lord told him to take his family to a costal area where he would later embark on a trip to a choice and promised land. After four years, he built eight unique barges for the ocean trek, but he had a problem. What about light? He presented 16 molten stones to the Lord in hopes the Lord could make them glow. When the Lord reached forth his hand, the brother of Jared was shocked to see His finger.

The brother of Jared's writings eventually ended up in the hands of the Nephites and became part of the abridged record prepared by Mormon. As for the real name of the brother of Jared, here is how we leaned it.

"WHILE RESIDING IN KIRTLAND Elder Reynolds Cahoon had a son born to him. One day when President Joseph Smith was passing his door he called the Prophet in and asked him to bless and name the baby. Joseph did so and gave the boy the name of Mahonri Moriancumer. When he had finished the blessing he laid the child on the bed, and turning to Elder Cahoon he said, the name I have given your son is the name of the brother of Jared; the Lord has just shown (or revealed) it to me. Elder William F. Cahoon, who was standing near, heard the Prophet make this statement to his father; and this was the first time the name of the brother of Jared was known in the Church in this dispensation." (*Juvenile Instructor*, Vol. 27, May 1, 1892)

The first pioneer company to arrive in Salt Lake moved an average 8-1/2 miles a day.

WHERE WE GOT 'EM: LECTURES ON FAITH

Brother Paul observes we don't hear much about the Lectures on Faith *any more. That's too bad, because that little collection is loaded.*

Shortly after the Church was organized in 1830, the Lord wanted a School of the Prophets. It was formally organized in 1833 at Kirtland and stayed open for three months until mob problems forced Church leaders to close the school temporarily. About a year later it was reopened and "was now well attended," Joseph Smith wrote in 1834.

WITHOUT PURSE OR SCRIP? At first, the School of the Prophets relied heavily on the instructor's knowledge and inspiration. Instruction was held in the open woods, often up to 50-60 elders were in attendance, and the classes were taught by Joseph Smith Jr., Parley P. Pratt, and others.

THE WRITTEN WORD: During the winter-spring session of 1834-35, some curriculum was prepared to facilitate the instruction. The Prophet Joseph Smith did the gathering of materials and writing, and his completed work comprised seven lectures in all. These were included in the first edition of the Doctrine and Covenants taking up the first 75 pages of that book.

NOT REVELATION! An important distinction that must be made is that although these lectures were carefully prepared, no one made claim that they were revelations from the Lord. The early brethren made it clear the lectures were Joseph's own materials, not direct revelations as were the sections in the Doctrine and Covenants. Regardless, wonderful insights can be gained with a prayerful reading of the Lectures on Faith. For example,

• Faith is not just a trite word, it is the foundation of everything. It is necessary, powerful, and the beginning place for all things.

- You can't have faith in something you don't know anything about. You've got to first have a little knowledge of its behavior, reliability, and promises, or there can be no faith.

- All elements obey God because they have faith in Him.

- Adam's personal and firsthand eyewitness account of walking and talking with the Lord was passed from father to son, uninterrupted, down to Abraham.

- With no ancient artifact to trigger an inquiry after God, it was this testimony from Adam to Abraham that excited the rational mind to go looking for God and gain a knowledge of Him.

- Faith plus knowledge is necessary to grow in truth.

- We cannot be saved in ignorance. We must know what we're signing on to.

- Three things necessary to exercise faith in God: the idea that He actually exists; a correct idea of His character, perfections, and attributes; actual knowledge that the course we pursue is according to His will.

- A person must know he's on God's errand or he won't lay down his all for the building of God's kingdom. A high level of knowledge produces a high level of faith. (So, let's study a lot!)

- Those who won't sacrifice never benefit from the resulting powerhouse of faith.

- Without the revelations God has given us, no searching by man would ever find out God.

- Attributes of God that make Him perfectly trustworthy: merciful, gracious, slow to anger, doesn't vary, one eternal round, no crooked paths, honest, cannot lie, loving, no respecter of persons, accepts those who fear him, forgiving, existed before the

Word, is the same yesterday, today, and tomorrow. He beckons to all people to seek Him out.

• Satan lacks all of God's wonderful attributes; therefore no one can have faith in Satan.

• Fear and doubt means having no faith. Doubt and faith cannot exist in the same person at the same time.

• Those of weak faith will not be strong enough to deal with contention.

• All that builds a confidence in God should be practiced by us daily (prayer, study, fasting, service).

• In the Fifth Lecture, we see an underdeveloped comment when Joseph says the Father is of "spirit, glory and power." We know from Joseph's First Vision and subsequent statements that he knew that God was also of flesh and bone. Critics of the Church like to point at this as a flaw in Joseph's testimony. It's not. Everything Joseph taught supported Father's physical body.

• Also in the Fifth Lecture, Joseph mentions there are two personages (not three) in the Godhead. Another out-of-context attack by critics comes from this but is easily dismissed. Joseph observed all along that the Holy Ghost was a spirit who dwelt in men's hearts, obviously separating the Father and Son as physical beings or personages.

****

In 1990, David Robinson's home teaching route in Australia was 1,000 miles round trip.

HOW NOT TO DO IT

There are many ways to eke out an existence on this planet and even more ways to impress Heavenly Father that we're not complete idiots. But if one were to pick something to prove to Father that yes, we are indeed idiots with a capital I, it would be to do what Mark Hofmann tried to pull.

MARK HOFMANN: Born Dec. 7, 1954
CURRENT RESIDENCE: Utah State Prison (for life)
MISSION: 2 years, England
MARRIAGE: His wife divorced him and took the children.
CRIME: Murder, forgery

STORY: Hofmann grew up in an LDS home and served a mission. He married in the temple and had four children. He was apparently a great guy until somewhere along the line, he decided to make some money by forging historical documents. He started by altering coins, books, and banknotes by adding a signature or something to increase the value. Finding he had a real talent for forging, he moved up into more serious projects, such as historically significant "discoveries."

ANTHON TRANSCRIPT
His first "discovery" that he sold to the LDS Church was the so-called Anthon Transcript. Charles Anthon was the professor who was shown a copy of the reformed Egyptian characters from the golden plates. The Church had some experts validate the signature of Joseph Smith on Hofmann's discovery and bought the transcript in an exchange for cash and collectibles worth $25,000, including a $5 Mormon gold coin, banknotes, and a first-edition copy of the Book of Mormon.

JOSEPH SMITH, III
Hofmann's second major forgery was a made-up Thomas Bullock letter making reference to a blessing given to Joseph Smith III, administered under the hands of Joseph Smith Jr., setting him apart as his rightful heir to lead the Church. Hofmann handed it over to the Church at no charge, under the guise of being a faithful Church member not wanting to see this embar-

rassing information leak into the public. Another forgery of the actual blessing was also "discovered," and led to an exchange with the Reorganized LDS Church for an original copy of the Book of Commandments.

DON'T MESS WITH THE LORD

Hofmann thought the Church's acceptance of these forgeries was clever proof that the brethren were not prophetic enough to divine the truthfulness of what he was doing. Hofmann failed to understand that the Lord's chosen are not given gifts of the spirit so they can be tour guides in "Book of Mormon land" or serve as document-forgery experts. Such gifts are strictly for guidance and leadership over the affairs of His Church, of which old letters, coins, and South American ruins are not a part. In other words, this is not a sign-seeking Church and never has been. But that doesn't discount the very obvious interest in historical documents that all of us share.

Nevertheless, Hofmann gained encouragement to continue the forging and deceit. He also forged works by Emily Dickinson, Mark Twain, Abraham Lincoln, and the "Oath of a Freeman," which was the Mayflower compact supposedly printed on an old press shipped from England to America aboard the Mayflower and potentially worth more than $1 million.

SALAMANDER LETTER

In 1984, Hofmann sold his most famous forgery called the Salamander Letter for $40,000 to Steve Christiansen, an LDS bishop and the son of Mac Christensen of Mr. Mac clothing-store fame. In this letter, Joseph Smith supposedly told of practicing folk magic and tells of his obtaining the golden plates with a completely different story than the commonly accepted version. It was all a fake.

THE OATH OF CAIN

In 1984, Hofmann was in serious financial difficulties, despite the great deal of money he was making from his forgeries. To bail himself out, he promised several buyers access to the so-called McLellin collection, a collection of writings from a disaffected general authority, William McLellin. Turns out the Church already had bought the McLellin papers back in 1908! (They were stacked away in the vaults.)

MURDER IN THE FIRST DEGREE

To buy time while he frantically tried to forge the McLellin collection, he planted two pipe bombs filled with nails. The first killed Steven Christiansen on Oct. 15, 1985. A second bomb that same day killed Kathy Sheets, the wife of Christiansen's boss. The following day, word came that Hofmann himself was severely injured when a bomb went off in his car. When police searched his basement, Hofmann's house of forged cards came tumbling down. They found enough evidence of forgery, bomb making, and deceit to send him to prison. He was immediately arrested for forgery and murder and pled guilty to reduced charges to avoid the death penalty. He received life in prison.

TOOLS OF HIS TRADE

• **Paper:** Hofmann tore out blank paper from books dating back to the period of his forgeries to create his fakery.
• **Ink:** Hofmann's clever ink recipe fooled most, but not all!
• **Forgeries:** Authentic Hofmann forgeries are now considered collectors' items.

FORENSIC SUMMARY OF HOFMANN'S DOCUMENTS:

• Number examined: 443
• Authentic: 268 (60%)
• Forged: 107 (24%)
• Undetermined: 68 (15%)
• Sold/donated to the Church: 48

THE FOLLOWING LIST of non-LDS names are those forged or part of forged documents created by Hofmann (based on his own admittance, and from strong suspicion and implication):

John Adams, John Quincy Adams, William H. Bonney (Billy the Kid), Daniel Boone, Jim Bridger, John Brown, Emily Dickinson, Button Gwinnett, Nathan Hale, John Hancock, Andrew Jackson, Francis Scott Key, Abraham Lincoln, Jack London, Thomas Lynch Jr., Herman Melville, John Milton, Robert Leroy Parker (Butch Cassidy), William C. Quantrill, Paul Revere, Betsy Ross, Haym Solomon, Myles Standish, Mark Twain, George Washington, Martha Washington, and more.

MORMON WAS HERE

The Book of Mormon is the world's greatest missionary. Over the years, this important work has been placed in some amazing locations. Brother Paul takes a look.

OUTER SPACE
Jake Garn and Don Lind each carried a copy of the Book of Mormon into space in 1985.

TITANIC
In 1912, Sister Irene Colvin Corbett was on a return trip from England, having studied nursing, when the Titanic struck an iceberg and sank. Sister Corbett perished, and her belongings, along with her Book of Mormon, sank into the icy depths.

WORLD TRADE CENTER
After the terrorist attack in New York on Sept. 11, 2001, an Episcopal priest recovered a copy of the Book of Mormon from among the piles of rubble at ground zero. It smelled of burnt plastic but was still in good shape. An owner was not found.

PRESIDENT LINCOLN'S DESK
In 1861, Abraham Lincoln checked out the Book of Mormon and four other books on Mormonism from the Library of Congress. He returned them about 8 months later.

MARK TWAIN
American humorist Mark Twain met Brigham Young in the early 1860s, and tells of getting a copy of the Book of Mormon. He didn't care for it much, calling it "chloroform in print."

LEO TOLSTOY
Russia's amazing author of "War and Peace," and "Anna Karenina," among others, owned the Book of Mormon and predicted if the LDS Church endured unmodified until its third and fourth generation, it would become the greatest power the world has ever seen.

1847: The first advance pioneer party camped at 400 South and State Street.

THE SECOND ESTATE

So, you think you can get away with it, huh? Well, take a look at what Alma and Amulek learned as they watched the innocent people of Ammonihah (Alma 14) sent to their deaths.

This is one of the few scriptural passages in which the important function of the Second Estate is clearly set forth. From our point of view, this present earth life is an opportunity to qualify for the highest degree of glory in the kingdom of our Heavenly Father.

EVIL IS AS EVIL DOES

But from the Father's point of view, this life also must be engineered in such a way that it clearly exposes the Cains and Judases, the Nehors and the Korihors. These are they who apparently went through the motions of being obedient servants during the first estate, but secretly harbored a nest of serpents in their breasts. By the same token, these people of Ammonihah who not only rejected the gospel but wanted to murder God's servants were of this caliber.

EXPOSED!

The task of the Lord was to expose them to a situation where their innermost satanical selves would be manifest in all their diabolical fury. When exercising their free agency to choose Satan over God, there had to be victims. Were there no victims, there could be no exposure and, therefore, no cleansing of this corrupt element from the ranks of the more faithful.

INNOCENT TESTAMENTS TO TERROR

God is working with the demands of an eternal pattern of progress, and one of those demands is the absolute necessity to shake loose the treacherous and irresponsible spirits from their pretentious moorings and let them sink to their proper level as a result of their conduct in the Second Estate. As the violent and vicious vehemence of these ugly mentalities lashes out among men, it is bound to leave a multitude of wounded and

Joseph Smith said: "Knowledge does away with darkness, suspense, and doubt; ...

abused strewn in its wake. God has special blessings "in glory" for those patient, humble and faithful souls who have had to endure this wholesale brutality.

LIFE IS SHORT, STAY STRONG
 Thus, all things work for the ultimate good of those who love and serve the Lord, especially when they are victims of wretches such as these apostate murderers of women and children in Ammonihah.

—W. Cleon Skousen, *Treasures from the Book of Mormon, Vol. 2*

****

AIRBORNE SACRAMENT CUP DELIVERY
When the Kangaroo Island Branch needed more sacrament cups in 1987, President Stef McCann requested several hundred from the Marion Australia Stake.

• **UNFORTUNATELY,** no boat could deliver the cups in time for the next Sunday's services, so stake executive secretary Michael Thorton volunteered to deliver them by air.

• **UNFORTUNATELY,** the Kangaroo Island airport was shut down by bad weather when Brother Thorton flew over, so he did the next best thing: he buzzed President McCann's home.

• **UNFORTUNATELY,** no one heard the plane. But after three fly-bys, McCann finally understood what the noise was all about and came out to receive the package as it dropped from the sky. He had planned to give fresh fish to the pilot to show thanks but ...

• **"UNFORTUNATELY,** I couldn't throw that high."

****

IN JUST 66 YEARS!

It's amazing what happened in just 66 years after the Wright brothers showed us how to control powered flight in air. And in just 66 years, we were flying aircraft with wingspans longer than the first airplane flew!

	Wright Flier	Boeing 747	Apollo 11/Saturn V
DATE	Dec. 17, 1903	1969	July 16, 1969
PLACE	Kitty Hawk, North Carolina	Washington state	Earth to the Moon, and back!
COST	$1,000	$21 million	$375 million
DURATION	12 seconds	13+ hours non-stop	195 hours, 19 minutes, 35 seconds
ALTITUDE	15 feet	39,000 feet	242,000 miles
DISTANCE	120 feet	7,260 miles on 1 tank of fuel	952,700 miles
FUEL WEIGHT	3 pounds 3 ounces	126,000 pounds	6.6 million pounds
FUEL	Gasoline	Jet fuel	Liquid oxygen, liquid hydrogen, and kerosene
POWER	12 horsepower	20,000 hp per engine (x's 4)	192,000,000 horsepower (7,600,000 pounds thrust)
ENGINE LIFE	10 hours	10,000 hours	17 minutes!
CRAFT WEIGHT	605 pounds	875,000 pounds	6.4 million pounds
SPEED	10 feet/second (31 mph)	567 mph	35,000 feet per second (23,863 mph)
WITNESSES	5	thousands	500,000,000

Colonial Flag of Sandy, Utah, made a U.S. flag covering 45,000 square feet.

COLONIA DUBLAN

The Mormon Colonies in northern Mexico were the scenes for some of the most amazing miracles and events in modern Church history. Here is the Night of the Lights.

KEY PLAYERS

PANCHO VILLA: Bandit, soldier, rebel, and famous revolutionary general.

ANSON B. CALL: Bishop of Colonia Dublan.

THE STORY

These were bloody, no nonsense times during the Mexican uprising and ultimate revolutionary war. In 1910, Pancho Villa joined forces with Mexican revolutionary Madero to free their country from the iron grip of a thousand or so men who ruled the country. Villa and Madero were champions of the poor, and led a grand struggle for three years.

ASSASSINATION

In 1913, Madero was assassinated by the pro-wealthy General Huerta. Villa joined with another army led by General Carranza, and together they drove out Huerta. However, problems between the two victorious generals erupted in fighting and Villa was defeated and he went into hiding. When Carranza won legal backing as Mexico's new leader, Villa was officially an outcast. Making matters worse, Villa tried to obtain arms and supplies through the U.S., and was turned down. He was branded a bandit.

VENGEANCE

Pancho Villa was angry. Americans would die, he vowed. With 400 men he left his hideout on March 9, 1916, and attacked Columbus, New Mexico, killing 20 people and burning part of the town. He stole all the provisions he needed and turned south towards the Mormon settlement, Colonia Dublan. It lay directly in his path to his main camp, and would be easy for the taking. The alternative was through rough terrain over cow paths and rocks with no resting places. What great general would miss such an ideal opportunity to extract more vengeance on Americans and take their badly needed supplies?

"DEATH RIDES HERE ON HORSEBACK"
Hearing of the attack in New Mexico, and knowing Villa was headed their way, the brethren of Colonia Dublan went to Bishop Anson B. Call, who calmed his nervous ward members, saying, "Let's go home, say your prayers, turn out your lights, and retire." With fasting and prayer, the Saints obeyed the counsel of their bishop.

AN AMAZING SIGHT
It was 3 a.m. when Pancho Villa and his men sat on horseback overlooking the settlement of Colonia Dublan. But what the men saw and what Villa saw were two different things. To Villa, the village was ablaze with lights and activity, possibly, he feared, with the presence of troops to protect the village. Villa's troops protested. "We see nothing, Generale. The town is asleep!" But Villa saw otherwise. He ordered his troops to detour around the community and headed off into the night, leaving the town unmolested.

LEGACY OF FAITHFULNESS
When the Saints awoke and discovered that Villa's army had indeed passed by in the night, they fell to their knees to thank God.

The details of the passover would not have become known had it not been for a desserter from Villa's army. He went to the town leaders and told of the strange events of that fearful night, of how Pancho Villa saw a town lit up and maybe filled with alert guards and protection, while all the troops saw nothing.

The night of the lights has since become legendary among the Saints in northern Mexico, a testimony of the inspired leadership that was pressing forward to build the kingdom in that great country during those dangerous years of lawlessness, bloodshed, and revolution.

To learn about Pancho Villa's conversion, see page 57.

In the U.S., Utah typically ranks 50th in smoking, drunk driving, cancer, sick days.

CHOCOLATE'S SWEET SEDUCTION

*Brother Paul is occasionally asked by his non-member inquisi-
tors, Why do Mormons eschew coffee, tea and caffeine
and yet consume unfathomable quantities of
chocolate which also contains caffeine?
Here's what Brother Paul discovered.*

CHOCOLATE'S NATURALLY-OCCURRING CAFFEINE IS NEGLIGIBLE!

Active ingredient: Theobromine

STORY: Chocolate, the "food of the gods," comes from the cacao bean, native to the tropical rainforest areas of the northern Amazon basin. Cacao trees love the shade, moisture and steady temperatures of these wet forests. Natives of Venezuela probably cultivated the trees more than 3,000 years ago, to produce the large cacao pods that are harvested today, just as the Peruvian natives cultivated the potato thousands of years ago from a root. Several high-value foods were invented by these early Americans: potatoes, maize (corn), squash, bananas, cacao.

ENERGY IN A DRINK

Early on, the cacao bean was discovered to offer significant benefits to the consumer. It gave energy to fortify soldiers when traveling or fighting. It gave users a sort of narcotic effect that energized them in ways not before experienced. People used the bean as a bitter spice for food, as a base for pasta and breads, and as a drink. The beverage usually was made by drying the cacao beans, and then roasting and grinding them to a powder that was mixed with extremely hot water and a few other ingredients such as vanilla, chilies, or maize. This is from where the popular Latin American phrase originates, "like water for chocolate," a phrase still used in Mexico today. The popular bean spread northward to the Maya in Mexico, the Aztecs, and finally to the Spanish Conquistadors who took it to Europe.

The cacao seeds were also used as currency in Mesoamerica. When English traders came on the scene, they're probably responsible for a misspelling that changed the Mayan word for the plant, "cacau," to the more familiar "cocoa."

A BIG HIT IN EUROPE

The bitter flavor of cocoa was remedied in Spain by adding flavorings—cinnamon, vanilla, black pepper, and cane sugar. By 1569, Pope Pius V declared the drink safe to consume during the fast, not realizing at the time that the cocoa beverage was loaded with nutritional value. Its popularity grew across Europe and throughout the Catholic countries, prompting economic changes as chocolate houses opened up even before coffee houses. Evidence of its popularity popped up 200 years later when chocolate became the medium in 1774 for murdering Pope Clement XIV when he was given a cup of poisoned cocoa.

KEEP YER POWDER DRY!

The popular way to make chocolate in Europe was to crush the whole bean, add hot water and sugar, and whip it into a foam. This being a little too fatty for some folks prompted the Dutch in 1828 to develop a press that forced out 98 percent of the fat. Left behind was the cocoa powder that we are familiar with today. The Dutch mixed in milk instead of water, and the great drink of hot chocolate (or cold!) was here to stay.

WHERE'S THE FAT?

An important by-product from the cocoa bean, after the Dutch press knocked out the real serious calories, was cocoa butter. The folks at the Joseph Fry factory (in England) learned they could mix the cocoa butter back into the Dutch chocolate powder and ta-dah! The first chocolate bar was created.

AN INDUSTRY IS BORN

In 1875, Swiss researchers Henri Nestlé and Daniel Peter had developed sweet condensed milk for babies, and discovered how to combine it with chocolate to create milk-chocolate. Rudophe Lindt invented a process to roll and knead the milk-

Hindus don't eat beef so the New Delhi McDonald's makes burgers with mutton.

chocolate paste into a creamy, smooth texture, and that is the chocolate we know today.

By the late 1800s, most companies that started making chocolate did so for religious purposes—to create a suitable replacement for alcohol. In 1900, Milton Snavely Hershey, a Pennsylvania Mennonite, was anti-alcohol and started producing milk-chocolate bars and "kisses" with fantastic success. His empire grew huge. He even talked the U.S. government into including four Hershey bars with each soldier's daily rations during World War I.

CHOCOLATE WARS

The problem with chocolate is that it is very bitter. Most consumers over the centuries have used it that way, and added other ingredients to alter the flavor. For chocolate's 3,000 years of existence, sugar has been used for only the last 300 of those years. Rule of thumb: the sweeter the chocolate, the less cocoa is in the product. Today's milk-chocolate treats taste nothing like real chocolate. A Hershey's Bar is only about 11 percent cocoa, and that ratio is mandated by U.S. law that states chocolate must contain at least ten percent cocoa solids. The narcotic effect of original chocolate has long since been replaced by the amazing rush created from sugar.

In 1994, the European Union responded to the declining "purity" of chocolate and waged discussions with manufacturers to reach a viable solution. The expensive part of chocolate was the cocoa bean at about a dollar a pound, pushing smaller manufacturers to reduce the quantity in their "chocolate" bars. The EU Food Standards discussion resulted in no minimum levels of cocoa, but the percentages had to be labeled on the chocolate bars. Chocolate connoisseurs are careful to buy imported bars containing 40-70 percent cocoa—the real stuff.

WHAT ABOUT CAFFEINE?

Most references to chocolate confuse caffeine and theobromine. The chemical theobromine is named from the genus name of the cacao tree (theobroma cacao). It is related to caffeine and the two chemicals have similar molecular structures, but they have very different origins, properties and effects.

Gabriel, Michael, and Lucifer are the only angels mentioned by name in the Bible.

The health risks of caffeine are not associated with theo-bromine. A lot of caffeine can decrease the sperm count in rats. One study points to perhaps 2 percent of miscarriages possibly due to caffeine in coffee. Most headaches are caused by dehydration, and in America our dehydration problems stem from our huge intake of caffeine. Cola drinks, then, don't quench your thirst, they actually increase it. Heart trouble and stress are two other problems associated with caffeine. None of these result from the intake of theobromine.

However, chocolate has more than theobromine to keep you happy. Other chemicals are naturally occurring that cause the blood pressure and sugar-levels to rise, this gives you a great feeling of alertness and contentment (these chocolate-lover ingredients include [brace yourself] phenylethylamine, theophylline, tele-methyl histamine, and pheyethylamine. Go look them up.)

Noticeable differences between chocolate and cola's impact on the consumer:

Theobromine	Caffeine
gentle	intense
mild effect	strong effect
very slow onset	fast acting
long lasting	rapid dissipation
50% in bloodstream after 6-10 hrs	50% in bloodstream after 2-5 hrs
increases feeling of well being	increases alertness
mild antidepressant	increases emotional stress
gentle, smooth, sensual stimulation	jagged, nervous stimulation
stimulates cardiovascular system	stimulates cardiovascular system
stimulates muscular system	stimulates respiratory system
mild effect on central nervous system	strong effect on central nervous system
almost no one is allergic	many people allergic
not addictive	physically addictive
no withdrawal symptoms	many proven withdrawal symptoms
mild diuretic	extreme diuretic
stimulates the kidneys	requires large intake of fluids to balance the diuretic effect

RALPH RAMSAY

Another of the great converts to the early Church whose contributions are revered, but whose name is almost forgotten.

Ralph Ramsay was born in Ryton, England, with an amazing skill: he could work wood like very few in his day, and took an apprenticeship in 1824, with a local artisan named WIlliam Hobbs. Learning the business of woodworking, and some new refinements and disciplines from the old master, he opened a shop of his own and started into his adult life.

When he was 25, the LDS missionaries knocked on his door and introduced him to the Gospel. He loved it and was baptized in the River Tyne on July 8, 1849. He was very active, serving in his branch presidency and doing a great deal of missionary work. He soon found a bride, married, had children, and settled down. But the call to Zion soon reached him, and the family packed up for a permanent move across the ocean.

In 1856, they boarded a sailing ship for the 7-week voyage to Boston. From there they took a train to Iowa City and then linked up with a handcart company that was just departing for the distant Rocky Mountains. The trek across the great plains was particularly difficult and tragic for Ralph and his bride. They had to bury two of their children along the way.

Arriving in Salt Lake, the loss-weary couple was grateful for employment with President Brigham Young. He put Ralph to work making furniture and carving various pieces for the Beehive and Lion Houses. His talents were also put to work for the building of the Salt Lake Temple and the Tabernacle.

Sometime around 1858, Truman O. Angell shot a large eagle in City Creek Canyon. The beautiful bird was hauled down to the valley where Brother Ramsay used it as a model for his most prominent wood project of all, a mighty eagle that would stand guard over the gate east of President Young's house. Standing on a beehive, the mighty bird was bound to it with iron and endured bitter cold winters and summer's scorching heat for many years. In 1891, the majestic bird was sent back east where it was electroplated for added protection. Additional treatments have kept this State Street icon in excellent condition for the past 150 years, an enduring monument to Brother Ramsay, another early stalwart of Mormonism.

Q. What is the most common disease in the world? A. Tooth decay.

TWO BOOKS

History changed dramatically when a big volcano named
Mount Tambora in the Dutch East Indies blew its top
in 1815. On April 5, the thunderous explosion was
heard a thousand miles away as 1.7 million tons of debris was
blasted into the sky. In its wake was a crater four miles across
and ½ mile deep, and a hurricane of hot ash that had roared
down in obliterating power to destroy villages and uproot trees.
Hot lava finished the job by burying 8,000 hapless victims who
couldn't escape to neighboring islands.

ASH WEDNESDAY ... AND THURSDAY ... AND ...

For several days, Tambora's gaping chimney belched black
smoke. Three columns of fire appeared rising from the crater,
uniting into a single putrefying funeral pyre that continued for
days. Hundreds of miles downwind to the west, a 2-foot blanket
of ash buried crops, animals and villages. Some 82,000 people
would soon die from starvation, disease and exposure.

It took a whole year for the massive grey cloud of dust to
spread around the globe, shrouding an entire growing season
with cold. In 1816, the cloud hit Europe. It was "the year without a summer."

NUCLEAR WINTER

Temperatures across Europe in 1816 plummeted and it
rained or snowed almost every day. Farmlands were ruined, and
riotous starving people panicked in Britain, France and
Switzerland. Ireland was hit hard with cold rain falling for 143
days in a 153 day stretch. The human toll continued to climb
with 65,000 more perishing from starvation and the resulting
typhus epidemic.

THE LORD WORKS HIS WONDERS

Along the American East Coast, 1816 was the coldest year
ever recorded in two centuries. On June 8, Montpelier, Vermont
had a foot of snow on the roads, and by August a killer frost

Mormon pioneers founded more than 600 western communities.

swept across the crops at harvest time, destroying farms and gardens.

For the Joseph Smith, Sr. family, it was the third and final year of crop failures. They surrendered to whatever forces of disquieting demise insisted on plaguing them and packed up their Vermont home to follow other farmers to a new wheat belt under development in western New York.

With the Smith family finally nudged into position near Palmyra, New York, they were at last in the shadow of Cumorah's golden plates and The Book of Mormon. Within a dozen years, these plates would be delivered to Joseph Smith Jr., the translation work would begin, and the impact of Mount Tambora would give birth to the world's most important book.

TWO BOOKS

But Mount Tambora's 1816 freeze gave birth to another book. Some 4,000 miles from the Smith's failed farm, five European friends sat gloomily in the light of a fire-warmed Swiss chalet because it was too rainy and cold that summer to venture out. The hours were whiled away with conversation that soon turned to fanciful story telling. The creative plots eventually thickened with tales of ghosts and terror and horror. When the holiday ended, Lord Byron bid farewell to his creative friends and all of them returned to their lives.

Except for Mary. Her contribution to the group's cold-summer story telling stayed with her, and within two months of that Geneva trip in 1816, she had expanded her story into a book that was put to press in 1818. The resulting masterpiece horrified an unsuspecting public as her gruesome rendering of dead flesh—the epitome of a holiday lost to Mount Tambora's dusty gloom—was given life in the form of a monster intent on avenging his master's cruel creative powers. It was Mary Shelley's spine-tingling Swiss invention that has scared the bejeebers out of all of us ever since: *Frankenstein*.

****

B. H. ROBERTS

It's a name we've all heard and usually associate with Church scholarship and history. Who was this great man who is referred to as the first "Defender of the Faith"?

BRIGHAM HENRY ROBERTS
BORN: 1857, Warrington, Lancashire, England.
DIED: Sept. 17, 1933, Salt Lake City, Utah, from complications of diabetes.

STORY: Young Brigham Roberts had a tough beginning. When his mother joined the Church, she left him in the care of friends in England and immigrated to Utah. At age 9, he boarded a sailing ship and headed for Utah. His ship landed in 1866, and he walked across the plains to join his mother in Salt Lake.

Brother Roberts had a hard upbringing, working as a semi-literate miner and blacksmith before he decided at age 18 to attend school and become a teacher. He worked hard at school and graduated from the University of Deseret the top of his class. He was a self-taught scholar who thirsted for knowledge. He served a mission in Iowa, the southern states and Great Britain and earned a reputation early on as being a stalwart defender of the Book of Mormon and the gospel because of his great knowledge and understanding.

CALLED TO SERVE

At age 31 he became a general authority in the First Council of Seventy, and he served faithfully all the rest of his life.

His great crowning works included editing the six-volume *History of the Church*, authoring the six-volume *Comprehensive History of the Church*, and his magnus opus, *The Truth, The Way, The Life*.

- **HE SERVED AS EDITOR** of the *Millennial Star* and the *Salt Lake Herald*.
- **HE WAS MARRIED** to three women and served six months in prison in 1889 for co-habitation.
- **HE WAS A DEMOCRATIC** member-elect of Congress

All of the coal, oil, gas and wood on Earth would keep the sun burning only a few hours.

from 1899-1900, but had his seat taken because he practiced polygamy.

- **HE WAS MISSION PRESIDENT** to the Eastern States Mission, 1922-1927. (His choice so he could study Church historical sites!)
- **HE SUFFERED** from diabetes and lost part of a foot as a result, and was sometimes bedridden in his later years.
- **HE IS IDENTIFIED BY SOME** as the most eminent intellectual in the history of the Church.
- **HIS PERSONAL LIBRARY** consisted of 1,385 books.
- **HE BELIEVED** that intellect and faith must go hand in hand in the search for truth.
- **HE REJECTED BLIND FAITH** and believed "brain sweat" was a necessary and life-long requirement for learning, and he supported that belief by declaring that nowhere do the scriptures excuse people from studying all truth from God and truth discovered by man, because truth is truth.
- **HE WROTE** more than 30 books, 300 articles, numerous tracts and pamphlets, and gave more than a thousand sermons and discourses (many of which were published in newspapers and magazines)—a volume of work far outstripping the output of any other general authority.
- **HE BELIEVED** in a simple faith, pure, uncluttered, but founded on bedrock of knowledge that was ever growing and ever expanding. He wasn't afraid to ask hard questions, even questions that might change the foundation of his faith. He believed that intellectual honesty strengthened the validity of the Book of Mormon and the restored gospel.
- **"MORMONISM,"** he said, "calls for thoughtful disciples who will not be content with merely repeating some of its truths but will develop its truths. ... Not half—not one-hundredth part—not a thousandth part of that which Joseph Smith revealed to the Church has yet been unfolded, either to the Church or the world. ..."
- **HIS QUINTESSENTIAL WORK** was *A Comprehensive History of the Church*, published in 1830. It remains the best history of the Church yet written, and even though new research has uncovered added detail, nothing surpasses this history work by B.H. Roberts.
- **SOME CRITICS THOUGHT** B.H. Roberts' testimony of the Book of Mormon faltered during his lifetime. Exactly the

opposite took place. He was honest enough to ask hard questions and admit when the answers were not yet available, but his testimony was unshakable. "It [The Book of Mormon] has survived all the ridicule and mockery of those who have scorned it .... Its voice is testimony of the Christ as Eternal God."

FRUSTRATION WITH SCHOLARSHIP

• Towards the end of his life, and after his three years as mission president in the Eastern States Mission, B.H. Roberts wrote a book called *The Truth, The Way, The Life*. In it he brought together all of the great breakthroughs, discoveries, and conclusions he gained from his lifetime of study. He had hoped the Church would publish it as the priesthood manual for 1929. However, it had to be approved by a reading committee from the Quorum of the Twelve. Joseph Fielding Smith was a member of that committee and he put the brakes on.

• **THE MAIN STICKING POINT** had to do with Adam and the creation. Brother Roberts said there were eons of living creatures prior to Adam, all of them living and dying, and following a cataclysmic destruction of life, Adam was sent as a "translated being" to replenish the Earth.

• **JOSEPH FIELDING SMITH** of the Twelve didn't like that, and insisted that there were no pre-Adamites, that Adam was the first man of all men on the Earth, and that there was no death on Earth prior to Adam.

• **LONG DEBATES** and discussions with the Quorum of the Twelve ensued, and sometimes these leaked to the public. Roberts was promised that if he would remove these offending ideas that the book would be published. Roberts refused. He believed truth was truth, and the findings of modern science should not be ignored but reconciled with the Scriptures. Smith felt that such acceptance would lead to an undermining of the scriptures and faith in the Lord. The final outcome was an official declaration that neither of the brethren's views was official doctrine, and it was better to leave the matter unresolved than to risk being in error by commiting to one side or the other.

• **THE TRUTH, THE WAY, THE LIFE** was tucked away until BYU published it in 1994 in a large compilation that included all three drafts of the book that Roberts wrote.

• **B.H. ROBERTS DIED** Sept. 17, 1933, to his last day standing loyal as a powerful and devoted "Defender of the Faith."

TOP TEN ANIMALS

Think hard about references to living creatures and which of them come to mind? Here are Brother Paul's Top Ten.

1. LAMB—Used 286 times in the scriptures, it frequently points to Christ as the Lamb of God that is given in sacrifice for the sins of the world.

2. DONKEY—Or ass in Biblical terms, this animal carried Christ and numerous other important figures in the Bible.

3. OXEN—Hauled the pioneer wagons and hold up the baptismal fonts in LDS Temples (represent the 12 tribes of Israel).

4. CUMOMS—This unidentified animal from the Book of Mormon always catches Brother Paul's attention. What were the journal keepers describing with the word cumoms?

5. CURELOMS—Same as above, an unidentified Book of Mormon animal with good qualities as to be a beast of burden. These two, cumoms and cureloms, make for great pickup lines for our single brethren at singles ward events. "Say, did you see any cureloms walking past in the last hour?"

6. BEE (Deseret)—Okay, not an animal, but watch one work for a day and you'd declare it was!

7. SHEEP—Often used as a metaphor for humble followers of Christ.

8. GOATS—Often referred to as stubborn, prideful, independent people. Among flocks, the goats are always wandering.

9. LION—Associated with power and integrity, or destructive.

10. DOVE—Emblem of peace; sent by Noah to find land; an acceptable sacrificial offering by the poor; a great chocolate!

THE OLDEST

OLDEST LDS FEMALE PARACHUTE jumper was Norma Gustafson, of Skyline Ward in Richland, Washington, who jumped from 11,500 feet to celebrate her 80th birthday.

OLDEST WORKING AMERICAN in 2003 was Brother Russell Clark, 102. His secret? "I don't take medications, go easy on the sweets and carbohydrates, and I eat plenty of fruits and vegetables."

OLDEST LDS WOMAN was 118 years old at the time of her baptism. Encarnacion Banares Rampas of Cuzco, Peru, was born in March of 1865, in Anta, Peru. She was baptized October 1983.

OLDEST LDS MAN was 116 years old at the time of his baptism. Nicholas Santucho of Canada de Gomez, Argentina, was baptized in the fall of that year; his wife was baptized a week later at the age of 86.

OLDEST MARRIED COUPLE was Peter (100) and Celestia Terry Peterson (99) who had been wed a record 82 years in 1960.

OLDEST TWINS in the Church turned 93 April 17, 1991. Margaret Olson Davidson and Mabel Field Nielson made their Utah homes in Manti and Pleasant View, respectively.

OLDEST MALE-FEMALE TWINS were Orlando Erickson and his twin sister, Amanda Binks, both Utah LDS, who celebrated their 92nd birthday on Jan. 28, 1991.

OLDEST SCOUT in America was Brother George Freestone, still active in Scouting at age 104 when he died in 2003.

OLDEST TOWN CRIER in the United Kingdom, as of 2003, was Brother Vic Garth, 90.

OLDEST WARD CHOIR is the Fountain Green Ward Choir, near Moroni, Utah, at 143 years old in 2005.

OLDEST MAN TO ROW THE ATLANTIC was Richard Jones, a 57-year-old high priest from Sandy, Utah, whose 4,579-mile trip took 133 days in 2000-01.

OLDEST GENERAL AUTHORITY was Elder Joseph Anderson who lived 102 years 113 days.

OLDEST BYU GRADUATE was Brother Laird Snelgrove graduated from BYU at age 91, on Feb. 13, 2003.

OLDEST TO BREAK 4-MINUTE MILE for the first time was Brother Henry Marsh, who reached his childhood goal in 1985 at age 31 with a time of 3:59.31.

OLDEST RODEO CLOWN in the World in 1985 was Earl W. Bascom, who was still going strong as an 89-year-old high priest in the Apple Valley 4th Ward, Victorville California Stake.

****

PROPHETIC UTTERANCE: In a letter to Jared Sparks, founding father Thomas Jefferson wrote: "...Thinking men of all nations rallied readily to the doctrine of one only God, and embraced it with the pure morals which Jesus inculcated. If the freedom of religion, guaranteed to us by law in theory, can ever rise in practice under the overbearing inquisition of public opinion, truth will prevail over fanaticism, and the genuine doctrines of Jesus, so long perverted by his pseudo-priests, will again be restored to their original purity. This information will advance with the other improvements of the human mind, but too late for me to witness it." This letter was dated Nov. 4, 1820, some six months after the boy Joseph Smith Jr. experienced the First Vision—the exciting first step of the restoration.

If you had $10 billion in $1 bills, at a dollar per second, you could spend it in 317 years.

"MR. BROWN, I PRESUME?"

Beginning in 2005, teaching the gospel made a full circle back to how it was taught in the days of Joseph Smith. In the 175+ years in between, the Church tried an assortment of approaches.

The Church's first missionaries had little help. Typical was what Parley P. Pratt described: "We carried on our backs our changes of clothing, several books, and corn bread and raw pork. We often ate our frozen bread and pork by the way, when the bread would be so frozen that we could not bite nor penetrate any part of it but the outside crust."

To this meager back pack of supplies and difficult trials might be added a bible, maybe some copies of the Book of Mormon, and a burning testimony in their hearts to just endure.

THE FIELD IS WHITE

Most new converts in those days were ready for the gospel message—they were attracted by hearing the ancient religion taught as they had read it in the Bible, and many of them felt there had been an apostasy from the true gospel of Jesus Christ.

HOW DID THEY TEACH?

The early missionaries relied heavily on the Spirit and taught from their own conversion stories. As their knowledge and experiences grew, they spoke historically about the great apostasy and the restoration afterwards. At one point, some tried to expound on things they didn't understand, such as the beasts spoken of in Revelations. Joseph Smith chastised them for it and told them to stay with the basics and leave such mysteries alone.

These early efforts were not the most effective approaches available, but the kingdom grew relatively fast.

1830-1900

Missionary techniques changed slowly during the first 70 years of the Church. Tracting literature was sparse but was always being improved, and missionary training courses were developed at six colleges and academies in Utah and Arizona. The main teaching tool remained street meetings, and most entered the field without purse or scrip. They had to rely on the Lord and the goodness of others for their sustenance.

Missionaries were typically married men who left wives and children behind. The first sister missionaries were called in 1898, and mission presidents quickly found them just as effective as the brethren.

HUNDREDS OF MISSIONARIES A YEAR!

At the turn of the century (1900), new missionaries were better prepared than their fathers with health exams, financial considerations, and worthiness interviews. They passed out Charles W. Penrose's *Rays of Living Light* as their primary tool of teaching, in addition to copies of the Book of Mormon.

Within a decade, missionaries had another publication to help them, the small *Ready Reference Guide* that contained scripture references listed by topic. "Let the Spirit guide" continued to be their primary mode of teaching.

Most missionaries at this time were either from the Seventies Quorum, or were ordained Seventies. In 1900, for example, 92 percent of all missionaries were Seventies. By 1927, the numbers of Seventies decreased and more missionaries were called from among the ranks of young, unmarried elders.

PRE-WAR JITTERS

The missionary program was hampered in 1939 when pamphlets with doctrine contrary to Hitler's Nazi propaganda were not permitted to be circulated in some European countries. The Saints in Germany had to abandon the Boy Scouts in favor of the Hitler Youth program. And missionary funds from America often failed to reach the elders. Nevertheless, the work carried on through the war.

DISCUSSIONS TO THE RESCUE!

In 1937, LeGrand Richards created an experimental missionary tool called *Message of Mormonism*. It was a mimeographed outline that combined the best teaching techniques from other missions and Church schools. He later expanded it into the book, *A Marvelous Work and a Wonder*.

Missionaries felt inadequate in teaching the gospel and loved Elder Richards' program. They developed their own plans using tried and true lessons with well-known salesmanship ideas. As baptisms increased through the use of such discussions, the Church gave the approach its official backing.

In 1952, the "Systematic Program for Teaching the Gospel" hit the mission home with a series of 7 discussions to help new elders teach in a systematic fashion. By 1955, the famous flannel board with pictures was introduced. Though popular and widely used, many mission presidents were reluctant because the "teach by the spirit" aspect was being replaced by rote memorization.

"HELLO MR. BROWN"

By 1961, the systematic approach was made official Church-wide. "A Uniform System for Teaching Investigators" gave elders a large collection of hypothetical situations in 6 discussions, with answers to deal with most tough questions. This was the birth of the mythical "Mr. Brown" and "Every Member a Missionary" was the new slogan as a means to help missionaries spend more time teaching instead of hunting for investigators.

FLIP CHARTS

In 1973, a more direct baptism challenge was tried along with a beautiful flip chart to encourage children's participation. Another similar face lift came in 1986.

BACK TO BASICS

In 2003, reliance on memorized text and pre-planned reactions was taken out. The brethren didn't put as much emphasis on the apostasy, placed more emphasis on the First Vision, and had the missionaries work from the positive angle. A heavier reliance on the guidance of the Spirit was created by taking away much of the memorized parts so prevalent in prior decades.

In 2005, a beautiful new book was finished, *Preach My Gospel*. It is a wonderful piece of inspired work and gives missionaries plenty to draw from both before and during the mission. Its main message? "Teach by the Spirit," not from a script. At long last, the circle is complete, and we're back to the start—but this time, with a lot more knowledge, experience, resources and understanding. Get your copy today for just a few bucks at a Church Distribution Center, because this part hasn't changed: "Every member is STILL a missionary!"

...a gold- and silver-plated iron spike from Arizona, and a newspaper's gold spike.

PROPHETIC THEMES

*If we were to attach the major assignment, theme or achievement
by which a prophetic leader contributed or is remembered,
what would that be? Here are some ideas.*

ADAM – The Fall—beginning of the Second Estate.
NOAH – The Flood—universal cleansing.
ABRAHAM – The Covenant—a line of righteous leadership and Priesthood.

ENOCH – Prophet of the Translated City.

DAVID – King of Israel's conquest of its inheritance.

SOLOMON – King of Wisdom; Solomon's Temple.

ELIJAH – Prophet of the sealing power.

ISAIAH – Prophecy.

JEREMIAH – Prophet of Jerusalem's destruction.

LEHI – Prophet of the Dispensation in America.

MALACHI – Prophet of the Second Coming.

JESUS – Reformation of the Law of Moses; The Atonement.

JOSEPH SMITH – The Restoration; the Book of Mormon.

BRIGHAM YOUNG – Prophet of the Exodus west.

JOHN TAYLOR – In vision saw the cleansing of America.

WILFORD WOODRUFF – Manifesto.

LORENZO SNOW – Tithing.

JOSEPH F. SMITH – Work for the Dead.

HEBER J. GRANT – Church's financial stability.

GEORGE ALBERT SMITH – Improving Public Relations.

DAVID O. MCKAY – Strengthening home and family.

JOSEPH FIELDING SMITH – Great leader and scholar.

HAROLD B. LEE – Welfare program.

SPENCER W. KIMBALL – "Do it!" and Lamanite program.

EZRA TAFT BENSON – Constitution; Flood the Earth with the Book of Mormon.

HOWARD W. HUNTER – Great leader and scholar.

GORDON B. HINCKLEY – Temples; positive Public Relations.

THE NAKED COMMUNIST

Brother Paul recalls as a young lad in 1958, there was a lot of hoopla over his father's book, *The Naked Communist*. As he later learned, this book did a world of good, serving as the "bible" for the FBI and early intelligence groups in the U.S. and internationally who were fighting that dangerous philosophy, government and power known as communism. While events over the past quarter century render impotent the word "communism" in most people's minds, the goal to imprint its failure formula on the free world continues by other means. How many of their original goals are now reality?

• **FIRST MAJOR PREMISE OF COMMUNISM:** Everything in existence came about as a result of ceaseless motion among the forces of nature. There is no design, no law, and no God.

• **SECOND MAJOR PREMISE OF COMMUNISM:** Human beings are only graduate beasts, and, therefore, human life is no more sacred than that of a centipede, a caterpillar or a pig.

• **THIRD MAJOR PREMISE OF COMMUNISM:** There is no such thing as innate right or wrong. To lie, is that wrong? Not for a good cause. To steal, is that wrong? Not for a good cause. To kill, is that wrong? Not for a good cause.

• **FOURTH MAJOR PREMISE OF COMMUNISM:** All religion must be overthrown because it inhibits the spirit of world revolution. Religion prevented new followers of communism from capturing the revolutionary spirit, from lying, stealing and killing when leaders commanded it. Marx said, "Religion is the opium of the people." Another wrote, "Atheism is a natural and inseparable part of Marxism."

ALMOST 50 YEARS AND A MILLION copies later, *The Naked Commuist* is still read, quoted, and available.

Tract (as in tracting): vast stretch of land, or short written political or religious work.

MORMON MYTH BUSTERS, Part III

Brother Paul continues his debunking of popular LDS legend and lore. To read from the start, see page 22.

CLAIM: A beast roams the Great Salt Lake
STATUS: Only true for youthful campers on Antelope Island who sneak out of their tents at night.
STORY: Beware the beast that roams the waters of the Great Salt Lake! Indeed it has been seen by reputable members of the Church since the year the Saints settled the valleys of the Rockies. Moving from Bear Lake to Utah lake, the beast has risen its alligator-shaped head many times. It once charged early settlers near the Great Salt Lake shore, and getting caught in the rushes, it rolled and rolled bellowing like an enraged bull. In 1868, the *Deseret News* printed the dispatch of Apostle Charles C. Riche's son Joseph, who told of early settlers in Bear Lake Valley seeing a serpentine-like animal with fur like a seal's that could swim through the waters at incredible speeds. In July of 1877, J.H. McNeill was with co-workers at a saltworks plant at the north-eastern end of the lake, when they were startled by a frightful bellow. Glancing up, they stared in horrified fascination as a huge and fearsome creature out in the lake came charging in upon them. They dashed into the mountains where they spent the night. Even among the Indians, some nameless animal carried off red men venturesome enough to swim in the blue mountain lake; the Indians said it had short 18" legs and would crawl onto land for short times. Though the beast hasn't been seen for decades, its origins and fate remain a mystery.

CLAIM: The Mormons sank a government ship
STATUS: False
STORY: This myth states that when Johnston's Army was approaching Salt Lake City in 1857, the Saints sank a government ship on the Colorado River near Las Vegas. The ship supposedly carried troops and arms needed to conquer any resist-

ance the Saints might muster from the Utah headquarters. "Not true" said researcher Elbert Edwards, Boulder City 1st Ward, Henderson Nevada Stake.

While a ship did indeed go up the Colorado to determine if it was navigable, on the way it met up with Jacob Hamblin and an exploring party of Mormon pioneers. The meeting was not unfriendly and nothing of a warlike nature erupted.

CLAIM: Brigham's spittoon and Masonic symbols are or were in his official portrait
STATUS: Unprovable, so far
STORY: For many decades, a rumor circulated that Brigham Young's original portrait included a spittoon at his feet, and several evil Masonic symbols on his clothing or in the background. The rumor goes on to say that members of the Daughters of the Utah Pioneers were offended by the spittoon and connection to the Masons, and all related images were subsequently painted out.

But X-ray studies put all these rumors to rest when it could be proven that the original painting was never touched.

CLAIM: The ninth horseman to enter Salt Lake Valley was a mystery man
STATUS: Solved
STORY: For years, it was not known, or at least forgotten, who the ninth horseman was who preceded the advance of the Mormon pioneers into Salt Lake Valley on July 22, 1847. When the "This is the Place" monument was being finished, the ninth horseman was still unknown, and was so listed on the granite slabs of the monument.

And then in 1952, a descendant of Lyman Curtis submitted evidence to the monument commission proving it was his ancestor. Among the records offered by Dr. A.L. Curtis of Payson Utah, were diary entries that listed Lyman Curtis as a member of Apostle Orson Pratt's company, which arrived two days before the main party in 1847.

The past tense of the English word "dare" is "durst."

CLAIM: President Ezra Taft Benson declared "the end is near"

STATUS: False

STORY: In the 1980s, a rumor began that President Benson was at the Jordan River Temple one Thursday and chanced upon a newly wed couple. "Where are you going for your honeymoon?" he asked. The couple then responded they were headed to Hawaii. "If I were you," he allegedly warns the young man and woman, "I would save that money and buy food storage ... You're going to need it in six months." This myth, and variations of it, traveled far and wide for many years during President Benson's administration. A quick call to the Office of the First Presidency put it all to rest. "Not true!" was the reply. "The prophet never makes declarations in private that he hasn't made to the Church in general. This story is a rumor."

Mormon Myth Busters Part IV begins on page 351.

GREAT MARRIAGE PROPOSALS
In 1975, Marty Shurtz was sitting in the BYU stadium during the annual and very heated football match between BYU and rival University of Utah. Suddenly, the card section on the opposite side of the stadium flashed the words, "Mary Shurtz, will you marry me? Love, Lyle." BYU stomped the U 51-20, and Mary said 'yes.'

PROVO CITY POLICEMAN ROBY DYER had a surprise in store when he took Lisa Blocher to a movie theater in 1982. Just after the coming attractions were previewed, and just before the movie began, these words flashed across the screen: "Will you marry me? Guppo." Guppo, Sister Blocher's nickname, was the only clue. It took three reads before she got the message: she said 'yes.'

WHEN PAUL STOUT, a freshman at BYU in 1980, stumbled over the finish line after running in the St. George Marathon for 26+ miles, he handed Teryll Kresge the baton he had carried the entire race. Attached was an engagement ring. "I told her to be sure and be at the finish line," he said. "She didn't know what to think. She was ecstatic!"

The Pantheon is the largest building from ancient Rome that survives intact.

WHAT WE EAT

Our Mormon culture offers a variety of foods that could accurately be called the best in the world because of the international contributions by early immigrant converts from around the globe. If we are what we eat, we eat because of what we are!

PRODUCT: Lime green Jell-0
USAGE: Dinner time and lunch-time snacks
STORY: In 1845, Peter Cooper won the first patent for a gelatin dessert that he packaged in a cardboard box with simple instructions. He did little to market it, but it was a huge improvement over the old way cooks made gelatin.

In 1897, Pearle B. Wait, a cough medicine manufacturer, learned how to mix flavors into Cooper's gelatin and invented a fruit-flavored treat that his wife named Jell-O. A revolution in 1930 came with the invention of lime-flavored Jell-O. It invaded America from one end to the other and quickly became a required ingredient in nearly a third of all cookbook entries on salads. Lime Jell-O was especially well suited for salads, appetizers, relishes, and entrees, and was often prepared with shredded carrots or cabbage, or cottage cheese and pineapple chunks.

The treat was popular among large LDS families and by the 1950s, Salt Lake City had became the largest consumer of lime-flavored Jell-O per capita of any city in the world. In 2001, the Utah legislature declared it the State's "Official State Snack." During the 2002 Winter Olympics, one of the most popular trading pins was the Green Jell-O pin.

PRODUCT: Postum
USAGE: A hot drink taken in place of coffee or hot chocolate
STORY: After 40 years of extreme work and resulting fatigue, C.W. Post broke his health several times over. From jobs such as farm equipment manufacturing to cattle to paper making, his health was finally in such decline from overworking and sleepless nights, he moved to Battle Creek, Michigan, for help. There he met Dr. John Harvey Kellogg, who was treating patients

---

Mormon mid-wife Patty Bartlett Sessions delivered 3,977 babies, and died at age 97.

with pure foods at a health institute established by the Seventh Day Adventists. The treatment worked, and Post regained his strength. He was fascinated by the pure foods idea, and started experimenting in 1894 with a brew that could be a coffee substitute. The damage from caffeine was already known in that day.

Post finally unveiled a combination of wheat, bran and molasses that mimicked the taste of coffee, but was a 100% natural, 100% caffeine-free hot beverage that was both healthy and satisfying. He named it Postum. Using his genius to market the product, he launched a nationwide advertising program and, within three years, sales of Postum neared a million dollars a year.

Jump ahead 50 years and we find some members of the Church liking Postum. It offered a more mature-tasting alternative to sugar-laden hot chocolate. Pushing the popularity was a paid advertising campaign on the back of LDS Church magazines that showed Salt Lake City's Chief of Police, W. Cleon Skousen, enjoying a cup of hot, caffeine-free Postum. Today's purists like to say, 'It's not a coffee table, it's a Postum table.'

PRODUCT: Funeral Potatoes
USAGE: A side dish popular at dinner or for post-funeral gatherings at Church.
STORY: Funeral potatoes might have been so named by Latter-day Saints, but the dish was not invented in Utah or among Mormons. Nevertheless, the dish has proven to be a delicious, inexpensive yet large-volume serving that can feed even the largest of Mormon families.

The traditional recipe is fairly basic: sliced boiled potatoes baked with the proper portions of cream of chicken soup, sour cream, cheddar, butter, onions, and topped with crushed Cornflakes. Variations? Yes—thousands! Other dishes of similar ilk probably took on the name of their inventors, but in the 1960s the unique popularity of the potato dish at Mormon funeral gatherings gave it the moniker, "funeral potatoes."

Today, funeral potatoes can be found in cookbooks around the world, yet only a handful of people really know the relative recent origins of its name and place in LDS culture. If you hear the name "funeral potatoes," this much you can count on: its genealogy will trace back to good ol' Mormon tater roots.

PRODUCT: Casseroles
USAGE: A popular dinner dish for large Mormon families
STORY: The word casserole evolved from ancient Greek meaning "cup," to Latin meaning "pan" and "ladle," then to Old French meaning "sauce pan." Casseroles are combinations of foods cooked together slowly in one pot or pan. The Greeks used the casserole to serve leftover vegetables after a huge harvest banquet. The American Indians had their version of meats slow cooked and added over rice or other filler. Immigrants from the north countries, the Swedes and Finns, brought recipes that combined foods of abundance with rice, potatoes, pasta and vegetables. The casserole was a great economic value because it was a one-dish meal combining foods with sparse portions of meat in a way that produced many servings. In the 1950s, the casserole really caught on thanks to the advent of new lightweight metal or glassware dishes. Our large LDS families love this economic dinner-in-a-dish. Mormon favorite: tuna casserole baked with crushed potato chip topping. Yum!

****

CHARLES MANSON INVITES THE HOME TEACHERS?
In 1984, the FBI revealed that notorious killer and cult-leader Charles Manson had a hit list containing the names of two LDS. This list, taken from Squeaky Fromm after she tried to assassinate President Gerald Ford in 1975, included

• Oliver Holt, Northridge 1st Ward, California. Brother Holt helped the forest service thin out overcrowded pine forests and then sold them as Christmas trees. He speculated that Manson saw this action as anti-environmental.

• Thomas Barnes, Long Beach, California, worked for the Arizona State Game and Fish Department; he was on Manson's list probably for the same reasons.

****

THE NEPHITES AND SOLOMON'S TEMPLE

The prophet Alma mentions that his people built temples. These were patterened after Solomon's Temple, but not so ornate!

SOLOMON'S TEMPLE was two stories high (about 45 feet). It was 30 feet wide and 90 feet long. It had a porch in front with two massive bronze pillars. The first part of the lower floor was called the "holy place" and it was here that the Aaronic Priesthood ordinances were performed.

NO SMOKING ALLOWED

The famous sacrifices that we read so much about were always burned on a huge altar in front of the temple (outside). The inner "holy place" was 60 feet in length, beyond which was the Holy of Holies which was 30 feet in length. In the Holy of Holies, the High Priest would go before the Ark of the Covenant to petition the Lord and receive revelations.

UPSTAIRS

There was a circular stair in the wall of the temple leading to the upper floor. This upper area was also divided into two sections by the holy veil. These two rooms would compare with the Terrestrial and Celestial rooms of our modern temples. It would appear that a select few were allowed to receive the higher endowments of the Melchizedek Priesthood in the upper rooms of Solomon's temple just as they are today. However, the sealing powers of the higher Priesthood were taken away completely with the death of Elijah (800 B.C.) about a century after Solomon's temple was built.

SMALLER BUDGET

So, just how did the Nephites get plans for their temples? A clean description of Solomon's Temple was taken from Laban's original brass plates (today's I Kings), and adopted to fit the materials and location in which the Nephites dwelt.

Snow job: In some Utah mountain valleys, snow totals can reach 40-50 feet.

THE BRETHREN SAID IT!

Part VI

All is not always sober and somber at the podium.
For more, see page 297.

Of government officials sent to Utah to put down Mormonism, John Taylor said, "They want to cause a quarrel ... Don't give it to them. They are bent on provoking a quarrel and mischief ... It takes two to make a quarrel, don't you be one of them ... They offer themselves to be kicked. Don't do it, have some respect for your boots."—*John Taylor*

"I REMEMBER MY COMPANION was dismissing. We had our eyes shut and our hands up. I thought he would never get through; and when he said, Amen, we looked back, and there were four men standing behind us with guns on their shoulders. I said to my companion, 'That is another lesson, from this time on in the South, I shall pray with one eye open.'"—*J. Golden Kimball*

"A PRESIDENT OF AN ELDERS QUORUM told this story of a man whom they had called on many times, a good man who had good intentions. He welcomed them to his home, listened to them, and he would usually say, 'Well, I will. I intend to. I will do it. I will come to Church when I get straightened out.' Then they would go back another time. The same story, 'Well, when I get straightened out, I'll come to Church.' Then the elders president said, 'I was called on to speak at that man's funeral. He was in church all right, and he was surely straightened out.'"—*Elray L. Christiansen*

AT A SUNDAY MEETING after arriving in the Salt Lake Valley, John Taylor rose to speak: "What was your object in coming here? Was it to rebel against the general government?" Seated behind Taylor was Brigham Young who spoke out, "To get away from Christians." The congregation roared with laughter.

Origin of saluting: Armored knights raised visors to identify themselves to the king.

EZRA TAFT BENSON ONE-LINERS

"You cannot do wrong and feel right—It is impossible!"

"Some of the greatest battles will be fought within the silent chambers of your own soul."

"Bad experience is a school that only fools keep going to."

"Be right, and then be easy to live with, if possible, but in that order."

"The proud cannot accept the authority of God giving direction to their lives."

"I have a vision of the whole Church getting nearer to God by abiding by the precepts of the Book of Mormon."

"Pride is a sin that can readily be seen in others but is rarely admitted in ourselves."

"Our will in competition to God's will allows desires, appetites, and passions to go unbridled."

"We must cleanse the inner vessel by conquering pride."

"The high cost of low living."

"Ingratitude is one of our great sins."

"Thoughts lead to acts, acts lead to habits, habits lead to character—and our character will determine our eternal destiny."

"Think of what pride has cost us in the past and what it is now costing us in our own lives, our families, and the Church."

"The God of heaven sent some of His choicest spirits to lay the foundation of this government—and he has sent other choice spirits to preserve it."

"Let us be in a position so we are able to not only feed ourselves through home production and storage, but others as well."

"I have noted within the Church the difference in discernment, in insight, in conviction, and in spirit between those who know and love the Book of Mormon and those who do not—that book is a great sifter."

Each human generates about 3.5 pounds of trash a day, mostly paper.

ANTI-MORMON FILMS

It's a waste of energy, but somebody had to do it. From 1905-
1945, more than 30 anti-Mormon movies were produced. And
more since then. Such films exploited stereotypes and fantasy, but
after creating a stir, they just went away. Here are a few.

FILM: A Trip to Salt Lake City – 1905
DETAILS: 2 minutes, black & white, silent
STORY: This first anti-Mormon spoof portrayed a polygamous family riding a train with the father struggling to feed
his many children. He solves the problem by giving them a
drink from a large milk canister with dozens of straws.

FILM: A Victim of the Mormons – 1910
DETAILS: 3 reels, black & white, silent
STORY: A young elder is serving in Copenhagen when he lures
the fiancee of a friend to elope with him to Utah. She is "baptized" in the Salt Lake Temple and kept locked up in the elder's
basement. The girl's lover arrives on the scene and rescues her.
This film ignited a huge legal and public effort by Utah
Governor William Spry to have the film banned, which it eventually was.

FILM: A Mormon Maid – 1917
DETAILS: 60 minutes, black & white, silent
STORY: A family is rescued from the Indians by the Mormons.
Then it gets ugly. Threats to join the cult's polygamous families
are pressed upon father and daughter. The mother commits suicide when the father is forced to take a second wife. Handsome
convert Tom rescues father and daughter, and they all escape
into the desert. Paramount was going to release the film but
declined, citing quality concerns.

FILM: The Rainbow Trail – 1918
DETAILS: 6 reels, black & white, silent
STORY: A Texas Ranger's cousin seeks to rescue little Fay who
has been trapped for 12 years in "The Secret Valley." Now
grown into a beautiful young woman, the local evil polygamist

Oldest working American in 2003 was Latter-day Saint Russell Clark (103) , Orem, Utah.

seeks to imprison her in his "City of Sealed Wives." The cousin rescues her just in time, only to be caught by the evil polygamist and his gang. The sheriff frees them, and Fay and the cousin fall in love.

FILM: Trapped by the Mormons – 1922
DETAILS: 97 minutes, black & white, silent
STORY: Mormons travel around the world to entrap young ladies for their wives, a tale of woe from professional anti-Mormon novelist, Winifred Graham of Britain. Banned from the United States after its release in 1922 following intense lobbying efforts by LDS Church leaders and U.S. Senator Reed Smoot (R-Utah). Though the silent film is today seen as a fantastic comedy and farce, it was serious business when it first appeared. The film created a hatred of Mormons by people in the United Kingdom and other places where it showed.

FILM: Hands Up – 1926
DETAILS: 6 reels, black & white, silent
STORY: It's the Civil War, and Lincoln sends a spy to secure gold from a western mine owner. A Confederate spy intercepts the other man and after eluding prison, Indians, and bullets, he is about to be hanged when the mine owner's daughters save his life. The girls and the spy all travel to Salt Lake City to set up house in blissful bigamy.

FILM: The Godmakers – 1983
DETAILS: $100,000 budget, full-feature, 59 minutes
STORY: Advertised as the hottest expose' on the truth behind the Mormons, *The Godmakers* eventually fell beneath an avalanche of discredit and ridicule. Based on the book, *"The Godmakers,"* the script was subsequently exposed and discredited in the book, *"The Truth About The Godmakers."* Additionally, several of the inactive LDS portrayed in the film returned to full fellowship in the Church and denounced the film as a hodgepodge of lies and deception. "The Godmakers II," released in 1992-93, became the subject of threatened court action by the Church because of gross hearsay and slander that the producers flowed into the final edited version.

The only LDS Temple with five spires: Oakland California Temple.

KNOW YOUR DEAD SEA SCROLLS

We've all heard of them, but what's so important that we should care? Brother Paul takes a look.

Ancient scrolls of calfskin and sheepskin were discovered in jars between 1947-1956 in 11 caves in Israel in the upper-northwest region of the Dead Sea's western shore. Five cache caves were discovered by Bedouin and six by archaeologists, from more than 250 caves searched nearby. With the discovery of the first jars, ancient religious history has stood to benefit from an exciting injection of re-discovery and confirmation.

• **THE DEAD SEA**, about 15 miles east of Jerusalem, has dry lifeless cliffs on its western side in which natural caves exist. The sea itself is 1,300 feet below sea level, and (this is interesting!) scientists believe an ancient earthquake altered the terrain so that the northern end of the Dead Sea flowed out and covered the cities of Sodom and Gomorrah, and three others.

• **NEAR THE WESTERN-SHORE CAVES** are the ruins of Qumran, an ancient community that dates to at least 150 B.C. Their connection to the scrolls is the scroll jars—these are the same as jars manufactured in Qumran.

• **THE SCROLLS APPEAR** to be part of a library of a Jewish group that might have hidden them in the caves after the Jewish-Roman War of 66 A.D. Some think these people were the Essenes (literally "healers"), a religious order with very rigid monastery-like communal living. Others see evidence of less rigid living. The "who" remains unanswered right now.

• **AMONG THE SCROLLS DISCOVERED**, more than 900 documents have been found that are part of at least 350 separate works duplicated several times over. More than 100,000 fragments were found in total. Cave 4 had 15,000 fragments (the most of any cave) that were painstakingly sorted into 520 texts.

- **THE SCROLLS INCLUDE** complete or partial copies of all books in the Old Testament except Esther, non-scripture books such as the Book of Enoch, and sacred writings by the Qumran people themselves (rules and commentaries on the scriptures). There are some stories and historical figures that fit into Jewish, Christian and Muslim sacred writings.

- **IN CAVE 3**, archeologists found the Copper Scroll that listed several dozen places where other scrolls were hidden along with gold, silver and sacred objects.

- **THE SCROLLS MOST INTACT**, found in Caves 1 and 11, were published in the late 1950s, and can be seen in the Shrine of the Book museum in Jerusalem.

- **MOST OF THE SCROLLS** were in Jordanian hands for preservation and translation via a group of Christian scholars. This group was hard to work with, too secretive and gave the whole project a "you can't touch this" reputation. After the 1967 war, Israel took charge but left that team intact. Publication of materials still came slow. In 40 years, they put out 8 volumes. By the 1980s, Jewish scholars were added to the team and more openness was, thankfully, imposed on the work.

- **THE VAST MAJORITY** of the remaining scrolls are mostly fragments, and remained hidden away until the world complained in the 1980s. Finally, photos of fragments began to appear in publications in 1991. A team of 55 international experts pushed hard for a few months a year to bring the work to light. Microfilm copies of all the fragments held by the Huntington Library were promised to be released shortly afterwards. By 2001, 37 volumes had been published.

- **BOTH CHRISTIANS AND JEWS** stand to benefit from the scrolls. The writings describe an ancient and non-traditional form of Judaism, and contain information that supports the presence and growth of Christianity.

- **SURPRISINGLY,** the information in the Dead Sea Scrolls is similar to that found on scrolls at Masada, the famous Herodian fortress that Jewish Zealots commandeered after the Romans destroyed Jerusalem in 70 A.D. The Romans scaled the mountain and retook the fortress in 73 A.D., but found no one to take prisoner. The Jews had killed each other and the last committed suicide rather than be taken by the Romans.

• **WHO HAS THE FINAL SAY** of what means what in the scrolls? Nobody, yet. The term "The Son of God" was found on one scroll and everybody has their own answer. The Christians see an obvious reference to Jesus. The Muslims see the phrase in a Jewish context as meaning someone other than God himself. The Jews see it as reference to a messiah, not The Messiah who is yet to come. And so it goes with the rest—interpretation, discussion, argument, counter argument. If only the Dead Sea Scrolls weren't so *dead* ....

****

WHEN STAKES IN EAST GERMANY don't get 100 percent home teaching, they have the best excuse in the Church: All their families are at the temple!

That was the word from President Thomas S. Monson after a trip there in 1988. He reported that the Saints in East Germany had been especially faithful in attending the new Freiberg Temple ever since it was dedicated in 1985.

In fact, he said, every seat at every endowment session was filled.

Added President Monson, "One stake president said, 'I'm having a little difficulty with my stake members with their home teaching, because all my stake members are in the temple.' I thought to myself that if every stake president could have all his members attending the temple, one of the chief purposes of home teaching would have been achieved.'"

****

"THEY ASKED [SISTER DAVID O. MCKAY] how she managed with 7 children and a husband whose time to help was so limited. Kindness was reflected in her reply: 'Through our struggling years I didn't expect much, so I was rarely disappointed.'"—*Russell M. Nelson*

MISSIONARY TOOLS

When the world's greatest message needed delivering to folks not all that interested, various Church members invented some creative means to help the deliverers and deliverees!

HAMSTER: To encourage Mesa Arizona 27th Ward members to do some kind of missionary work, "Buck" the hamster was sent home teaching, cage and all. Buck stayed at a member's house until the family performed some kind of missionary task such as give out a Book of Mormon or give the missionaries a referral, and then he was passed along. Buck's longest stay was a month before being transferred!

SEMAPHORE: Ray N. Taylor was practicing his semaphore messaging at Camp Gilmore in Farragut, Idaho in 1945 when he grabbed his Church News to relay a speech by President Heber J. Grant. Some distance away, a salty old chief was reading the message, located Taylor and started taking missionary lessons.

CAB-TIVE AUDIENCES: Martin Kerper, an LDS cab driver in New York played dramatized stories from the Book of Mormon to his fares who often asked, "Isn't that Nighttime Theater on the air?" In Phoenix, Arizona, Brother Bill Arnett became the first U.S. cab operator to offer non-smoking cabs.

ON ANGEL WINGS. During the Vietnam war, LDS soldiers used available aircraft to transport scriptures, supplies and members to Sunday meetings. A chopper emblazoned with "Hereafter 727" was the workhorse. LDS group leader Loyal D. Hastings painted "TEMPLE SQUARE" on his F-4C Phantom and became one of the best Church advertisements in the air.

OCEAN ROW. In 2000, the rowboat Richard Jones used to row across the Atlantic Ocean gained international fame with its Jaredite name, "The Brother of Jared." Curious press from around the world learned all about the Book of Mormon every time one of them asked, "Why the strange name?"

The last person to meet Joseph Smith, Mary Field Garner, died in 1943.

JOHN MORGAN, MISSIONARY

Oftentimes some of the greatest stalwart Saints of old get lost in the history of progress in the Church. Meet one of the thousands whose innovations we mustn't forget.

JOHN MORGAN WAS A STRONG organizer and supporter of good causes. After serving valiantly as a soldier in the Union Army, he created the first college west of the Mississippi in 1866. Located in Salt Lake City, it was called Morgan College with prominent alumni including future general authorities Heber J. Grant, Orson F. Whitney, Mathias F. Cowley, J. Golden Kimball, and Brigham H. Roberts.

EARLY PAMPHLETS

Brother Morgan did a lot for the early Church. In 1878, he wrote the first mission tract. He called it *The Plan of Salvation*, and it remained one of the most popular pamphlets for missionaries for decades thereafter.

MEET THE MORMONS

In 1878, he also organized the first mission of the Church in the U.S.—the Southern States Mission, in Heywood Valley, Georgia. He served as its first president. And several years later, at the request of President Lorenzo Snow, he opened up the first Bureau of Information on Temple Square.

MAY I LEAVE MY CARD?

Many missionaries use a calling card nowadays to make contact with investigators. Today, we recognize those cards as having a picture of a temple on one side and the Articles of Faith on the other. And who was the first to begin using these "Articles of Faith" calling cards? It was Brother Morgan, in 1878. He was serving as a member of the Council of Seventy at the time. Six years later, he contracted typhoid-malaria, and died suddenly in 1884 at the premature age of 52.

AMAZING GRACE

The gospel net draws in people from all walks of life. Oh my heck, it even drew in Brother Paul. But here are some converts from unexpected realms.

AFFILIATION: Punk Rock
NAME: Arthur "Killer" Kane
STORY: "Punk Rock" music started as a radical departure from the prior generation's post-war rock and roll led by Elvis, The Rolling Stones, The Beatles, and others. By the mid-1970s, garage bands and rock star wannabes began a new trend that rebelled against classic rock with "sex, drugs and rock 'n' roll." It was anti-establishment, irreverent, vulgar, shocking, loud, mean, raucous, dissonant, sexually and politically confrontational ... and millions of kids loved it.

One of the first pioneering punk bands that was the very definition of "punk rock" was the legendary *New York Dolls*. The lead bass for the group was Arthur "Killer" Kane. After years of indulgence and a years-long haze of alcohol addiction, he was drunk in 1989 when he attacked his wife and fell out of his Los Angeles apartment third-story window. While recuperating in the hospital, he saw an ad in *TV Guide* for a free Book of Mormon. "I prayed about it, hoping the Book of Mormon was true," he said in a documentary made of his life. "I got an answer quickly," he said, explaining that it was "like an LSD trip from the Lord, like a drug trip without the drugs."

Kane gives credit to the Church for saving his life. He stopped drinking, got a job at the Family History Center, and straightened out. After a reunion tour with his former band in 2003, he was diagnosed with leukemia and died July 13, 2004.

AFFILIATION: Black Panthers
NAME: Eldredge Cleaver
STORY: In the 1960s, a new black militant group called The Black Panthers became part of the fight for civil rights in America. This paramilitary and self-defense group sought to overthrow capitalism, install communism, and use warfare and violence to get its way.

George Washington loved cream of peanut soup and mashed sweet potatoes.

Leroy Eldredge Cleaver was an angry young man who hated whites and used rape as his personal form of revenge against racism. He was in correctional institutions in California most of his junior and high school days for crimes that ranged from possession of marijuana to assault with intent to murder. While incarcerated, he did a lot of reading and became a follower of Malcolm X. He wrote the black rights classic, *Soul On Ice* while in prison and won parole in 1966. His book was published two years later. In 1968 he was wounded in a shootout with police and jumped bail to leave the country for Cuba and then Algeria. In 1975, he returned to the U.S. a changed man, saying "I'd rather be in jail in America than free under communism."

He pled guilty to his 1968 assault charges in exchange for having the charges dropped, but he was put under 5 years probation. During his rediscovery years, he found the gospel and was baptized into the LDS Church on Dec. 11, 1983, at the Oakland, California, Stake Center. "I feel real good," Cleaver said. "I'm sure and clear about it ... It was worth waiting seven years for." He wrote a sequel to his first book and told of his awakening to the realities of the Lord and the importance of getting life squared away, under the title of *Soul on Fire*. He later ran unsuccessfully for several political offices in California, and died May 1, 1998.

****

"IN A BASKETBALL GAME when the outcome was in doubt, the coach sent me onto the playing floor right after the second half began. I took an inbounds pass, dribbled the ball toward the key and let the shot fly. Just as the ball left my fingertips, I realized why the opposing guards did not attempt to stop my drive: I was shooting for the wrong basket.

"I offered a silent prayer: 'Please, Father, don't let that ball go in.' The ball rimmed the hoop and fell out.

"From the bleachers came the call: 'We want Monson, we want Monson, we want Monson–OUT!' The coach obliged."
—*Thomas S. Monson*

THE INQUISITION

Even its simple pronunciation ignites the sounds of screaming, tortured souls and reminds Brother Paul of his interview with the Bishop. "The nursery? ME? Are you nuts?"

INQUISITION comes from the Latin "inquiro," meaning to "inquire into." The intent of the Inquisition was not to wait for a complaint, but to go looking for evil offenders injecting heresy into the Church and wandering off from the true faith.

HERETIC: One who believes differently than how they're told to believe.

MIDDLE AGES: Period of European history from about 500 to 1450 A.D.

ORIGINS: Pope Gregory IX started the Inquisition in 1231 to root out heretics.

STORY: For 600 years after the fall of Rome in 476 A.D., the Roman Catholic Church was the main stabilizing force in western Europe. Schools, commerce, religion, science, defense, and just about everything else was rooted in the stability of the Church. The problem was that not everybody wanted to be a Catholic or a Christian and live in that religion-dominated society. And for some who were Catholics, they didn't like the political power of the Church. In addition, strange doctrines were always entering the mainstream, and various local Catholic leaders had for centuries tried to suppress the problems, but without much success.

GOING ON THE OFFENSE

Pope Gregory IX was worried that heretics among the sheep were stirring the European Christians into rebellion or otherwise injecting false doctrine into the Church. So he tried to root out the rabble rousers in 1231 A.D. with something he called the "Inquisition."

Q. What is the shortest verse in the Bible? A. "Jesus wept." (John 11:35)

HOW IT WORKED

Somebody preaches a non-Catholic doctrine as truth, or otherwise sins, and local Church authorities discover him. The sinner is arrested and hauled before an inquisitor to confess and absolve himself. If this doesn't work there might be a trial where witnesses are called forward. After 20 years of trying to extract confessions the old fashioned way, they decided to try one-time-only torture beginning in 1252. It worked really well, but confessions from torture didn't win a lot of confidence from most level-headed judges. And some over-zealous inquisitors justified additional torture by claiming with every new piece of evidence, 'Ah-ha, you lied! Back to the rack for you.'

Once somebody was tortured into spilling the beans, their penalties ranged from prayers and fasting, to losing their property or being thrown in prison, sometimes for life. Prison was nasty—Little to no food and water, no cleanliness, often chained to a chair or wall. Those refusing to repent or those who repeated their offense were turned over to the secular authorities who alone could execute a person.

WHERE IT WORKED

The Inquisition was used all over northern Europe, but not as severely as in northern Italy, southern France, and Spain from around 1300-1500 A.D.

SPANISH INQUISITION

The most severe of all Inquisition periods was that started in 1478 and carried out by the number-one bad guy, Tomás de Torquemada. He was a pious man, but his passion for the letter of the law ruined or exposed his lack of compassion. He was ruthless when necessary.

Born in 1420, Torquemada became an advisor to King Ferdinand II and Queen Isabella I, telling them that they should not trust those Jews and Muslims in Spain who joined Christianity just to avoid religious persecution. By 1492, his influence paid off when Jews and Muslims were kicked out of Spain. With that problem gone, the king and queen could focus on other things, such as financing Christopher Columbus's attempt to reach Asia by sailing west.

Meanwhile, Torquemada set up a supreme council and a whole group of regional Inquisition offices, himself being in charge of all. He quickly "reproved" himself out of control, using torture and confiscation to terrorize his wayward flock. As guidance to other inquisitors, he issued a new and improved list of offenses for which an inquisition could be called: alchemy, witchcraft, sorcery, heresy, sodomy, polygamy, blasphemy, usury, and others. He was happy to apply torture as needed, and during his reign an estimated 2,000 people were burned at the stake.

Four years before Torquemada's death in 1498, Pope Alexander VI grew tired of the complaints about Torquemada's sinister treatment of others, and assigned four assistant inquisitors to manage the program while restraining Torquemada's tirade.

INQUIRING MINDS WANT TO KNOW

The Inquisition kept folks in line until freedom finally caught up with it and the Inquisition lost its intense practice. As the church took more of a backseat to politics, any act of Inquisition was reduced to a relatively harmless way for running the church government and excommunicating heretics.

By the 1800s it was just another church office. In 1908, the word "inquisition" was dropped and it became known as the "Holy Office." In 1965, Pope Paul VI reorganized the church government and renamed the "Holy Office" to "Congregation for the Doctrine of the Faith."

CATHOLIC VIEW

Most of us have a very negative view of the Inquisition period, and non-Christians will cite it as proof that Christians are hypocrites with their "turn the other check" talk. But in the day, the heretics were viewed as more malignant than acts of treason. Their view that eternity never yields for mortality is not too foreign of a thought to Mormons. But as the emphasis on the Godly dwindled, so did the ability to police the doctrines of the early church. Today, there is less regard for purity of the faith in the Catholic Church as there once was, so dealing with it harshly seems grossly obscene nowadays.

Brother Paul is grateful the Bishop delivers lectures and not the rack ... though the outcome is often the same. "The Nursery? Sign me up, Bishop!"

MORMONS ON HIGH

People look up to Mormons—and with good reason ...

HIGHEST MOUNTAIN
Larry Nielson of the Olympia Washington 4th Ward was the first American to climb Mount Everest without the aid of oxygen, and the first Mormon in history to conquer that mountain. He reached the summit on May 7, 1983.

HIGHEST ALTITUDE JET: In 1990, explorer John Goddard, La Canada, California, took the controls of an F-106 and flew it to an altitude of 63,000 feet (almost 12 miles high), making him the only civilian to pilot an aircraft to that altitude.

HIGHEST BALLOON FLIGHT: On Nov. 11, 1935, two BYU graduates, Capt. Orvil A. Anderson and Capt. Albert W. Stevens, set a new world's record for altitude when they piloted an Army Corps balloon, the *Explorer II*, to 72,395 feet.

HIGHEST IN SPACE: Jake Garn, Don Lind and Richard Searfoss have all flown through space aboard the space shuttle at altitudes averaging 200 miles high. Garn and Lind flew in 1985, and Searfoss flew three times—1993, 1996 and 1998.

HIGHEST KITE: In 1967, Dr. Philip Kunz and his son sent a 29-cent drug store kite aloft to 28,000 feet over Laramie, Wyoming, using 33,000 feet of fishing line. It set a new world record.

HIGHEST FLAG: In 1986, a U.S. flag placed aboard the Space Shuttle Challenger by Church-sponsored Troop 514 in Colorado Springs was one of the few items found intact, floating in the ocean, after the shuttle was destroyed when its engine exploded.

HIGHEST HIGH JUMP: In 2001, Charlie Clinger and Lorin Farr, Ogden Utah Stake, set a world record for the high jump by clearing 7 feet 8-1/2 inches.

A pound of potato chips cost two hundred times a pound of potatoes.

A FACE-OFF WITH FACE CARDS, PART III

Brother Paul continues his exploration into the banishment of face cards in the LDS home. To read this story from the beginning, turn to page 43.

TAROT CARDS The earliest names for tarot cards were Italian and meant "triumph," and they were invented in the early A.D. 1400s. When another card game of "triumphs" came along that used ordinary playing cards, people starting using the name "tarocchi" or "tarocco" to separate their special game from ordinary playing cards. The German form of the "tarocco" is "tarock," and the French form is "tarot." Nobody knows exactly what "tarot" means except its roots are Italian for "triumph."

22 "LIFE" CARDS

The tarot deck was the same as regular playing cards except for an additional 22 not belonging to any suit. These cards had symbolic pictures of life as defined by European Christendom. Much of this art work is found elsewhere in paintings and books, so tarot card design was not really that unique in the beginning. Images included The Wheel of Fortune, Death, the Devil, the Emperor, the Pope, and the Moon. For card players, these cards had power over the regular deck of 56 or 52 cards, something a seasoned card player would appreciate by the term "permanent trump." A tarot card could be played no matter what suit the player had, and outranked the rest of the cards.

NO FORTUNES IN FORTUNE TELLING

For a couple of centuries, there was no fortune telling or occult connection to the tarot cards.. They were simply an extension of the hugely popular playing cards. The Inquisition in the 1500s makes no mention of the cards as being evidence of heresy, and card printers made their living from both religious cards and playing cards, without drawing scorn from the

Old Testament books average 30 pages while New Testament books average 14 pages.

Church. While regular playing cards were restricted or outlawed because of their connection to gambling, tarot cards were sometimes exempted. After the Reformation in the 1500s, the church didn't like cards showing the Pope so card makers replaced them with other figures.

THE WAITE IS OVER

For 350 years, tarot cards are not mentioned as tools of fortune telling. The best evidence comes in the early 1700s. And where were the gypsies? They were known more for their palm reading and other fortune telling long before they started using tarot cards in the 1800s. The Waite-Smith deck of tarot cards was created in 1909 with unique illustrations said to be of ancient and mysterious origin. It was the only such deck available in the U.S. for many years, and that's the deck that most of us have seen or heard about as "those devil cards."

THE FOOL CARD. A popular myth about the Joker found in today's playing cards is that it descended from The Fool found in the original tarot deck. This is not true. The Fool has always been so named—in Italian "il matto," in French, "le mat" and sometimes "le fou." This card was amazingly useful for the game player. Sometimes given the label of "0," and other times, "XXII," it was the least and the most powerful of all. It was played as a "wild card," but not like today's Joker. The Fool can't beat other cards, but it is worth a lot of points. Having one at the end of a game guarantees a high score, so it was worth keeping.

The Joker showed up in the U.S. card playing public around 1850, probably to add spice to the game of Poker. Perhaps the Joker's inventor was aware of The Fool, but The Fool never had the adaptability given the Joker. Scholars do not see any viable connection.

And now to gambling and a look at the puzzling dilemma facing us today, see our concluding chapter on page 378.

The curvature of the Earth is 8 inches every mile, or 66 feet in 100 miles.

MORONI'S PROMISE!

PART IV

*More famous people who received a copy
of the Book of Mormon.*

READER: Mark Twain (1835-1910)
DATE: 1861-66
CIRCUMSTANCE: Mark Twain's many adventures
took him through Salt Lake City in the 1860s where he met
Brigham Young and picked up a copy of the Book of Mormon.
He told of the event in his book, *Roughing It*. In his typical
Mark Twain style of biting sarcasm and genteel blasphemy, he
declared the Book of Mormon to be "chloroform in print." And
then he comments on the frequent use of "And it came to pass."

READER. Nikita Khrushchev (1894-1971) and family
DATE: September 1959
CIRCUMSTANCE: During his visit to the United States,
Soviet Premier and Cold War adversary Nikita Khrushchev and
his family were given a tour of Washington, D.C. Ezra Taft
Benson's son, Reed, hosted Mrs. Khrushchev and family. When
the conversation turned to the Mormon Tabernacle Choir, Reed
told them of the Church and the Book of Mormon. They
agreed to receive copies and six were delivered within the year.
Khrushchev's son-in-law told Reed, "Come to Russia and do
some missionary work for your Church!" (See page 135)

READER: Jesse Jackson
DATE: 1987
CIRCUMSTANCE: Arizona Governor Evan Mecham present-
ed a copy of the Book of Mormon to Jesse Jackson while
Jackson was in Arizona to persuade Mecham not to drop the
Martin Luther King holiday. "I committed him to read it,"
Mecham says.

To read more about Moroni's Promise, see page 348.

The first full English translation of the Bible was made in A.D. 1382 by John Wycliffe.

PROPHECY SCORECARD

A little book published in 1938 called Prophecy and Modern Times *by W. Cleon Skousen summarizes nearly all of the major prophecies pertaining to modern times that are found in scripture and in talks by the brethren. Where do you think we stand on the prophecy time line? Check the box!*

PROPHECY	Done	Underway	Not yet
The Church is cast into the wilderness.	☐	☐	☐
The Church is established in the tops of the mountains.	☐	☐	☐
All manner of new religions start.	☐	☐	☐
Gentiles gather to Salt Lake City.	☐	☐	☐
Salt Lake is known as a very wicked place.	☐	☐	☐
Speculation and extravagance infests the Saints.	☐	☐	☐
Persecution of Saints follows. True LDS are tested to their limits.	☐	☐	☐
Pressures on Church are so great, the righteous begin praying day and night for deliverance.	☐	☐	☐
Pride of America exceeds whole world.	☐	☐	☐
America becomes a nation of liars, hypocrites, and murderers, and is full of secret combinations.	☐	☐	☐

In earlier days, the prophet was called, "Prophet, Seer and Translator."

PROPHECY	Done	Underway	Not yet
Gospel is taken from the gentiles.	☐	☐	☐
America suffers political and financial collapse.	☐	☐	☐
Constitution teeters on the edge of destruction.	☐	☐	☐
Elders of the Church work diligently to spare the Constitution from collapsing.	☐	☐	☐
Righteous (the converted) Lamanites rise up and cleanse the land of wicked gentiles.	☐	☐	☐
Jews build their temple and offer a blood sacrifice in righteousness.	☐	☐	☐
In America, the New Jerusalem is started.	☐	☐	☐
The keys of the priesthood are passed to Adam and to Jesus Christ.	☐	☐	☐
The Ten Tribes return and join the Saints.	☐	☐	☐
Lucifer's church dominates the Earth. A mark on the hand or forehead is needed to buy and sell.	☐	☐	☐
Saints from all over the world are warned to escape their homes and flee to America.	☐	☐	☐
Major wars break out, pestilence, famine. Only those in Zion escape the ravages.	☐	☐	☐
144,000 sent to issue final call for the truth seekers to embrace gospel and flee to America.	☐	☐	☐

In the Bible: There's no mention of three wise men, only three gifts.

PROPHECY	Done	Underway	Not yet
Earthquakes, thunderings, lightnings, tempests; waves of seas heave beyond their bounds; all things in commotion; men's hearts fail them.	☐	☐	☐
Earth staggers in its path; stars fall from heaven; sun darkened & moon turns to blood.	☐	☐	☐
American continent is cut off.	☐	☐	☐
Parable of Ten Virgins—only half the Church is worthy.	☐	☐	☐
Jews return to their homeland.	☐	☐	☐
Gog dominates Europe and Asia—his army and people are called Magog.	☐	☐	☐
Gog marches on Palestine; holds it under siege for 3-1/2 years; two Jewish witnesses keep Gog at bay; they are killed and lie in the street 3 days, and are then resurrected.	☐	☐	☐
Lord intervenes. All but 1/6th of Gog's army is destroyed.	☐	☐	☐
With Earth cleansed and the New Jerusalem built, the Savior appears to the Jews and the sign of the coming of the Son of Man is witnessed all around the Earth; a great earthquake hits, righteous Saints are drawn up to greet the Savior as He comes for the second time.	☐	☐	☐

****

PROPHET JOSEPH SMITH: "This morning, I read German, and visited with a brother and sister from Michigan, who thought that 'a prophet is always a prophet;' but I told them that a prophet was a prophet only when he was acting as such." (*History of the Church*, Vol. 5:265)

Apples, not caffeine, are more efficient at waking you up in the morning.

FIRE HEROES

FIRE
In 1986, RaNelle Wallace, Bakersfield 1st Ward, Bakersfield California East Stake, barely survived a fiery plane crash and was finally released to convalesce at home. A few days later, she saw out of her window her neighbor's home in flames and raced to warn them of the pending doom. In the process, she became trapped in their garage but managed to escape. She lived to tell about her fiery ordeals and *Newsweek* listed her in its special edition, "100 New American Heroes."

GUNFIRE

In 1934, Latter-day Saint and FBI agent Sam Cowley was in a high-speed car-chase, hot on the tail of that dirty coward and multi-murderer Baby Face Nelson and his body guard. With cars skidding to a stop and men leaping for cover in a blaze of gunfire, Nelson was shot dead, Cowley's partner was dead, and Cowley lay mortally wounded atop his machine gun. As Nelson's body guard came to turn Cowley over, Brother Cowley pulled up his gun and emptied it into the body guard and then collapsed. As Cowley lay dying in a hospital bed a few hours later, word came to him that Cowley "got his man." FBI director J. Edgar Hoover called Sam Cowley "The bravest man I ever knew."

HOUSE FIRE

In 1984, youth from the Little Rock, Arkansas 2nd Ward were just cleaning up when somebody noticed a nearby nursing home was ablaze. The youth and leaders dashed to the building and began removing the elderly patients, relocating them in the cultural hall of the Stake Center. By the time fire fighters and police arrived, most of the patients were safely evacuated and being tended to in the Church. When word of the fire spread, LDS from all around descended on the meeting house with food, blankets, bedding and supplies. Said one elderly woman, "There's not anything better than going to a church to be saved." And said one fireman, "Little Rock is going to really sit up and take notice the next time you Mormons have one of these firesides!"

In case you need any, bamboo can grow up to 36 inches in a day.

ABRAHAM LINCOLN

A close encounter with the Mormons came to Abraham Lincoln back in 1840 when, as a newly re-elected Illinois state representative for the fourth time, he voted to approve Nauvoo's petition for city status.

NO POLYGAMY ON MY WATCH

One of Abraham Lincoln's platform positions while campaigning for president in 1860 was a promise to eradicate what he sometimes called, "the twin relics of barbarism"—namely, slavery and polygamy. He was really more preoccupied with slavery and focused on that for most of his stumping about the country.

MEET THE MORMONS

Lincoln finally had opportunity to meet up with an official representative of the Church, a Brother T.B.H. Stenhouse. Said Lincoln, "Stenhouse, when I was a boy on the farm in Illinois there was a great deal of timber on the farm which we had to clear away. Occasionally we would come to a log which had fallen down. It was too hard to split, too wet to burn, and too heavy to move, so we plowed around it. You go back and tell Brigham Young that if he will let me alone I will let him alone."

THE FIRST "INSTANT MESSAGING"

The next year, Brigham Young wired Lincoln to inaugurate the recently completed transcontinental telegraph system, and sent, "Sir, permit me to congratulate you." In April of 1862, Lincoln wired back and asked President Young to support the Union by guarding the telegraph and overland mail system. President Young was happy to help.

****

A t the cost of $150 per mile, the Church built 500 miles of telegraph lines in 1865-67 to connect LDS settlements throughout Utah, and a few in Nevada and Idaho. In 1900, the line was merged with the Western Union system.

Lawn fertilizer? Bunny rabbits poop almost everytime they hop in newly-explored areas.

WHERE WE GOT 'EM: NEW TESTAMENT

*The foundation document for Christianity that we know today
didn't appear on the heels of the death of Jesus as some
might think. It took a good 12 decades before
this portion of the Bible became a book.*

The death of Jesus probably came as a great shock to the young, fledgling Church that He organized, starting in 30 A.D. But it was His follow-up work that energized the apostles to exchange their grief and burdens for the positive of zealous missionary work. This labor largely fell on the backs of Peter and the apostles. But where was the written history and teachings of this religion? The Jews certainly had theirs, but a Christian record would have to wait for several decades.

PAUL THE AUTHOR!
First on the author scene is Saul, who became Paul. About ten years after the crucifixion of Christ, Paul did missionary work all over the Mediterranean region. During his treks to Asia Minor and Cyprus in 40-51 A.D., he wrote the first surviving letters or epistles addressed to those churches. Were these his first? We don't know. Dates are such hard things to nail down this far beyond the events, but some say Paul wrote his epistle to the Thessalonians in 49 A.D. and one to the Galatians in 51 A.D. His letters to the Corinthians and Romans came a few years later.

OTHER WRITERS GET ON BOARD
Around 70 A.D., Mark's testimony was written or found. Some 15 years later, Luke's Gospel was secured. And some time after that, about 60 years after the crucifixion, Acts and Revelation were gathered into the fold.

Authorship and timing of the remaining New Testament books get a little blurry towards the turn of the century in 100 A.D. The "Pastoral Epistles" (Hebrews, Timothy, Titus and

Peter), Matthew's record, and after that, the Gospel of John were written. Were these writings actually created at these late dates, or is this when surviving versions were grabbed to be included in the Book? Nobody knows.

THE NEW CONVERTS HAD LITTLE MONEY

The letters by these great early Christians were carefully passed around from church to church. The problem was poverty. It was expensive to hire a scribe and pay for ink and a scroll. Instead, letters were shared without copying them. Those that survived were probably preserved because they were short and cheap to copy. The longer letters probably crumbled with the ages.

BRINGING IT ALL TOGETHER

About 120 years after the crucifixion, the churches started gathering the various letters, starting first with the four gospels (Matthew, Mark, Luke and John). There was a library of material to choose from to create a Christian book, but most of these documents were copies of copies. About 200 A.D., the New Testament as we know it today was more or less together—all in Greek.

Not until 367 A.D. did the list of 27 New Testament books become finalized.

Our friend St. Jerome finished translating the New Testament into Latin in 405 A.D. His version also contained the Old Testament, and was known as the Vulgate (for vulgar version, or one for the common man).

A BOOK FOR THE MASSES

The rest of the story is pretty well known. In 1380 A.D, John Wycliffe began an English translation of the Bible, and 140 years later, Martin Luther created his German translation of the New Testament. The so-called Geneva version (1560) was used by Shakespeare and the pilgrims who came to America aboard the *Mayflower*. And then in 1604, the King James translation was started.

Zebras are white with black stripes (the black stripes end at their white bottoms.)

SAINTS & SLAVES

It's an ugly sore spot in America's history, but slavery carried over into early Church history. Here's the story.

When the pioneers were just setting up camp in Salt Lake valley, the issue of slavery was rearing its ugly head. The U.S. had acquired huge new territories from Mexico, and California was boiling over with gold-rush speculators. California wanted to be a state. Should slavery be allowed?

As it turned out, Congress passed the "Compromise of 1850" that allowed California to enter the union as a free state, and the territories of Utah, Nevada, Arizona and New Mexico would be allowed to vote on slavery when they petitioned Congress for statehood. In exchange for the southern states' support of the Compromise, Congress passed the Fugitive Slave Act requiring citizens to help in the recovery of fugitive slaves.

The Compromise was only a temporary fix. Tensions grew for another decade until finally the Civil War broke out.

Meanwhile, back among the Saints....

• **THE CHURCH** had no official policy for or against slavery. In 1836, the Prophet Joseph Smith counseled slave holders to treat them humanely, and under those circumstances, the slaves should be obedient to the laws of that period.

• **DURING HIS RUN** for president in 1844, Joseph made it clear he was most certainly anti-slavery.

• **IN 1847,** three slaves traveled to the Salt Lake valley in the first pioneer company: Green Flake, Hark Lay, and Oscar Crosby. Their names are on the Brigham Young Monument located in downtown Salt Lake.

• **THE ARRIVAL** of the pioneers in Salt Lake disrupted an active slave-trading business of American Indians. Our local Chief Walker and his band of Utes helped supply Indian slaves for Spanish, Mexican, American and American Indian slave traders who wanted cheap labor for their fields, mines and households.

• **THE COMPROMISE OF 1850** came along and basically made slavery in Utah legal, although it wasn't encouraged.

• **IN 1850,** the census showed 26 black slaves in Utah, and 29 in 1860. However, there is some debate as to whether those numbers are accurate.

• **MORMON CONVERTS** from the South brought slaves with them to Utah where some were freed. Others traveled on to California and had to free their black slaves there.

• **AT BRIGHAM YOUNG'S URGING,** the Legislature passed an act in 1852 to stop the Indian slave trade, but it did just the opposite. The Act declared that white "owners" of Indians could keep them as indentured servants for no more than 20 years. This accidently encouraged more slavery as Ute traders would sell stolen Indian children to the Saints. If the Saints refused, the traders would threaten to kill the children.

• **IN 1853, BRIGHAM HAD FINALLY HAD ENOUGH.** He called on the local militia to drive the slave traders out of the territory. The Ute traders were angry at the disruption of their lucrative business. This and other tensions came to a head during a trade dispute between Indians at James Ivie's home near Springville. Ivie entered the frey to prevent it from spreading into his cabin and in the process, accidently killed one of the Indians. This led to the so-called Walker War in 1853. When the war ended the next year, and Chief Walker died a short time later, the slave trading activities involving American Indians was brought to an end in Utah.

Thanks to researcher Jeffrey D. Nichols and others for these amazing details.

IT'S A MYSTERY!

Brother Paul is sometimes chastised with this finger-shaker:
"You shouldn't delve into the mysteries, young man."
What is the story behind this admonition that
is both widespread and mysterious?
According to the authorities ...

DEFINITION: A mystery is something God has revealed that man has not yet discovered.

THE RUMOR GETS STARTED
Talking about missionary work, Joseph Smith said: "Declare the first principles, and let mysteries alone ... Never meddle with the visions of beasts and subjects you do not understand." Was this statement meant to steer all of us away from "mysteries"?

THE CONVERTED SHOULD KNOW BETTER
Apostle Paul was frustrated with the early Church members because they were not preparing themselves to move from milk to meat. Said he: "I have fed you with milk, and not with meat: for hitherto ye were not able to bear it, neither yet now are ye able."

THE LORD SAID:
"And I command you that you preach naught but repentance ... For they cannot bear meat now, but milk they must receive; wherefore, they must not know these things, lest they perish." D&C 19:21-22

BROTHER PAUL OBSERVES:
Joseph Smith, the Apostle Paul, and the Lord say the same: the real meat, the mysteries of the Kingdom, are only for those who are ready. And hmmmmm—one wonders who that might be?

SCRIPTURES SAY:
- "It is given unto you to know the mysteries." Matt. 13:11.
- "For he that diligently seeketh shall find; and the mysteries of

God shall be unfolded unto them, by the power of the Holy Ghost." 1 Ne. 10:19

• "It is given to many to know the mysteries of God ... and he that will not harden his heart, to him is given the greater portion of the word, until it is given unto him to know the mysteries of God until he know them in full." Alma 12:9-10.

• "To such is given to know the mysteries of God." Alma 26:22.

• "Yea, he that repenteth and exerciseth faith, and bringeth forth good works, and prayeth continually without ceasing—unto such it is given to know the mysteries of God." Alma 26: 32

• "Seek not for riches but for wisdom; and, behold, the mysteries of God shall be unfolded unto you, and then shall you be made rich. Behold, he that hath eternal life is rich." D&C 11:7

• "If ye ask, ye shall receive revelation and know the mysteries of the kingdom." D&C 42:61, 65 (1 Cor. 2: 7, 11-14).

• "He who keeps the commandments will be given the mysteries of the kingdom." D&C 63:23.

• "To them will I reveal all mysteries." D&C 76:7.

• "The greater priesthood holds the key of the mysteries." D&C 84:19.

• "The Melchizedek Priesthood is to have the privilege of receiving the mysteries of the kingdom." D&C 107:19.

MYSTERIES ARE MEAT
Those who reject revealed mysteries as "forbidden" must not be striving to learn them as the Lord commands. A good way to prepare for the mysteries is to wear out the Book of Mormon with deep, prayerful study. Said the Lord through Joseph Smith:

"AND YOUR MINDS IN TIMES past have been darkened because of unbelief, and because you have treated lightly the things you have received—Which vanity and unbelief have brought the whole church under condemnation. And this condemnation resteth upon the children of Zion, even all. And they shall remain under this condemnation until they repent and remember the new covenant, even the Book of Mormon and the former commandments which I have given them, not only to say, but to do according to that which I have written." D&C 84:54-57

ARTIFACTS OF THE BOOK OF MORMON

STONE BURIAL BOX According to Palmyra scholar Willard Bean, early scavengers found the original stone box that held the Golden Plates for 1,600 years, and dug it up looking for treasure. The stones ended up at the bottom of the hill where they lay for decades. In 1935, President Heber J. Grant was filmed by Movietone cameramen pointing out the enlarged hole, but the stones were long gone. Brother Bean speculates that local farmers took them away for fences or mantel pieces.

GOLDEN PLATES

They measured six inches wide, eight inches long, the overall stack was six inches deep with an estimated 40-50 plates in the unsealed portion, and some 30-50 pounds total weight. They had the appearance of gold. Recent archeological discoveries hint that the plates might not have been pure gold, but tumbaga.

Tumbaga is an alloy, a mixture of copper and gold. It is strong and versatile and can be hammered, rolled, welded, molded and shaped. Apply a simple acid, such as citric acid, and the surface copper dissolves leaving a pure-gold gilding of maybe .0006 inches thick. Ancient South American plates made of tumbaga showed this thin gold gilding that would be softer to inscribe, yet more durable than softer pure gold because of the large copper content. Such plates would be less prone to damage, easier to handle, and much lighter than pure gold.

WOODEN TOOL BOX

Joseph Smith first stored the plates in a lockable wooden lap desk made by his brother Alvin. The desk later disappeared and was lost for more than a century until it was found filled with old board nails in an old Smith-family barn in Salt Lake. The lid was cracked where a horse had stepped on it. How did anyone know this was THE box? Scratched on the lid in large letters, now faded with time and wear, is the capital name "ALVIN."

THE URIM AND THUMMIM

Sometimes called "the Nephite Interpreters," this instrument of translation is described as a silver bow twisted into the shape of a figure eight with two transparent crystals between the rims of the bow connected by a rod to a breastplate. This instrument held the crystals conveniently positioned in front of Joseph's eyes so that his hands were left free to hold the plates. For Joseph, the stones were too far apart, indicating they were made for a man larger than Joseph Smith. This tool remained with the plates when Joseph returned them to safe keeping.

FOOLSCAP PAPER

The name "fool's cap" came from the stationer's watermark in the upper right hand corner of this particular type of fine writing paper. Foolscap also refers to a size of paper that measured 16 inches by 13 inches, and was folded in half to provide four sides of writing on pages that were 8 x 13 inches. Horizontal lines were about ½ inches apart.

Foolscap paper was created by pouring the paper slurry over a wire screen and pressing the water out. It was considered fine stationery, sometimes called "Bible paper." Compared to standard paper that was thicker and rougher, it was used for a more delicate, neat and professional appearance needed for letter writing or other fancy printing needs. It was on 116 pages of this foolscap paper that Joseph Smith's first translation effort was painstakingly written—and ultimately lost by Martin Harris.

PENS

Pencils were not very refined in Joseph Smith's day, and probably were not used for the serious work of translation.

Ink pens available during the 1820s were quill and steel-tipped. The steel-tipped pens were relatively new and pretty fancy but not widely available. But what a huge improvement! The goose quills wore down much too fast. Royal Skousen reports the printer's manuscript of the Book of Mormon shows clear evidence of quill pens in use, wearing and sometimes splitting before a new one was employed, or the old one sharpened. Between the quill and its constant repair, the slow and tedious work to transcribe dictation was never too slow for Joseph.

EXTERMINATION ORDER

Full text of the infamous order issued to drive the Saints out of Missouri, or kill them. It was later rescinded (see next page).

OCTOBER 27, 1838—TO GEN. JOHN B. CLARK

Sir: Since the order of this morning to you, directing you to cause four hundred mounted men to be raised within your division, I have received by Amos Rees, Esq. of Ray county and Wiley C. Williams, Esq., one of my aids, information of the most appalling character, which entirely changes the face of things, and places the Mormons in the attitude of an open and avowed defiance of the laws, and of having made war upon the people of this State. Your orders are, therefore, to hasten your operations with all possible speed. The Mormons must be treated as enemies, and must be exterminated or driven from the State if necessary, for the public peace—their outrages are beyond all description. If you can increase your force, you are authorized to do so, to any extent you may consider necessary. I have just issued orders to Maj. Gen. Willock of Marion county, to raise five hundred men, and to march them to the northern part of Daviess, and there unite with General Doniphan, of Clay, who has been ordered with five hundred men to proceed to the same point for the purpose of intercepting the retreat of the Mormons to the north. They have been directed to communicate with you by express, you can also communicate with them if you find it necessary. Instead, therefore, of proceeding as at first directed to reinstate the citizens in their homes, you will proceed immediately to Richmond and then operate against the Mormons. Brig. Gen. Parks of Ray, has been ordered to have four hundred of his Brigade in readiness to join you at Richmond. The whole force will be placed under your command. I am very respectfully,

Your Ob't Serv't, L. W. BOGGS, Commander-in-Chief.

"Ma is as selfless as I am," reads the same forwards and backwards.

INFAMOUS EXTERMINATION ORDER RESCINDED

Missouri Governor Christopher Bond was invited to an RLDS Stake Conference in 1976, and as a gesture of Bicentennial good-will, he offered this resolution (Also see prior page).

WHEREAS, on October 27, 1838, the Governor of the State of Missouri, Lilburn W. Boggs, signed an order calling for the extermination or expulsion of Mormons from the State of Missouri; and

WHEREAS, Governor Boggs' order clearly contravened the rights to life, liberty, property and religious freedom as guaranteed by the Constitution of the United States, as well as the Constitution of the State of Missouri; and

WHEREAS, in this bicentennial year as we reflect on our nation's heritage, the exercise of religious freedom is without question one of the basic tenets of our free democratic republic;

NOW, THEREFORE, I, CHRISTOPHER S. BOND, Governor of the State of Missouri, by virtue of the authority vested in me by the Constitution and the laws of the State of Missouri, do hereby order as follows: Expressing on behalf of all Missourians our deep regret for the injustice and undue suffering which was caused by the 1838 order, I hereby rescind Executive Order Number 44, dated October 27, 1838, issued by Governor W. Boggs.

In witness I have hereunto set my hand and caused to be affixed the great seal of the State of Missouri, in the city of Jefferson, on this 25 day of June, 1976.

(Signed) Christopher S. Bond, Governor.

4-month trips: Nauvoo to Missouri River (250 miles), and Missouri R. to Utah (1,032 miles)

MELCHIZEDEK

*This great man stood head and shoulders above most folks,
and was so honored by the Lord that we are permitted to call the
higher priesthood after him. Here's a summary of his life.*

MELCHIZEDEK was a faithful and great High Priest.
As king of Salem he was a contemporary of Abraham,
but somewhat older. The two men lived about 2000
B.C.

• **AS A YOUTH, ABRAHAM** sought out Melchizedek to
receive the holy priesthood, and desired also to be called a
"prince of peace" just like Melchizedek.

• Melchizedek came from a royal family with a large kingdom
in the middle of Canaan.

• **HIS FATHERS** brought the descendants of Shem to this
region and built a capital at Salem, today's Jerusalem. "Salem"
means peace. "Jeru" means "city" or comes from "Jebu," a
Canaanite tribe living in the area several centuries before being
conquered by King David.

• Melchizedek grew up around the same sacred Mount Zion or
Mount Moriah where Jesus would later be crucified and resurrected some 2,000 years later.

• **AS A CHILD,** Melchizedek was righteous and faithful: he
feared God, stopped the mouths of lions, quenched the violence
of fire.

• **HE WAS ORDAINED** a High Priest after the same covenant
God made with Enoch.

• Melchizedek came to power over his people at a time of terrible wickedness. He brought peace to his people by encouraging
and enticing them to become humble and repent. And they did.

• **ABRAHAM'S OWN FATHERS** were wicked, even sacrificing children. So Abraham went to THE fathers for his priesthood. And from Joseph Smith we learn, "So Melchizedek ordained Abraham and sent him away. Abraham rejoiced, saying, Now I have a priesthood." (DHC, Vol. 5, p. 555)

• **AT AGE 75,** Abraham moved to Hebron, about 16 miles south of Jerusalem and enjoyed a friendship with Melchizedek. Some 25 or 30 years later, Abraham welcomed Isaac into his family but was commanded to sacrifice "the lad" on Mount Moriah, in Salem. When Abraham arrived, there was no city of Salem, the place was empty and uninhabited. From the inspired version comes the astonishing truth that Melchizedek and Salem were translated and taken up into heaven, similarly to the city of Enoch! (Inspired Version, Gen. 14)

• **IN DOCTRINE AND COVENANTS 107,** another honor is explained: "Why the first [or higher Priesthood] is called the Melchizedek Priesthood is because Melchizedek was such a great high priest. Before his day it was called the holy priesthood, after the order of the son of God. But out of respect or reverence to the name of the Supreme Being, to avoid the too frequent repetition of his name, they, the Church, in ancient days, called that priesthood after Melchizedek, or the Melchizedek Priesthood." (D&C 107:2-4)

****

SOMETIMES WOMEN ARE OVERLY SUSPICIOUS of their husbands. When Adam stayed out very late for a few nights, Eve became upset. "You're running around with other women," she charged.

"You're being unreasonable," Adam responded. "You're the only woman on Earth." The quarrel continued until Adam fell asleep, only to be awakened by someone poking him in the chest.

It was Eve. "What do you think you're doing?" Adam demanded.

"Counting your ribs," said Eve.

HOW THEY DIED

Early apostles and latter-day apostles—a difference of 1,800 years.

IN APPROXIMATE ORDER OF THEIR POSITIONS, this list shows that the early apostles met a much more severe fate than our brethren of the 1800s. And while the Savior had to deal with one bad apple, seven of the brethren helping Joseph Smith apostacized (three were rebaptized).

- Simon Peter – Crucified upside down.

- Andrew—Whipped and crucified on an x-shaped cross

- James—Beheaded

- John—Translated

- Philip—Crucified

- Nathaniel—Flayed to death by whip.

- Matthew—Stabbed by a sword

- Thomas—Speared by four soldiers.

- James—Pummeled with stones and a fuller's club.

- Thaddaeus—unknown

- Simon—killed for his beliefs while on his mission

- Judas—Suicide

- Thomas B. Marsh—Old age and effects of palsy

- David W. Patten—Shot in stomach, died from wounds

- Brigham Young—Ruptured appendix

- Heber C. Kimball—Subdural hematoma

- Orson Hyde—Declining health in old age, died at home

- William E. McLellin—death details unknown

- Parley P. Pratt—Shot and stabbed by a jealous husband

- Luke S. Johnson—death details unknown

- William Smith—death details unknown

- Orson Pratt—Complications from diabetes

- John F. Boynton—death details unknown

- Lyman E. Johnson—Drowned in the Mississippi River

What's for dinner? The second wagon train into Salt Lake brought 716 chickens.

ERNEST WILKINSON

I t will always be said of Ernest L. Wilkinson, "A giant has passed this way."

Though small in stature, the former BYU president, politician, religious leader and attorney, cast a shadow that falls across the lives of countless thousands who worked, learned and aspired under his leadership.

He left an array of monuments to a life devoted to service. The man who worked hardest at getting too many things done, died of a heart attack on April 6, 1978, a month before his 79th birthday.

SELFLESS, BULL-HEADED SERVICE!

The first 13 of his 20 years at BYU were without salary. After his first three years he invited Church officials to BYU to dedicate not one but 22 modern buildings. Three years later, the brethren were invited again to dedicate 12 more. By his retirement, his careful nurturing of hundreds of millions of donated dollars helped beautify and expand the campus with 300 new structures.

He worked hard for the faculty, winning them raises and benefits. Creating a learning atmosphere with strong LDS standards, enrollment exploded from 4,654 in 1950 to more than 25,000 in 1972. Eight new colleges were organized, and the faculty grew from 98 to 1,070.

SURVIVING THE WORLD

Growing up in Ogden's "Hell's Half Acre," Brother Wilkinson was strong in the faith. While he was a student at BYU, the influenza hit in 1918. Praying for recovery he promised the Lord if his life was spared, he would "do something great for the Lord's university." He pursued the promise with vigor. After law school, he left his reputation in New York as "Bishop of Wall Street," and headed back to Provo. As a busy, focused executive, he seemed cold and impersonal to some. "If I sometimes offend people it is not because I want to, but because I am determined to get something done." Ben E. Lewis, an executive with the Marriott Corporation said, "I've heard it said by members of the Board of Trustees that he's just too hard to turn down. He comes so well prepared they couldn't disagree."

OBEY OR ELSE!

Wilkinson was very concerned about students and went out of his way to help individuals experiencing problems, oftentimes offering financial aid out of his own pocket. But he also wouldn't hesitate to tell students if they wanted to stay at BYU they had to get their hair cut.

His sense of humor was legendary. At one unveiling of the mascot Cosmo, who should it be but Ernest. He performed in school plays as a custodian and an elderly Indian, complete with long hair, an old hat and a feather. He entered the annual greased pig contest and ruined a good suit catching the animal. He also would do pushups during basketball games as the students counted, and at one game he did 44 nonstop!

MONUMENTS

Wilkinson believed his greatest accomplishment was establishing wards and stakes on BYU's campus. His peers thought his greatest achievement was representing the Ute Indian Tribes in a law suit against the U.S. government—he won them $31.5 million, one of the largest settlements in history.

But to his students and faculty, Brother Wilkinson's greatest accomplishment was BYU.

RESIGNMENT

"Between five and seven this morning," he said at his retirement from BYU, "I had a number of calls asking if I was retiring. I gave a resounding NO. I'm just changing jobs. There's a big difference between resigning and retiring. For one thing, they're spelled different."

Ernest Wilkinson left a shadow that continues to fall across the successes of the ever-growing BYU campus and student body. It was hard to see him go. But for him, it wasn't too hard. He just changed jobs.

Non-LDS estimates: by 2080, Church membership should be about 265 million.

SURPRISE!

How would it be? The Lord calls you to the most important leadership roles in the Church, and you hear about it second hand, by surprise, or with no advance warning.

WILFORD WOODRUFF: In 1838, Brother Woodruff had just baptized his father's family in Connecticut and was on his way back to Maine when a letter arrived on August 9. It was from Thomas B. Marsh, president of the Twelve Apostles. It's nice to get mail, but this was an unusual letter. Elder Marsh reported that the Lord had spoken through the Prophet Joseph Smith. In response to vacancies created when four members of the twelve had apostatized, Wilford and three others were called by name to fill the voids, and he was to return to Far West immediately. Said Brother Woodruff, "The substance of this letter had been revealed to me several weeks before, but I had not named it to any person."

FRANCIS M. LYMAN: In 1880, Elder Lyman was a member of the Council of Fifty and was on assignment hundreds of miles from home with Erastus Snow when his call came. At the end of the day, he happened upon a copy of the Deseret News and was reading the report of the recently concluded general conference. Down in the section dealing with new callings, he saw his own name there as having been sustained a member of the Quorum of the Twelve!

DAVID O. MCKAY: In 1906, Elder McKay and his family were enjoying lunch when the phone rang. "Come immediately to the office of the Quorum of the Twelve," he was told. Thinking he was being considered for the Church Board of Education, Elder McKay met up with Elder George Albert Smith who took Elder McKay to Elder Lyman's office. "So, you're David O. McKay," Elder Lyman said upon first meeting him. "Well, David O. McKay, the Lord wants you to be a member of the Quorum of Twelve Apostles." The stunned educator was sworn to secrecy, and that afternoon he sat next to his wife, Emma

Ray, at general conference anxiously anticipating his call from the podium. And it came.

EZRA TAFT BENSON: In 1943, Elder McKay was serving as a counselor to President Grant when he was sent to bring Elder Benson to the prophet's bedside. Wrote President Benson, "So I went in, and [President Grant] was reclining on the bed—dressed reclining. He asked me to pull my chair right up to his bed, which I did. Then he took both of my hands in his and looked me in the eye. He said, 'Brother Benson, the Lord bless you. You have been chosen as the youngest member of the Council of the Twelve Apostles.'" Elder Benson wrote, "I just could not believe it. It just seemed as though the whole world had caved in on me."

BRUCE MCCONKIE: Brother McConkie was on the job as a news reporter for the *Deseret News* covering general conference in 1946 and had just sat down at the press table when Elder David O. McKay, then a counselor in the First Presidency, approached him. Right there he called Elder McConkie to the Quorum of the Seventy, and Elder McConkie was still seated at his table as his name was read from the pulpit.

DELBERT L. STAPLEY: It was 1950, and Elder Stapley was in Salt Lake for the October general conference. While in the Hotel Utah, he took the elevator to the ground floor. Just as he left the elevator, President George Albert Smith happened to be right there. "You are just the man I'm looking for" he said, and called him to join the Quorum of the Twelve.

N. ELDON TANNER: In October 1960, Elder and Sister Tanner were in Salt Lake for general conference and were enjoying the tremendous growth in the Kingdom. Since Elder Tanner's calling as Stake President in 1953, the Church had added half a million members, 87 new stakes and more. When the first day's session ended, Elder Tanner's uncle Hugh B. Brown invited him to his home for the evening. After a cordial time together and, almost as an afterthought, Elder Brown said, "President McKay would like to see you tomorrow morning at 9

... to make 10,000 million million, million, million, million bottles of whisky.

o'clock," and, he suggested, get some sleep! That next morning, President McKay called Elder Tanner to be an assistant to the Twelve. He was called into the Twelve a few years later.

L. TOM PERRY: It was in Provo, Utah, in 1972 and Elder Perry was in the dorm of his son, and was growing impatient. "Where is my boy?" he wondered.. Suddenly, a police car pulled up out front and out jumped his son. We're looking for you, his son said, and explained that President Harold B. Lee had been trying to find him. Elder Perry immediately left for Salt Lake City and an interview with the prophet, and was called into the Twelve.

RUSSELL M. NELSON: It was spring Conference in 1984 when Elder Nelson arrived at a regional representative's seminar for some enjoyable training. As the meeting got underway, he felt a tap on his shoulder and a good brother told him that President Gordon B. Hinckley, second counselor at the time, wanted to see him. When he arrived at President Hinckley's office and sat down, the first question was, "Brother Nelson, is everything in your life in order?" Elder Nelson was relieved to say, "Yes." And then, "Good! Tomorrow we will sustain you as a new member of the Quorum of Twelve Apostles!" Writes a stunned Elder Nelson: "In one short moment, the focus of the last forty years in medicine and surgery was changed to devote the rest of my life in full-time service to my Lord and Savior, Jesus the Christ."

****

WHAT WOULD THE "WORLD" SAY TO THIS?

"I SUBMIT TO YOU that no power, priesthood or otherwise, is given by God so universally to so many with virtually no control over its use except self-control. And I submit to you that you will never be more like God at any other time in this life than when you are expressing that particular power." BYU President Jeffrey R. Holland, speaking about procreation at a BYU devotional in 1988.

Junk yard? There are more than 8,000 pieces of man-made junk in orbit around the earth.

THE BRETHREN SAID IT!

Part VII

All is not always sober and somber at the podium.
For more, see page 341.

"One man had an inscription prepared for his tomb stone which said, 'I knew it would happen.'"—*Sterling W. Sill*

"A MAN SAID, 'I can call spirits from the vast deep!' 'So can I,' shouted another, but they won't come.'"—*John Taylor*

"'THEN SAID THE KING to the servants, Bind him hand and foot, and take him away, and cast him into outer darkness; there shall be weeping and gnashing of teeth. (Matt. 22:2-13)' I used to be a little puzzled about that last part, and now I think I know why we have so many Latter-day Saint dentists."—*Paul H. Dunn*

"WHEN I LOOK OVER this body of men, I do not discover that you are very distinguished in appearance. Why, you are no better looking than I am, and I look pretty bad. I am only a remnant of what I ought to be. I am not very well groomed, and I do not look distinguished; neither do you."—*J. Golden Kimball*

"ONE OF OUR MORMON BOYS out on a mission was confronted with this question. He had just been preaching that the Father and the Son appeared to Joseph Smith, when a voice rang out: 'No man hath seen God at any time.' The boy had his wits about him. 'Of course not,' said he, 'God is a businessman—you can't see him at any time; you have to make a special appointment with him.'"—*Orson F. Whitney*

"IN LISTENING to this very generous introduction of Dr. Bernhard's, I thought of a man who said to his wife, 'How many really great men do you think there are in the world?' And she said, 'I don't know, but I am sure of this: there is one less than you think there is.'"—*Sterling W. Sill*

Blacks in the Civil War: 200,000 served; 38,000 were killed; 22 won Medal of Honor.

WINE & WATER

When Jesus attended the wedding feast at the start of his ministry, he miraculously changed water to wine. In 1830, he did it again, but this time, it was wine to water!

The sacrament prayer initially included a blessing on the bread and wine as emblems of Christ's body and blood. For the first four months of the Church's existence, wine was always used for the sacrament.

In August 1830, the Prophet Joseph Smith had just returned home from Harmony. With the company of his wife, Newel Knight and his wife, and John Whitmer, Joseph gathered the group for the purpose of confirming Emma Smith to her newly-revealed calling to make a selection of hymns for the Church.

JOSEPH WANTED THE SACRAMENT to be a part of that special meeting, but there was no wine to be found. He left the house and was on his way to secure some wine from neighbors when he was stopped by a heavenly messenger who proclaimed,

• **"LISTEN TO THE VOICE** of Jesus Christ, your Lord, your God, and your Redeemer, whose word is quick and powerful. For, behold, I say unto you, that it mattereth not what ye shall eat or what ye shall drink when ye partake of the sacrament, if it so be that ye do it with an eye single to my glory—remembering unto the Father my body which was laid down for you, and my blood which was shed for the remission of your sins. Wherefore, a commandment I give unto you, that you shall not purchase wine neither strong drink of your enemies; Wherefore, you shall partake of none except it is made new among you; yea, in this my Father's kingdom which shall be built upon the earth."

JOSEPH RETURNED HOME and administered the sacrament using "wine of our own making ... The Spirit of the Lord was poured out upon us, we praised the Lord God, and rejoiced exceedingly."

Shortly after this experience, Joseph instructed the Saints to use water instead of wine in the sacramental services.

Utah's official fruit is the cherry, but most believe it's my wacky neighbor.

HIGH FLY'N FLAGS!

Latter-day Saints encourage patriotism in whatever country they find themselves. Here are some important flag firsts and facts by Saints in the U.S.

IWO JIMA

The famous photo of Marines raising a flag in 1943 over the captured island of Iwo Jima is immortalized in a statue at Arlington National Cemetery. The first flag raised was small and not dramatic enough for the photographer, so Elder A. Theodore Tuttle was sent to retrieve a larger flag from his ship. That's the famous flag caught in the most famous of all WWII photographs.

HIGHEST FLYING

When the Space Shuttle *Challenger* exploded after take-off in 1986, the heavens rained debris for an hour afterwards. One of the few items retrieved intact and floating on the surface of the ocean was a plastic-enclosed American Flag, placed on board by Boy Scout Troop 514, sponsored by Monument Ward in Colorado Springs, Colorado.

LARGEST FLAG

Colonial Flag, owned by LDS brothers Paul and David Swenson, created a U.S. flag that is 300 feet by 150 feet in size (45,000 square feet of fabric), large enough to cover a football field goal line to goal line, and five feet shy of the sideline boundaries. The stars are 7-1/2 feet across and the stripes are 12 feet wide.

LARGEST DISPLAY

To honor those killed in the 9/11 terrorist attacks, and all soldiers fallen in the war against terror, Colonial Flag puts up a display of flags, one for each life lost, in Sandy, Utah each September. The display is called "The Healing Field," and covers several acres with a total number of flags now exceeding 4,000. The idea of Healing Fields has caught on across America.

In 1987, Marvin Ezra Clark ended his streak of 100% home teaching of 85 years!

A GREAT FLOOD STORY

SCIENTISTS RECENTLY DISCOVERED an ancient coastline about 550 feet underwater in the Black Sea, leading them to believe a sudden flood may have occurred as told in the Sumerian account of Gilgamesh and the Old Testament account of Noah. They estimate the flood took place about 7,500 years ago.

FISHING WITH CAMERAS

In August 1999, maritime explorer Bob Ballard (famous for discovering the sunken Titanic) lowered a camera into the Black Sea and found a mound of dirt with plants on it and a sandbar on the bottom that had remained undisturbed for what they estimated to have been thousands of years. This sandbar formation seemed a little out of place at the bottom of an ancient sea, so they sent down a scooper to investigate.

SNOOPER SCOOPER

As the scooper dumped silty debris on the deck of their boat, they were shocked to find freshwater mollusk shells and rounded stones like those found along lakes and rivers. And all of this only 2-3 feet beneath the top layers of sediment. What was fresh-water aquatic remains doing buried at the bottom of a salt sea?

GUESSING GAME

Radio-carbon dating showed the freshwater mollusks lived about 5500 B.C., and sometime afterwards, probably about 4900 B.C., the various saltwater species of aquatic life showed up. What possibly happened? The theory right now is that after a period of melting glaciers and then a season of high moisture monsoons, the oceans rose so high that the Mediterranean Sea breached the natural dam separating it from the Black Sea. With the force of 200 Niagara Falls, the sea gushed over thousands of square miles and replaced the small freshwater lake with a massive inland sea. Each day the Black Sea rose another six inches. The event probably killed thousands of people and millions of land and sea creatures with the initial flooding, and everyday it spread its damage many miles more.

AWASH IN THEORIES

Scientists believe the event was probably so sudden at the outset, so terrible and destructive over the long run while the sea filled to its present-day capacity, that it was burned into ancient legend and lore. Scientists speculate that the legend grew and was added to from generation to generation until writing was invented. It might have then entered the Sumerian literature in the Epoch of Gilgamish and the Hebrews' Old Testament.

THE PERFECT STORM IN ANY LANGUAGE

Stories of a great flood are in just about every culture. Each story usually has these five main parts: humans do something wrong, a god sends a flood as punishment, someone is spared death by a boat or raft, a sample of all living things is preserved, and afterwards, the Earth is repopulated with goodness.

THE WIDE, WIDE WORLD OF ORAL HISTORIES

Such stories were circulated among people in Sumer, Babylon, Australia, Chaldea, China, Peru, Hawaii, Scandinavia, New Guinea, and Thailand. They are also among the Hindu, Zoroastrians, Greeks, Romans, Apache, Mayan, Aztec, Yakima, Chippewa, Navajo, Hopi, and the list goes on.

HOUSE FOR SALE?

In 2000, Ballard and his team went searching again, this time for signs of ancient life on the bottom of the Black Sea. What they found, on the submerged beach 311 feet under the sea's surface, was a rectangular structure 12 miles east of the Turkish city of Sinope. The 39 ft. by 13 ft. building appeared to be of traditional Black Sea "wattle and daub" construction, that is, with walls made of wood branches and sticks embedded in a clay matrix. So, thousands of years ago, humans lived on the sea shore of a fresh water lake some 300 feet below the water level of today's salty Black Sea. Regardless of any connection to Noah or Gilgemesh, Brother Paul thinks this is a Really Great Flood Story!

OBEY THE SABBATH

How tough is it to live your religion when you are a stand out in your sport, and your belief tells you, "NO Sabbath play"? Here are some champion Mormons who chose their right from wrong—and lived with the outcome.

SUPER ACHIEVER: Eli Herring, Provo, Utah
OPPORTUNITY: NFL football and millions of dollars
STORY: Herring was a world class football lineman coming out of BYU. The pros expected the 6-foot-8, 300-pound tackle to be a first-round draft pick in 1995, with millions in contract money. But Herring had to choose between Sunday play for the NFL, or keeping the Sabbath a holy day. "It wasn't easy, but it wasn't just the money," he told the Church News after turning down a lucrative career in sports. "I was walking away from something I was good at and that I enjoyed doing and that I'd made a big investment in. That's probably harder for me than actually not having money—wondering what I could've done." What he did was become a low-paid high school math teacher, football coach, and fathered his five children with his wife. "I've had opportunities to serve in my church and be with my family on the Sabbath that I would never have had if I'd had a long professional football career. So I guess as the years go by, I'm more grateful that I've had all that time doing those things."

SUPER ACHIEVER: Bradley Morrison, of Ottawa, Canada
OPPORTUNITY: Leading his team to a championship game
STORY: Morrison was only 10 years old, but he was the star full-back, punter and special team leader of his city league football team in Ottawa, and led his team to three consecutive championships. Because the championship games were held on Sunday, he didn't play in them. Teammates criticized him and his brother, Brandon, but the boys held to their standards. But the final outcome was rich: dozens of gospel discussions among other team members and their families, and a couple of boys joined Bradley at his ward youth activities. The team coach said,

---

The farthest ward from Salt Lake City is 13,000 miles away in Albany, Western Australia.

"I don't know what you do in your church, but the people I've met are the finest people I know." In 2001, the first time Bradley missed a Sunday championship game, he stood in testimony meeting to express his feelings. If the team won that day, they would be city league champs. "But I know I'm a winner. I'm at Church where my Heavenly Father wants me to be." Bradley was voted as his team's offensive player of the year, and nominated for the Ottawa Outstanding Youth Award.

SUPER ACHIEVER: Mitch Nelson, of Salt Lake City, Utah
OPPORTUNITY: Snowboarding championships
STORY: Nelson's talent for snowboarding was so well documented, it was usually his photo that captured the sport's most popular cover photos and story spreads. And he never had to buy his equipment—the manufacturers donated it for publicity purposes. That's why the whole sport was shocked when Nelson abandoned his snowboarding prestige and expertise for a mission. Immediately upon his return two years later, the calls and letters poured in asking for endorsements, appearances, interviews and photos. Newly returned Elder Nelson resumed his beloved sport, but without Sunday participation. The decision has cost him a mountain of money, but created huge missionary opportunities among his followers. "I think that's what keeps me in snowboarding, the fact that I'm helping other kids," Mitch said.

SUPER ACHIEVER: BYU athletes
OPPORTUNITY: NCAA championship games
STORY: For 35 years, the so-called "BYU rule" kept college playoffs and championship games from being scheduled on Sundays. But in recent years, the NCAA began resisting the BYU rule and finally voted to rescind it. Did BYU knuckle under? "We have a very strong belief in keeping the Sabbath Day holy," said Merrill J. Bateman, BYU President at the time. "As a Church institution, it would be inappropriate for us to encourage our young people to play on the Sabbath." BYU Athletic Director Rondo Fehlberg observed, "If LDS athletes want the right to not participate on Sunday, BYU is a place where they will not be put into the difficult position of having

to violate deeply held personal beliefs or violate a sense of loyalty to their teammates." Is it working? So far, so good!

SUPER ACHIEVER: Four 9-year-old football players from Fontana, California
OPPORTUNITY: League championship game
STORY: The Fontana Generals had four LDS primary-aged boys on its winning team, along with two others of another faith who helped their team to a 11-0 record for the season. When the championship game was scheduled on a Sunday, the boys had a dilemma. They decided to pull out of the team rather than play on the Sabbath. And the team supported them by voting unanimously to forfeit the game. The local media got a hold of this story, and the whole community rose up to demand the game be rescheduled. And it was, for a Tuesday night. Interestingly, the undefeated Fontana Generals lost 12-0. Said Assistant coach Chad Edington, "Heavenly Father answered our prayers that we could play the game, but He never said we were going to win." It turned out to have created a huge missionary opportunity and positive exposure for the Church. And as some onlookers observed, despite the games' final score, the boys turned out winners after all.

SUPER ACHIEVER: Jade Hafen, 11 years old
OPPORTUNITY: A $1,000 saddle
STORY: Jade was a natural. He did so well at the junior rodeo competitions that youth and adults alike were enthused that he'd take the nationals. But after all the competitions, and with plenty of points to win, he just needed to show up and the saddle was his. But the championship was on a Sunday. Despite the best persuasions and encouragement by others to compete, Jade held to his commitment about Sunday sports, and declined. It hurt his overall annual scores and he finished lower than he might have, but he stuck by his decision. "I know I will be able to get blessings by doing what I know is right," he told the *Church News.* "I wish it wasn't so hard being Mormon." A pretty mature acknowledgment from a young 11-year-old.

MEAT VS. MILK

*The Gospel comes in two wonderful forms: the delicious milk
that everybody loves, and the more satisfying meat that is
sometimes hard to chew. Here is one of Brother Paul's
favorite multi-layered skewers of shish-kabobed
"milk" and "meat," each worthy of a lengthy discussion.*

MILK: GOD CREATED THE UNIVERSE
MEAT: The Gods *organized* the Universe. The D&C says there are two building blocks in the universe: intelligence and matter (D&C 93:29-35). One is to act, the other is to be acted upon (2 Ne. 2:14). Once united, these little units can exercise agency and allow themselves to be organized with other such units to create atoms. From atoms and their components come everything: spirits, dirt, rocks, gases, elements, plants, living beings, planets, stars, and bathroom books.

MILK: GOD GAVE US OUR FREE AGENCY
MEAT: God *protects* our free agency. Brigham Young taught that all things are free to act for themselves, including the most basic elements. God never forced anything to obey him, but invites all things to join him. For those that obey him, he expands their opportunities to exercise their agency, to join him in a wonderful pursuit of joy and growth. For his children, that path included learning his Godly principles of right and wrong, sin and obedience, joy and sorry, worry and peace.

MILK: ANYTHING GOD WANTS HAPPENS NOW!
MEAT: Obedience in the creation process always takes time. At the creation, the Gods observed in at least five references whether or not they were being obeyed. In one reference, they even had to wait. "And the Gods watched those things which they had ordered until they obeyed." (Abr. 4:18). Why wait? Because all things exercising their agency require time to obey.

MILK: THE PRIESTHOOD IS THE POWER OF GOD
MEAT: The Priesthood is God's power of organizing. Whether it be the gathering of elements to create water and land, or the gathering of elders to move a family into a home, it is the same.

The Priesthood is the power of God's loving influence to organize all things large and small, and things microscopic and macroscopic.

MILK: GOD'S POWER IS BEYOND UNDERSTANDING
MEAT: God's power is well defined in scripture. Father explains His source of power in D&C 29:36 where He says Satan demanded, "Give me thine honor, which is my (God's) power," and Moses 4:1-3: "Wherefore, give me thine honor," Satan said, which God defines in verse 3 as "my own power." How does "honor" equate to "power"? When home teachers home teach, when sunday school teachers teach, when deacons collect fast offerings, when people honor their callings, we say, "My, what a great bishop!" When the U.S. president sends troops overseas, we say, "My, what a powerful president." If ward members refused service, if troops refused to budge, we'd think, "our bishop isn't very good," or "We have a weak president." God is powerful because all things choose to obey (honor) Him. To win that obedience in all things, He must be honorable in every way so that all of creation will follow. "My honor is my power."

MILK: MIRACLES ARE GOD'S MYSTERIOUS WAYS
MEAT: Miracles are really God-science in operation. When Jesus turned water to wine, he was asking the elements to reorganize themselves from water molecules to wine molecules. When he healed the blind, he was ordering the atoms in the tissues of the eye to return to their normal state of organization. When he raised Lazarus from the dead, he asked the elements of Lazarus' body to start functioning again, and the spirit of Lazarus to return. None of this would be possible if the intelligence in matter didn't exercise their agency to obey God and his appointed representatives (holders of the priesthood).

MILK: ONLY JESUS CAN "SAVE" US
MEAT: God the Father would lose His power if He accepted our sinful selves into His kingdom. In Alma 42, Mormon 9, D&C 1, He says He would cease to be God if He looked upon sin with any degree of allowance. "I God cannot look upon sin with the least degree of allowance," and if so, He would dishon-

or Himself and "God would cease to be God." Why does Father want us to know he could cease to be God? To learn three principles: He can't "save" us in our sins (allow imperfection into Heaven) or he'd risk an awful downfall. Second, Father's power is predicated on all things honoring him as a trustworthy, perfect judge and leader in all things. And third, to be "saved," a separate and important principle must be brought to bear: a mediator or advocate who can plead our case before Father and bring salvation that won't require Father to look upon sin with any degree of allowance.

MILK: JESUS PAID FOR ALL OF OUR WICKED DOINGS
MEAT: "There is not any man that can sacrifice his own blood which will atone for the sins of another," said Amulek in Alma 34:11. If that is true, what then did Jesus do if not die and "pay" for our sins? Amulek explains how the atonement works with these seven points: (1) We're all responsible for our own sins, no one can take that responsibility from us. (2) Justice demands we suffer the consequences of our sins. (3) Surprisingly, we learn that the demands of justice can be satisfied with compassion. (4) The suffering of Jesus was ugly and painful enough that it aroused compassion and mercy for all things in which he played a part in their creation. (5) Mercy can satisfy the demands of justice. (6) Jesus begs mercy of the Father, not for our sakes but for his; not because of our works, but because of his. "Listen to him who is the advocate with the Father, who is pleading your cause before him—Saying: Father, behold the sufferings and death of him who did no sin, in whom thou wast well pleased; behold the blood of thy Son which was shed, the blood of him whom thou gavest that thyself might be glorified; Wherefore, Father, spare these my brethren that believe on my name, that they may come unto me and have everlasting life." (D&C 45:3-5) (7) Before we can have the Savior plead our individual cases, we must first win his sincere trust by proving we are his closest and loving friends by working hard, doing our best, and humbling ourselves and repenting.

For sources to the above meaty shish kabob, dig them out of the scriptures, Journal of Discourses, and the Doctrinal History of the Church. Or, to save time, see W. Cleon Skousen's "A Personal Search for the Meaning of the Atonement," "Days of the Living Christ," or the appendix of his "The First Two Thousand Years."

WHY MEN ARE JUST HAPPIER PEOPLE

Sisters of the Church, are not men just pathetic? Is life really fair? Probably not. This list has been floating around the Internet for years, in various forms. Its origin is unknown to Brother Paul. Nevertheless, he shares this version because it feels so right. ...

Your last name stays put.

The garage is all yours.

Wrinkles add character.

Wedding plans take care of themselves.

Chocolate is just another snack.

You can be president.

Car mechanics tell you the truth.

You never have to drive to another gas station because this one's just too icky.

Same work, more pay.

You know stuff about tanks.

A five-day vacation requires only one suitcase.

You can open all your own jars.

Wedding dress - $5000; tuxedo rental - $100.

The occasional well-rendered belch is practically expected.

New shoes don't cut, blister, or mangle your feet.

One mood, ALL the time.

Phone conversations are over in 30 seconds flat.

You get extra credit for the slightest act of thoughtfulness.

If someone forgets to invite you, he or she can still be your friend.

Your underwear is $8.95 for a three-pack.

Everything on your face stays its original color.

Three pairs of shoes are more than enough.

You don't have to stop and think of which way to turn a nut on a bolt.

You almost never have strap problems in public.

You are unable to see wrinkles in your clothes.

The same hairstyle lasts for years, maybe decades.

You don't have to shave below your neck.

Your belly usually hides your big hips.

One wallet and one pair of shoes, one color, all seasons.

You can "do" your nails with a pocketknife.

You have freedom of choice concerning growing a mustache.

You can do Christmas shopping for 25 relatives, on Dec. 24 in 45 minutes.

Challenge to missionaries: There are more than 40,000 characters in Chinese script.

MORE DUMB "LDS" CRIMINALS

A judge ruled that a man accused of taking hostages at the Washington Temple in 1986 was mentally competent to stand trial even though he wanted numerous dead prophets to testify in his defense. Clarence Leake, 30, was arrested Oct. 23, 1986, after holding two men hostage overnight in the top floor of the temple. Leake had his defense subpoena 14 witnesses, all of whom were dead LDS prophets. The judge read four scriptures dealing with the LDS belief that dead spirits come back to illustrate the reason for his decision of finding the defendant competent. Leake was later found guilty on four of six counts of assault and false imprisonment.
—*Latter Day Sentinel, July 9, 1988*

A PROVO, UTAH, MAN was arrested and charged in 1988 with swindling a Cedar City woman out of $20,000. He reportedly gained her trust by telling her he had been a high councilor in the Church. The 50-year-old suspect then allegedly became romantically involved with the woman and talked of marriage, while talking her out of cash and credit cards for "emergencies." He had since left her and married another woman, who at the time of the arrest was expecting a baby.
—*Latter Day Sentinel, July 9, 1988*

AN IDAHO MEMBER of an unidentified "fundamentalist Mormon" sect (okay, not really LDS, but remotely related) filed a $10,000 law suit against Sanpete County, Utah, claiming that jail officials violated his religious freedom. Myron Hamilton was jailed on drunk driving charges, and was sentenced to be incarcerated for a long period of time. His complaint? Hamilton says he was ordered to remove his religious undergarments and dress in jail-house garb, a violation, Hamilton complained, of his 1st and 14th amendment rights.
—*Latter Day Sentinel, June 26, 1988*

TOP TEN LDS MOVIE$

LDS cinema has come a long way, Sister! In the past five years, a huge investment has brought forward some great and not so great alternatives to the usual Hollywood fare. In order of highest grossing to least, here are the recent top ten.
Check out www.ldsfilm.com for updates.

THE OTHER SIDE OF HEAVEN—2001
BOX OFFICE GROSS: $4,720,112
BUDGET: $7,000,000
STORY: A film adaptation of Elder John H. Groberg's missionary travels to Tonga. Rich photography, strong story, humor and great casting made this movie a winner for both members and non-LDS alike.

THE WORK AND THE GLORY—2004
BOX OFFICE GROSS: $2,793,391
BUDGET: $7,500,000
STORY: Film adaptation of Gerald N. Lund's "The Work and the Glory," a fictional story of early Saints caught in the religious intolerance of the 1800s.

GOD'S ARMY—2000
BOX OFFICE GROSS: $2,628,829
BUDGET: $300,000
STORY: A huge hit with LDS, this is an inside look at missionary life, set in Los Angeles, that brought back humorous, painful and great memories to Brother Paul who enjoys watching it every other Sunday.

THE BOOK OF MORMON MOVIE—2003
BOX OFFICE GROSS: $1,672,730
BUDGET: $2,000,000
STORY: A nice attempt to tell the opening chapters of the Book of Mormon, but it needed a better touch. Most viewers went because of the subject matter, but didn't return. Hopefully the next installment will smooth off the rough edges.

THE SINGLES WARD—2002
BOX OFFICE GROSS: $1,250,798
BUDGET: $500,000
STORY: Great spoof on LDS culture and mystique, poking fun at the single life with great cameo shots of famous and legendary Church members. Good for many laughs.

THE BEST TWO YEARS—2004
BOX OFFICE GROSS: $1,163,450
BUDGET: $400,000
STORY: Best portrayal of missionary work yet done. Touching, realistic, subtle humor, and well crafted. This one is a keeper.

SAINTS AND SOLDIERS—2004
BOX OFFICE GROSS: $1,162,730
BUDGET: $780,000
STORY: Outstanding story of an LDS missionary meeting a former convert, a German soldier, while on patrol during WWII. Well crafted, acted, and told. We want more of this kind!

THE R.M.—2003
BOX OFFICE GROSS: $1,111,615
BUDGET: $500,000
STORY: Funny sequel to "The Singles Ward," but a little overboard on the slap-schtick. Worth seeing at least once.

BRIGHAM CITY—2001
BOX OFFICE GROSS: $905,073
BUDGET: $900,000
STORY: A shockingly great murder mystery that leads viewers through a dark journey of twists and surprises. Lot's of blood, however, so it's a little hard to watch more than once. The closing scene is the most meaningful portrayal of the sacrament ever put to film.

JACK WEYLAND'S CHARLY—2002
BOX OFFICE GROSS: $814,666
BUDGET: $950,000
STORY: Great love story built on a conversion story that touches, inspires and entertains. Well worth a good look.

World Record: LDS Violet Gison, Australia, typed nonstop for 264 hours.

OLD HEADLINES

Brother Paul is a bit of pack rat (his eternal companion would say he's more like a pack mule, but that's another story). And among his collections are these interesting newspaper headlines with the opening paragraph, from the past quarter century.

IT IS MOURNING AGAIN IN AMERICA
LOS ANGELES – Ronald Reagan, the cheerful crusader who devoted his presidency to winning the Cold War, trying to scale back government and making people believe it was "morning again in America," died Saturday after a long twilight struggle with Alzheimer's disease. (*Deseret News,* June 6, 2004)

SHE'S HOME!
After nine months of sleeping in the wilds and on the floors of strangers' homes, Elizabeth Smart crawled into her own bed to sleep Wednesday night—the same bed from which she was snatched at knife-point. (*Deseret News,* March 13, 2003)

ATTACK—U.S. BEGINS ITS AIR AND GROUND ASSAULT
U.S. warplanes unleashed a second wave of Baghdad bombing Thursday, moving from precision strikes to a wider attack while the ground war began with U.S. infantrymen cheering as how-itzers boomed scores of artillery shells at Iraqi troops. (*Deseret News,* March 20, 2003)

GORE SURRENDERS
WASHINGTON – Al Gore decided Wednesday to concede the country's overtime election, aids said, clearing the way for George W. Bush to become 43rd president and leader of a nation sharply divided along political lines. The vice president acted after a split Supreme Court ruled against recounts in contested Florida. (*Deseret News,* Dec. 13, 2000)

SCOUTS GET OK TO BAR GAY LEADERS
WASHINGTON – The Boy Scouts can bar homosexuals from serving as troop leaders, the Supreme Court ruled Wednesday, placing a limit on how far the courts should go to force open admissions upon private organizations. (*Deseret News,* June 28, 2000)

Honey is the only food that doesn't spoil.

2000—A MILLENNIUM DAWNS
Two thousand years after Christ's obscure birth in a dusty town in Judea, the world's 6 billion people—most of them non-Christian and many of them preoccupied with terrorism, computers, diets, bank accounts, politics and the perils of the future – rode their turning blue planet across time's invisible line Friday and, by common consent, looked into the dawn of a new millennium. (*New York Times*, Jan. 1, 2000)

'GOODBYE TO AN OLD FRIEND'
As he closed the 169th Semiannual General Conference Sunday afternoon, President Gordon B. Hinckley "bid goodbye to an old and wonderful friend ... If present plans hold, this is the last time we will meet in this Tabernacle for a general conference." (*Church News*, Oct. 9, 1999)

SLAUGHTER AT COLORADO SCHOOL
LITTLETON, Colo. – Two heavily armed students dressed in black stormed through a suburban Denver high school Tuesday in a bloody rampage that left as many as 25 students and teachers dead. (*Salt Lake Tribune*, April 21, 1999)

PRESIDENT IMPEACHED
WASHINGTON – Casting a permanent stain on a man who once dreamed of a gloried place in American history, the House of Representatives on Saturday impeached President Clinton and urged the Senate to remove a president from office for only the second time the nation's history. (*Salt Lake Tribune*, Dec. 20, 1998)

FEDERAL BOOKS BACK IN BLACK—WITH FISCAL 1998 ALMOST OVER, A BUDGET SURPLUS—THE FIRST IN 29 YEARS—IS A NEAR CERTAINTY
WASHINGTON – With just the month of September remaining in fiscal 1998, the first federal budget surplus in 29 years looks virtually assured. (*Salt Lake Tribune*, Sept. 23, 1998)

MCGWIRE SLUGS WAY INTO HISTORY
ST. LOUIS – History wasn't made with one of his magical moonshots or majestic arcs. Mark McGwire simply lined a laser to left Tuesday night—his shortest home run of the season at 341 feet—and the biggest, most glamourous record in sports was his ... his historic 62nd homer, breaking Roger Maris' 37-year-old record. (*Salt Lake Tribune*, Sept. 9, 1998)

Humans shed 600,000 particles of skin every hour—105 pounds by age 70.

MILLENNIUM MYSTERY: WILL COMPUTER CHAOS CRIPPLE CIVILIZATION?
WASHINGTON – Inside a suburban home darkened by a power outage from a summer thunderstorm, the top bureaucrat hired by President Clinton to make sure the nation's computers survive past 2000 was just trying to survive the evening's muggy weather. (*Salt Lake Tribune*, August 19, 1998)

'GIVING IT THEIR ALL'WEARY JAZZ IN MUST-WIN GAME 6 TONIGHT
CHICAGO – Physical and mental fatigue has gripped the NBA Finals, just as certainly as the Bulls have wrested control from the Jazz. ... Game 6 is tonight, and neither team did much in the way of preparation Thursday. (*Salt Lake Tribune*, June 13, 1997)

O.J. SIMPSON ACQUITTED
LOS ANGELES – O.J. Simpson was acquitted Tuesday of murdering his ex-wife and her friend, a suspense-filled climax to the courtroom saga that obsessed the nation. ... With two words, "not guilty," the jury freed the fallen sports legend to try to rebuild a life thrown into disgrace. (*Deseret News*, Oct. 3, 1995)

THOUSANDS COME TO PAY RESPECTS
Long before dawn, even before a touch of pink began to lighten the skies over Salt Lake City, friends and admirers of President Howard W. Hunter began gathering Tuesday to pay their respects to the 87-year-old Church leader. (*Deseret News*, March 7, 1995)

THE SOVIET UNION IS FINISHED
MOSCOW – The Soviet Union today begins the process of re-creating itself after a historical vote to transfer power from the central government to newly sovereign republics. (*USA TODAY*, Sept. 6, 1991)

GORBACHEV DEPOSED
Soviet leader Mikhail Gorbachev was ousted as president Monday in a coup by hardline right-wingers and replaced by Soviet Vice President Gennady Yanayev. (*USA TODAY*, Aug. 19, 1991)

RUSSIA RECOGNIZES LDS CHURCH
MOSCOW – The Russian Republic has granted official recognition to The Church of Jesus Christ of Latter-day Saints. (*Deseret News*, June 25, 1991)

SALT LAKE STRIKES OLYMPIC GOLD
Salt Lake City is the U.S. Olympic Committee's choice to bid for the 1998 Winter Olympics. (*Salt Lake Tribune,* June 5, 1989)

IRAN'S AYATOLLAH KHOMEINI DIES – BEIJING ERUPTS INTO BLOOD BATH
BEIJING – Troops backed by tanks and armored cars fought pitched battles with thousands of civilians Saturday and Sunday as a crackdown on the pro-democracy movement (in Tiananmen Square) exploded into a citywide insurrection leaving more than 500 people dead and 464 wounded, witnesses and hospital officials said. (*Salt Lake Tribune,* June 4, 1989)

BUNDY'S EVIL TRAIL ENDS IN CHAIR
STARKE, Fla. – Theodore Robert Bundy's trail of missing and murdered women ended Tuesday at 7:07 a.m. in Florida's electric chair. (*Salt Lake Tribune,* Jan. 25, 1989)

U.S. SAYS SOVIET DOWNED KOREAN AIRLINER; 269 LOST; REAGAN DENOUNCES 'WANTON' ACT
A South Korean airliner missing with 269 people on a flight from New York to Seoul was shot down in the Sea of Japan by a Soviet jet fighter near a Soviet island off Siberia, the United States said yesterday. (*New York Times,* Sept. 2, 1983)

REAGAN WOUNDED BY ASSAILANT'S BULLET; PROGNOSIS IS 'EXCELLENT'; 3 OTHERS SHOT
President Reagan survived an assassination attempt yesterday when a revolver-wielding gunman waiting among reporters and photographers on the sidewalk outside the Washington Hilton hotel fired a bullet into his chest. (*Washington Post,* March 31, 1981)

FREED AMERICANS LAND IN W. GERMANY; REAGAN SWORN IN AS THE 40TH PRESIDENT
Ronald Reagan, his first moments in office accompanied by a happy ending for the nation, assumed the powers of the president of the United States yesterday amid emotional circumstances unmatched in America's 48 previous inaugurations. (*The Washington Post,* Jan. 21, 1981)

REAGAN TAKES OFFICE—HOSTAGES NOW FREE
Symbolically facing West and the shrines to the nation's giants, Ronald Wilson Reagan became the nation's 40th president today—three minutes early. (*Washington Star,* Jan. 20, 1981)

If the whole world moved to Texas it would be less densely populated than NY City.

SCRIPTURES IN CONTEXT: THE ROCK

Almost 2,000 years ago the Savior built a rock-solid case against paganism with an important declaration.

SCRIPTURE: Matthew 16:13-17 (quoted below)
PLACE: Caesarea Philippi, a once thriving pagan community built on the slopes of Mount Hermon.

BROTHER PAUL'S NO-CHARGE WORD GUIDE:
Caesarea = Ses'uh-REE-uh
Philippi = Fuh-LIP-i

STORY: Caesarea Philippi is the most northern part of Jesus' ministry. It is situated on a terrace 1,150 feet high on the slopes of Mount Hermon, and overlooks a beautiful valley. Only about 25 miles north-east of the Sea of Galilee, it was a place where there were no Jews. Jesus could teach his twelve apostles in peace and quiet without the glaring judgements of others.

It is also a historical place mentioned in the Old Testament as a boundary of Joshua's conquests. The Hivites who remained as a "test" for ancient Israel also lived here, as did the half-tribe of Manasseh.

WATERY CAVE
The prominent feature of this area is a small but mysterious cave. It is not very deep, but was considered to be the birthplace of Pan, the Greek god of nature, forests, mountains, fields, shepherds and flocks. Pan's origin was actually in Greece, and Pan worshipers who traveled to Palestine found the landscape similar to home so they set up this place as a sanctuary to worship Pan.

They carved five niches in the rock wall on the right side of the cave wherein they placed statues and carved inscriptions that made mention of Pan and other Greek pagan gods.

THE ORIGINAL NAME of Caesarea Philippi had been Panias, after Pan. Its modern name of Banias is an Arabic corruption of Panias.

Mount Hermon is the only place in Israel with snow skiing.

GOING TO THE SOURCE

The beautiful Jordan River has four primary sources. Its easternmost spring is the Cave of Pan where water is constantly flowing out of the cave and travels beneath solid rock for several yards through underground cavities and channels, back into the open, down some short waterfall steps, and then funnels into a cool rushing stream.

OUT WITH THE NEW, IN WITH THE OLD

In 20 B.C., King Herod took ownership of Paneas and built a temple of white marble in front of the cave. Beneath it, the cold spring water flowed. Down the hill from this cave King Herod's son Philip built a small village, and included at least 14 additional pagan shrines.

Around 2 B.C., Philip renamed the place Caesarea in honor of Caesar Augustus. But there was already a Caesarea Maritima, so Philip put his own name there, and that's how it came to be called Caesarea Philippi. About 360 years later, the city would collapse in an earthquake, but that's getting ahead of our story.

CALLING ALL GODS, CALLING ALL GODS ....

The Pan pagans used the human sacrifice of a child or an animal to appease their god. The killing took place near the mouth of the cave and the body was cast into the waters inside the cave. The worshipers would hurry a few steps down from the cave and gather around the little waterfalls and pools. If the sacrifice was accepted by Pan, no blood would be seen in the water. If it was rejected, the priests would find diluted red blood polluting the cool, fresh water.

CHECKING OUT THE PAN-DAMONIUM

Jump ahead many years and Jesus is seen traveling through the area with his apostles.

He stops with his back to the reddish rock walls of the pagan temple and its many followers. As recorded in Matthew 16, Jesus then asked his disciples an interesting question:

"Whom do men say that I the Son of man am? And they said, Some say that thou art John the Baptist: some, Elias; and others, Jeremias, or one of the prophets.

"He saith unto them, But whom say ye that I am?"

That's when Peter speaks his heart: "Thou art the Christ, the Son of the living God."

To which the Lord responded, "Blessed art thou, Simon Bar-jona: for flesh and blood hath not revealed it unto thee, but my Father which is in heaven. And I say also unto thee, That thou art Peter, and upon this rock I will build my church; and the gates of hell shall not prevail against it."

A GREAT CONNECTION!

Brother Paul loves the connections here. With the Temple of Herod and the pagan symbols of Pan standing in all their glory, those gentle spring waters rushing by, and the great red rocks and cliffs towering behind the Savior, he teaches that no sacrifice of flesh and blood is needed to reveal *his* truth.

Instead, His Church will be built upon something more solid, reliable, stronger, more sure than *these* rocks. Unlike the sign-seeking cave of Pan, Jesus would build His kingdom upon the real rock foundation of revelation. And the gates of hell would not prevail.

It was the perfect setting to establish contrast between the world of man and the heaven of God.

NO PAN JUST PANTING

In 363 A.D., an earthquake destroyed the village at Caesarea Philippi. The ruins remained undisturbed for many centuries until excavation work began in 1967. Today, the visitor can see the fallen columns of the white temple and the column stumps that remain. The five niches carved into the cliff are clean, and the engravings visible. Other ruins can be seen as you walk around the site. The water from the cave is refreshing after a long day on the bus, and the locals are happy to sell you drinks or souvenirs for only 20 American dollars—evidence that there remains yet *some* strong degree of paganism!

****

First English translation of the Bible was started by The Venerable Bede about 700 A.D.

WILFORD WOODRUFF'S EMINENT MEN, Part II

This is a continuation of the story involving Wilford Woodruff and departed people demanding their temple work be done. Listed here are the names of the men who either appeared to President Woodruff or were part of the group that had its work done. For the list of women, see page 367. Read this story from the start on page 119.

The "Eminent Men" whose Temple work was performed vicariously following the appearance of the signers of the Declaration of Independence to Wilford Woodruff and his counselors in August 1877 (listed in alphabetical order)—

1. Adams, John (1735-1826), Massachusetts, 2nd US president; signer of the Declaration of Independence
2. Adams, John Quincy (1767-1848), 6th president of US
3. Adams, Samuel (1722-1803), of Massachusetts, signer of the Declaration
4. Agassiz, Louis (1807-1873), brilliant Swiss/American natural ist, firmly anti-evolution
5. Bartlett, Josiah (1729-1795), New Hampshire, signer of the Declaration
6. Bonaparte, Napoleon I (1769-1821), military genius, restored civility and order to France after revolution had spawned anarchy
7. Braxton, Carter (1836 1897), Virginia, signer of the Declaration
8. Brougham, Lord Henry Peter (1778-1768), Scottish parliament member; anti-slavery
9. Bulwer, Edward George Lytton (1803-1873), English, wrote *Last Days of Pompeii*
10. Burke, Edmond (1729-1797), influential political thinker and writer
11. Burns, Robert (1759-1796), Scottish poet; wrote "Auld Lang Syne, Comin Thro' the Rye"
12. Byron, Lord George Gordon (1788-1824), English poet
13. Calhoun, John C. (1782-1850), Vice President, strong advocate of States' rights

Three Latter-day Saints have orbited the earth (that NASA knows of!).

14. Carroll, Charles (1737-1832), of Maryland, last surviving signer of the Declaration
15. Cavour, Count Di (1810-1861), Prime Minister of Sardinia, helped unify Italy
16. Chalmers, Thomas (1780-1847), founder Free Church of Scotland
17. Chase, Samuel (1741-1811), of Maryland, signer of the Declaration
18. Clark, Abraham (1726-1894), of New Jersey, signer of the Declaration
19. Clay, Henry (1777-1852), Kentucky congressman and leader known as "The Conciliator"
20. Clymer, George (1739-1813), Pennsylvania, signer of the Declaration
21. Cobden, Richard (1804-1865), English parliament member who supported tariff-free trade
22. *Columbus, Christopher (1451-1506), credits Holy Ghost with guiding him to discover America
23. Curran, John Filpot (1750-1817), famed Irish orator and trial lawyer; Parliament member
24. Custis, Daniel Park (died 1757), first husband of Martha Custis Washington, George Washington's wife
25. Custis, John Park (1754-1781), son of Daniel and Martha Park Custis
26. Ellery, William (1727-1820), Rhode Island, signer of the Declaration
27. Faraday, Michael (1791-1867), English chemist/physicist who discovered electromagnetic induction
28. Farragut, David Glasgow (1801-1870), Union officer and hero: "Damn the torpedoes! Full speed ahead!"
29. Fillmore, Millard (1800-1874), 13th US president
30. *Franklin, Benjamin (1706-1790), Pennsylvania, signer of the Declaration
31. Frederick II (The Great) (1712-1786), benevolent King of Prussia who Voltaire nicknamed "Philosopher King"
32. Fulton, Robert (1765-1815), American inventor remembered for first steamboat
33. Garrick, David (1717-79), famous English actor of his day

The most rare signatures in the Church are those of the early brethren's wives.

34. Gerry, Elbridge (1744-1814), Massachusetts, signer of the Declaration

35. Gibbon, Edward (1737-1794), wrote *Decline and Fall of the Roman Empire*

36. Goethe, Johann Wolfgang von (1749-1832), German writer, author of *Faust*

37. Goldsmith, Oliver (1730?-1774), Irish writer: *She Stoops to Conquer, Vicar of Wakefield*

38. Grattan, Henry (1746-1820), Irish patriot secured free Irish Parliament and Catholic voting rights

39. Gwinnett, Button (1735-1777), Georgia, signer of the Declaration

40. Hall, Lyman (1724-1790), Georgia, signer of the Declaration

41. Harrison, Benjamin (1726-1791), Virginia, signer of the Declaration

42. Harrison, William Henry (1773-1841), 9th US president

43. Hart, John (1711-1779), New Jersey, signer of the Declaration

44. Hewes, Joseph (1730-1779), North Carolina, signer of the Declaration

45. Heyward, Thomas Jr (1746-1809), South Carolina, signer of Declaration

46. Hooper, William (1742-1790), North Carolina, signer of Declaration

47. Hopkins, Stephen (1707-1785), Rhode Island, signer of the Declaration

48. Hopkinson, Francis (1737-1791), New Jersey, signer of the Declaration

49. Humboldt, Baron Alexander von (1769-1859), German scientist and geographer

50. Huntington, Samuel (1731-1796), Connecticut, signer of the Declaration

51. Irving, Washington (1783-1859), wrote *Rip Van Winkle, Legend of Sleepy Hollow*, others

52. Jackson, Andrew (1767-1845), 7th president of US

53. Jackson, Gen Thomas "Stonewall" (1824-1863), famous Confederate leader, also anti-slavery!

54. Jefferson, Thomas (1743-1826) 3rd president of US, Virginia, signer of the Declaration of Independence

55. Johnson, Andrew (1808-1875), 17th US president

The most rare edition of the Book of Mormon is a first edition in Hawaiian.

56. Johnson, Samuel (1709-1784), famous English writer, wrote *Dictionary of the English Language*
57. Juarez, Benito Pablo (1806-1872), Mexican patriot who set up constitutional govt. and established religious freedom
58. Kemble, John Philip (1757-1823), famous English actor
59. Lee, Francis Lightfoot (1734-1797), Virginia, signer of the Declaration
60. Lee, Richard Henry (1732-1794), Virginia, signer of the Declaration
61. Lewis, Francis (1713-1802), New York, signer of the Declaration
62. Liebig, Baron Justus von (1803-1873), German chemist started organic chemistry; co-discoverer of chloroform
63. Lincoln, Abraham (1809-1865), 16th US president
64. Livingston, Philip (1716-1778), New York, signer of the Declaration
65. Livingstone, David (1813-1873), famous missionary/explorer in Africa, discovered Victoria Falls
66. Locke, Francis, Massachusetts, unable to identify
67. Luther, Martin (1483-1546), started the great Protestant reformation; wrote "A Mighty Fortress is Our God"
68. Lynch, Thomas Jr (1749-1779), South Carolina, signer of Declaration
69. Macauley, Thomas Babington (1800-1859), famous English author of history and *Horatius*
70. Madison, James (1751-1836), 4th US president
71. McKean, Thomas (1734-1817), Delaware, signer of the Declaration
72. Middleton, Arthur (1742-1787), South Carolina, signer of Declaration
73. Monroe, James (1758-1831), 5th US president
74. Morris, Lewis (1726-1798), New York, signer of the Declaration
75. Morris, Robert (1734-1806), Pennsylvania, signer of the Declaration
76. Morton, John (1724-1777), Pennsylvania, signer of the Declaration
77. *Nelson, Lord Horatio (1758-1805), British naval hero who defeated Napoleon's navy

78. Nelson, Thomas Jr (1738-1789), Virginia, signer of the Declaration
79. O'Connell, Daniel (1775-1847), Irish statesman; symbol of Ireland's liberation and emancipation
80. Paca, William (1740-1799), Maryland, signer of the Declaration
81. Paine, Robert Treat (1731-1814), Massachusetts, signer of Declaration
82. Peabody, George (1795-1869), foremost philanthropist of his time; set example of philanthropy which others emulated
83. Penn, John (1741-1788)North Carolina, signer of the Declaration
84. Pierce, Franklin (1804-1869), 14th US president
85. Polk, James K (1795-1849), 11th US president
86. Powers, Hiram (1805-1873), famous American sculptor; most famous work was "Greek Slave"
87. Read, George (1733-1798), Delaware, signer of the Declaration
88. Reynolds, Sir Joshua (1723-1792), famous English painter called "Painter to the King"
89. Rodney, Caesar (1728-1784), Delaware, signer of the Declaration
90. Ross, George (1730-1779), Pennsylvania, signer of the Declaration
91. Rush, Benjamin (1745-1813), Pennsylvania, signer of the Declaration
92. Rutledge, Edward (1749-1800), South Carolina, signer of the Declaration of Independence
93. Schiller, Friedrich von (1759-1805), German writer whose work inspired freedom and dignity among German people
94. Scott, Sir Walter (1771-1832), Scottish author of *Ivanhoe*, and *Waverly Novels*
95. Seward, William Henry (1801-1872), Secretary of State for Lincoln and Johnson; believed in "manifest destiny" of US
96. Sherman, Roger (1721-1793), Connecticut, signer of the Declaration
97. Smith, James (1819-1806), signer of the Declaration from Pennsylvania

Foot breath? Rub garlic on your sole—it will absorb and show up in your breath!

98. Stephenson, George (1781-1848), Father of English railways system; inventor who built "Puffing Billy," and "Rocket"

99. Stockton, Richard (1730-1781), New Jersey, signer of the Declaration

100. Stone, Thomas (1743-1787), Maryland, signer of the Declaration

101. Taylor, George (1716-1781), Pennsylvania, signer of the Declaration

102. Taylor, Zachary (1784-1850), 12th US president

103. Thackeray, William Makepeace (1811-1863), English novelist who wrote "Vanity Fair"

104. Thornton, Matthew (1714-1803), New Hampshire, signer of Declaration

105. Tyler, John (1790-1862), 10th US president

106. Vespucci, Amerigo (1454-1512), famous explorer after whom America is named

107. Walton, George (1741-1804), Georgia, signer of the Declaration

108. *Washington, George (1732- I 799), great leader in US war for independence; 1st US President

109. Washington, John, great-grandfather to George Washington

110. Washington, Sir Henry

111. Washington, Lawrence (1718-1752), brother of George Washington

112. Washington, Augustine (1794-1743), father of George Washington

113. Washington, Lawrence, grandfather of George Washington

114. Washington, Lawrence, unknown namesake

115. Webster, Daniel (1782- 1852), US congressman, helped put off civil war for ten years; Secretary of State

116. *Wesley, John (1703-1791), Episcopal minister, founder of the Methodists

117. Whipple, William (1730-1785), New Hampshire, signer of the Declaration

118. Williams, William (1731-1811), Connecticut, signer of the Declaration

119. Wilson, James (1742-1798), Pennsylvania, signer of the Declaration

In 10 minutes, a hurricane releases more energy than all nuclear weapons combined.

120. Witherspoon, John (1723-1794), New Jersey, signer of the Declaration
121. Wolcott, Oliver (1726-1797), Connecticut, signer of the Declaration
122. Wordsworth, William (1770-1850), famous English poet whose works inspired goodness in people
123. Wythe, George (1726-1806), Virginia, signer of the Declaration, teacher and mentor to the early founders and two presidents

* *Indicates he was ordained a High Priest*

****

GREAT WORDS FOR TROUBLED TIMES

GEORGE W. BUSH speaking to European leaders during a summit meeting: "The world is speaking with one voice when it comes to making sure that democracy has a chance to flourish in Lebanon and throughout the greater Middle East," he said. "Freedom is on the march. It's a profound period of time. So I look forward to continuing to work with friends and allies to advance freedom—not America's freedom, but universal freedom, freedom granted by a Higher Being." —*Washington Times*, March 2, 2005

****

OUR CUPS RUNNETH OVER ...

The Church's main printing press facility in Salt Lake City also produces some of the plastic sacrament cups needed for worldwide distribution.

• In one second, the machine presses 32 plastic cups.

• That's 115,200 sacrament cups in an hour.

• And, in one year, that's 136 million sacrament cups, just barely enough to meet the need!

Okay, one more time: In Casablanca, Humphrey Bogart never said, "Play it again, Sam."

C.S. LEWIS
ONE-LINERS

"Badness is only spoiled goodness."

"Now is our chance to choose the right side. God is holding back to give us that chance. It won't last forever. We must take it or leave it."

"Christ died for men precisely because men are not worth dying for; to make them worth it."

"Every poem can be considered in two ways—as what the poet has to say, and as a thing which he makes."

"The modern idea of a Great Man is one who stands at the lonely extremity of some single line of development."

"Surely what a man does when he is taken off his guard is the best evidence for what sort of man he is."

"In the midst of a world of light and love, of song and feast and dance, [Lucifer] could find nothing to think of more interesting than his own prestige."

"The heart never takes the place of the head: but it can, and should, obey it."

"If God thinks this state of war in the universe a price worth paying for free will ... then we may take it it is worth paying."

"Without the aid of trained emotions the intellect is powerless against the animal organism."

"[God] is not proud ... He will have us even though we have shown that we prefer everything else to Him."

"No doubt those who really founded modern science were usually those whose love of truth exceeded their love of power."

"Tribulations cannot cease until God either sees us remade or sees that our remaking is now hopeless."

"[Pain] removes the veil; it plants the flag of truth within the fortress of a rebel soul."

"Joy is the serious business of Heaven."

Bibliomancy: opening the Bible at random and living that day by the first verse seen.

'X' ALMOST MARKS THE SPOT!

A tour to Israel is the Mormon equivalent of a pilgrimage to Mecca! It's probably second on the list after visiting Carthage, Cumorah and Nauvoo. But do you really get to see the real McCoy when walking "where Jesus walked?"

OUR GUIDE: Helena (249-329 A.D.)
CONTEXT: Constantine (280-337 A.D.) conquered the eastern and western parts of the Roman empire, and made Christianity an official religion of Rome. In 326 A.D. he sent his mother, Helena (probably 76 or 77 at the time), to locate the historical sites of Jesus's life.

PROBLEM: For almost 300 years, the sites where Jesus was born, lived and died were trampled beneath an influx of Roman and pagan construction, activity and fighting. The sites Helena found were not those preserved from the past, but were selected based on tradition and guesses. Helena's sites are worth visiting, but don't forget to sit outside and read the associated scriptures because the events described happened somewhere nearby. 'X' may not mark the spot, but there's a great feeling in this land!

• **THE CHURCH OF THE NATIVITY** in Bethlehem, was dedicated in 339 A.D. and stands over the traditional place where Jesus was born. A gold star marks the "exact spot."

• **CHURCH OF THE DISCIPLES**, or Eleona, was erected on the Mount of Olives in 326 A.D., close by, Helena thought, to where Jesus taught his disciples The Lord's Prayer.

• **GARDEN OF GETHSEMANE**—Helena built a church here in 326 A.D., the site where Jesus prayed. Today's Olive Trees are some of the oldest and largest in Palestine, but neither history nor botany can reveal their age. No one knows if they were razed during the Roman siege of Jerusalem in 70 A.D.

In 1985, an LDS couple gave birth to septuplets (seven).

When the crusaders left, the Christian significance was lost to time. By the 1200s, it was known as the "Flowery Field." By the 1600s, pilgrims described the olive trees there as burnt, uprooted or dead of old age. Today, the place evokes wonderful feelings of oneness with the Savior who, somewhere nearby, did indeed come for fervent prayer. Maybe it was that very place.

• **CHURCH OF THE HOLY SEPULCHER** is actually three churches in one. Constantine built a church over Jesus's tomb, a site "discovered" by Helena. A second church was built over Golgotha where Jesus was crucified, also identified by Helena. A third church was built behind these two where it was claimed the "true cross" was discovered. The three were combined into one called the Church of the Holy Sepulcher.

• **GOLGOTHA AND CALVARY:** *Gulgoleth* is Hebrew for skull. When translated into Latin, it becomes Calvaria, from *Calva* which means skull. And from this comes the English term, Calvary. So, Golgotha and Calvary are two names for the same place.

• **BASILICA OF THE ANNUNCIATION** was built on a site identified by Helena as the place where Jesus ascended into heaven. The latest church to be built there has an open courtyard allowing visitors to see where Jesus was thought to have stood, with an unobstructed view of the heavens above.

• **THE VIA DOLOROSA,** The Way of the Cross, The Way of Suffering, or The 14 Stations of the Cross, is the path, Helena said, that Jesus took on his way to his crucifixion. It includes the places thought to be where Jesus was condemned to death, received the cross, fell under it the first time, etc.

• **MOUNT SINAI:** Venturing into Old Testament territory, Sinai is actually a collection of mountain peaks. In this range is Mount Horeb, and its southern peak is called Jebel Musa, or Mount Moses. Tradition held that this was where God gave Moses the Ten Commandments. Helena had a church known today as The Monastery of St. Catherine built on the foothills.

TOP EIGHT LDS PLACES TO VISIT

1 **THE SACRED GROVE** – Where it all began. Joseph's humble prayer was answered with the power and majesty of Celestial beings visiting him to begin the restoration of God's kingdom in these latter days. Said Joseph, "All I wanted to know was which church to join." Is this the actual place? U.S. Forest Service markers designate existing trees that would have been mature at the time of Joseph's humble prayer.

2. JERUSALEM/CHRIST'S TOMB – We don't know where Jesus was buried. Tradition holds that the popular Garden Tomb is the site, and countless thousands have visited, sung, wept and prayed there. Other scholars dispute the conclusion citing historical and archeological reasons, and place the actual tomb elsewhere in Jerusalem. Regardless, pilgrims there can feel of its spirit, walk where Jesus walked, and return home edified.

3. CARTHAGE JAIL – The place of martyrdom. Joseph and Hyrum Smith were both killed by a mob of about 150 men on June 27, 1844, while confined in the upper room of Carthage Jail in western Illinois. A beautiful visitor's center provides a cool rest from the hot summer heat, with cold water to drink before proceeding out doors for a tour of the actual jail.

4. TEMPLE SQUARE – This monument to inspired leadership and determination remains the largest tourist attraction in Utah and ranks high among all tourist stops in the United States. Visitors can enjoy a walk through the Salt Lake Tabernacle (built 1864-67) where the Saints have gathered for more than 135 years, the Assembly Hall (1877-82) built of cast-off stone from the Temple where smaller services and meetings are held, and around the massive Salt Lake Temple (1853-93)—with its basement and three stories above ground, it is the gleaming jewel among Temples built in these modern days.

Sid Walker bakes more than 10,000 cookies in his kitchen to give away each Christmas.

5. NAUVOO – The "City Beautiful" was Joseph Smith's final earthly effort to unite the American Saints in a single city where peace, freedom and the restored Gospel could grow unfettered. After Joseph's death, the beautiful Nauvoo Temple was destroyed and the city largely abandoned by the Saints. Today, it is coming back. The Temple is rebuilt, the original houses are restored, tourists feed the local economy, and it stands as another monument to the faithful pioneer spirit that runs like a ramrod through the minds and souls of determined present-day Saints.

6. INDEPENDENCE HALL, PHILADELPHIA – Is this a Mormon tour stop? Oh, Yes! Daniel 2 talks about a stone cut out without hands that fills the whole Earth. Some say this is the Gospel, others say it's freedom. The birthplace of the greatest freedom formula on Earth, talked of in the Book of Mormon and the Old Testament, can be visited here in Pennsylvania. It was the founders who gathered in this place to sign our freedom documents who later visited Wilford Woodruff in the St. George Temple asking for their Temple work to be done.

7. CUMORAH – This silent witness to history past and prophecy fulfilled in western New York State was the place where the Book of Mormon plates lay hidden. When the Hill Cumorah Monument was dedicated in 1935, President Heber J. Grant posed for Movietone films in front of a depression dug into the hill, the time-worn remnant of where the plates had once been buried. For decades, the hole was preserved in the middle of the "O" created with shrubs spelling "Cumorah."

8. BRIGHAM YOUNG UNIVERSITY – Never mind the lackluster sports program in recent years (beware you U of U fans!). This world-class university is host to top rankings in almost every category including its Law School, its ability to create, invent and win patents, its academic prowess among schools its size, and a proud ranking as the most stone-cold sober university in America. In the catacombs of its special collections are relics thousands of years old. The famed and famous deposit their papers here, and the nationalities of its 30,000+ students reads like the phone directory at the U.N. It's worth a visit someday!

First temple designed for film rather than live presentation was the Bern Switzerland Temple.

THE BOOK OF PROPHECIES

Between his third and fourth voyages to the Americas, Christopher Columbus wrote a book called the "Book of Prophecies" wherein he declared his divine calling to find the New World. The book reveals an amazingly religious and well-read theologian.

BOOK: "Libro de las profecias," known as the *Book of Prophecies*, by Christopher Columbus.
WRITTEN: 1501-1502, and largely ignored for 460 years.
THE ORIGINAL: Resides in Spain in the Biblioteca Colombina at the Cathedral of Seville.

TRANSLATED INTO ENGLISH: Two translations published in 1991—one by Kay Brigham (Barcelona, Spain), and the other by Delno C. West and August Kling (Gainesville, Florida); both books are quoted below.

CONTENT: More than 200 biblical and religious passages compiled by Columbus.

STORY: Columbus had found the New World. It came at the cost of hard and amazing work, plus a few lucky accidents, but he made it. When he returned from his third voyage he wrote down those things closest to his heart that he had been saving since each of his prior risky ventures. In the end, he offered the book to King Ferdinand and Queen Isabella—a personal collection of letters, scriptures, quotations from Biblical scholars, and more. The book was written in four parts: an introduction followed by "Concerning the Past," "Concerning the Present and Future," and "Concerning the Future In the Last Days."

SAID LEHI, "And I looked and beheld a man among the Gentiles which were separated from the seed of my brethren by the many waters; And I beheld the Spirit of God, that it came down and wrought upon the man; And he went forth upon the many waters, even unto the seed of my brethren which were in the promised land." 1 Nephi 13:12

SAID COLUMBUS, "Our Lord opened to my understanding (I could sense his hand upon me), so that it became clear to me that it was feasible to navigate from here to the Indies; and he unlocked within me the determination to execute the idea ... Who doubts that this illumination was from the Holy Spirit? I attest that he [the Spirit], with marvelous rays of light, consoled me through the holy and sacred Scriptures ... encouraging me to proceed, and, continually, without ceasing for a moment, they inflame me with a sense of great urgency." (Brigham 1991:179)

HOLY GHOST: "Who can doubt that this fire was not merely mine, but also the Holy Spirit who encouraged me with a radiance of marvelous illumination from his sacred Scriptures, ... urging me to press forward?" (Libro de las profecias, p. 105)

A NEW EARTH: "God made me the messenger of the new heaven and the new earth of which he spoke in the Apocalypse of St. John after having spoken of it through the mouth of Isaiah; and he showed me the spot where to find it." (Ibid)

PROPHECY FULFILLED: "For the execution of the journey to the Indies I was not aided by intelligence, by mathematics or by maps. It was simply the fulfillment of what Isaiah had prophesied." (Ibid)

GATHERING OF ISRAEL: "[Columbus related the writings of Abbot Joachim who] taught that ... there would be ... an age of restoration and renewal for the kingdom of Christ" and that "the restorer of the House of Mt. Zion would come out of Spain." (Ibid)

OTHER SHEEP: Columbus included John 10:16 in his Book of Prophecies: "I have other sheep that are not of this sheep pen [fold], and I must bring them also; they will hear my voice, and there shall be one flock and one shepherd." Brigham points out

Columbus believed the flock would not just be "Israel after the flesh" but that a "spiritual Israel" would result from all who came unto Christ. (Brigham 1991:208-9, 264-5)

LAST DAYS: Columbus calculated that "there are but 155 years left for the fulfillment of the seven thousand [years from creation] ... at which time ... the world will come to an end. Our Savior said that before the consummation of this world, all that was written by the Prophets must be fulfilled." (Brigham 1991:181).

MORE PROPHETIC EVENTS: Columbus wrote that with many prophecies fulfilled, there were many that "remained yet to be fulfilled ... great events for the world." (West and Kling 1991:111)

GOSPEL TAUGHT WORLD-WIDE: "I believe that there is evidence that our Lord is hastening these things. This evidence is the fact that the gospel must now be proclaimed to so many lands in such a short time." (West and Kling 1991:111)

SHORT TIME LEFT: Writing in retrospect of his discovery, he said, "The sign which convinces me that our Lord is hastening the end of the world is the preaching of the gospel recently in so many lands." (Brigham 1991:183)

AN OTHERWISE VERY RELIGIOUS MAN: He was "an exceptionally pious man," writes historian Delno C. West. "Throughout his journals and letters, we find him constantly in prayer, invoking the names of Christ, Mary, and the Saints and solemnly giving praise to God."

And, according to his son Ferdinand, "He was so strict in matters of religion that for fasting and saying prayers he might have been taken for a member of a religious order."

****

97% of all earth's water is salty. Of the remaining 3%, 2/3rds of it is locked up in the ice.

HEAVYWEIGHT MORMONS

HEAVIEST HOUSE CAT: Sneaky the Cat, owned by the Alma Didra family in 1990, put on weight fast. By 1992, the cat's weight fluctuated from 39 to 55 pounds, a world record heavy weight ... but he never got the "heaviest" crown because at weighing time, Sneaky had snuck off too many pounds.

HEAVYWEIGHT BOXING CHAMP: Jack Dempsey took the world heavyweight crown when he knocked out Jess Willard in 1919 and defended it until the infamous "long count fight" with Gene Tunney in 1926. Dempsey was not active in the Church but was proud of his Mormon roots. Before he died in 1980, he starred in 16 movies, most often as himself.

HEAVIEST MURAL: A huge mural painted by Harvey Jackson, elders quorum counselor in Gillette, Wyoming, is the heaviest in the Church at 16 tons. Mounted on the side of a large steel building, the mural measures 56 feet tall and 220 feet wide, and is made of 286 panels weighing 112 pounds each. The mural depicted western themes and took 2 years to create.

HEAVIEST LOAD MOVED BY WAGON. In 1874, the Saints had the chore of moving the baptismal font built in Salt Lake City to its new home in the St. George Temple. Several teams of oxen were needed to haul the 18,000-pound load.

HEAVIEST LOAD MOVED BY TRUCK. Stanley Jones, San Jose 13th Ward, San Jose California Stake, moved the largest legal load in American history in November 1979 when he transported a 107-ton magnet 2,200 miles from Illinois to Palo Alto, California.

PROPHETIC CONSTITUTION

The U.S. Constitution is the greatest freedom document ever put to paper. If the Saints are to bear it away from destruction, we'd better get with it. Here's a start.

THE LORD: "I established the Constitution of this land, by the hands of wise men whom I raised unto this very purpose." (D&C 101:80)

ABRAHAM LINCOLN: "Let [the Constitution] be taught in schools, in seminaries, in colleges; let it be written in primers, spelling-books, and in almanacs; let it be preached from the pulpit, proclaimed in legislative halls, and enforced in courts of justice. And, in short, let it become the political religion of the nation."

JOSEPH SMITH: "Even this nation will be on the very verge of crumbling to pieces and tumbling to the ground, and when the Constitution is upon the brink of ruin, this people will be the staff upon which the nation shall lean, and they shall bear the Constitution away from the very verge of destruction." (July 19, 1840)

THE LORD: "I, the Lord, justify you, and your brethren of my church, in befriending that law which is the constitutional law of the land." (D&C 98:6)

THE LORD: "May those principles, which were so honorably and nobly defended, namely, the Constitution of our land, by our fathers, be established forever." (D&C 109:54)

BRIGHAM YOUNG: "How long will it be before the words of the Prophet Joseph will be fulfilled? He said if the Constitution of the United States were saved at all it must be done by this people." (*Discourses of Brigham Young*, p. 360)

Something to write home about: About 100 people choke to death on ballpoint pens annually.

BRIGHAM YOUNG: "When the Constitution of the United States hangs, at it were, upon a single thread, they will have to call for the 'Mormon' elders to save it from utter destruction; and they will step forth and do it." (*Discourses of Brigham Young*, p. 361)

DAVID O. MCKAY: "Next to being one in worshiping God, there is nothing in this world upon which this church should be more united than in upholding and defending the Constitution of the United States." (*Instructor*, 1957 91:34)

BRIGHAM YOUNG: "I expect to see the day when the elders of Israel will protect and sustain civil and religious liberty and every Constitutional right bequeathed to us by our fathers, and spread these rights abroad in connection with the gospel for the salvation of all nations. I shall see this whether I live or die." (*Discourses of Brigham Young* p. 361)

BRIGHAM YOUNG: "[The Constitution] is a progressive—a gradual work"; the founders "laid the foundation, and it was for after generations to rear the superstructure upon it." (*Journal of Discourses* 7:13-15)

JOHN TAYLOR: "When the people shall have torn to shreds the Constitution of the United States the elders of Israel will be found holding it up to the nations of the earth and proclaiming liberty and equal rights to all men." (*Journal of Discourses* 21:8)

EZRA TAFT BENSON: "I should like to pay honor—honor to the document itself, honor to the men who framed it, and honor to the God who inspired it and made possible its coming forth.

"For the past two centuries, those who do not prize freedom have chipped away at every major clause of our Constitution until today we face a crisis of great dimensions.

"The God of heaven sent some of His choicest spirits to lay the foundation of this government. And he has sent other choice spirits to preserve it."

10% OF OUR BRAIN?

How many times have you heard we only use ten percent of our brains? That idea is 100 percent laughable.

MYTH: People only use 10 percent of their brain power. **ORIGINS:** Unknown. In the late 1700s and 1800s, scientists debated whether or not basic functions of the brain were localized to certain parts of the brain.

EXPERIMENTS: In 1929 a researcher reported that rats could still solve mazes and make visual discriminations with only 2 percent of a fiber connecting parts of the brain used for such tasks. He also found that with 58 percent of the cerebral cortex removed, the rats showed no decline in the ability to learn certain tasks.

Somewhere in all of this, the idea that most of the brain is unused emerged and found popular support.

RECENT REPETITIONS:
• ABC television advertised a fall season lineup with the caption, "Men only use ten percent of their brains."
• National ads for *Satellite Broadcasting* showed a brain with the caption, "You only use 11 percent of its potential."
• Bryant Gumbel interviewed on prime-time television a psychic who said untapped psychic and intuitive powers lay hidden in everyone's "80-90 percent" of the subconscious mind.

VARIATIONS: Some purveyors of the myth convince people that the brain is neatly divided into the conscious and subconscious, be that a 10-90 split, 30-70 or 50-50. Even when shown evidence to the contrary, so deeply imbedded is this myth that some will dismiss the obvious activity as evidence of subconscious or random computations busy providing the ten percent of the conscious part with all the support it needs.

PET TO THE RESCUE:
PET scanning (positron emission tomography) is one of several modern tools used to map brain activity. Since their invention,

scientists have known that people use all of their brain. As people don't use every muscle at any given second, neither is the entire brain used at any given second. Some parts of the brain are used for particular tasks, but over the course of the day, the entire brain is well used and, for many of us, often feels well tired.

OTHER PROOFS

A person who has had a stroke or severe brain injury is often severely impaired. If only a small portion of the brain was really used, traumatic brain damage would be no more debilitating than having tonsils removed. People use 100% of their brains!

Thanks to psychologist Benjamin Radford, managing editor of the Skeptical Inquirer, *for helping us get back our lost 90 percent brain power with this information.*

****

A little girl and her mother went shopping in a very large mall one afternoon. After being in a major store for some time, the little girl grew tired and sat down on the floor to wait for her mother to finish the shopping. While she watched the people moving around her, the little girl's mother moved on to another part of the department, not knowing that the little girl didn't follow her. Soon the little girl realized that her mother was no where to be seen and she started to cry. One of the clerks soon heard her and came to ask her why she was crying. The little girl sobbingly told her that she had lost her mommy. The clerk took her by the hand, and they set out to find the lost mommy. After a few minutes had gone by the clerk had an idea. She asked the little girl if she thought that her mommy would recognize her voice, and the little girl nodded her head. The store clerk took her to the counter and lifted her up so that she could reach the microphone for the store PA system. The clerk told her to talk into the mike, and her mother would hear her voice and come to get her. The sweet little girl held the mike close to her face and with tears running down her cheeks and a sob in her voice she said, "I would like to bear my Testimony...."

HUGH NIBLEY

We've all heard the name and perhaps read a book or paper of his, but who is this man? Here's a snapshot of a great life.

SELF DEFINITION: "I call myself an observer," he said in his last interview on Sept. 22, 2004. "What we're doing in this life is observing; we came into this life to get experience."

LDS MISSION: Germany

EDUCATION: Studied in California, and finished his doctorate at the University of California, Berkeley.

MILITARY: Master sergeant (military intelligence) for the 101st Airborne Division of the U.S. Army during World War II. He participated in the D-Day invasion on Omaha Beach, and visited the liberated Nazi concentration camps.

LANGUAGE FLUENCY: Aramaic, Arabic, Coptic, Dutch, Egyptian, French, German, Greek, Hebrew, Italian, Latin, Old Norse, Russian, and other languages at sight.

LANDMARK RESEARCH: Nibley's research covered Egyptian, Hebrew, and early Christian histories; he was one of the earliest scholars to examine the Book of Mormon as an ancient document.

NOTE TAKING: Nibley's notes are a mix of Gregg shorthand, Arabic, Hebrew, Greek, and Egyptian.

REPUTATION: "Defender of the Faith," a title shared only with LDS historian and leader B. H. Roberts.

POPULAR WORKS: Nibley's vast assortment of writings have been compiled into 14 volumes. These include *Lehi in the Deseret*; *Since Cumorah*; *Abraham in Egypt*; responses to anti-Mormon literature such as Fawn M. Brodie's *No Man Knows My History*, which was titled *No Ma'am, That's Not History*; and thousands more.

340

FAVORITE STORY: (from the last interview of he and his wife) *How did you two meet?*

[Sister Nibley] "By the time he was finished with the war (1946), and ready to go back to teaching, Hugh went to the Church offices. Brother Widtsoe offered Hugh a position at Brigham Young University and then said, 'But you need to be married.' So, Hugh said, 'All right, if you arrange it so the first girl I meet on campus be my intended wife, I'll do it.' He came to BYU in June after the term had ended, and the campus was almost empty. He came looking for a room and I was working in the housing office, so he asked me for addresses. So, I was the first girl he met. ... He asked me to go on a picnic with him, we took walks together, ate dinner together in the cafeteria, and he asked me to marry him and we got married in September before Fall term started." They raised a great family of 8 children.

HIS DRIVING FORCE:
What does it take to feed your hunger for knowledge?
[Brother Nibley] "The Spirit. The Spirit tells you where you're supposed to go. If the Spirit tells you you're supposed to go to Egypt, you go there."

SCHOLARLY WORKS collected in several big books (so far!):
Vol. 1: *Old Testament and Related Studies*, 1986
Vol. 2: *Enoch the Prophet*, 1986
Vol. 3: *The World and the Prophets*, 1987
Vol. 4: Mormonism and Early Christianity, 1987
Vol. 5: *Lehi in the Desert/The World of the Jaredites/There Were Jaredites,*1988
Vol. 6: *An Approach to the Book of Mormon*, 1988
Vol. 7: *Since Cumorah*, 1988
Vol. 8: *The Prophetic Book of Mormon*, 1989
Vol. 9: *Approaching Zion*, 1989
Vol. 10: *Ancient State: The Rulers & the Ruled*, 1991
Vol. 11: *Tinkling Cymbals and Sounding Brass: The Art of Telling Tales about Joseph Smith and Brigham Young* (includes *No, Ma'am, That's Not History*), 1991
Vol. 12: *Temple and Cosmos: Beyond This Ignorant Present*, 1992
Vol. 13: *Brother Brigham Challenges the Saints*, 1994
Vol. 14: *Abraham in Egypt*, 2000

A hamlet is a village without a church; a town is not a city until it has a cathedral.

THE BRETHREN SAID IT!

Part VIII

All is not always sober and somber at the podium.
For more, see page 383.

Walking into a clothing store, the tall and skinny J. Golden Kimball asked the clerk, "I'd like to see a suit that will fit me." Replied the clerk, "So would I."

"POLITICS REMINDS ME very much of the measles. The measles don't hurt much if you will take a little saffron tea or something to keep them on the surface, but if they once set in on you, they turn your hide yellow and often make you cross-eyed. So don't let politics set in on you."—*Heber J. Grant*

"WE WENT on a six weeks' trip through the southern part of the state. We held two or three meetings each day. At Kanab conference I listened to Brother Francis M. Lyman for a long time. Then I dozed off and had a dream. I dreamed I was falling over a cliff one hundred feet high. I wondered how long it would be before I hit the bottom. Finally I landed stretched out on the platform, helpless and discomfited before four hundred people. Brother Lyman turned and said, 'Young man, you have ruined one of my best sermons.' It cured me of sleeping in church."—*J. Golden Kimball*

"I HEARD A MAN SAY that he did not care what was said, against this people, he was ready to believe it."—*Ezra T. Bensen*

"I AM READY to confess that I am keyed up to a pretty high tension, and the only thing I am afraid of is that I will say just what I think, which would be unwise, no doubt."—*J. Golden Kimball*

"ANOTHER OF HIS LURID TALES was to the effect that the Mormon men killed off their old wives by giving them a strong alkali drink which destroyed them gradually, thus making way for younger wives, recruited through the labors of the missionaries. Needless to say, alkali was not the only kind of lie used in his statement."—*Orson F. Whitney*

CAFFEINE, PART II

*Let's settle it once and for all: is it okay to drink caffeinated
sodas, yes or no? Here's how some of the brethren
have been voting over the years.*

FROM THE PRIESTHOOD BULLETIN for February
(1972) "With reference to cola drinks, the Church has
never officially taken a position on this matter, but the
leaders of the Church have advised, and we do now specifically
advise, against the use of any drink containing harmful habit-
forming drugs under circumstances that would result in acquir-
ing the habit. Any beverage that contains ingredients harmful to
the body should be avoided." (*Church News,* February 12, 1972)

PRESIDENT HEBER J. GRANT – YES___ NO ✓
"I am not going to give any command, but I will ask it as a
personal, individual favor to me, to let Coca-cola alone. There
are plenty of other things you can get at the soda fountains
without drinking that which is injurious. The Lord does not
want you to use any drug that creates an appetite for itself."
(*Conference Report*, April 1922, p.165)

BISHOP H. BURKE PETERSON – YES___ NO ✓
"We know that cola drinks contain the drug caffeine. We
know caffeine is not wholesome nor prudent for the use of our
bodies. It is only sound judgment to conclude that cola drinks
and any others that contain caffeine or other harmful ingredients should not be used." (*New Era*, Oct. 1975)

ELDER BRUCE R. MCCONKIE – YES___ NO ✓
"There are many other substances which have a harmful
effect on the human body, though such particular things are not
specifically prohibited by the Word of Wisdom. Certainly the
partaking of cola drinks, though not included within the measuring standard here set out, is in violation of the spirit of the
Word of Wisdom. Harmful drugs of any sort are in a like category." (*Mormon Doctrine*, p. 845)

The Eucalyptus can grow 35 feet in one year; the Sika Spruce can grow 11 inches in 98 years.

PRESIDENT SPENCER W. KIMBALL – YES___ NO ✓

"Generally when we speak of the Word of Wisdom, we are talking about tea, coffee, tobacco, and liquor, and all of the fringe things even though they might be detrimental are not included in the technical interpretation of the Word of Wisdom. I never drink any of the cola drinks and my personal hope would be that no one would. However, they are not included in the Word of Wisdom in its technical application. I quote from a letter from the secretary to the First Presidency, 'But the spirit of the Word of Wisdom would be violated by the drinking or eating of any-thing that contained a habit-forming drug.' With reference to the cola drinks, the Church has never officially taken any attitude on this but I personally do not put them in the class as with the tea and coffee because the Lord specifically mentioned them [the hot drinks] ... I might say also that strychnine and sleeping pills and opium and heroin are not mentioned in the Word of Wisdom and yet I would discourage them with all my power." (*The Teachings of Spencer W. Kimball*, p. 202)

BISHOP VAUGHN J. FEATHERSTONE – YES___ NO ✓

"Speaking of those who rationalize the Church's stand on cola drinks, Bishop Featherstone said, 'We can find loopholes in a lot of things if we want to bend the rules of the Church.'" (*The Church News*, Conference Issues 1970-1987, p.9)

ELDER SAMUEL O. BENNION – YES___ NO ✓

"I heard President Grant say, recently, that he would consider it a favor to him, if men and women would abstain from the use of tea and coffee, tobacco, liquor, and Coca-cola; that they would have power given them to establish themselves in the faith, and save themselves from debt, sickness, and disease. And he read from the revelations, that the destroying angel would pass them by; and he is a prophet of God." (CR, April 1922, p.140)

ELDER JOHN A. WIDTSOE – YES___ NO ✓

"Whenever a drink is advertised to 'give you a lift,' the 'lift' is likely to be caused by the drug which it contains. Such soft drinks are decidedly harmful and habit-forming, even though sold by the millions. Such caffeine-containing drinks, offered by

If ice did not float, oceans and lakes would fill up with ice and all life would die.

every soda fountain and most eating places, and consumed in large quantities, should be known and avoided." (*The Word of Wisdom: A Modern Interpretation*, p.97)

ELDER MARK E. PETERSON – YES___ NO _✓_

"And then there are some soft drinks which contain harmful or habit-forming ingredients. The leaders of the Church have not attempted to add to the list of prohibitions in the Word of Wisdom to include all such items, but they teach that in the spirit of the Word of Wisdom, if not in the letter, we should avoid anything which contains ingredients which are harmful and habit forming." (*A Word of Wisdom*, p.15)

ELDER WIDTSOE, PART II – YES___ NO _✓_

"The poison caffeine is not confined to China tea leaves and coffee berries. ... It should be well remembered that caffeine in cola drinks is more harmful than in coffee." (explanation given) (*Gospel Interpretations*, pg. 177-178)

"The result of the investigation furnishes another evidence against the use of caffeine in any form. It also adds evidence as to the correctness of the 'Word of Wisdom,' which advises against such 'hot drinks.'" (Ibid, pg. 186)

"Intelligent, devoted Latter-day Saints will refrain from using anything which injures the body, and is, therefore, contrary to the spirit of the Word of Wisdom. The attempt to justify the use of beverages, found harmful by modern investigation, because they are neither tea nor coffee, is quibbling." (Ibid, pg. 181)

KNOWN PROBLEMS connected to the casual use of caffeine or the excessive use of caffeine:
- Can cause allergic reactions
- Can cause arrhythmia (irregular heart beats)
- Can increase incidence of breast cysts
- Can impair fertility
- Increases risk of heart disease
- Increases risk of miscarriages
- Possible link to birth defects
- Can contribute to panic disorder
- Worsens symptoms of thyroid disease

About 1,800 thunderstorms are raging at any given moment, day or night.

SWORD OF LABAN

What became of the famous Sword of Laban talked about in numerous places in the Book of Mormon?

SPEAKER: Brigham Young in Davis County to dedicate a stake
DATE: June 17, 1877 (see *Journal of Discourses*, vol. 19, p. 38)

Brother Brigham said: "I tell these things to you and I have a motive for doing so. I want to carry them to the ears of my brethren and sisters, and to the children also, that they may grow to an understanding of some things that seem to be entirely hidden from the human family. Oliver Cowdery went with the Prophet Joseph when he deposited these plates. Joseph did not translate all of the plates; there was a portion of them sealed, which you can learn from the Book of Doctrine and Covenants. When Joseph got the plates, the angel instructed him to carry them back to the Hill Cumorah, which he did.

"**OLIVER SAYS** that when Joseph and Oliver went there, the hill opened, and they walked into a cave, in which there was a large and spacious room. He says he did not think, at the time, whether they had the light of the sun or artificial light, but that it was just as light as day. They laid the plates on a table; it was a large table that stood in the room. Under this table there was a pile of plates as much as two feet high, and there were altogether in this room more plates than probably many wagon loads; they were piled up in corners and along the walls.

"**THE FIRST TIME THEY WENT THERE** the sword of Laban hung upon the wall; but when they went again it had been taken down and laid upon the table across the gold plates; it was unsheathed, and on it was written these words: 'This sword will never be sheathed again until the kingdoms of this world become the kingdom of our God and his Christ.' I tell you this is coming not only from Oliver Cowdery, but others who were familiar with it, and who understood it. ... I take the liberty of referring to those things so they will not be forgotten and lost."

In 1860, "Godey's Lady's Book" told women to cook tomatoes a minimum of 3 hours.

FIRST EDITIONS

Does your family have any first editions in the family library?
You do now with Brother Paul's Mormon Bathroom Reader *book.*
But that's nothing compared to today's Mormon
memorabilia market.

THE BOOK OF MORMON—1830
In 1830, a first edition of The Book of Mormon could be bought for $1.25. And if you really wanted it badly, you could probably get a copy for free from Brother Joseph. With some 500 or so copies known to exist out of the original 3,000 printed, the price among rare book traders has grown from $5,000 in the 1980s to $82,000 for an exceptionally clean version in 2004.

THE BOOK OF COMMANDMENTS—1833
This little book was made valuable by its scarcity. The two dozen or more copies that were salvaged after the mob destroyed the Saint's printing press in Independence, Missouri, were actually assembled and bound by hand. The brethren had planned to print several thousand, and had it gone to market, it probably would have sold for less than a dollar. In 1987, one of these books sold for $32,000, and by 2001, another sold for $391,000.

THE DOCTRINE AND COVENANTS—1835
After the loss of the original Book of Commandments, the brethren regrouped and expanded the work to include additional revelations (100 total), the *Lectures on Faith*, and the minutes of the first High Council on February 17, 1834, and the General Assembly of August 17, 1835. Of the 1,000 copies originally printed that were sold for $2.00 apiece, there are only about 50 complete copies known to exist. A beautifully preserved copy sold in February 2005 for $210,000.

THE PEARL OF GREAT PRICE – 1851
Published by Elder Franklin D. Richards in Liverpool, England, this short book was to support new converts who

asked for more information about the Church they just joined. It included "Selections from the Book of Moses," "The Book of Abraham," Joseph Smith's corrections to Matthew 24, "A Key to the Revelations of St. John" (now D&C 77), other revelations given to Joseph Smith (all or parts of D&C 20, 27, 87, 107), the thirteen articles of faith, and the poem "Truth" that later became the LDS hymn "Oh Say, What Is Truth?" The Pearl of Great Price originally sold for $2.10, but a first edition copy sold among rare book collectors in 1999 went for $32,000.

JOSEPH SMITH TRANSLATION OF THE BIBLE (JST)

The Prophet Joseph Smith began making inspired corrections, additions, deletions, rearrangements and other fixes to the King James Version of the Bible beginning in 1830. By 1833, he had completed the majority of his work, though he continued working on it until his death. The Reorganized Church of Jesus Christ of Latter-day Saints published the complete version in 1867. In all, Joseph added or changed 3,410 verses in the Old and New Testaments. A first edition, second printing of JST recently sold for $1,200 in 2004.

****

"Professor Heber S. Goddard is now teaching me to sing, Who's on the Lord's side, Who?' I do not know how many months it will take him, but I propose to learn it some day, whether it takes six months or six years. ... From the standpoint of a singer, I have lost thirty-three years of my life. I was told when ten years old that I could never learn to sing. I did not learn until forty-three years of age, and I have spent four or five months trying to learn to sing the hymns, 'God Moves in a Mysterious Way,' and 'O My Father.' I have learned one because of the sentiments and my love for the author, and the other because the late President Wilford Woodruff loved it better than any other hymn in the hymn book. Now all singers say it is a mistake to speak before you sing, and therefore if I do not sing very well, it is because I spoke first."—*Heber J. Grant*

The Angel Moroni faces west on the Seattle, Nauvoo, and Taipei Taiwan temples.

MORONI'S PROMISE!

PART V

*More famous people who received a copy
of the Book of Mormon.*

R EADER: Sir Winston Churchill (1874-1965)
DATE: August 1954
CIRCUMSTANCE: Sir Winston Churchill was at his
400-year-old country estate when Elders G. Edwards Baddley
and Rodney H. Brady stopped by as escorts to a visiting digni-
tary. At the appropriate time, they presented Churchill with a
handsome leather-bound triple combination. Churchill
thumbed through the volume and thanked the givers by raising
his glass and making a toast to their good health.

READER: Queen Elizabeth and Prime Minister Margaret
Thatcher
DATE: July 24, 1987
CIRCUMSTANCE: At a commemoration of the 150th anniver-
sary of the first Church missionary work in Great Britain,
President Wendell J. Ashton of the England London Mission,
along with other Church representatives, presented to aides of
Queen Elizabeth and Prime Minister Thatcher a modern
quadruple combination of the LDS scriptures and a replica of
the Book of Mormon that was given to Queen Victoria in 1841.

READER: Elvis Presley (1935-1977)
DATE: Unknown
CIRCUMSTANCE: Elvis received at least two copies of the
Book of Mormon. The first from his newly befriended body
guard, Ed Parker, a member of the Church in Pasadena,
California. The other was handed to him through the gates of
his Graceland mansion. He read them, underlined passages, and
made marks in the margins. One of the books eventually ended
up in the Church archives in Salt Lake City.

To read more about Moroni's Promise, see page 393.

A single drop of water contains one hundred billion billion atoms.

IT'S THE LAW!

Every community in America has its share of silly laws, some that are pretty goofy and astounding. Here are a few collected from around and about Utah—all legally of course.

NUCLEAR WEAPONS: In Utah, you may own a nuclear weapon, apparently, but you better not try to detonate it or you could be faced with a severe fine, possibly jail time, too, if any are left. The law says that causing a catastrophe is definitely a felony.

BIRD CROSSING: The Beehive State also demands a courteous yield to birds crossing the road. Take special care if their beaks are stuffed with crickets.

FISHING: It is against the law to fish from horseback, but accordingly, it is probably okay to fish from a camel or giraffe (or even a curelom or cumom).

MARRIAGE: It sounds as if the point of no return is age 50, because an interpretation of a Utah law says that when a person reaches the age of 50, he/she can then marry their cousin. Just don't try to have kids (like that's going to be easy).

DANCING: If you live in Monroe, don't dance too close to your sweetie, because local law demands there must be daylight visible between partners on a dance floor.

BOXING: Those mouth guards are important safety fixtures, apparently, to prevent biting, because opponents engaged in any full-contact fighting that by rule allows biting their opponent are subject to a fine and jail time.

ALCOHOL: Nothing silly about restricting these "spirits" in Utah. On the books are laws stating no booze allowed in an area of declared emergency (nothing more funny than a drunk rescue worker); for retailers, no beer is allowed in containers

Hard night? Ancient Egyptians slept on pillows of stone.

larger than two liters or with an alcohol content of more than 3.2 percent may not be sold; and restaurants may serve wine with meals, but the customer must first ask for the wine list.

ANIMALS: The law is very specific here—it is unlawful to tease, molest, annoy, disturb or otherwise irritate an animal on its owner's property unless you are a cop or dog catcher. So, if you're mad at your cat, call a cop and have him bring a lot of rubber bands and Scotch tape.

AUCTIONS: Salt Lake is pretty strict about people holding auctions and attempting to draw crowds. Any attempt to interest shoppers to crowd the street or sidewalk is illegal, and by definition outlaws the hiring of trombone players.

COWS: Ogden doesn't mess around when it comes to Mrs. Moo. A city resident may have no more than one cow on his or her property, and the barn had better be clean or you could be fined.

CURSING: It's pretty clear that the use of assorted and offensive language is unfortunately common place all over television, school yards, and at fast food emporiums. But don't mess with the bus—it can cost you a fine and/or jail time if you cut loose with a bad word on our public conveyances. And Brother Paul is just nerdy enough to applaud this law.

WOMEN: Speaking of foul language, falsely accusing a woman of being unchaste is slander and punishable by up to six months in jail and a fine of $1,000. But on the flip side, if a woman commits a criminal act in the presence of her husband, he is responsible. Hey, wait a second, how does that work again?

AND AMONG THE SAINTS IN IDAHO:
- No merry-go-round riding on Sunday, it's a crime.
- Gift chocolate or candy had to weigh 50 pounds or more!
- No grouchy faces in public; it's against the law.
- In 1912, no concealed weapons unless they could be seen.
- Do not sweep dirt from your house into the street—it's illegal.
- And *never* sleep in a dog kennel; it's the law.

MORMON MYTH BUSTERS, Part IV

Brother Paul continues his debunking of popular LDS legend and lore. *To read more, see page 412.*

CLAIM: Our youth were Generals in the War in Heaven
STATUS: False
STORY: The rumor goes that a leader of the Church supposedly said at a temple prayer meeting that today's youth were generals in the pre-existence, and that one day eternal beings would worship the youth, who would fall into hushed silence of respect when they learn that such youth lived during the times of President Gordon B. Hinckley. This statement was typically attributed to President Boyd K. Packer, but sometimes to President Monson, Elder Eyring, or Elder Maxwell.

On April 28, 2001, President Packer issued an official statement saying he didn't say this, nor did any other Church leader, and, furthermore, he doesn't believe what it says at all!

CLAIM: The face of Christ in a painting was recognized by a girl
STATUS: False
STORY: Another rumor states that Del Parson went to the brethren with several drafts of his painting of Christ, and the efforts were rejected because they didn't reflect the true face of Christ. Furthermore, the finished work supposedly was recognized by a little girl who identified the man in the painting as He who watched over her when her folks died in a car crash.

Brother Parson says it's typical to have artwork commissioned by the Church reviewed several times before completion, but in no way was it because they wanted a near-photographic image of the Savior. And, the whole "little girl" story is pure fabrication.

CLAIM: Catholic priest prophesies restoration in 1739
STATUS: Unverifiable
STORY: The LDS urban legend typically begins with, "The fol-

The original name for butterfly was flutterby.

lowing was written by a Catholic priest by the name of Lutius Gratus. It is in a book called *Hope Of Zion*, written in the year 1739. This book can now be found in the library at Basel, Switzerland." And then the priest supposedly tells that the old true gospel was lost, false doctrine filled the earth, and that an angel would return within a hundred years to restore the truth, that his followers would build a great city but be driven out to the shores of a great lake, etc.

This legend apparently appeared in LDS periodicals in both English and German in 1893. Efforts to find the book or any other details have failed.

CLAIM: Jaredite Barge found in Lake Michigan
STATUS: False
STORY: On January 25, 1999, *The Chicago Tribune* published an article about a mysterious object found on the bottom of Lake Michigan. "If one set out with the preposterous goal of making an oak zeppelin 31 feet long, ten feet in diameter, pointed at its ends, complete with an 18-inch hatch to crawl inside, this is pretty much what they'd get. Those who have strapped on air tanks and visited the thing say the craftsmanship used to build it is remarkable--four-inch-thick oak boards bent and fitted together and caulked watertight, like nothing built today." The rumor among LDS was that this was a long-lost "Jaredite barge" and the "proof" of the Book of Mormon spread like lightning! The object was later identified as a floating fuel tank built in the 1940s.

CLAIM: Patriarchal Blessing for a Downs Syndrome child
STATUS: False
STORY: Supposedly shared during Stake Conference that children with Downs Syndrome were those who escorted Satan out of heaven, and because of this treasonous act, Satan swore vengeance on them during their earthly lives. Downs Syndrome was given to such as a protection through their earthly lives.

First, patriarchal blessings are never shared from the podium, even "with permission." Second, Heavenly Father didn't need anybody's help kicking Satan out of His kingdom! This is a nice story, but it has no prophetic or factual foundation.

The first pioneers into Salt Lake brought 17 dogs.

WHERE WE GOT 'EM: THE BOOK OF ABRAHAM

Finding the Book of Abraham is the closest to a real-life Egyptian-buried treasure story as we'll get. It all began in the hot desert near Luxor, Egypt.

Our story begins with a mystery man named Antonio Lebolo. He apparently was an adventurous sort and managed to take pretty good care of himself in dangerous situations. For example, when Napoleon occupied Italy in the early 1800s, Lebolo managed to stay safe by serving as a French officer in the emperor's military police. This backfired when Napoleon was driven out, and Lebolo was threatened with prison. He chose voluntary exile and fled for Egypt—and a new line of work.

NOT THE GOLDEN AGE OF TREASURE!
Egypt wasn't a bad place to be in those days. In fact, there was an active industry of excavating ancient and lost Egyptian artifacts and mummies. Lebolo became the supervisor of some profitable excavations near ancient Thebes—today's Luxor. The tomb raiders of those days were certainly no learned archeologists. They were looters. And with their trade came plenty of fierce competition, thievery, and sometime violence. They stole what they could, sold it to European museums, and went back for more. Documents prove Lebolo was there in 1820-1830 as a buried treasure hunter, and that he had a reputation for finding well preserved papyri documents buried with assorted mummies.

STRIKING IT POOR
On June 7, 1831, Lebolo and his crew of 422 diggers struck it rich, or so they thought. They found an opening into a massive catacomb. Stepping carefully into the darkened cavern, Lebolo was disappointed to see about 300-400 mummies. He had hoped

for a solitary king or queen with all their accumulated riches surrounding a sarcophagus in resplendent glory.

ENTERING PIT TOMB 33

As Lebolo and his crew crawled through the mass of mummies, crushing a body here, a pottery jug or jar there, he surveyed the collection and noticed about 100 caskets upright in niches, buried after the manner of the first order. Only eleven of these were in good enough shape to be moved, and off they went by ship to France. Call it the mummy's curse, or just a bad case of tomb dust, but something made Lebolo sick on his trip to Paris. He put in at Trieste to rest up, but after ten days, he died. It was February 19, 1830.

MAKING MONEY FROM MY MUMMY

Lebolo had authorized a friend to sell the mummies in his behalf, and the cargo was shipped to New York City. Proceeds from the sale were supposed to go to Lebolo's heirs. Now our story gets a little murky as we meet Michael H. Chandler.

CHANDLER WHO?

Where and how Chandler fits in has not been clearly established. An Italian man in Philadelphia was hired to sell the mummies in the U.S., and somehow, somewhere, Michael H. Chandler came into possession of them. The story goes that Chandler was Lebolo's nephew, but this has not been proven. Chandler opened the mummies and found ancient papyri and writings in black and red ink. This could be a real money-maker, Chandler thought, so he worked hard to find buyers. BYU professor H. Donl Peterson found proof of this hard work when he located 61 newspaper advertisements for the "Chandler exhibits" in Philadelphia alone. For two years, Chandler sold off the mummies one at a time.

FINDING JOSEPH SMITH

When Chandler arrived in Kirtland, Ohio, he was down to four mummies. Recognizing the potential value of the ancient papyri, two members of the Church—Joseph Coe and Simeon

---

Fitness expert Paddy Doyle did more than 2,400 pushups in one hour—one-armed!

Andrews—contributed $800 of the $2,400 purchase price. Other Church members contributed the rest.

WHY SUE AN INNOCENT MAN?
Did Chandler really come by the mummies honestly, and was he really Lebolo's nephew? Nobody knows, but Brother Peterson found evidence that Chandler was hounded by lawsuits after the mummies were sold. One lawsuit was filed in the same county where Kirtland is located. Apparently, the suits didn't catch up with Chandler because he bought a nice farm in Parkman, Ohio, and raised a family of 12 children. He died there in 1866.

SURPRISE, IT'S ME!
Meanwhile, the papyri was delivered to the Prophet Joseph Smith in 1835. With W.W. Phelps and Oliver Cowdery as scribes, Joseph began translating the first set of papyri. It began, "In the land of the Chaldeans, at the residence of my father, I, Abraham..."—Joseph and the brethren were elated. The writings of Abraham! The second scroll appeared to be a continuation of the first and contained the writings of Joseph who was sold into Egypt. Of this second scroll, Parley Pratt recorded that it described the creation, the fall, the Godhead, the pillars of Enoch (mentioned only in Josephus, not the Bible), the great flood, patriarchs, ten tribes, and events of the last days. William S. West later interviewed Joseph and published a pamphlet on the upcoming book, saying it would be a big book, perhaps the size of the Old Testament.

PUTTING IT ALL TOGETHER
Joseph's translation of the Abraham papyri is today's Book of Abraham. Mob action prevented him from translating the Book of Joseph, and after his death, the scrolls were apparently left behind in Nauvoo as the Saints fled. It was thought the papyri were destroyed in the great Chicago fire of 1871. But in 1967, a scholar looking through ancient manuscripts at the New York Metropolitan Museum of Art stumbled on a few of the papyrus manuscripts, including Facsimile No. 1, which is reproduced in the Pearl of Great Price.

Animators claim: You'll see 6,469,952 black spots when you watch "101 Dalmations."

MORE MORMON INVENTIONS

INVENTION: World's First Traffic Light
INVENTOR: Lester Farnsworth Wire
STORY: In 1912, a Salt Lake City traffic cop invented the first electric red-green traffic light. He hoisted it atop a pole at an intersection in downtown Salt Lake, and operated it by hand from the curb. The large box looked a lot like a birdcage and each side was 20-square inches. The yellow light didn't come for several years later when it was realized that people needed reaction time when trying to stop for the red light.

INVENTION: World's First Television
INVENTOR: Philo T. Farnsworth
STORY: Philo came up with the idea of television while plowing crops on his parent's Idaho potato farm. Looking at the long furrows gave him the idea of breaking an image into a long string of signals sent through the air and repainted on a screen of some sort. On Sept. 7, 1927, Farnsworth demonstrated his invention to one of his financial backers. His creation included a camera tube and a television receiver, both inventions of his. When the first faint, foggy image appeared to move (it was a piece of glass with a scratch in the middle), his amazed witnesses heard the humble Philo simply say, "There you are—electronic television." There are more than 1 billion television sets or monitors in the world today.

INVENTION: Audio communications
INVENTOR: Harvey Fletcher
STORY: Brother Fletcher's insights into communications were powerful yet simple. Having invented the first real hearing aid, stereophonic sound and more, he said this in his timeless text, *Speech and Hearing*: "The processes of speaking and hearing are very intimately related, so much so I have often said that we speak with our ears. We can listen without speaking but cannot speak without listening. People who are born without hearing learn to talk only with the greatest difficulty, and none of them has yet succeeded in producing what most of us would call nor-

mal speech." And with this simple philosophy, he gave the world of sound to the deaf and a world of rich enhanced sound to the hearing.

INVENTION: Hawaiian or Pedal Steel Guitar
INVENTOR: Alvino Ray
STORY: Brother Ray was born in California and married into the famous King Sisters singers. He had a huge following during the big band era. His innovations before World War II led to the electric guitar and pedal steel guitars widely used today.

INVENTION: The magnetic toy, Wheelo
INVENTOR: Harvey Job Matusow
STORY: Brother Matusow was toying around with some magnets one day and invented what he first called his "stringless yo-yo." It was an appropriate name, too, because during the 1950s, the yo-yo was one of the fastest selling toys, and Matusow's stringless version was right behind it. The toy is a looped wire track with a spinning wheel on a magnetic shaft. It continues to sell today, more than 50 years after its introduction to America.

INVENTION: Anti-lock Brakes
INVENTOR: Andrew K. Watt, co-inventor
STORY: Brother Watt spent years in research to take advantage of a problem that the car industry was dealing with: the fact that a skidding tire let a car slide farther than if the brakes were hit intermittently. This seemed to work on both dry and wet pavement. His original ideas were developed over the years as the forerunner of today's anti-lock brakes.

INVENTION: Scrapbooking
INVENTOR: The Mormons
STORY: It's really tough to say who started the scrapbooking craze that has spread around North America for the past decades, but many credit the LDS Church. The reason? The Church's emphasis on genealogy and keeping journals. In an effort to encourage the Saints to keep journals, various creative minds began to make journal keeping a craft project. A few enterprising members enlarged the ideas into small businesses and suddenly—WHAMO! Scrapbooking became a huge nation-wide hobby with craft stores stocking all kinds of paper, shape cutters, scissors, stamps, glue-ons, stick-ons—you name it!

A cheetah at full speed takes strides of more than 30 feet.

"KILL NEPHI!"

These guys were bad. Laman and Lemuel, with help from Ishmael's kids, were out to kill that young whipper-snapper Nephi, and they nearly succeeded four times.

AS RECORDED in I Nephi, Lehi sent his boys back to Jerusalem for the family of Ishmael. The trip went fairly well until, during the return trip, Laman and Lemuel and a couple of Ishmael's daughters and sons began to clamor and complain. Whine, whine, whine. Too hard, no water, crummy food, smelly camels, fleas, bugs, hot weather, we wanna go home. Nephi pled with them to stay faithful, but that just made them more mad. They wrestled Nephi down, bound him with cords, and left him to be devoured by wild beasts. The Lord loosened his cords and he was freed. (See I Nephi 7:16-17)

SHORTLY AFTER NEPHI'S STEEL BOW BROKE and a new one was made, Ishmael died. All the bad people started complaining again and plotted to kill Lehi and Nephi "who has taken it upon him to be our ruler and our teacher, who are his elder brethren." The Lord sent words of reason, calmed them down, and Nephi was spared again. (See I Nephi 16: 37)

DURING THEIR BOAT VOYAGE to the Americas, Laman and Lemuel bound Nephi with cords, swearing again that he would never be a ruler over them. When the ball or compass (Liahona) stopped working and they were driven back 3 days, they were humbled and let Nephi go. (See I Nephi 18:11-12)

AFTER LEHI'S DEATH, Laman and Lemuel had had it with Nephi and his words of repentance. Their anger grew to the point that they were ready to murder him, especially now that dad was dead. They refused to let Nephi rule them, believing that the rightful rulers should be the eldest brothers. The Lord told Nephi to take his families, plus Sam, Jacob and Joseph, and Zoram, and flee into the wilderness. Nephi brought with him the sword of Laban, the brass plates, and the ball or compass. When Laman and Lemuel found Nephi and his friends all gone, and all the good loot taken, they were pretty angry. And so began 1,000 years of bloody warfare. (See 2 Nephi 5)

Can you read this? In 1780, Benjamin Franklin invented bifocal lenses for glasses.

MORMON COLLOQUIALISMS

We Latter-day Saints have our own lexicon of words and phrases that mean little to an outsider. Here's a sampling.

COLLOQUIALISM: Informal words, phrases or pronunciations that reflect a locale or culture.

SPECIAL – In 1225 A.D., it originally meant "better than ordinary," or having distinguishing qualities. It became part of LDS lore and culture when well-meaning adults applied it to the more valuable inner traits of a youth who otherwise suffered with obviously negative outward traits. *Special Spirit* was rudely abused to refer to an overweight or otherwise unattractive Sister. Shame on you elders who might have used that while serving in northern Belgium during, say, about 1974-1975 ... ahem.

HUMP DAY – In 1901, the word *hump* applied to a mound in a railway yard over which the cars had to be pushed. This is probably the origin of its meaning as a critical point or juncture during a process. Hence, a missionary's *hump day* is his half-way point. This is, perhaps, the very worst day for an old girl friend to call long distance and encourage her elder along for his last remaining whole, entire, 12-month, 52-week, 365-day year.

DUNKED – The Pennsylvania Dutch used the word to mean *dip*. More modern LDS missionaries might use it casually to mean baptize. In 1756, an American-German Baptist group was called the *Dunkers* because they triple-baptized their converts.

INVESTIGATOR – To *investigate* means to track or trace the footprint. The word dates to at least the days of Columbus. To the missionaries, an *investigator* is a contact who is anxiously tracking the footprint of the gospel and needs tender loving care during this important journey.

STICKS – Missionary slang for their scriptures. It makes reference to the Stick of Judah and the Stick of Joseph, the idea being that their records were written on scrolls and rolled on rods, shafts, poles or sticks.

TESTIMONY – From the Latin *testis,* meaning to witness, and *monium* meaning action, state, or condition. It also meant "the Ten Commandments" as used in the Vulgate version of the Bible. For Latter-day Saints, it's an irrefutable heart-felt message that something is true (gain a *testimony* or have a *testimony*), and to bear a *testimony* is to put that belief and knowledge into words and share it with others.

STORIMONY – Relating a *story* that is primarily of very personal interest or more suitable for a speech, under the guise of bearing a real testimony. "And then the king said to the pauper, 'It was good of you to move that rock, because now my treasure is yours....'"

TRAVELMONY – Bragging about a recent trip, usually one that nobody else can afford, during fast and testimony meeting. "I know that the spirit was there on that Sabbath morning on the sunny, wind-swept deck of our luxury cruise ship during our 28-day boat trip to New Zealand and all of those lovely surrounding islands, populated with thousands of converted villagers ...."

PRAYERALOGUE – Unlike a monologue when a person simply speaks solo to a crowd, a *prayeralogue* is a stolen opportunity to give one of the meeting's keynote speeches disguised as the opening/closing prayer. These can go on for 6, 7, maybe ten minutes. High Priests have been known to doze off before the end.

MORMON STANDARD TIME – At least 5 minutes but not more than 15 minutes late arrival or delayed start time for meetings and gatherings. Its invention is unknown, although thought to have originated either for the accommodation of large families with 8 or more children, or with the advent of the first female teenager whose dawdling in the bathroom is blamed on her discovery of the alluring impact of makeup on the otherwise unappreciative Aaronic Priesthood brethren. Circa late-1870s.

INACTIVE IS WORSE

Why do some people fight so hard against the Church when they drop out? Why not just leave it alone and move on? Research shows they'd live longer if they did!

ACCORDING to some fascinating research performed at the University of Utah Medical Center, it appears active LDS and non-LDS may be healthier than less-active LDS.

In other words, you're better off "hot" or "cold" rather than "lukewarm."

DR. JOSEPH L. LYON was an associate professor in the Division of Epidemiology and Biostatistics in the Department of Family and Preventative Medicine at the University of Utah's School of Medicine at the time this study was made.

Over a period of several years, Dr. Lyon and his colleagues compiled research data on LDS and non-LDS in Utah, their risk of infant mortality and their risk of developing cancer, strokes or heart disease.

Among their amazing conclusions—

INFANT DEATHS: 4.1 per thousand among active LDS.
7.8 per thousand among non-LDS.
20.5 per thousand for inactive LDS.

LOW BIRTH WEIGHT: 31 per thousand among active LDS.
58.4 per thousand among non-LDS.
63.7 per thousand among inactive LDS.

LUNG CANCER: 85 percent less likely among active LDS.
26 percent less likely among non-LDS.
17 percent less likely among inactive LDS.

KIDNEY CANCER: 29 percent less likely among active LDS.
39 percent less likely among non-LDS.
64 percent MORE likely among inactive LDS.

WHO SAYS "INACTIVE"?

"Determining Church activity was very difficult," Dr. Lyon said, adding the only real way to determine that was to look at men's progression through the ranks of the priesthood.

Said Dr. Lyon: "From baptism to deacon, teacher, priest, elder, missionary, temple marriage and high priest, we had seven or eight checkpoints over a large number of years to confirm activity in the Church."

TOUGHER TO FIND "INACTIVE" WOMEN

Among the women, no such Priesthood-progress comparison with advancement existed.

"We looked for those (women) baptized and later married in the temple," Dr. Lyon explained. "Sometimes we found women who had served missions, but this number was too small to significantly alter the data. And sometimes, extremely active women had not yet married."

As a result, he had to rely heavily on obituary notices and other sources to determine the level of activity.

"The Church was very helpful," Dr. Lyon says. "We would submit the names of cancer patients from the Utah Cancer Registry, and the Church would link them up with their membership records. They sent back numbers indicating how many were members, their ages and other significant information (marriage, ordinations, etc.), without revealing individuals' names."

BE SMART, DON'T DEPART!

Dr. Lyon gave one possible explanation for the data. He speculated that many who leave the Church often abandon it for its strict life-style requirements. To prove that they are no longer under the rigid supervision of so many commandments, meetings, and expectations, Dr. Lyon looked at the tendency of inactives or dropouts to go overboard with their new independence. Many will start drinking and smoking in excess, and engaging in unsafe life styles just to prove, "I'm free!" In reality, the statistics show an apparent fatal difference between those who haphazardly exceed the life styles of LDS and non-LDS who have learned to deal with life's vices with a level of prudence, restraint and wisdom.

At age 57, George Washington had all his teeth pulled.

363

THE MYSTERY OF DESERET

PART II

On page 15 we talked about the beehive in Utah and Mormon culture. But what triggered this whole curious question about Deseret and the honeybee? It's a connection you won't bee-lieve!

SCHOLARS in and out of the Church have uncovered a great mystery about bees. It's a neat journey that starts before the founding of Egypt. Take a look:

IN THE BEE-GINNING
Egypt's first pioneer settlers came from Babylonia and brought with them a culture that had secrets. The most important of these secrets was symbolized in the honeybee. In fact, there seems to have been an entire "cult of the bee" in early Egypt that was super secret. But the bee was more than secret, it was sacred.

• **RESURRECTION:** The bee, they believed, was the preserver and restorer of life. Bees coming out of dead animals was a sign of the resurrection. Do bees build hives in road kill? In Judges we read that Samson "turned aside to see the carcase of the lion: and, behold, there was a swarm of bees and honey in the carcase ... he took thereof in his hands, and went on eating [the honey]."

• **RESTORER:** After cataclysmic destructions or desolation, the Egyptians believed it was the bee that went forth to invigorate the land and get the cycles of life going again by pollinating plants and making honey—the food of the gods.

• **MIGRATIONS:** The honeybee was also seen as the helper on great migrations. Ancient tradition from the Hittites tells of honeybees going with Adam and Eve out of the Garden into the dreary world because the bees had lived there and knew their way around. This departure of Adam and Eve was viewed as the first of all migrations, headed up by our friends the honeybees.

First white woman buried in Salt Lake Valley: Caroline Grant, wife of Jedediah M. Grant.

- **CHRISTIANITY:** So pervasive was this culture of the honey-bee and its connection to amazing things such as a resurrection of the dead that even St. Jerome in 384 A.D. expressed puzzlement that come Easter time, Christians were always swarmed with amazing bee stories. Why bee stories, he wondered?

SO, WE HAVE THE EGYPTIANS using the bee just about everywhere but refusing to talk about it openly. It was a sort of double talk. Take a look at these interesting efforts to avoid the super secret yet keep it out in plain sight:

- The first land settled in Egypt was named "the land of the bee," and has been so known since then. The hieroglyph associated with that was the image of the bee.

- Although the bee was super important, the Egyptians intentionally refused to provide its name in writing. It was left "unreadable," according to scholars. Is that strange? Not terribly so. The Jews, for example, avoid the actual name of God in print and use YHWH instead of writing out Jehovah, or they'll simply use "Adonai."

- However, we get a hint of the bee's name from another image they often used in place of the bee – a red crown. This is so very interesting! Look at old hieroglyphics and you'll be surprised that you can identify this crown on numerous images.

- The red crown had an antenna sticking up from it, symbolic of the bee. The crown's name was "Deshret." (Say this part slowly, say it out loud. Deshret sure sounds like Deseret to Brother Paul!). This name comes from research by Egyptologists who attempted to give expression to the actual Egyptian alphabetic letters that accompany the red crown, which are "dsrt."

- Kings of Lower Egypt wore the red crown as their emblem of power. This wasn't to say they were bees, but rather that they were after the order of the bee. When Upper and Lower Egypt were united under one king, his "unspeakable" association with the cult of the bee became more public in his official title: "he who belongs to the sedge and the bee."

Cheery thought: There are seven suicides mentioned in the Bible.

SO, WHAT'S SO SECRET about the bee that the Egyptians won't even say its real name, and when alluding to its role in power and authority, they replace it with a Red Crown which they do indeed talk about as "Deshret"? Very suspicious. Maybe we can find the reason.

THE LADY IN CHARGE!

The book of Abraham explains that Egypt was first discovered and settled by a woman named Egyptus and her sons (Abr. 1:23-24). From the Egyptologists, we're told that the founding woman in Egypt was named Lady Neith. If these two gals are one and the same, then our first Egyptian leader, the true Queen Bee, is the actual namesake for Egypt after all!

If she founded Egypt, then it was she who gave the land its name (Egypt), and it was she who brought the cult of the bee to this land and gave it to the kings that followed her to protect and pass along. And it was she who gave power to the government along matriarchal lines. In the ancient Egyptian imagery, we see Lady Neith wearing the red crown, the sign of the bee—Deshret.

TO BEE OR NOT TO BEE

All of this detail may be too much information for one sitting, but it is provided for one purpose: to show that when Joseph Smith presented the Book of Abraham, he gave us a *real* Egyptian word he did not know (DESERET), a *real* definition he did not know (honeybee), a *real* place in time for this word that he could not have guessed (pre-Abraham), and placed it *precisely* in the Old World portion of the Jaredites' journeys, not in their travels to the new world. And with a few simple sentences out of Ether 2:3 and Abraham 1:21-27, Joseph Smith amazingly linked together Egyptian religion, myth, cult, ritual, imagery and history that in his day was simply unknown by anybody anywhere. Almost makes you think he really might possibly just have perhaps received divine help to translate ancient records ....

For more information, see Kerry A. Shirts' article "To Bee, or Not to Bee" (do an Internet search), and Hugh Nibley's "Lehi in the Desert and the World of the Jaredites."

JEALOUS BROTHER

In Gospel Doctrine class, Brother Paul's former Bishop posed this question about the Prodigal Son: "I've always wondered," he asked, "why the brother who stayed home was jealous?"

PARABLE: The Prodigal Son

CONTEXT: Jesus sits at supper with known sinners, drawing mocking criticism from the Pharisees who are watching. Jesus responds with three parables: the lost sheep, the lost piece of silver and the lost son—the prodigal son.

SUMMARY: A son demands of his father his inheritance. He spends it on months of wild living. Having exhausted all, he crawls home starving and impoverished. The father embraces his boy, slays the fatted calf and celebrates his return. The other son who remained faithful at home is jealous of all the attention.

JOSEPH SMITH COMMENTS: All three parables speak of the joy that comes when something lost is found again. But only in the Prodigal Son parable is the Pharisees' hypocrisy addressed—they are represented in the eldest son. The sinners are represented in the prodigal son. And the Lord is represented in the father.

MIXED MESSAGE: The sub plot in this parable, that of the jealous brother, illustrates that hypocrisy is as serious as blatant sin. The prodigal son came forward, humbled, confessing and was welcomed back. The jealous brother, appearing otherwise faithful, righteous and obedient to inherit Father's kingdom, exposes his flaw when he demonstrates his jealousy. Were he all that he appeared to be, were he converted as his father, he would have been joyful and full of love towards his brother. Although jealousy is natural, it can't be excused. The natural man is an enemy to God—always has been, always will be, the Lord said.

GNAWING AT HYPOCRISY: The genius of the prodigal son message as it was delivered to the Pharisees, and now to us, is that it's not about just one son gone astray, it is about two sons gone astray—one publicly, the other in his heart.

The largest hailstone ever recorded: 17.5 inches in diameter—larger than a basketball.

WILFORD WOODRUFF'S EMINENT WOMEN, Part III

An amazing event involving Wilford Woodruff happened in 1877. In part III, we list the names of the women who either appeared to President Woodruff, or were part of the group that had its temple work done. The list of men is on page 319. Turn to page 119 to read this story from the start.

The "Eminent Women" whose temple work was performed vicariously following the appearance of the Signers of the Declaration of Independence to Wilford Woodruff and his counselors in August 1877 (listed in alphabetical order). There were 73 in all.

1. Antoinette, Marie (1755-1793), wife of Louis XVI
2. Armour, Jean (1767-1834), of Scotland, wife of Robert Burns (1759-1796)
3. Austin, Jane (1775-1817), first great English novelist
4. Ball, Mary (1707-1789), mother of George Washington
5. Barnard, Sarah (1800-1879), wife of Michael Faraday
6. Bronte, Charlette (1816-1855), author of Jane Eyre; her sister Emily wrote "Wuthering Heights"
7. Browne, Felecia Dorothea (1793-1835), poet
8. Browning, Elizabeth Barrett (1806-1861), wife of Robert Browning
9. Burney, Francis "Fanny" (1752-1840), of England, Madam d'Arbley
10. Butler, Jane (died 1728), wife of Augustine Washington
11. Caldwell, Martha (died 1802), wife of Patrick Calhoun, parents of John C. Calhoun
12. Calvert, Eleanor, (1757-1811), wife of John Parke Custis (1757-1781)
13. Carpenter, Charlotte Margaret (1770-1826), wife of Sir Walter Scott
14. Charlotte, Princess (1717-1797), daughter of Leopold I (Belgium) and wife of Maximilian, emperor of Mexico

15. Corday, Charlotte (1768-1793), heroine of French revolution, and died by guillotine
16. Creagh, Sarah (1750-1817), wife of John Philpot Curran
17. Custis, Martha Park (1755-1773), daughter of Martha Washington
18. Dandridge, Martha (1732-1802), wife of George Washington
19. Donelson, Rachel (1767-1828), wife of Andrew Jackson
20. Dykes, Elizabeth (1795-1865), wife of Thomas Moore
21. Eastman, Abigail (1737-1816), wife of Daniel Webster
22. Eden, Mary Ann (died 1865), wife of Henry Lord Brougham
23. Edgeworth, Maria (1767-1849), famous Irish novelist,
24. Elizabeth, Christina (1715-1797), wife of Frederick II (1712-1786)
25. Fackrell, Maria, unable to identify
26. Fairfax, Anne, wife of Lawrence Washington, unknown dates
27. Fitzgerald, Henrietta, unknown dates
28. Fletcher, Grace (1781-1828), betrothed to Washington Irving
29. Ford, Sarall (1769-1859), wife of Samuel Johnson
30. Fuller, Sarah Margaret (1810-1850) of Massachusetts
31. Gibbs, Mrs Elijah, unable to identify
32. Gurney, Elizabeth (1780-1845), English, daughter of John Gurney; married to a "Fry"
33. Henderson, Francis (1768-1805), England
34. Herbert, Frances (1758-1831)
35. Hoffman, Matilda, (1791-1809)
36. Hopkins, Priscilla, (1755-1845)
37. Huntley, Lydia (1791), Connecticut, unable to identify
38. Hutchinson, Mary (1770-1859), wife of William Wordsworth
39. Judson, Emily Chubbuch (1817-1854), New York, can't identify
40. Junkin, Eleanor (1825-1854), first wife of "Stonewall" Jackson
41. Kemble, Sarah, wife of Roger Kemble, mother of 12, many of whom became famous actors/actresses
42. Landon, Lititia Elizabeth (1802-1838), English poet/novelist
43. Lingefeld, Charlotte Von (1766-1826)
44. Livingston, Sarah Van Bough (1757-1802), New York, wife of John Jay
45. Locke, Francis (1811-1849)

Thank you! Insulin was discovered in 1922 by Frederick Banting and Charles Best.

46. Maria, Theresa (1717-1780), archduchess of Austria and daughter of Emperor Charles VI
47. Mazza, Margarita (1826-1871)
48. Melbourne, Emily Mary (1787-1869), wife of Lord Palmerston
49. Milbanke, Anne Isabella (1792-1860), wife of Lord Byron
50. Mitford, Mary Russell (1787-1855), from England
51. Morgan, Layd Sydney (1780-1859), Irish, famous novelist and wife of Sir Thomas Charles Morgan, a surgeon
52. Murphy, Anna (1794-1816), Ireland, unable to identify
53. More, Hanna (1745-1833), English, unable to identify
54. Nugent, Jane, (1734-1812)
55. O'Connell, Mary (1775-1836), wife of Daniel O'Connell
56. Packenham, Lady Catherine (1727-1831), wife of Duke of Wellington
57. Parepa, Euphrosyne, (1836-1874), famous opera singer
58. Parepa, Countess Demetricus (1815-1870), mother of Euphrosyne
59. Payne, Dorothy (1772-1849), North Carolina, can't identify
60. Philipse, Mary (1728-1822), English patriot, friend of George Washington
61. Pope, Ann, wife of John Washington, great grandfather of George Washington
62. Sedgewick, Catherine Maria (1789-1867), possibly wife of Gen. John Sedgewick, Union Army
63. Shawe, Isabella (1818-1894), wife of William Thackeray
64. Siddons, Sarah Kemble, (1755-1831); English actress, John Phillips Kemble's sister
65. Smith, Abigail (1744-1818), wife of John Adams
66. Somerville, Mary Fairfax (1780-1872), Scottish, mathematician, scientist
67. Veigel, Eva Maria, (1724-1822), wife of David Garrick (1717-1779)
68. Vulpius, Christiane, (1764-1816), wife of Goethe (1749-1832)
69. Warner, Mildred (died 1701), mother of Augustine Washington grandmother of George Washington
70. Washington, Mrs. Henry
71. Wayles, Martha, (1748-1782), wife of Thomas Jefferson
72. Bushrod, Hannah, wife of John Washington
73. Washington, Mrs Lawrence (not same as other Lawrence)

MORMON PRIMER ON ISLAM

Shove aside the radical extremists and terrorists claiming allegiance to Islam, and there remain hundreds of millions of Muslims with family-friendly values that are surprisingly similar to Mormonism.

RELIGION: Islam
ADHERENTS: Muslims (or Moslems)
HOLY BOOKS: Koran, an Arabic word meaning "reading" or "recital"
FOUNDED: 610 A.D. when Muhammad (570-632 A.D.) received a revelation from God to preach religion.
ISLAM: Arabic for "to submit" to God.
MUSLIM: Arabic for "one who submits to God."

BACKGROUND: At age 40, a Saudi Arabian merchant and businessman named Muhammad was visited in a cave in 610 A.D. by an angel who instructed him to write down the words of God. This dictation continued for another 23 years. The hundreds of principles, commands, and prohibitions Muhammad wrote down were later put into one book that was not to be translated into any other language because followers believed it was the direct and unalterable word of God to mankind.

• **TO READ THE KORAN,** converts had to learn Arabic. This became a huge unifying force that finally brought together thousands of scattered bedouins and tribesmen, all speaking with one voice—and once unified they became a feared and powerful force in the Middle East and Mediterranean areas.

• **BY 710 A.D.,** Islam had spread like wildfire among Arab cultures. Their armies conquered most of the Middle East as far as Morocco and Spain. It spread eastward to India and Central Asia, and then Indonesia and the Philippines. The great Ottoman empire kept them in charge of the Holy Land up until the 1800s.

- **THE HOLY LAND:** First called the *Land of Canaan* by Abraham, it was named the *Promised Land* by Moses. The Romans called it *Palestine*. Today we call it *Israel*, named after Jacob's title he received from the Lord. Local Jews call themselves Israelis, and local Arabs call themselves Palestinians.

- **COMMON ANCESTOR:** The Arabs descended from Abraham. God's promise to Abraham that his seed would number as the stars in heaven found a humble fulfillment through Hagar, Sarah's handmaid, who gave birth to Ishmael. A squabble between Hagar and Sarah forced Abraham to send Hagar and Ishmael off into the desert. Ishmael grew, married, had twelve sons, and these people became the nations now known as the Arabs. Muhammad is a descendent of Ishmael, and considered by Muslims to be the last prophet from God to give His message to mankind.

- **KORAN:** Also spelled qur'an, the Muslims' holy book is the size of the New Testament and is divided into 20 portions, one to be read each day of the month of Ramadan. Smaller sections called "prayers" or "surahs," have short introductions and a title such as "The Poets," "The Cow," or "The Bee." The Koran contains many of the same stories found in the Bible.

- **THEIR EQUIVALENT TO OUR 13 ARTICLES OF FAITH** is called the Five Pillars of Islam: (1) Belief in the one True God; (2) Prayer offered five times a day; (3) Every year give money and help to the poor; (4) During the month of Ramadan, fast from food, drink and evil desires from sunup till sundown; (5) visit Mecca at least once in your lifetime.

- **PRACTICES:** no pork, eats only kosher type meats; prays five times daily; dresses modestly (women especially are covered up); no alcohol, drugs, or pornography; seeks good educations strives to be kind to others regardless of others' beliefs; respects all forms of work; sees marriage as God-given and a spouse is always for life; all good performed for the betterment of others is a form of worship of God.

In 2000, Utahns ate an average of 6.3 gallons of ice cream per person.

- **THE BIBLE:** Muslims believe Adam was the first prophet followed by others such as Noah and Abraham; Isaac was the first of many true prophets in the Jewish line, including Moses, David and Jesus; Jesus is the second-to-last prophet, and Muhammad is the very last.

- **A FEW WORDS:** *Allah*–the one true God; *Mosque*–an Islamic place of worship; *Jihad*–means "to struggle" towards closeness with God, also means "holy war" to defend the faith; *Ramadan*–the ninth month set aside for fasting; *Salah*–the prayers given five times daily; *Zekah*–a tithing or charity given annually to the poor; *Al-Hajj*–a pilgrimage to Mecca.

- **TODAY** there are 1.3 billion Muslims in the world: Asia has 780 million, Africa 310 million, and Europe 32 million.

- **POPULATION IN THE U.S.:** About 6 million Muslims total: 20 percent live in California, 16 percent in New York, 8 percent in Illinois.

- **PROFESSIONS IN THE U.S.:** Ten percent are in engineering and computers; 8 percent are in medicine; 4 percent are in finance.

- **BUILDINGS:** In the U.S., Muslims have about 3,000 Islamic centers, mosques and prayer locations; 200 Muslim schools; six schools of Islamic higher learning.

- **IN COMPARISON,** there are—Christians: 2 billion
    Hinduism: 900 million
    Secular/Nonreligious/Agnostic/Atheist: 850 million
    Buddhism: 360 million
    Chinese traditional religion: 225 million
    primal-indigenous: 150 million
    African Traditional & Diasporic: 95 million
    Sikhism: 23 million
    Juche: 19 million
    Spiritism: 14 million
    Judaism: 14 million

HOW DID MOSES DEAL WITH MURDER?

Was it really "eye for an eye and tooth for a tooth"?

The Law of Moses made a lot more sense than people give it credit. Most people only know it by the slogan "An eye for an eye, and a tooth for a tooth." And many folks believe that under the Law of Moses, if you poked out your neighbor's eye, your punishment was to lose yours. What good is that to have two half-blind men walking around?

DON'T MESS WITH THE LORD'S LAW

Obviously the half-blind man can't get his eye back, but the guilty party can be forced to make satisfaction. How? With money. And the money went to the victim, not the court or state (as it is today). The money was to compensate the victim for his loss. If the offender refused to pay, or fell behind in his payments, he did so at the risk of losing his own eye, tooth, or whatever.

SO, LET US ALL REPEAT TOGETHER, what the law of Moses really taught was "The value of an eye for an eye, and the value of a tooth for a tooth."

WHAT IF NO SATISFACTION IS POSSIBLE?

For murder, there can be nothing (no money) that will satisfy the Lord and justice short of the life of the murderer. The Lord declared in Numbers, "Moreover ye shall take no satisfaction for the life of a murderer, which is guilty of death: but he shall be surely put to death." (Num 35:31)

WHAT ABOUT MURDER and accidental homicide? The law clearly distinguished between premeditated killing and accidental homicide. There were four types of homicide problems that the Law of Moses covered:

The Mexico City Mexico Temple is the largest outside of the United States.

MURDER: This is the premeditated, deliberate killing of another. The penalty was death. No amount of "satisfaction" could ameliorate the crime of murder: "He shall surely be put to death." A murder conviction had to be on the testimony of two or more witnesses, otherwise the matter must wait on God's judgment.

The victim's nearest kinsman had the responsibility of bringing the murderer to trial and avenging his death.

ACCIDENTAL HOMICIDE: The accidental killing of another was not punishable.

If the victim's kinsman accused the accidental killer of murder, then the latter was to flee to the altar of the temple or to a city of refuge where he was to remain until he could have a fair trial. He had to be returned to the city where the killing occurred for his trial. If he were found innocent of deliberate homicide (murder) but the kinsman would not believe the findings of the judge, then the accused was to be sent back to the city of refuge and remain there until the High Priest died.

CITY OF REFUGE
Once assigned to a city of refuge he was not allowed to give "satisfaction" to the avenger of blood in order to return home before the high priest died. It was felt that he might be tricked. However, if he wandered from the city of refuge before the appointed time and was slain, the kinsman would not be punished because the accused had violated the limits of his sanctuary. After the high priest died the accused could return to his own city and the avenger of blood or kinsman had to leave him unmolested. The application of this law was the same for "strangers" as it was for Israelites.

EXCUSABLE HOMICIDE: "If a thief be found breaking up [into a building], and be smitten [at nighttime] that he die, there shall no blood be shed for him." In other words, it is considered excusable.

"If the sun be risen upon him, there shall be blood shed for him." To kill a person in broad day light was not excusable because the thief could be identified and apprehended with much greater facility than at night.

UNSOLVED MURDERS: In order to preserve the sanctity of human life, the Lord required that every murder be treated as a major issue whether the perpetrator were found or not. In those cases where "it be not known who hath slain him," the elders of the city nearest to the place where the body was found were required to take a heifer into "a rough valley, which is neither eared nor sown, and shall strike off the heifer's neck."

They would then wash their hands over the heifer and say, "Our hands have not shed this blood, neither have our eyes seen it. Be merciful, O Lord, unto thy people Israel, whom thou hast redeemed, and lay not innocent blood unto thy people of Israel's charge." The Lord said that in this manner "shalt thou put away the guilt of innocent blood from among you."—By W. Cleon Skousen, *The Third Thousand Years*

****

JACOB HAMBLIN'S 8 GOOD RULES OF DEALING WITH INDIANS

1. I never talk anything but the truth to them.

2. I think it useless to speak of things they cannot comprehend.

3. I strive by all means to never let them see me in a passion.

4. Under no circumstances show fear.

5. Never approach them in an austere manner; nor use more words than is necessary to convey my ideas; nor in a higher tone of voice, that to be distinctly heard.

6. Always listen to them.

7. I never allow them to hear me use any obscene language.

8. I never submit to any unjust demands or submit to coercion.

****

In 1979, a Latter-day Saint mother gave birth to a baby 16 lbs. 13 oz.

WHERE ARE THEY NOW? Part II

Brother Paul looks at the faces and names that meant so much to us baby boomers, and wonders, where are they now?
To read Part I, turn to page 169.

MAN'S SEARCH FOR HAPPINESS (1964)
THE FATHER: Bryce Chamberlain
STORY: Since the famous and favorite of all missionary film strips, *Man's Search for Happiness* appeared in 1964, Brother Chamberlain has gone on to appear in more than 55 movies, including several Disney films, plus dozens of television shows, and more than 200 theatrical productions. In various settings he has played the role of Christopher Columbus, George Washington, Johann Gutenberg, Thomas Jefferson, Joseph Smith, Brigham Young and Moroni. His most recent major film role was the part of Lehi in Gary Roger's 2003 Book of Mormon movie. He remains active in media arts to this day.

THE FIRST VISION, 1976
JOSEPH SMITH: Stewart Petersen
STORY: Brother Petersen was only 15 when he was cast for the part of Joseph Smith. This first of many Church films about important events in Church history, was a good fit for Petersen because he was the same age as Joseph Smith was when he had his experience at the Sacred Grove. Prior to *The First Vision*, Brother. Petersen had experience with major or minor roles in *Where the Red Fern Grows* (1974), *Seven Alone* (1974), *Against a Crooked Sky* (1975), and *Pony Express Rider* (1976). He served his mission to the Netherlands and now works ranching and construction with his wife and kids.

BRIGHAM YOUNG—FRONTIERSMAN, 1940
BRIGHAM YOUNG: Dean Jagger
STORY: Brother Jagger was a very accomplished veteran of theater, film, and television, and won an Academy Award for best

---

George Eastman invented the portable camera way back in 1888.

supporting actor in the 1949 war film, *Twelve O'Clock High*. After his energetic portrayal of Brigham Young in 1940, he continued a career that included more than 90 films, including the much enjoyed role of General Thomas F. Waverly in the box office hit *White Christmas* (1954). He was a familiar face on "Mr. Novak," "The Twilight Zone," "Bonanza," "The Fugitive," and others.

In 1972, Jagger joined the Church and was an active member of the Santa Monica 2nd Ward, Los Angeles California Santa Monica Stake. In 1975, he donated his papers, awards, theatrical files, correspondence and five volumes of personal journals and scrapbooks to BYU. Later years included regular roles on television including "The Waltons," "Alias Smith and Jones," "Kung Fu," and "The Patridge Family." He passed away Feb. 5, 1991 at age 87.

****

FOR ANYONE THINKING they have a good excuse to delay, forget, postpone or otherwise ignore journal keeping, read this revealing apology from Joseph Smith as he reaches out to generations yet unborn for reasons he couldn't do more.

"SINCE I HAVE BEEN ENGAGED in laying the foundation of the Church of Jesus Christ of Latter-day Saints, I have been prevented in various ways from continuing my journal and history in a manner satisfactory to myself or in justice to the cause. Long imprisonments, vexatious and long-continued law suits, the treachery of some of my clerks, the death of others, and the poverty of myself and brethren from continued plunder and driving, have prevented my handing down to posterity a connected memorandum of events desirable to all lovers of truth; yet I have continued to keep up a journal in the best manner my circumstances would allow, and dictate for my history from time to time, as I have had opportunity so that the labors and suffering of the first elders and Saints of this last kingdom might not wholly be lost to the world."—*History of the Church,* Vol.4, p. 470

A FACE-OFF WITH FACE CARDS, PART IV

Brother Paul finishes his exploration into the banishment of
face cards in the LDS home. To read this story
from the beginning, turn to page 43.

GAMBLING CARDS, PLAYING CARDS, OR BOTH?
Finally, face cards entered the Americas. Their first
arrival was probably with the crewmen who idled away
their time with card playing while aboard Columbus's first
ships to the Western Hemisphere. And along the way over the
ocean blue, the sailors probably were doing what countless
thousands of card players had done for 200 years before them:
keeping score with the loss or gain of playing pieces, money,
food, opportunity, etc. Gambling was as old as the cards themselves.

So intoxicating became this exchange of chance and skill,
card playing was soon condemned by early American colony
leaders. Like religious leaders before him, the good Christian
man was expected never to indulge in such a time-wasting and
risky activity as card playing when there was a fort to be built,
crops to plant, game to hunt, and Bible reading from a preacher
to be heard after supper.

THE BRETHREN SPEAK OUT

Can a game really be that habit forming? According to Elder
John H. Widstoe, the answer is a strong yes. "It has been
observed through centuries of experience," Elder Widstoe said,
"that the habit of card playing becomes fixed upon a person and
increases until he feels that a day without a game of cards is
incomplete. After an afternoon or evening at card-playing, nothing has been changed, no new knowledge, thoughts, or visions
have come, no new hopes or aspirations have been generated,
except for another opportunity to waste precious hours. It leads
nowhere; it is a dead-end road. Dull and deadly is a life which
does not seek to immerse itself in the rapidly moving stream of

The Book of Moses is actually an inspired translation of Genesis given in 1830-31.

new and increasing knowledge and power. Time is required to 'keep up with the times.' We dare not waste time on pastimes that starve the soul."

GOOD PROPHET QUOTES
Good quotes by the brethren affirm this stand, that card playing is bad because it wastes precious time. "We hope faithful Latter-day Saints will not use playing cards," said President Spencer W. Kimball in 1974.
• **President Joseph F. Smith** declared, "Card playing is an excessive pleasure; it is intoxicating and, therefore, in the nature of a vice. It is generally the companion of the cigarette and the wine glass, and the latter lead to the poolroom and the gambling hall... Few indulge frequently in card playing in whose lives it does not become a ruling passion ... A deck of cards in the hands of a faithful servant of God is a satire upon religion ... Those who thus indulge are not fit to administer in sacred ordinances ... The bishops are charged with the responsibility for the evil, and it is their duty to see that it is abolished ... No man who is addicted to card playing should be called to act as a ward teacher; such men cannot be consistent advocates of that which they do not themselves practice."

THE IRONY OF THE TIMES
In these modern times when the computer and television are the fulcrum of many lives, an odd change of seasons has come to our society. People sit in front of their screens and monitors and tick off the hours of their lives while absorbed with ingeniously-designed computer games, idle exchanges in chat rooms, instant messaging, sitcoms, reality TV, block-buster movies, and trips into the past and future through amazing technologies hardly tapped for their capabilities. The sacrifice paid for this amazing electronic world is human isolation. Sitting in the same house, in the same room, perhaps even within arm's reach are couples, families, friends, and classmates who can be totally absorbed into their computer monitor or television show, oblivious to the exciting and wonderful experience contained in a fellow human who might be sitting just inches away. And what amazing trick or awesome power do you suppose could pull people from their computerized addictions and back into

In a study of 200,000 ostriches over an 80 year period, not one put its head in the sand.

the fold of human interaction? What force for good could reunite family members back around the dinner table or fireside for conversation and some modicum of human interaction? Hummmm. How about a game of cards?

NOTE TO READERS: It was at this point in the reading that Brother Paul's wise and more finely attuned-to-the-infinite wife gave him *that look*, and said, "Not." Brother Paul must concur. And at the prodding of his special eternal and very wise companion, and at the risk of finding a pillow and blanket on the couch, he wishes to amend his final statement to include his opinion that Uno is a great card game ... and so is Go Fish and Old Maid. I'm sure there are others.

****

In 1841, a pocket of lonely saints in New Orleans offered to pay $10 for an elder from Salt Lake City to come preach to them. Elder Harrison Sagers was dispatched to share the gospel. A few months later, the First Presidency made New Orleans the official entry point for all emigrants coming to the United States from foreign lands. During the following 14 years, some 79 companies of saints, totaling 17,463, passed through New Orleans on their way west. After 1855, the destination point was moved to the eastern seaboard where Saints landed in New York, Philadelphia, and Boston.

****

Handcart rules: Adults could bring 17 pounds of belongings, children only 10 pounds.

10 QUESTIONS ABOUT: THE HOLY GHOST

How much do we know about this important member of the Godhead? Quite a bit, actually.

1. **IS THE HOLY GHOST** an "It," "He," or "She"? The Holy Ghost is referred to as "he," or in the masculine form, at least 20 times in the New Testament, for example, "He shall teach you all things" (John 14:26). "For as yet He had fallen on none of them" Acts 8:15. Heber C. Kimball made it clear in *Journal of Discourses* volume 5, page 179, "He is a man."

2. DOES THE HOLY GHOST have a body or is it just "an influence"?

• He is a spirit: "The Holy Ghost has not a body of flesh and bones, but is a personage of Spirit. Were it not so, the Holy Ghost could not dwell in us." (D&C 130:22). Joseph Smith also taught that all spirit is matter—very refined matter, but matter nevertheless. (D&C 131:7)

3. WHAT IS the Holy Ghost's relationship to us?

• He is an elder brother like Jesus Christ.

4. WILL the Holy Ghost be born and receive a physical body?

• Yes. A body is necessary to receive a fulness of joy (see D&C 93:33-34). "But the Holy Ghost is yet a Spiritual body and waiting to take to himself a body." (*Words of Joseph Smith*, note 26, p. 305)

5. CAN the Holy Ghost be in more than one place at a time?

• No. The Holy Ghost can be in only one place at one time, but his influence extends everywhere. (*Articles of Faith*, pg. 157-170) However, Joseph Smith points out that people often confuse the man with the mission. His role as communicator for Father is through the same mechanisms that Father organizes and controls all things. That medium isn't well described, but its operation and necessity is referred to frequently.

6. DOES the Holy Ghost have helpers?

• Yes. He uses the entire priesthood on the other side of the veil. (See John Taylor, Millennial Star 9:321-2; DHC 5:555)

7. WAS THE HOLY GHOST on earth before Christ?

• Yes. Several passages say this. Peter himself mentioned it regarding ancient prophets, "Holy men of God spake as they were moved by the Holy Ghost." (2 Peter 1:21) And while Elisabeth was expecting her baby, she was visited by Mary. Her baby "leapt in her womb" and she was filled with the Holy Ghost—and Christ had not yet been born. (Luke 1:41)

8. HOW DOES the Holy Ghost perform his role in Church services?

• First of all, if you are teaching or speaking and you don't get the Spirit you're not supposed to be up there yammering away, anyway (D.C. 42:12-14). And anything you say in that capacity that isn't validated by the Holy Ghost, it is not of God (D&C 50:13-18). However, if you are speaking by and led by the spirit, then whatever you feel directed to say is the word of the Lord. (D&C 68:3-4) This sounds daunting, but it happens more frequently than not. That's why Church is a good place to be whenever possible.

9. BY WHAT OTHER NAMES is the Holy Ghost known?

• Holy Spirit, Spirit of God, Spirit of the Lord, Comforter, Light of Christ, Spirit, Spirit of Truth, Still Small Voice, Testifier, and more, though such terms have also been applied to the power or influence of the Holy Ghost, not just the man himself.

10. IS THE HOLY GHOST an office, a person, or both?

• Both. When that member of the Godhood receives his body, as did Jesus, there is no mention of what his role afterwards then becomes. But going without a body so he can 'dwell in our hearts' and then receiving a body so he too can have a fulness of joy implies that another person fills the roll of dwelling in the hearts of unborn generations, rendering the Holy Ghost as both an office and a person. Early brethren also referred to him as "the office of the Holy Ghost." See *Journal of Discourses* Index for more.

THE BRETHREN SAID IT!

Part IX

All is not always sober and somber at the podium.
For more, see page 407.

"When an apostate lifts up his voice against this people, when he makes dastardly charges against the Latter-day Saints, he lies, and I have no patience with him. I have breathed this mountain air so long that I feel inclined to discard a little of the gospel and knock such men down, and repent afterwards."—*J. Golden Kimball*

"AS I HAVE TOLD THE ELDERS, so I will say here, Any man who goes on a mission in these times, to the European nations, to the United States, or to the islands of the sea, and returns home with his scalp on, I think he should certainly acknowledge the hand of the Lord in it."—*Ezra T. Benson*

"YOU KNOW there is no other man like me in all Israel and probably you are glad of it ... If I can be saved it is an encouragement to every man, woman and child in Israel to make the effort."—*J. Golden Kimball*

"MAYBE WE CAN EMPHASIZE this by relating President Tanner's statement of an incident which occurred while he was in England. Two of the missionaries were conversing with a minister. They didn't agree on very many things. Finally the minister said, 'Well, on this one thing we can agree. We are all trying to serve the Lord.' The missionaries replied, 'Yes. You in your way and we in his.'"—*Marion G. Romney*

"I LOVE GOD ... I know that He will deal justly with me; and the great joy I will have is that He will understand me, and that is more than some of you have been able to do."
—*J. Golden Kimball*

Easter is the first Sunday after the first Full Moon after March 21.

HARD TO ATMIT, BUT IT'S A MIRACLE!

Death by starvation is not an easy way out. The Church is mar-shaling its resources to do all it can to stave off death by hunger in Ethiopia and Tsunami-affected areas, among others. It's part of a world-wide effort to help famished third-world countries around the globe. Part of this food aid comes in the form of a strange nutritional drink with an even stranger name.

In 2003, the Church sent more than 5,000 tons of nutritional drink mixes to help the 13 million starving men, women and children in Ethiopia. During the Tsunami disaster of 2004, the Church sent more, not to mention other food, medical and hygiene supplies to people in desperate straits.

Untold thousands have been spared disease and death because of the Church's emergency relief and the sacrifices of its membership through fasting and fund raisers. Partnerships with other relief organizations around the world have created lifetime friendships and associations that prove their worth with each passing day. And the main food product we provide is porridge!

DRINK: Atmit
DEFINITION: Ethiopian (Amharic) for "soup-like"
PURPOSE: A primary food source for those suffering from severe starvation.
RECIPE: A centuries-old Ethiopian porridge mix of oat flour, powdered milk, sugar, salt and vitamins and minerals that can be mixed with water and cooking oil (optional).
PREPARATION: Two tablespoons of the powder mixed in 6-8 ounces of water provide the basic nutritional needs of one child for one meal. Serve warm, if possible.

STORY: People who are severely malnourished, especially children and the elderly, cannot digest regular food, especially whole grains and foods made with coarse flour. To bring them back from the brink of death, their digestive systems need tender loving care with frequent feedings of small amounts of food that is easily digestible until the people are recovered enough to take regular foods.

Atmit is the first stage. Once the digestion track is working, people can handle more grains and a good fortified blend of food that the Church is also providing under contract with producers in Africa. This heartier blend comes in an assortment of varieties that typically are referred to simply as *Unimix*.

DRINK: Unimix
RECIPE: A mixture of cereal grain flour, oil and sugar, and fortified with minerals and vitamins.
PURPOSE: Unimix is a blend of food especially helpful to pregnant and nursing mothers as well as infants and children. It has the consistency of porridge, cooks quickly so less wood is needed to heat it to boiling, and is packed with vitamins, minerals, and calorie power for starving people.

WANT TO MAKE SOME FOR HOME STORAGE?
Consider these requirements for providers of Unimix to third-world nations (the final product is a finely ground powder):

1. **FOR FOOD SAFETY PURPOSES,** Unimix is not "instant," but is designed to be boiled, cooked, fried or baked in 2-15 minutes to kill contaminants (for example, being forced to boil the water makes the water safe to consume).
2. **THE MIX** of ingredients must provide essential vitamins and minerals.
3. **YOUR BATCH SHOULD INCLUDE** 80 percent cereals such as maize, millet, wheat, sorghum, or a combination.
4. **YOU SHOULD ALSO INCLUDE** 20 percent soybeans.
5. **THE CEREALS** and soybeans do not have to be hulled, but should be pre-roasted.
6. **YOU MAY ADD** to either of the quantities some chickpeas, oilseeds such as groundnuts, hulled sunflower seeds, sesame, as well as vegetable oil.
7. **AND DON'T FORGET** some sugar (up to 10 percent) replacing an equivalent amount of cereal. And add some salt for taste.
8. **FROM THE LOCAL AGRICULTURE,** add leafy vegetables, fruits in season, and local grains such as fresh corn. Yum!!

The great "dust bowl" covered 50 million acres in south-central plains in 1935–1936.

SHOOT OUTS!

The lawless west has been portrayed in movies, literature, legend and lore as the scene of gritty showdowns on a deserted, dusty, wind-blown main street at the crack of noon. Were the Saints ever involved? Not exactly, but we did have some local shootouts.

GOOD AND BAD GUYS: Jack Watson and a gunman named "Ward"
PLACE: Price, Utah
DATE: 1890
STORY: Jack Watson was a Confederate soldier whose war wound gave him a life-long limp. But he was a tough guy and became a Texas Ranger. After a drunken spree in Montrose, Colorado in 1884, he shot up the place and the locals put out a $600 reward for his capture. Another brush with the law came shortly after when he was a miner at Crystal, Colorado and knifed a man. He was acquitted. Crystal's sheriff saw something good in Watson and hired him as a deputy, a job he fulfilled with integrity. By 1890, Watson was out hunting down horse and cattle rustlers and had, over the years, made plenty of enemies. Somehow, his cover was blown and a hired gun known as "Ward" went to Price, Utah, where Watson was doing undercover work. Drinking as usual, he stumbled out of the saloon and right into the gun sites of Ward who fired and wounded him. Watson tried to crawl back into the saloon for his guns, but before he could make it in, a second shot finished the job.

GOOD AND BAD GUYS: Utah ranch family and outlaw Joe Walker
PLACE: Thompson, Utah
DATE: 1898
STORY: Joe Walker's dad was a rancher who died when Joe was an infant. Managing the family herd was too much for Joe's mother, so she turned to Joe's Uncle Whitmore for help. This would have worked fine except that Uncle Whitmore was killed in an Indian raid. His widow and sons took the family herd to Utah where they established thriving businesses in ranching and banking. And then Joe showed up. He wanted his share of his father's herd but so many years had passed, the Whitmore family turned him down. This made Joe mad. He took a job

---

nearby and took opportunity to harass the Whitmores. In 1895, he shot up the town of Price in a drunken spree and was chased for 15 miles, gunshots exchanged all the way. He found refuge in Robber's Roost and hooked up with the Robber's Roost gang stealing horses, livestock and running from the law. In 1898, he joined Butch Cassidy's Wild Bunch and helped with the $8,000 Castle Gate robbery. After one such raid, he was out alone, met up with a passing cowboy and the two camped near the town of Thompson. That night, a posse of nine men surrounded the camp and as the sun rose, the posse riddled the two slumbering men with dozens of bullets. The innocent cowhand died along-side Walker.

Many thanks to researcher Becky Bartholomew
for this amazing information.

****

NOT LIKE YOU'RE LOOKING, but here's another important item to add to your "perfect mate" list.

The BYU Counseling and Development Center embarked on a study of marriages where one spouse is a morning person and the other spouse a night person to see if this had any significant impact on their marriage relationship. Overall, it appeared that such couples had lower marital satisfaction.

Jeff Larson, one of the counselors at the center said, "Couples also reported significantly fewer minutes spent in serious conversation per day, fewer minutes spent in shared activities each week, and less intimate contact."

However, the study showed important management and adjustment skills that grew from such "mismatched" marriages. The happily married "mismatched" couples reported better problem-solving skills than happily married "matched" couples.

The "mismatched" couples reported that they learned to compensate for their partner. One practice cited was that the morning person would take an afternoon nap so he or she would have plenty of energy for the night person.

****

... John Adams died the same day Jefferson died.

SPEAKING OF FAIRY TALES ...

The Christian Crusades were long, bloody battles to win back the Holy Land from the Muslims who occupied the holiest of Christian sites. One of the most tragic crusades is remembered in a familiar fairy tale.

THE CRUSADERS who were sent to liberate the tomb of Jesus and other sacred sites had been defeated time and again. It was a decades-long bloody battle that had been carried on by some of Europe's finest beginning in 1095 A.D. Frustrated that the Muslims kept control of the land, the Church began looking to other reasons for their failure to conquer. About this time there emerged a new idea: if fierce fighting wouldn't work, what was needed were children—those pure in heart and undefiled by the world or adulthood. These would conquer by love what the sword could not slay.

CHILDREN'S CRUSADE—THE ULTIMATE FIELD TRIP

It was 1212 A.D. when two boys, one in France, the other in Germany, had epiphanies that they should lead all the children of Europe on a holy quest to Jerusalem. The idea caught on and soon preachers were recruiting kids from all over rural France and Germany to serve as instruments in God's hands.

MYSTICAL MADNESS

The German children marched through the country sides in great columns led by 10-year-old Nicholas. Their presence drew awe, praise, and religious fervor from bystanders. The number of children grew daily. As the German contingent of children reached the German side of the Alps, their huge numbers estimated at 20,000 shivered over the 8,000 foot level among the icy fields, peaks and danger. Many froze to death. The survivors split into two groups, some disbursed among local towns, others boarded ship at Pisa, and some reached Rome. They all disappeared from history.

GDP compared: China (pop. 1.3 billion) $6.5 trillion; U.S. (300 mil.) $11 trillion.

THUS SPEAKETH THE LORD?

Meanwhile, Stephen of Cloves led his estimated 30,000 French children toward Marseille. When the survivors reached the Mediterranean Sea, Stephen raised his hands as did Moses to part the Red Sea, but nothing happened. With so many crowded at the seashore, numerous local traders negotiated passage for the stranded children aboard ships to the Holy Land. But when the ships pulled away from shore, they didn't go west to Jerusalem, they headed to the Arab slave markets in North Africa. The boys were sold as slaves, the girls were sold into prostitution.

A FAIRY TALE IS BORN

In 1284 A.D., an interesting story appeared among the German country folk and their legend and lore. As the tale goes, all the children of a particular town were lured away as punishment for the townspeople's errors. The leader of the march? A man who played a flute. His dress? Black and white – a style that in old English was called "pied," as in "magpie," a reference to the bird's black and white patchwork of feathers. And the town? A place called Hamelin! We've all heard of the Pied Piper of Hamelin, that cunning musician who could lead rats to their drowning deaths and children to their fate—could this tale be a memorialized retelling of the Mediterranean demise of tens of thousands of lost European children because their parents had not freed the Holy Land with their wealth, soldiers and Knights Templar? Legend says yes! For us it gives pause for ponder.

BOOK REBUKES

"SOME EDITORS are failed writers, but so are most writers."
—*T. S. Eliot (1888-1965)*

"THANK YOU for sending me a copy of your book—I'll waste no time reading it."—*Moses Hadas (1900-1966)*

"THIS IS NOT a novel to be tossed aside lightly. It should be thrown with great force."—*Dorothy Parker (1893-1967)*

Tallest building in the world (as of 2004) is in Taipei, Taiwan, and stands at 1,670 feet.

IS IT REALLY 666? Part II

On page 146, we talked all about an amazing imaging technology used by BYU experts to unlock invaluable treasures in ancient literature. We continue with more on the same cache of documents that addresses the interesting question of whether Revelation really says the mark of the beast is 666. Or is it 616?

From a cache of documents discovered in 1895 in an ancient garbage dump just outside of Egypt's city of Oxyrhynchuscomes came a fragment that is about the size of a postage stamp. Turns out this fragment is part of 20 other fragments covering nine chapters from the Book of Revelation—the oldest existing copies in the world dating to 250-300 A.D.).

Our interest is that this fragment is part of Revelation 13:18 which reads today as: "Here is wisdom. Let him that hath understanding count the number of the beast: for it is the number of a man; and his number is Six hundred threescore and six." (King James version).

IT SAYS WHAT IT SAYS

Dr. Daniel B. Wallace of the Center for the Study of New Testament Manuscripts in Frisco, Texas, viewed the postage-stamp-sized fragment under a microscope and confirms what others saw: the number is "616." However, as he points out, "The verdict is not in on this one yet. I am inclined to the view that the original wording here was 616, but a lot of work is needed to determine this. Although this is the earliest fragment for this portion of Revelation, the fragment's textual affinities and general reliability still need to be examined fully." In other words, we don't know if this is a valid copy of Revelation, or somebody's sloppy rewrite, etc. Dr. Wallace points out some tempting insights that make one wonder:

- The number 616 also had meaning in antiquity.
- 616 was discarded in the second century.

- Irenaeus was an ancient Christian scholar who wrote numerous works in Greek, and wrote about the "mark of the beast." He said 666 represented one striving for perfection (represented by the number 7), but was never able to achieve it (a traditional reference to Satan, the "beast").
- Irenaeus said the "better manuscripts" of Revelation used 666 instead of 616.
- Dr. Wallace wonders if Irenaeus is the reason later scribes used 666, simply on the *authority* of Iranaeus stating that 666 was used in the "better manuscripts." Oh heavens, get it straight!

During the Roman era, educated Greeks loved to play "popular parlor games" with words and numbers. In Greek, each letter corresponds to a number, so it is thought that the Emperor Nero's name was somehow tied in to 616, part of a game at the time. Nero really doesn't work, but the numbers could be the initials of three words. It's a wonderfully tantalizing pursuit for scholars, and with this new find, the jury is most definitely "out" until more analysis is done.

SO, IF THEY DECIDE that "666" isn't really the "mark of the beast," think of all the wasted fun we've had trying to pin "666" on the Internet, or buried in people's names, or sequences in the so-called "Bible Code," or part of heavy-metal groups' names, and in our own Sunday vernacular. Should on-going tests prove "616" was the original number, what will it all mean?

Basically nothing because the "beast" and his mark remain!

****

KNOW YOUR GROUPS!

A group of frogs is called an army. A group of rhinos is called a crash. A group of kangaroos is called a mob. A group of whales is called a pod. A group of geese is called a gaggle. A group of crows is called a murder. A group of officers is called a mess. A group of larks is called an exultation. A group of owls is called a parliament. And buzzards? A wake!

... you are less likely to snack and you'll eat regular portion sizes the rest of the day.

LARGEST
LDS-CARVED BEAR

- **IN 1998,** James R. Veater, a high priest in the Jordan River Ridge 3rd Ward, River Ridge Utah Stake, decided to carve a life-sized grizzly bear. He found a couple of old cottonwood stumps that had been standing in Riverton, Utah, for at least a year and thought they'd make an excellent carving.

- **WITH THE HELP OF A BACKHOE** and a truck, he brought the logs home and stood them up, one atop the other, with two feet of the logs buried in his front yard for support. Using a clay model he made and a drawing of the face he sketched out, he went to work.

- **THREE MONTHS** and three electric chain saws later, his finished work was ready for the final touches. He used a torch to darken the wood, and an electric chisel to detail the face, and a little sanding on the nose and eyes. Some linseed oil and a little stain, and he was done.

- **IT STANDS NINE FEET TALL** and averages 34 inches in diameter, and he estimates it took about 300 hours to carve it. Among his local ward members it's the prime landmark ("Sure, just drive past the bear one street and turn south ... "), and a frequent photo shoot for students from the local high school learning about photography. Little kids were scared of it when it first went up, he said, but over time their concern turned to amazement.

- **"WE CALL IT BALOU,"** he said. The bear stands outside in the weather, and so far people have been respectable of it. "We've found him diapered with toilet paper on two occasions, but otherwise, they just enjoy looking."

****

For the past 15 years, every day an average of 800 people have joined the Church.

MORONI'S PROMISE!

PART VI
More famous people who received a copy of the Book of Mormon. To see this list from the beginning, turn to page 7.

READER: Leo Tolstoy (1828-1910)
DATE: Unknown
CIRCUMSTANCE: Tolstoy was a tremendous reader and somehow obtained a copy of the Book of Mormon that today is on display with other of his books at the Tolstoy Museum in Chechnya. Of the Church he wrote: "If Mormonism is able to endure, unmodified, until it reaches the third and fourth generation, it is destined to become the greatest power the world has ever known."

READER: Sgt. Alvin C. York (1887-1964)
DATE: Summer of 1949
CIRCUMSTANCE: Elders Burke V. Bastian and L. Kent Bard wanted to meet the famous World War I hero and went to his Jamestown, Tennessee, home to pay him a visit. York was out tending his Hereford cattle, and seemed pleased to meet the elders. York told the elders he participated on a program in New York called "We The People." He remembered meeting one of the guests, the youngest daughter of Brigham Young. The elders took that opportunity to present a copy of the Book of Mormon to York, and related to him the history behind the book. York accepted the gift, saying, "I have been wanting to get one of these books. I'll take it home and study it some."

READER: Dr. Albert Schweitzer
DATE: 1961
CIRCUMSTANCE: A noted humanitarian, physician, and philosopher, Schweitzer was awarded the Nobel Peace Prize in 1952. Mrs. Richard O. Winkler, of the Garden Park Ward, Bonneville Utah Stake, had for so long admired Dr. Schweitzer and read so much about him that she felt he should be introduced to the gospel. She tracked down Dr. Schweitzer's location

---

The U.S. Constitution was prepared in secret, behind guarded & locked doors.

and sent a copy of the Book of Mormon to the mission president in France, asking him to send the book to Dr. Schweitzer. Dr. Schweitzer's nurse wrote back conveying his "heartfelt thanks and kindest thoughts" for Winkler's gift.

READER: Mangosuthu G. Buthelezi, Leader of six Million Zulus
DATE: January 1988
CIRCUMSTANCE: A Church delegation headed by Elder Spencer H. Osborn presented a copy of the Book of Mormon, which had just been translated into the Zulu language, to the chief minister of KwaZulu and Buthelezi who led this famous group known for their fierce independence and loyalty to their heritage.

****

There is a brown cow on a stake welfare farm that caretakers fondly named "Coffee." Of course, after she had her baby, they renamed her: "Decaffinated."—Jewel P. Skousen, SLC, UT

"SEVERAL YEARS into this project (of compiling and organizing the new standard works) we asked for a report. How were they progressing with the tedious, laborious listing of topics in alphabetical order? They responded, 'We have been through Heaven and Hell, past Love and Lust and now we're working toward Repentance.'"—*Elder Boyd K. Packer*

****

COUNTING OUR STARS

For her it's the 5:30 a.m. wind-up that begins with ten children who must be nudged from bed, dressed, fed, packed with lunch and books, and scooted off to buses, cars and work. For me it's shaking off the clingy scales of another late night and slogging from bed to shower to a kiss goodbye and a sleepy ride into work. The steady flow of adrenalin keeps me going through lunch and beyond until I drag home that night to a clean house, neat rooms, delicious dinner, teasing, running kids, and a few seconds of togetherness to eat. The moments flit by, and it's quickly 8:30—bedtime for the little ones. And then there's the complaining, confessions, extra drinks, and stories, prayers, and finally lights out. The older children park themselves about the house, attempting homework, or not. And suddenly it's 11 p.m. No more computer work for me, the second job is put away, and that tired look from her tells it all. A turned head says let's go. We take each other by the hand, step quietly to the door and disappear down the front steps and into the cool of the night. Out past the driveway we sneak into the dark, the quiet, the peace, our very own place where silence is disturbed only by our thoughts and hushed words. Walking too slowly to call it exercise, we gaze into the sky, the waning moon, the stars and clouds, and quietly stroll by as our neighbors' lights blink off to bed. Now it's just us. Around the cul-de-sac we walk, hand in hand, whispering the day away —what worked, what didn't, who called, who didn't, what it cost, what it didn't. Somehow we will find a way. And around we go, three, four, five times, maybe six or ten. Who's counting? With the day finally talked out, our feet tired, our hands still clasped, the fresh air crisp and cool, our minds take ease. All of those things that wound us up now slowly unwind with each turn of the cul-de-sac. We go around yet once more. Suddenly the magic of the night carefully turns the day upright and all seems okay—it was a good day, not too bad, productive; we made progress. We end the circle once more, beneath old branches, past crickets and cats, into the

Amniotic fluid and breast milk help pre-determine our likes and dislikes in foods.

moonlight and out, the day finally loosens its grip, and we pause in front of our peaceful home and decide. Yes, it's time to go in. I escort my bride back to the porch. A quiet kiss, a big hug, a loving look into each other's eyes, and we turn in. This has been our secluded escape for 29 years, and for every time we go walking, we create a nightly rekindling of our love that sparks new and bright once again. And the last time we looked? There's a billion stars yet to be counted.—*By PBS for KBS*

IS WORK KILLING YOU?

From Barbara Bailey Reinhold's book, *Toxic Work: How to Overcome Stress, Overload and Burnout and Revitalize Your Career* (Dutton, $23.95), stress can contribute to everything from back pain to heart disease. How's your work-place stress level? Take her quiz. Rate from 1 (almost never) to 4 (almost always):

- I'm worried I won't find another job if I lose this one.
- I wake up worrying about work.
- I'm upset about the increased demands at work.
- I find myself getting irritable or angry.
- I speed impatiently from one task to another.
- I don't have enough control over how I do my work.
- I'm worrying about whether I can keep up at work.
- I wonder whether I'm really doing a good enough job.
- It seems that nobody wants to know what I'm feeling.
- I have trouble knowing what I'm really feeling.
- I hold in my feelings until they finally erupt in some way.
- It's hard to make enough time for friends and family.
- People close to me complain that I'm not available enough.
- I'm too worn out to give much time to my relationships.

Score less than 25, you're managing stress well; 25-34, you could be in for some emotional and physical discomfort; 35-44, talk with others at work about ways to reduce stress; over 45, you're probably under a doctor's care but should also consider a career counselor as well.

LOST!

How would you fare if this true event had happened to you?

Ralph Flores, San Bruno Ward, San Mateo California Stake, was flying his passenger, Helen Klaben, 21, in the icy climes of the Yukon when his plane crashed. A blinding snowstorm blasted the little plane as it struggled to remain airborne on its fateful flight of 1963. Blown off course , the little plane crashed into a mountainside.

SURVIVING DEATH TO FACE DEATH AGAIN

The impact of the collision threw Brother Flores against the dashboard, dislocating his jaw and breaking his nose, cheekbone, two ribs, and sternum. His upper lip was ripped open. All he could do was to roll out of the wreckage and lie in the snow. When he discovered his jaw was dislocated, he put a stick in his mouth to reset it. Miss Klaben suffered a broken arm but otherwise was all right.

WE NEVER PLAN FOR THESE THINGS....

Finding shelter near the plane, the two fought to stay alive. In the first four days, they consumed their supply of food that consisted of two cans of sardines, two cans of fruit cocktail, and one package of crackers. They tried but failed to catch wildlife with slings, arrows and traps. There was no food, they were starving and their only intake was melted snow. They were gradually dying.

One day, after much prayer, Brother Flores promised his Jewish companion that, if she would read the Bible cover to cover, God would send them help. Flores determined from his maps that a highway lay about 65 miles away, a hike that would take him through waist-deep snow over rugged terrain. As a last desperate act to escape their frozen encampment, he headed off to find help. Left alone, Helen had nothing to do but read.

MIRACLE, PROPHECY OR TEST?

On March 24, 1963, as Helen finished the very last page in the Bible, a search plane appeared overhead and spotted the 70-

---

Black Hills, South Dakota: A place where Lakota Indians go on vision quests.

foot tall "SOS" that Flores had tramped sometime earlier in a frozen swamp. Seeing the plane circle, Flores returned to camp and a dog-sled rescue team arrived the next day. The pair became overnight celebrities, having survived on essentially nothing but their faith and water for 49 days in the freezing Yukon snow scape.

MADE FOR TV MOVIE

A movie was made of the incident some years later. After their rescue, Flores was able to complete his trip to California where he, his wife and six children went to the temple to be sealed as a family. As for Miss Klaben, she and Flores never met up again, but he credits the Lord for keeping them alive, and through this unusual missionary experience helping someone who had been lost to be found again.

****

A SALESMAN AT A downtown Salt Lake City photography store discovered that you're never too important or too busy to be a camera buff.

A gentleman showed up at his store wanting to purchase a camera for "his boss." After a few moments of routine questions and answers, the man said thank you and left.

Later that day, the man returned. What was needed, he began again, was a small, easy-to-use camera that could be taken anywhere and wouldn't require a lot of complicated and time-consuming adjustments to take good pictures.

Asking to borrow the telephone, the man then made a phone call, spoke a minute or two and paused to ask the salesman yet another question.

Becoming frustrated, the salesman finally blurted out, "Here, give me the phone and I'll get this thing straightened out!"

Then he took the phone and said, "Hello, may I help you?" At the other end he heard the down-to-business tones of a famous voice. "I need a camera I can take on my trips," the voice began. It was President Ezra Taft Benson.

THE FIRST MISSIONARY

*In any new endeavor, somebody has to lead out. What often is
lost to history is how difficult that first
pioneering trek really was.*

Samuel Smith, the Prophet Joseph's brother, was the
Church's first missionary. His first missionary experience
took place about three months after the Church was organized. His mother, Lucy Mack Smith, tells what happened:

"ON THE THIRTIETH OF JUNE [1830], Samuel started on
the mission to which he had been set apart by Joseph, and in
traveling twenty-five miles, which was his first day's journey, he
stopped at a number of places in order to sell his books [Book
of Mormon], but was turned out-of-doors as soon as he declared
his principles. When evening came on, he was faint and almost
discouraged, but coming to an inn which was surrounded with
every appearance of plenty, he called to see if the landlord
would buy one of his books. On going in, Samuel inquired of
him, if he did not wish to purchase a history of the origin of the
Indians.

"'I do not know,' replied the host; 'how did you get hold of
it?'

"'It was translated,' rejoined Samuel, 'by my brother, from
some gold plates that he found buried in the earth.'

"'You liar!' cried the landlord, 'get out of my house—you
shan't stay one minute with your books.'" And the young elder
was thrown out onto the street.

"Samuel was sick at heart, for this was the fifth time he had
been turned out of doors that day. He left the house, and traveled a short distance, and washed his feet in a small brook, as a
testimony against the man. He then proceeded five miles further on his journey, and seeing an apple tree a short distance
from the road, he concluded to pass the night under it; and here
he lay all night upon the cold, damp ground."

WHEN SAMUEL PASSED BY the same Inn some two weeks later, he spotted the sign "Small Pox" on the tavern and learned that the keeper and two of his children had recently died and other family members were severely ill with the pox. However, no one else in the surrounding village had contracted the fatal disease.

AT THE CONCLUSION of his difficult missionary trip, Samuel returned home with all of his books except two. He gave one to a kindly poor widow who fed him. The other he gave to a new acquaintance, John P. Green. And with that, he headed home.

FROM SMALL THINGS ....

Mr. Green was a Methodist minister and a brother-in-law to Brigham Young. After reading the book, Green gained a testimony of its truthfulness.

Green was so excited that he ran the book to his other brother-in-law, Phineas H. Young, who read the volume and gained a testimony. He in turn gave it to his brother Brigham who also devoured the book, gained a testimony and with the others, he sought baptism. This very book also helped convert Heber C. Kimball. Within the year, the Greens, the Kimballs, and the Youngs, with their families, were all baptized into the Church. And from these families came prophets, missionaries and leaders whose impact on the history of the Church is widely known and felt to this very day.

AND SO WENT the modern Church's very first missionary effort in the form of a doggedly determined, temporarily discouraged, but always faithful and obedient young man named Samuel Smith. He was true to the faith.

****

"... unity of our Country as the Railroad unites the two great Oceans of the world."

I'LL NEVER FORGET THE LOOK ON HER FACE WHEN I BURIED SWEET MAUDE

Brother Paul breaks into rhyme with his romantic tale of the old west. Better pull out the hankies. Or a saddle blanket.

She was purtiest in heels, perfume, and white lace,
She'd sigh and look lovely, when I took her embrace.
The prairie and ride'n kept us lean and not fat,
And at night by the fire she'd smile as we sat.

With me just guitar'n 'bout each other we cared,
There under the stars, fond memories we shared.
We'd sing of that night when our eyes met aglowed,
And the 20 years since, our love'n had growed.

Then up in Montana on one cold winter's day,
A blizzard came blow'n, deep snow started to lay.
I'd been drink'n the whiskey, a cure I was told
For whatever that ails you, yup, even the cold.

So I stammered about and went dig'n up sod
And built a small shelter; t'was for me but not Maude.
By morn'n I woke from my drunk'n bad deed,
Being too blind and stuck selfish, gave it no heed.

Then I found there just stand'n, a terrible sad sight—
In the cold Maude was frozed, must have died in the night.
I looked in her eyes, yes, her sweet smile still shown,
The love that rode with us, so fer from our home.

So I dug a big hole, working hard as I might,
Thinking this place was purty, a purty 'nuff site.
Then into the grave, I pushed my poor Maude,
And shoved in the dirt, the rocks, and the clod.

Duffel bags are named after the town of Duffel, Belgium, where the fabric was made.

The ground was frozen hard, my hole was not deep,
To hide her remains, my love, in her sleep.
But the place is most fine on a hill but this high,
And many visitor comes rev'rent, say'n goodbye.

Now stranger I warn you, be most tender, don't bawl,
When you come on a call'n to see Maude and her all.
Your way's a marked trail with a landmark you won't lose,
'Cuz pointing straight up, see her four frozen hooves.

****

A Sunday school teacher asked her class just before she dismissed them to return to sacrament meeting, "And why is it necessary to be quiet in church?" Little Jessie replied, "Because people are sleeping."

****

A Sunday school teacher was teaching her little five and six year olds about the Ten Commandments. After telling about the commandment to "honor thy father and thy mother," she asked "Is there a commandment that teaches us how to treat our brothers and sisters?" One little boy shot up his hand and answered, "Thou shall not kill."

****

Brother Fred asked, God, how much is a million dollars to you? God replied: It is but a penny. Brother Fred inquired, God, how long is a million years to you? God answered: It is but a second. Brother Fred asked, God, could you please give me a penny? God said, Sure, just a second.

During a housefly's lifetime, it will fly no farther than 100 feet from its birthplace.

TIME HEALS MOST WOUNDS

It was 1954, the year of the scandalous. And, it was the murder of the century, a deed that uncorked a mystery-whipped tale of stirred imaginations and accusations. This lurid drama carried headlines around the world with its sordid tale of forbidden crimes of the head and passions of the heart. But in the end ... well, in the end, which is now, that's what you'll need to read here.

The story of two young girls in Christchurch, New Zealand, began innocent enough. Juliet Hulme was 15, shy and reserved. Pauline Parker was 16 and pulling away from her parents' affection. They had met in school a couple of years earlier and found in each other a true and trustworthy soul-mate. They would spend hours and then days together, oftentimes sleeping over, and kept much to themselves. The parents were glad for the friendship as they had worried about their daughters' isolation from schoolmates.

CONFLUENCE OF LONELINESS AND CREATIVITY

Together the girls fashioned fantasy and make believe, creating in their journals pages of passionate escapades with dashing heroes and intimate explorations into forbidden love. As their friendship grew closer, Pauline's mother worried that the relationship wasn't very healthy for her daughter, and plans were announced to separate the girls. Juliet was horrified at the prospect that came just after she discovered her mother in bed with a lover, an event that triggered her parent's divorce. And Pauline's distance from her parents grew antagonistic when her mother demanded that the friendship with Juliet end.

THE GRAND DESIGN

The girls were distraught over the prospects of separation. They had planned to raise money and run away to America to publish their journal writings as love novels. But this would soon end if Pauline's mother had her way. The girls grew des-

---

In 2005, the Honda Civic GX was the least polluting with 30 mpg in the city.

perate and clung to one another with greater zeal because they knew there was but one way out: Pauline's mother had to go.

HATCHING MURDER

As recorded in Pauline's journal, the plan was to have a going-away holiday at Victoria Park. The plantation of trees and shrubs that filled the park with green and shadow was built along the slope of the foothills of Cashmere. The park's emerald green lawns and landscapes flattened to a plateau near the top upon which stood a home for the park's caretaker and his wife. They enjoyed treating visitors to tea as interlude when walking the grounds, and people could enjoy the views from their sunny tea rooms. A winding, four-foot pathway led through the trees and past overlooks, and a small stone wall separated the view from the steep drop to the valley below.

A DAY AT THE PARK

As the girls left for a walk with Pauline's mother, Juliet was up ahead when Pauline and her mother stopped in the path and argued. When Juliet hurried back, Pauline's mother was bent down—at least one blow to the head, probably more, and the fight was on. As planned, Pauline had half of a pink brick in a foot stocking and had struck her mother from behind. The blow did not kill her as planned. Juliet raced to help and the girls took turns holding the woman by the throat against the pathway as the other beat her with the brick. In the end 44 blows finally cracked her skull. The brick and stocking were found a few feet from the body, the girl's clothing was splattered with blood, and lying there very dead was Honora Mary Parker, aged 45, of 31 Gloucester Street.

It was 3:30 p.m. when the girls ran hysterically to the teahouses screaming and panting, "Please help us. Mummy has been hurt—covered with blood."

ACCIDENTS DO HAPPEN

The idea was to make it appear as an accident. The girls told the police that mummy had tripped on a brick and struck her head. When asked about the multiple blows, they explained she just bumped her head over and over until she died.

In 2005, the Dodge Ram SRT10 was the most polluting with 9 mpg in the city.

SHOCKING SCANDAL

The case was headline news around the world. The secluded cloistered community of Christchurch became a place on everybody's map, and the trial of the century drew stampeding crowds to the courthouse to see the two murderesses in person.

The defense pleaded not guilty by reason of insanity. "They are mentally sick girls," said their attorney, "more to be pitied than blamed." Followed by an examining doctor: "The whole thing," said Dr. Medlicott "rises to a fantastic crescendo. In my opinion they were insane when they attacked Mrs. Parker. Paranoia," declared the doctor, "is a form of insanity in which there is a surface of apparent normality. I consider Parker and Hulme certifiably insane."

EVIL AND SANE, OR EVIL AND INSANE?

And then the prosecution dug in. Dr. Francis Bennett testified, "There came the threat of separation. Anything that threatens the paranoiac makes him dangerous. They thought that by removing Pauline's mother the way would be clear. This idea was stupid but they have steadily maintained it was justified. Neither will admit contrition or regret. Pauline told me she would still feel justified today in killing her mother if she was a threat to their being together. Juliet Hulme was more outspoken. She not only considers the murder justified but also that other murders might be justified if there was a threat to the association of the two accused."

A total of five doctors testified that the girls knew what they were doing and the jury took only 2 hours and 15 minutes to find them guilty. Because the girls were under 18, the judge ordered that they be detained during her majesty's pleasure. The two were sent to prison.

FIVE YEARS AND FIVE DECADES

After five years, the girls were released and never saw each other again.

Now, some 50 years later, the case remains a grisly topic for locals and criminal investigators alike. Books, plays and even a movie have recreated the amazing events. In 1995, Miramax distributed *Heavenly Creatures*, starring Kate Winslet as Juliet and Melanie Lynskey as Pauline.

The busiest airport in 2004 was Atlanta where 83,578,906 passengers were received.

WHERE ARE THEY NOW?

In 1997, Pauline was found living near Rochester, Kent, in England. She had changed her name to Hilary Nathan and had been the deputy Headmistress at Abbey Court School for children with special needs. After retiring in 1994, she ran Abbots Court Riding School where she taught young girls to ride. The diminutive grey-haired spinster was a loner but well liked; eccentric, but very giving, and a devoted Catholic who went to the church once a day.

PRISON PURGING

As for Juliet Hulme, her life's course took a much different direction. She hated prison. "It was cold, there were rats, canvas sheets and calico underwear. I had to wash out my sanitary towels by hand and they put me on to physical labour until I passed out," she told the *Guardian* newspaper in 2003. "It was there that I went down on my knees and repented."

JULIET'S NOVELS

For three decades, Juliet lived quietly in Scotland under a new name, Anne Perry. For crime-mystery readers, it's a familiar name. She has published 40 books and is a leading crime novelist with more than ten million books in print. In 1967, she joined the LDS Church and has been a Gospel Doctrine teacher and young women's leader in her small branch in Scotland. When the movie came out in 1995, she worried about her past being uncovered. Talking to her branch president, she told the *Guardian* that he advised, "Your calling comes from God and He knows." She added, "He also told me I would not lose a single friend over it. It didn't seem possible, but I have learned how decent and compassionate people can be. Not a single friend has gone. That surprised me."

Time heals most wounds, but the Lord heals them all.

****

"CHILDREN'S MINDS are like banks—whatever you put in, you get back ten years later with interest."—*M. Russell Ballard*

THE BRETHREN SAID IT!

Part X

All is not always sober and somber at the podium. To start this compilation from the beginning, turn to page 16.

"I have forgotten to mention before, that the fleas are my best companions. I call them companions because they stick to me so close."—*Matthew Cowley*

"NOW, WHAT I AM TRYING to get at is this: it takes intelligent people to understand what I am trying to get at. ... If I give you a little chaff to get you to take a little wheat, my trouble has always been, you choose the chaff and lose the wheat."
—*J. Golden Kimball*

"IT IS MUCH EASIER to stand up and talk for an hour than to sit and listen—for everyone knows that the mind can't conceive what the seat can't endure."—*Brigham Young*

A SOBBING WOMAN once told Brigham Young, "My husband keeps telling me to go to hell." Brigham replied, "Don't go."

"DOUBTLESS MANY of the elders think that they are smarter than I am. As brother Kimball has said, some of the knowing ones marveled when we were called to the Apostleship. It was indeed a mystery to me; but when I consider what consummate blockheads they were, I did not deem it so great a wonder."—*Brigham Young*

"I REMEMBER HEARING about a saying of President Young to a brother who was terribly tried. His case came before the High Council, and the council had decided against the man. You know it happens sometimes, when the decision is not in your favor, you feel disgruntled. And some leave the Church because of the actions of men; they feel they have been dealt with unjustly. Brother Brigham, on the occasion referred to, said to the brother in sarcasm, 'Now apostatize and go to hell.' And the brother said, 'I won't do it; this is just as much my Church as it is yours, and I am going to stay with it.'" And the man stayed active, just to spite Brother Brigham.—*J. Golden Kimball*

92% of Americans own one Bible; the average household has three.

THAT FAMOUS PRIDE SPEECH

Here's a refresher on President Ezra Taft Benson's timeless advice for all future generations—beware of pride! Taken from his general conference talk in April, 1989

"Pride is a very misunderstood sin, and many are sinning in ignorance. In the scriptures there is no such thing as righteous pride—it is always considered a sin. Therefore, no matter how the world uses the term, we must understand how God uses the term so we can understand the language of holy writ and profit thereby."

WE DON'T RECOGNIZE IT
• "Most of us think of pride as self-centeredness, conceit, boastfulness, arrogance, or haughtiness. All of these are elements of the sin, but the heart, or core, is still missing."

HATRED
• "The central feature of pride is enmity—enmity toward God and enmity toward our fellow men. Enmity means 'hatred toward, hostility to, or a state of opposition.' It is the power by which Satan wishes to reign over us."

US VERSUS HIM
• "Pride is essentially competitive in nature. We pit our will against God's. When we direct our pride toward God, it is in the spirit of 'my will and not thine be done.' As Paul said, they 'seek their own, not the things which are Jesus Christ's.'" (Philip. 2:21.)

LOSE CONTROL
• "Our will in competition to God's will allows desires, appetites, and passions to go unbridled.... . The proud cannot accept the authority of God giving direction to their lives. They pit their perceptions of truth against God's great knowledge, their abilities versus God's priesthood power, their accomplishments against His mighty works."

From a 2001 study: Some people "happily eat spinach" while others cringe because ...

THE "LIST"

- "Our enmity toward God takes on many labels, such as rebellion, hard-heartedness, stiff-neckedness, unrepentant, puffed up, easily offended, and sign seekers. The proud wish God would agree with them. They aren't interested in changing their opinions to agree with God's."

MY ENEMY ME

- "The proud make every man their adversary by pitting their intellects, opinions, works, wealth, talents, or any other worldly measuring device against others. In the words of C. S. Lewis: 'Pride gets no pleasure out of having something, only out of having more of it than the next man... . It is the comparison that makes you proud: the pleasure of being above the rest. Once the element of competition has gone, pride has gone.'" (*Mere Christianity*, New York: Macmillan, 1952, pp. 109-10.)

IMAGE IS EVERYTHING

- "The proud stand more in fear of men's judgment than of God's judgment. 'What will men think of me?' weighs heavier than 'What will God think of me?'"

NOT MORE BUT LESS FREEDOM

- "When pride has a hold on our hearts, we lose our independence of the world and deliver our freedoms to the bondage of men's judgment. The world shouts louder than the whisperings of the Holy Ghost. The reasoning of men overrides the revelations of God, and the proud let go of the iron rod."

I'M NOT PRIDEFUL?

- "Pride is a sin that can readily be seen in others but is rarely admitted in ourselves. Most of us consider pride to be a sin of those on the top, such as the rich and the learned, looking down at the rest of us. There is, however, a far more common ailment among us—and that is pride from the bottom looking up. It is manifest in so many ways, such as faultfinding, gossiping, backbiting, murmuring, living beyond our means, envying, coveting, withholding gratitude and praise that might lift another, and being unforgiving and jealous."

... they firmly understand and believe that eating wholesome foods will benefit them.

TESTING, ONE, TWO, THREE ...

• "Disobedience is essentially a prideful power struggle against someone in authority over us. It can be a parent, a priesthood leader, a teacher, or ultimately God. A proud person hates the fact that someone is above him. He thinks this lowers his position."

LET'S TALK ABOUT ME

• "Selfishness is one of the more common faces of pride. 'How everything affects me' is the center of all that matters—self-conceit, self-pity, worldly self-fulfillment, self-gratification, and self-seeking."

PUT 'EM UP

• "Another face of pride is contention. Arguments, fights, unrighteous dominion, generation gaps, divorces, spouse abuse, riots, and disturbances all fall into this category of pride ... Contention in our families drives the Spirit of the Lord away. It also drives many of our family members away. Contention ranges from a hostile spoken word to worldwide conflicts. The scriptures tell us that 'only by pride cometh contention.'" (Prov. 13:10; see also Prov. 28:25.)

THAT STUPID GOOD FOR NOTHING IDIOT. . .

• "The scriptures testify that the proud are easily offended and hold grudges. They withhold forgiveness to keep another in their debt and to justify their injured feelings...The proud do not receive counsel or correction easily. Defensiveness is used by them to justify and rationalize their frailties and failures."

THE WORLD KNOWS

• "The proud depend upon the world to tell them whether they have value or not. Their self-esteem is determined by where they are judged to be on the ladders of worldly success. They feel worthwhile as individuals if the numbers beneath them in achievement, talent, beauty, or intellect are large enough. Pride is ugly. It says, 'If you succeed, I am a failure.'"

Weird food: giant water bugs, frogs, crocodile, fish eggs, rattlesnake, cooked pig's blood!

DEAD-END STREET
• "Pride is a damning sin in the true sense of that word. It limits or stops progression. The proud are not easily taught. They won't change their minds to accept truths, because to do so implies they have been wrong."

DOWNWARD SPIRAL
• "Pride adversely affects all our relationships—our relationship with God and His servants, between husband and wife, parent and child, employer and employee, teacher and student, and all mankind. Our degree of pride determines how we treat our God and our brothers and sisters. Christ wants to lift us to where He is. Do we desire to do the same for others?"

HURTS THE CHURCH
• "Unity is impossible for a proud people, and unless we are one we are not the Lord's."

LET'S FIX IT NOW
• "If we love God, do His will, and fear His judgment more than men's, we will have self-esteem."

ALSO: lift others as high or higher than we are; receive counsel and chastisement; render selfless service; go on missions; get to the temple more often; confess and forsake our sins; submit to God's will and put him first in our lives.

"MY DEAR BRETHREN AND SISTERS, we must prepare to redeem Zion. It was essentially the sin of pride that kept us from establishing Zion in the days of the Prophet Joseph Smith. It was the same sin of pride that brought consecration to an end among the Nephites ... Pride is the great stumbling block to Zion. I repeat: Pride is the great stumbling block to Zion. ...We must cleanse the inner vessel by conquering pride. We must yield 'to the enticings of the Holy Spirit,' put off the prideful 'natural man,' become 'a saint through the atonement of Christ the Lord,' and become 'as a child, submissive, meek, humble.'"

****

MORMON MYTH BUSTERS, Part V

Brother Paul concludes his debunking of popular LDS legend and lore. To start at the beginning, see page 22.

CLAIM: Arab scholar converted by Book of Mormon
STATUS: False
STORY: *"Reflections of Sami Hanna—as recorded by Elder Russell M. Nelson"* was the title of an e-mail message (and probably existed in printed form, too) that has been in circulation for many years. It is a fascinating read and alleges several amazing connections between the Arabic culture and the Book of Mormon, pulling out all kinds of interesting tidbits regarding phrasing, format and ordering of words and thoughts patterned in the ancient Semitic language. There's even a definition of "ziff," as mentioned a couple of times in the Book of Mormon. It makes good sense after a cursory read. ... But delve into any aspect of the claims, and things go south really bad and really fast.

A retraction supposedly written by Sami Hanna's son in an e-mail dated July 19, 2003, has appeared on the Internet. The son asks that the article be removed from the Internet because his father was no longer a member of the Church.

TRUTH: According to Elder Nelson's office at Church headquarters, he did not write this article. He did have a neighbor named Sami Hanna who was converted to the Church after translating the Book of Mormon.

Some of the message's false claims include a statement that Arabic was "the original language of the book" (an obvious untruth!), and says "ziff" was a "special kind of curved sword" when in reality the two Book of Mormon references to ziff always place it in a series of decorative metals—from Mosiah 11:8, "... precious things, of gold, and of silver, and of iron, and of brass, and of ziff, and of copper."

The "Reflections" memo is an interesting tale but not true.

CLAIM: Missionaries from three zones in New York all miraculously missed a mission conference planned to be held in the World Trade Center the morning of Sept. 11, 2001.

STATUS: False

STORY: Days after the 9/11 terror attacks in New York, Washington and Pennsylvania, variations of a message about a missionary conference began spreading around the Internet. The message said all the missionaries, from three zones, failed to get to the meeting due to flat tires, alarm clocks that didn't awaken them, missed busses or trains, empty gas tanks, etc.

TRUTH: The mission president and his wife, who presided over the New York New York North Mission that covers all the missionaries in Manhattan, had no conference scheduled for that day. And had there been one scheduled, they would not have held it in the World Trade office building.

CLAIM: Missionaries will be called home because of the outbreak of World War III.

STATUS: False

STORY: The Internet is the breeding ground for so many faith-promoting rumors! This one alleges that patriarchal blessings are telling future missionaries that they will, one day, be called home from their missions to fight in WWIII, or not even receive a missionary calling because of the explosive conflicts erupting around the globe.

TRUTH: There is no evidence of this anywhere. Stories such as these have been around ever since the prophecies of the last days have been around, and we're not talking just the modern Church, we're talking the Book of Revelation ... and Isaiah! Last Day scenarios have prompted speculation and even misguided action for centuries. Brother Paul says: "When the Lord doesn't need his missionaries in the field, he'll say so."

CLAIM: Missionaries have been secretly called to China.

STATUS: False.

STORY: The story goes that somebody gets his mission call and instead of a country listed in the usual missionary-call letter, there's a phone number. When the number is called, the prophet answers, asking them to serve 3 years in mainland China.

TRUTH: Service and welfare missionaries serve, but that's ALL!

LAST OF ALL...

LAST NAME

Who has the longest last name in the Church? In 1945, it was the district Aaronic Priesthood leader and first counselor in the Wailuku Branch presidency in Hawaii: Solomon Kekanakailokookoaihana (22 characters).

LAST WITH AN OUTHOUSE?

The last chapel in America with an outhouse was the Vernon Branch, Show Low Arizona Stake. It retained its outdoor accommodations well beyond the birth of modern indoor facilities. In 1985, when construction on a replacement church building began, workers didn't need to venture far for the bathroom—it was out back.

LAST APOSTLE

Orson Pratt was the last survivor of the original Council of the Twelve Apostles chosen in 1835. He died at age 70 in 1881, four years after Brigham Young's death.

LAST OF UTAH PIONEERS BEFORE 1850

James William McDaniel, age 100 on Sept. 13, 1946, was honored as the last of the pioneers to cross the plains from Illinois to Utah before 1850. At the age of three he came to Utah with his parents and served in the Blackhawk War when he was 18. His wife died just one day before their 70th wedding anniversary. Brother McDaniel died in January 1947.

LAST HANDCART COMPANY

The last handcart company to make the 1,300-mile trek from Missouri to Utah was led by Oscar Orlondo Stoddard. His company had 126 emigrants, 22 handcarts and 6 wagons. Brother Stoddard celebrated their arrival in Salt Lake by marrying his sweetheart, Elizabeth Taylor, on Oct. 2, 1860, only eight days after their arrival in Salt Lake City.

LAST PERSON WHO MET JOSEPH SMITH

Before her death in 1943 in Ogden, Utah, Mary Field Garner was thought to be the last living soul who personally knew the Prophet Joseph Smith. She had seen and heard him as a young girl. Shortly after Smith's 1844 martyrdom, Sister Garner recalled attending a meeting in the bowery to listen to Brigham Young address the Saints. She recorded in her diary that she was on her mother's knee and accidentally dropped a tin cup. As her mother stooped to pick it up and was momentarily distracted, they both suddenly heard the voice of Joseph. They looked up and saw the form of Joseph standing before the crowd. From that time on she had no doubt, she wrote, that Brigham Young was to be their new leader.

LAST SURVIVING CHILD OF BRIGHAM YOUNG

Mrs. Mabel Y. Sanborn, 87, the last surviving child of President Brigham Young, died Sept. 20, 1950. One of her last public appearances was in Washington, D.C., on June 1, 1950, where she unveiled the statue of her father which now stands in Statuary Hall in the Capitol. She was one of the last links with Utah's pioneer era.

LAST STATE TO GET A STAKE

With the dedication of the Fargo North Dakota Stake on Aug. 7, 1977, all 50 states in the United States had a stake center within its boundaries. The Fargo Stake was the 852nd to be organized in the Church. "This is a very historic day," Elder Boyd K. Packer said. "The tapestry is complete; the last piece is in place."

LAST CONFERENCE IN THE TABERNACLE

Oct. 3, 1999, was the last general conference session held in the Salt Lake Tabernacle on Temple Square. From that point forward, conference has been held in the Conference Center. President Gordon B. Hinckley ended the tradition that dated back to 1867 by saying goodbye to "an old and wonderful friend."

****

...the same mother, a female wild hamster found with a litter of 12 babies in Syria in 1930.

THIS LAST PAGE MEANS ROLL CALL!

BROTHER PAUL IS THRILLED. That was a lot of story telling for one book. But there will be more, and there will be others.

CONSUMERS UNITE!

As a seasoned reader of *Brother Paul's Mormon Bathroom Reader*, you are the ideal candidate to suggest topics, questions, and areas of research or concern that should be a part of the next installment.

In fact, those submitting articles that are used for the next edition may have their byline published with their article! And what is more amazing, offers such as this are frequently and expeditiously snubbed with the usual vapid expression of smoldering disinterest found only in such outlandish and exotic places as the halls of Congress, the Hollywood Walk of Fame, and the Astronaut Training Program in Houston, Texas! So don't be left out—send your idea TODAY.

You may reach Brother Paul at www.mormonworld records.com, and he'd be delighted to respond to submissions, corrections, suggestions and downright insulting commentary. Either way, he's delighted to hear from you (and that kind of obsessive cheeriness really annoys the heck out of the rest of us.)

AND NOW, YOUR QUIZ

As promised on the instructions page at the beginning of this book, it is now time for the promised quiz. Here you go:

"Long articles for extended periods of concentration are called
_____ articles."

If you got it right, very good. You are free to move on to other reading materials. If you got it wrong, go back to the beginning and start reading again. There will be another quiz when you finish—but you better watch out, it will be much HARDER.